CHARACTER

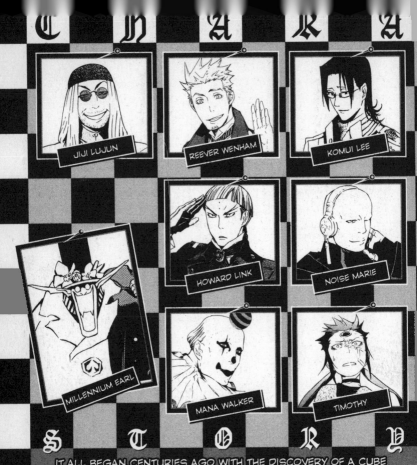

JIJI LUJUN

REEVER WENHAM

KOMUI LEE

HOWARD LINK

NOISE MARIE

MILLENNIUM EARL

MANA WALKER

TIMOTHY

STORY

IT ALL BEGAN CENTURIES AGO WITH THE DISCOVERY OF A CUBE CONTAINING AN APOCALYPTIC PROPHECY FROM AN ANCIENT CIVILIZATION AND INSTRUCTIONS IN THE USE OF INNOCENCE, A CRYSTALLINE SUBSTANCE OF WONDROUS SUPERNATURAL POWER. THE CREATORS OF THE CUBE CLAIMED TO HAVE DEFEATED AN EVIL KNOWN AS THE MILLENNIUM EARL BY USING THE INNOCENCE. NEVERTHELESS, THE WORLD WAS DESTROYED BY THE GREAT FLOOD OF THE OLD TESTAMENT. NOW, TO AVERT A SECOND END OF THE WORLD, A GROUP OF EXORCISTS WIELDING WEAPONS MADE OF INNOCENCE MUST BATTLE THE MILLENNIUM EARL AND HIS TERRIBLE MINIONS, THE AKUMA.

IN THE AFTERMATH OF ALLEN'S BATTLE WITH THE NOAH, HE FINDS HIMSELF UNDER SUSPICION WITH HIS SUPERIORS. BUT SOON THE ORDER SUFFERS A DEVASTATING ATTACK BY A LEVEL 4 AKUMA AND HAS TO MOVE TO A NEW LOCATION. THEN ALLEN LEARNS FROM GENERAL CROSS THAT THE FOURTEENTH'S MEMORY HAS BEEN IMPLANTED IN HIM, BUT SOON THEREAFTER THE GENERAL IS MURDERED AND HIS BODY STOLEN.

D.GRAY-MAN
Vol. 18

CONTENTS

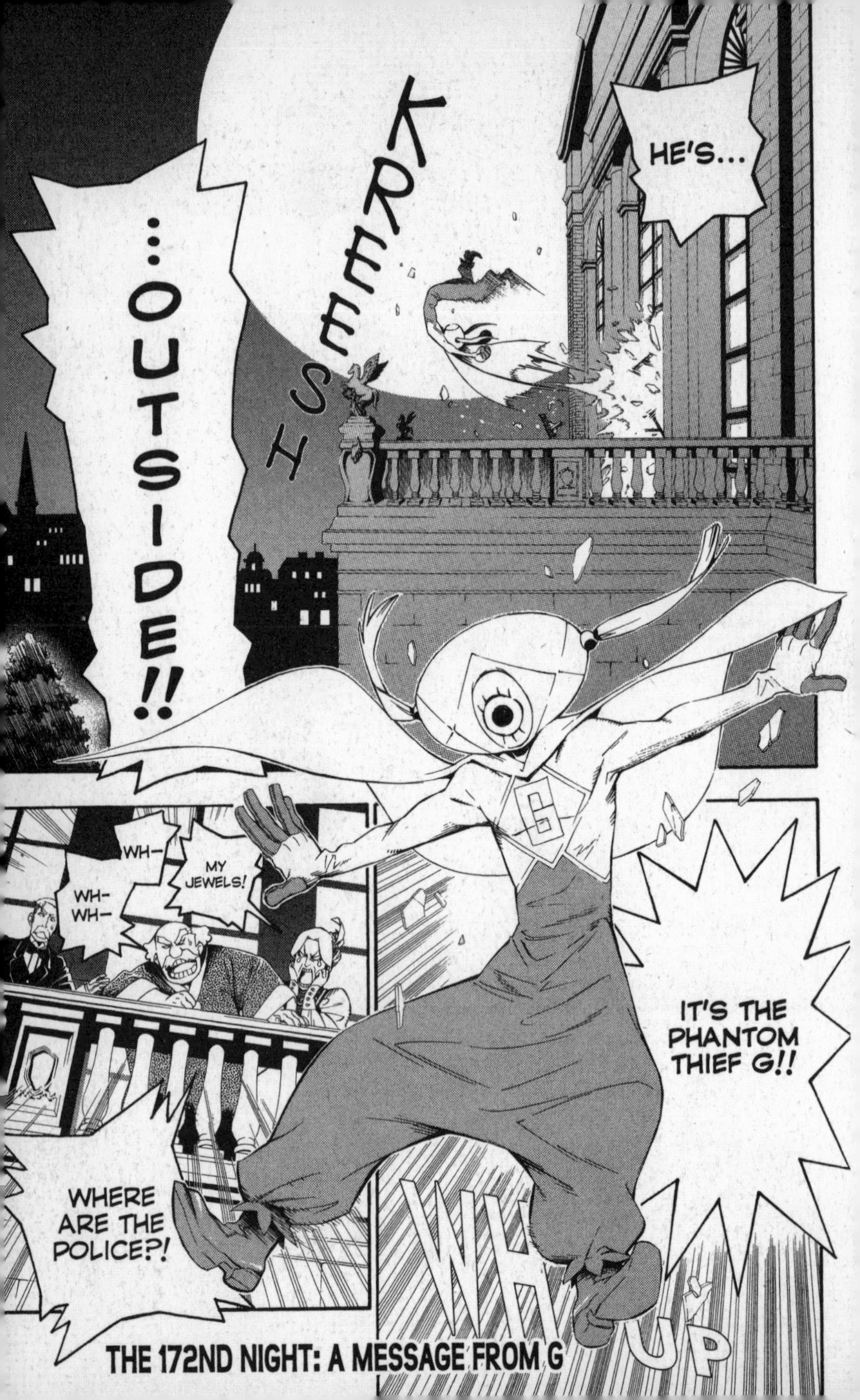
HE'S...
KREESH
...OUTSIDE!!
IT'S THE PHANTOM THIEF G!!
WHUP
MY JEWELS!
WH-
WH- WH-
WHERE ARE THE POLICE?!

THE 172ND NIGHT: A MESSAGE FROM G

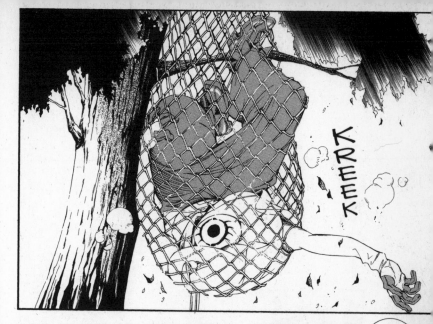

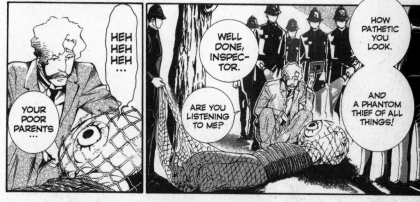

KREEK
HOW PATHETIC YOU LOOK.
AND A PHANTOM THIEF OF ALL THINGS!
WELL DONE, INSPECTOR.
ARE YOU LISTENING TO ME?
HEH HEH HEH ...
YOUR POOR PARENTS ...
THERE'S NO WAY YOU'LL EVER CATCH ME.
WHAT-EVER.
TAKE HIM AWAY.
YES, SIR!
SHWUFF SHWUFF

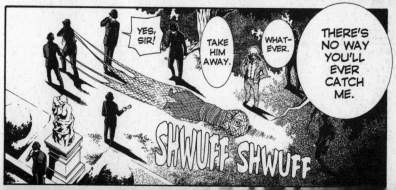

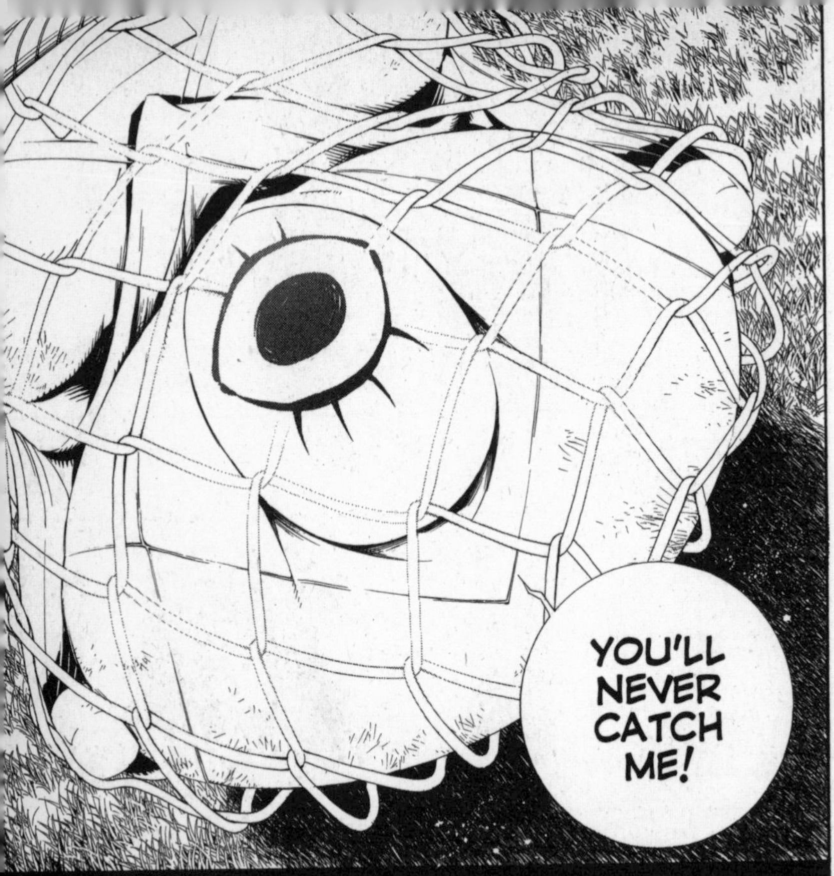
YOU'LL NEVER CATCH ME!

THE 172ND NIGHT: A MESSAGE FROM G

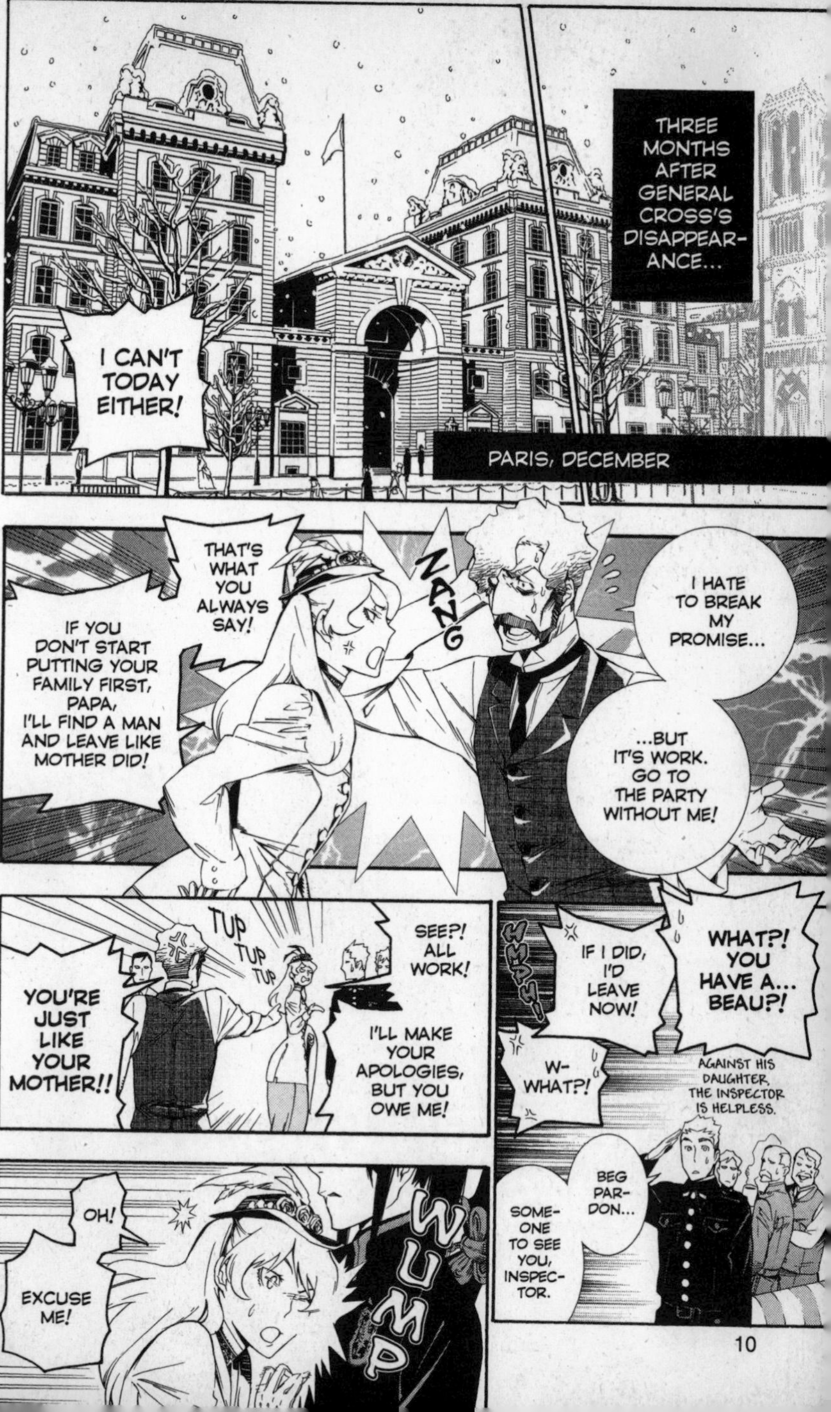
THREE MONTHS AFTER GENERAL CROSS'S DISAPPEAR-ANCE...
PARIS, DECEMBER
I CAN'T TODAY EITHER!
I HATE TO BREAK MY PROMISE...
...BUT IT'S WORK. GO TO THE PARTY WITHOUT ME!
ZANG
THAT'S WHAT YOU ALWAYS SAY!
IF YOU DON'T START PUTTING YOUR FAMILY FIRST, PAPA, I'LL FIND A MAN AND LEAVE LIKE MOTHER DID!
WHAT?! YOU HAVE A... BEAU?!
IF I DID, I'D LEAVE NOW!
HMPH!
W-WHAT?!
AGAINST HIS DAUGHTER, THE INSPECTOR IS HELPLESS.
SEE?! ALL WORK!
TUP TUP TUP
I'LL MAKE YOUR APOLOGIES, BUT YOU OWE ME!
YOU'RE JUST LIKE YOUR MOTHER!!
BEG PARDON...
SOME-ONE TO SEE YOU, INSPEC-TOR.
WUMP
OH!
EXCUSE ME!

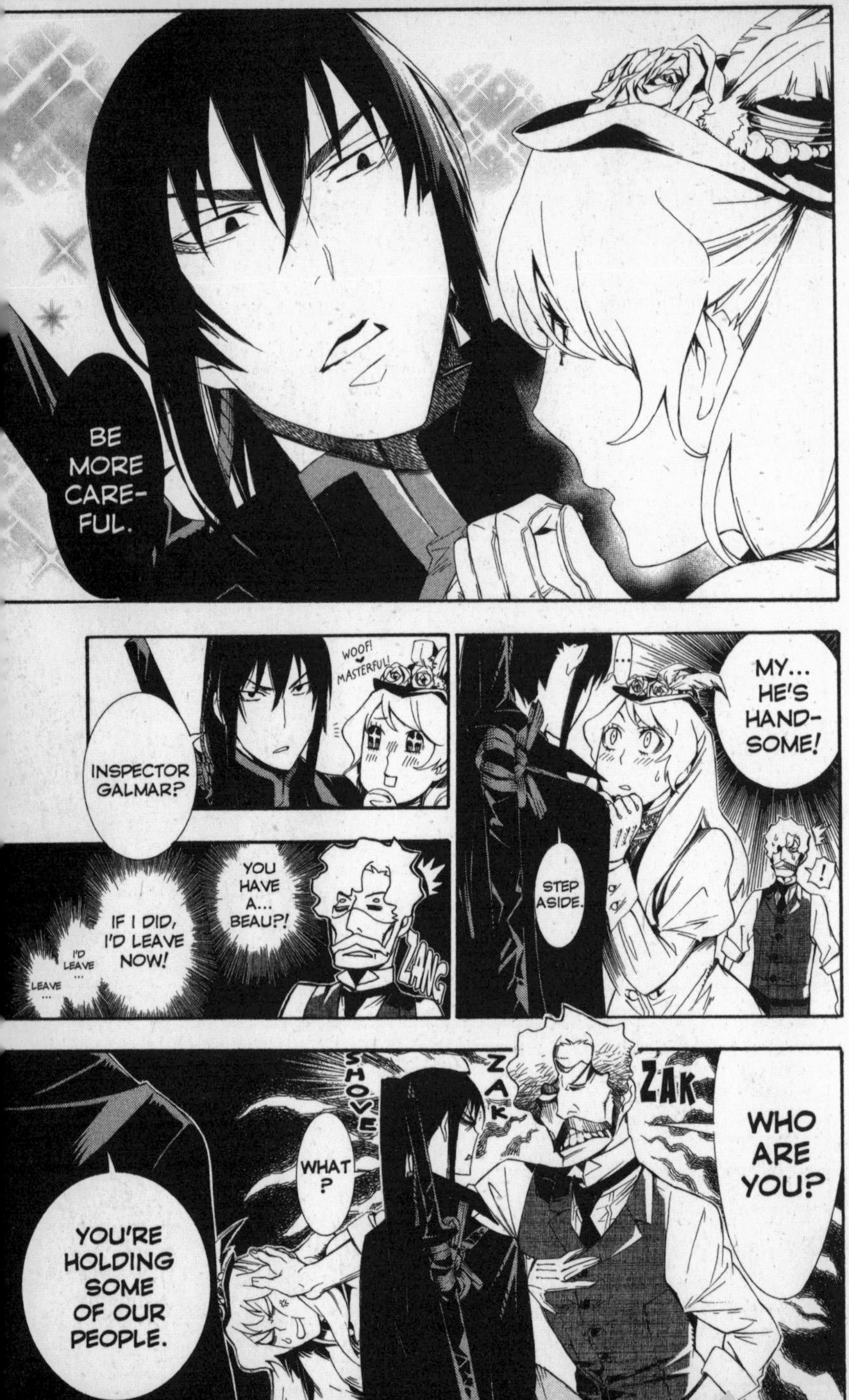
BE MORE CARE-FUL.
...
MY... HE'S HAND-SOME!
STEP ASIDE.
!
WOOF! MASTERFUL!
INSPECTOR GALMAR?
YOU HAVE A... BEAU?!
ZANG
IF I DID, I'D LEAVE NOW!
I'D LEAVE...
LEAVE...
WHO ARE YOU?
ZAK
ZAK
SHOVE
WHAT?
YOU'RE HOLDING SOME OF OUR PEOPLE.

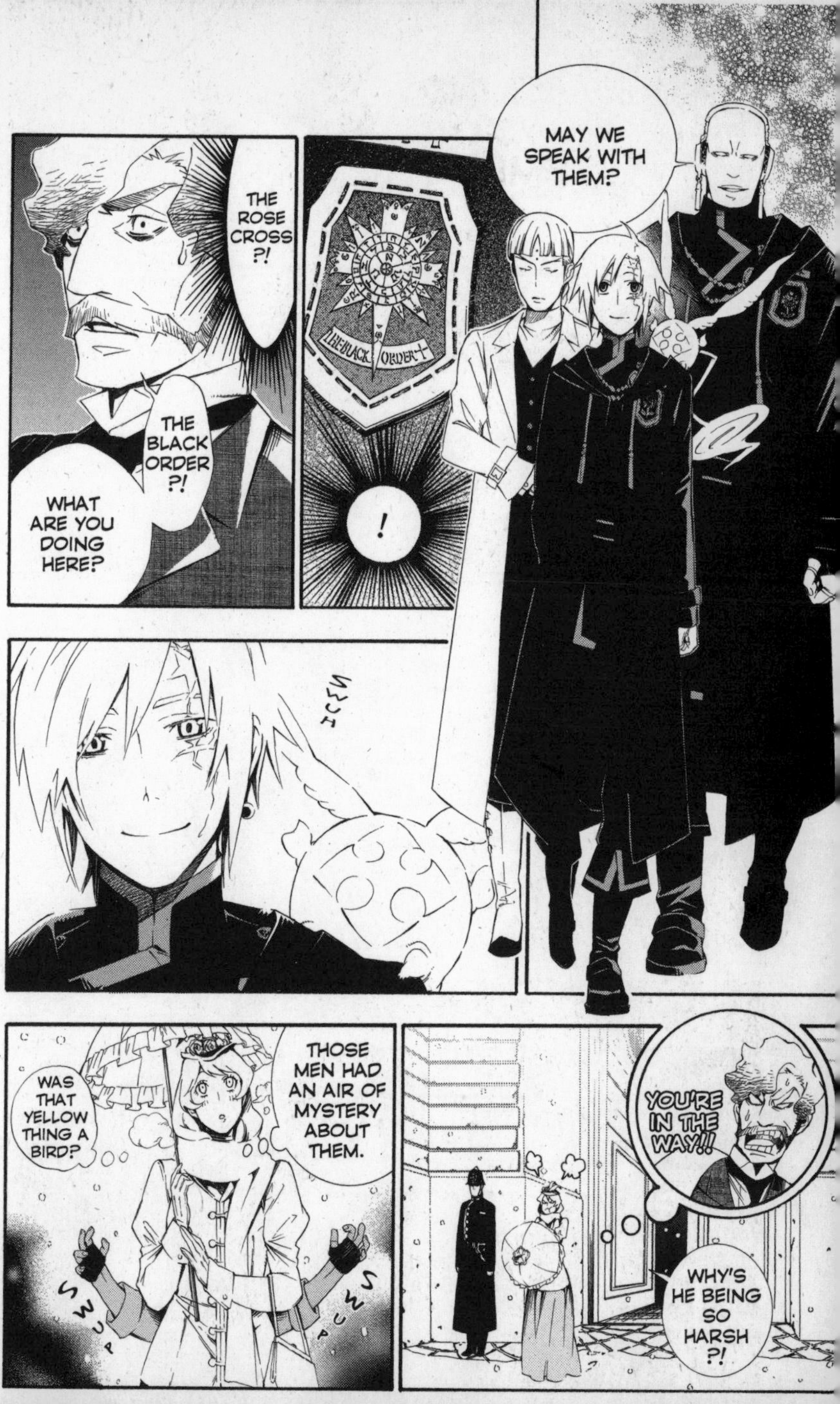
MAY WE SPEAK WITH THEM?
!
THE ROSE CROSS ?!
THE BLACK ORDER ?!
WHAT ARE YOU DOING HERE?
SWUH
YOU'RE IN THE WAY!!
WHY'S HE BEING SO HARSH ?!
THOSE MEN HAD AN AIR OF MYSTERY ABOUT THEM.
WAS THAT YELLOW THING A BIRD?
SWUP
SWUP

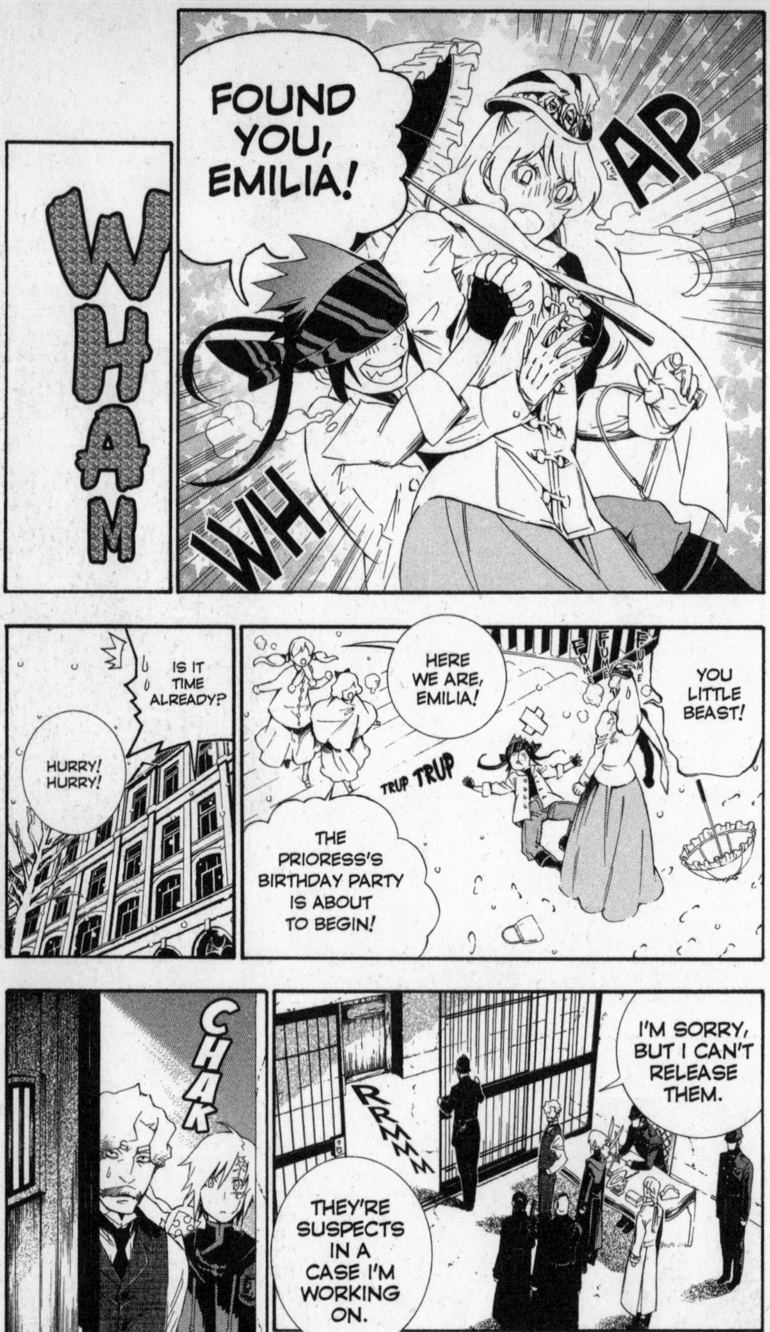
AP
FOUND YOU, EMILIA!
WH
WHAM
YOU LITTLE BEAST!
FUME FUME FUME
HERE WE ARE, EMILIA!
TRUP TRUP
THE PRIORESS'S BIRTHDAY PARTY IS ABOUT TO BEGIN!
IS IT TIME ALREADY?
HURRY! HURRY!
I'M SORRY, BUT I CAN'T RELEASE THEM.
RRMMM
THEY'RE SUSPECTS IN A CASE I'M WORKING ON.
CHAK

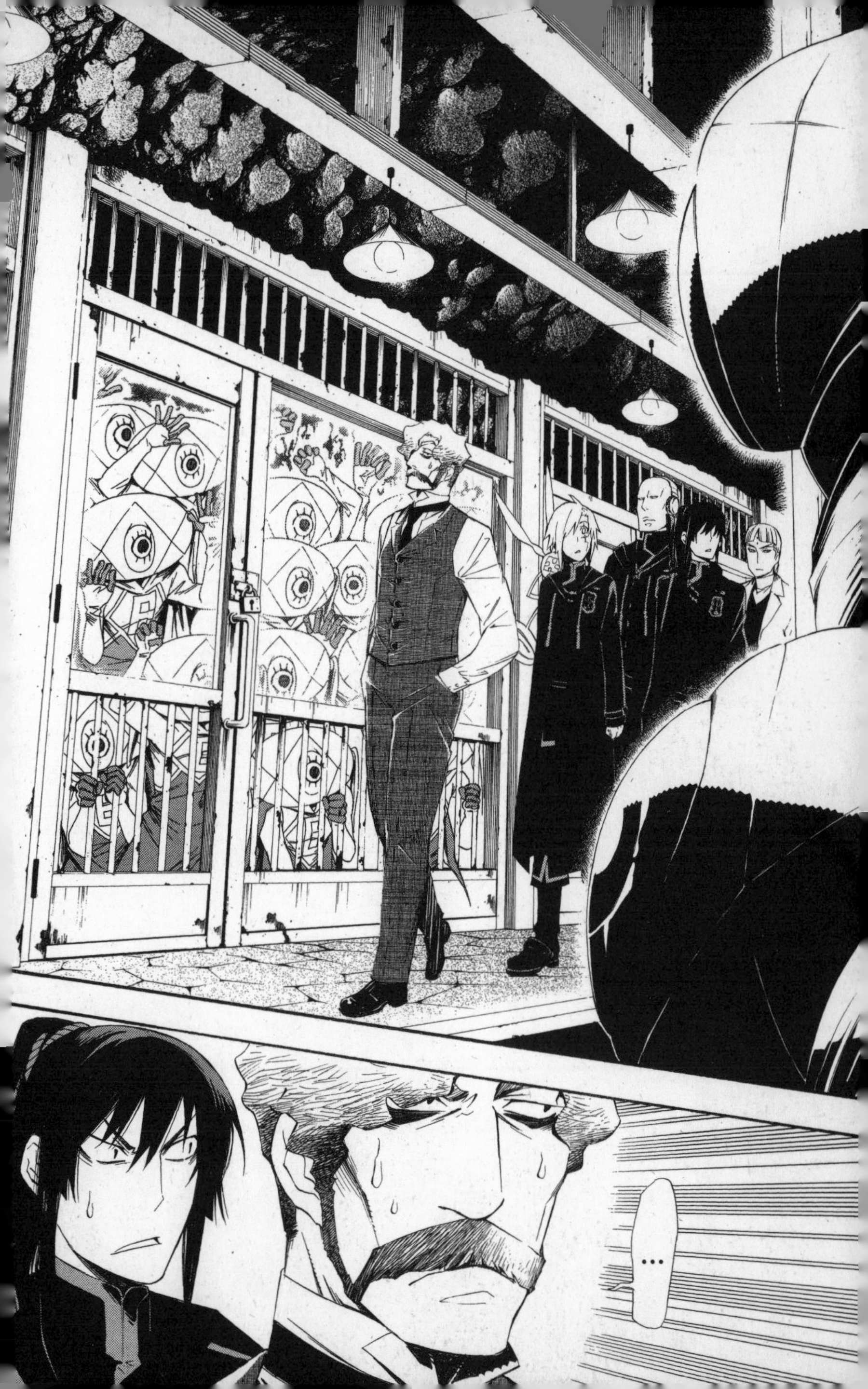
...

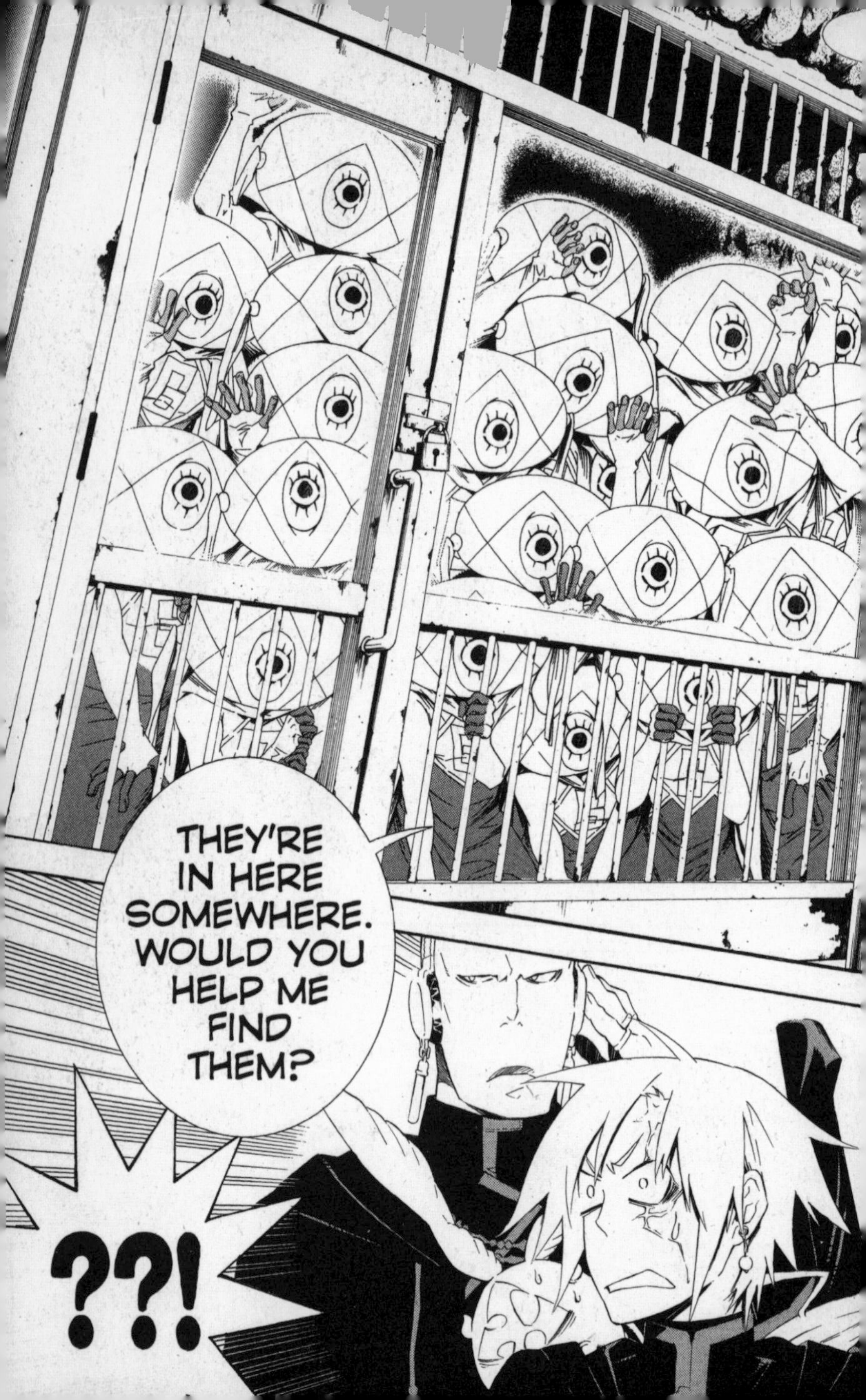
THEY'RE IN HERE SOMEWHERE. WOULD YOU HELP ME FIND THEM?
??!

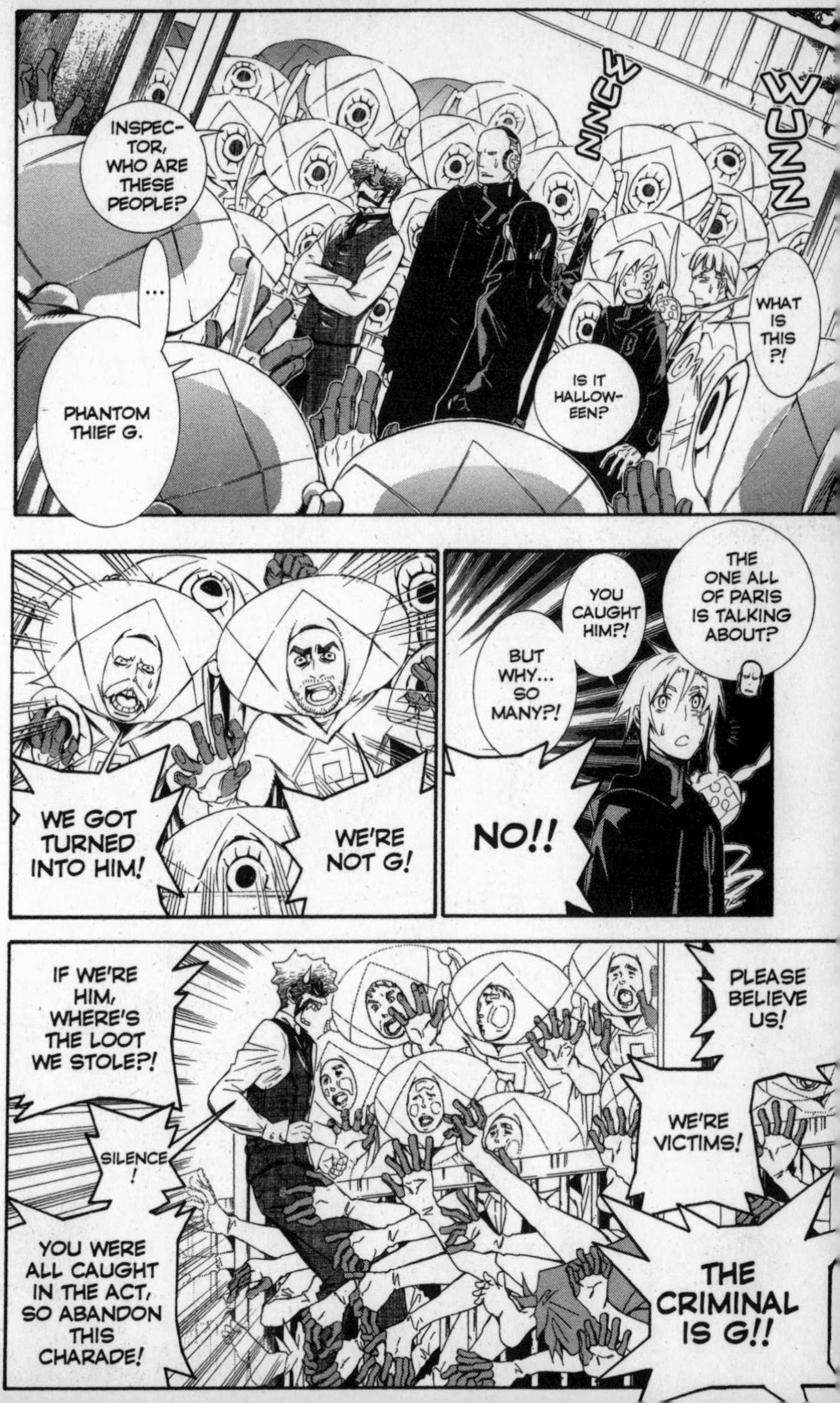
WUNN
WHAT IS THIS?!
WUNN
IS IT HALLOWEEN?
INSPECTOR, WHO ARE THESE PEOPLE?
...
PHANTOM THIEF G.
THE ONE ALL OF PARIS IS TALKING ABOUT?
YOU CAUGHT HIM?!
BUT WHY... SO MANY?!
NO!!
WE'RE NOT G!
WE GOT TURNED INTO HIM!
PLEASE BELIEVE US!
IF WE'RE HIM, WHERE'S THE LOOT WE STOLE?!
WE'RE VICTIMS!
SILENCE!
THE CRIMINAL IS G!!
YOU WERE ALL CAUGHT IN THE ACT, SO ABANDON THIS CHARADE!

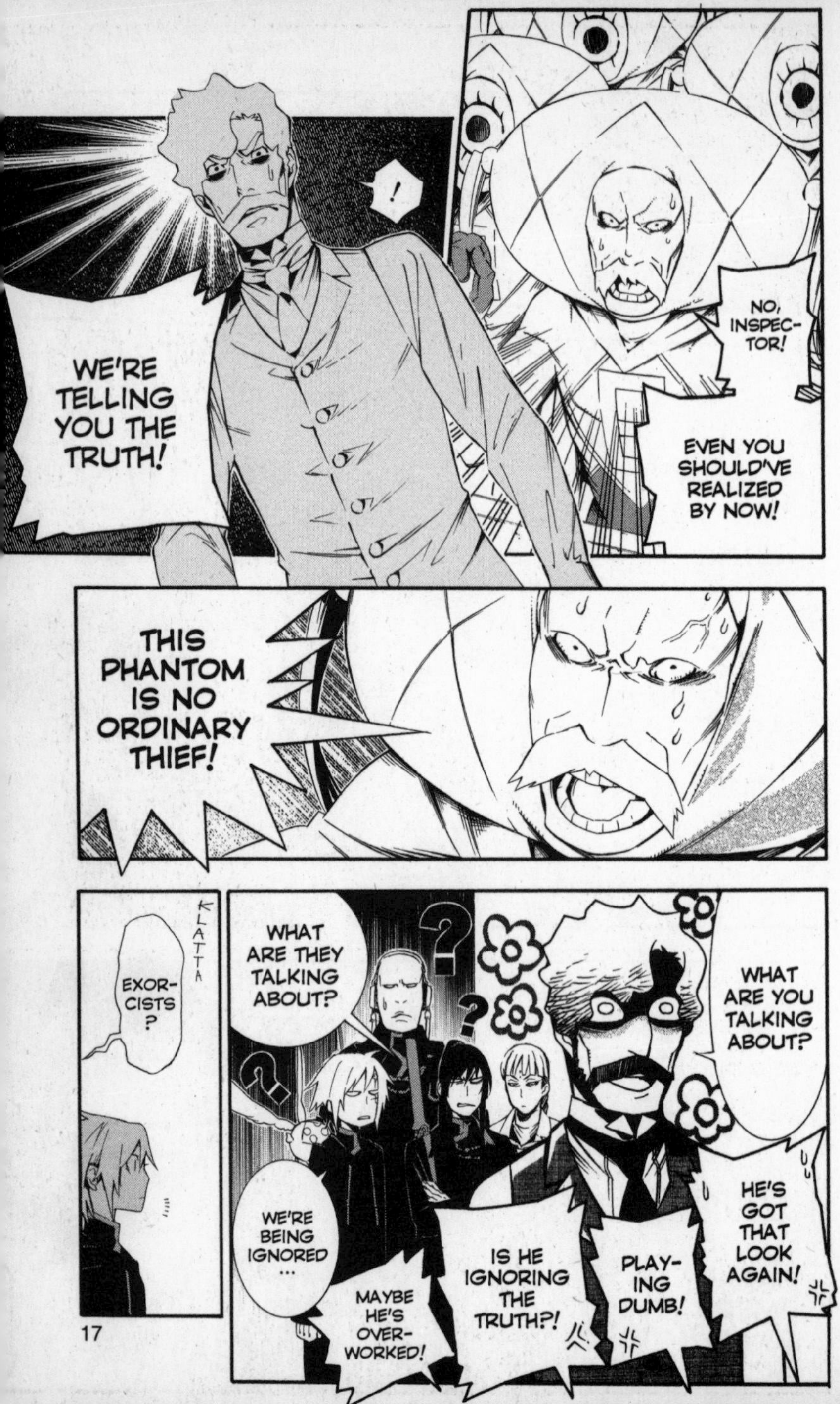
NO, INSPEC-TOR!
EVEN YOU SHOULD'VE REALIZED BY NOW!
!
WE'RE TELLING YOU THE TRUTH!
THIS PHANTOM IS NO ORDINARY THIEF!
WHAT ARE YOU TALKING ABOUT?
WHAT ARE THEY TALKING ABOUT?
HE'S GOT THAT LOOK AGAIN!
PLAY-ING DUMB!
IS HE IGNORING THE TRUTH?!
MAYBE HE'S OVER-WORKED!
WE'RE BEING IGNORED ...
KLATTA
EXOR-CISTS ?

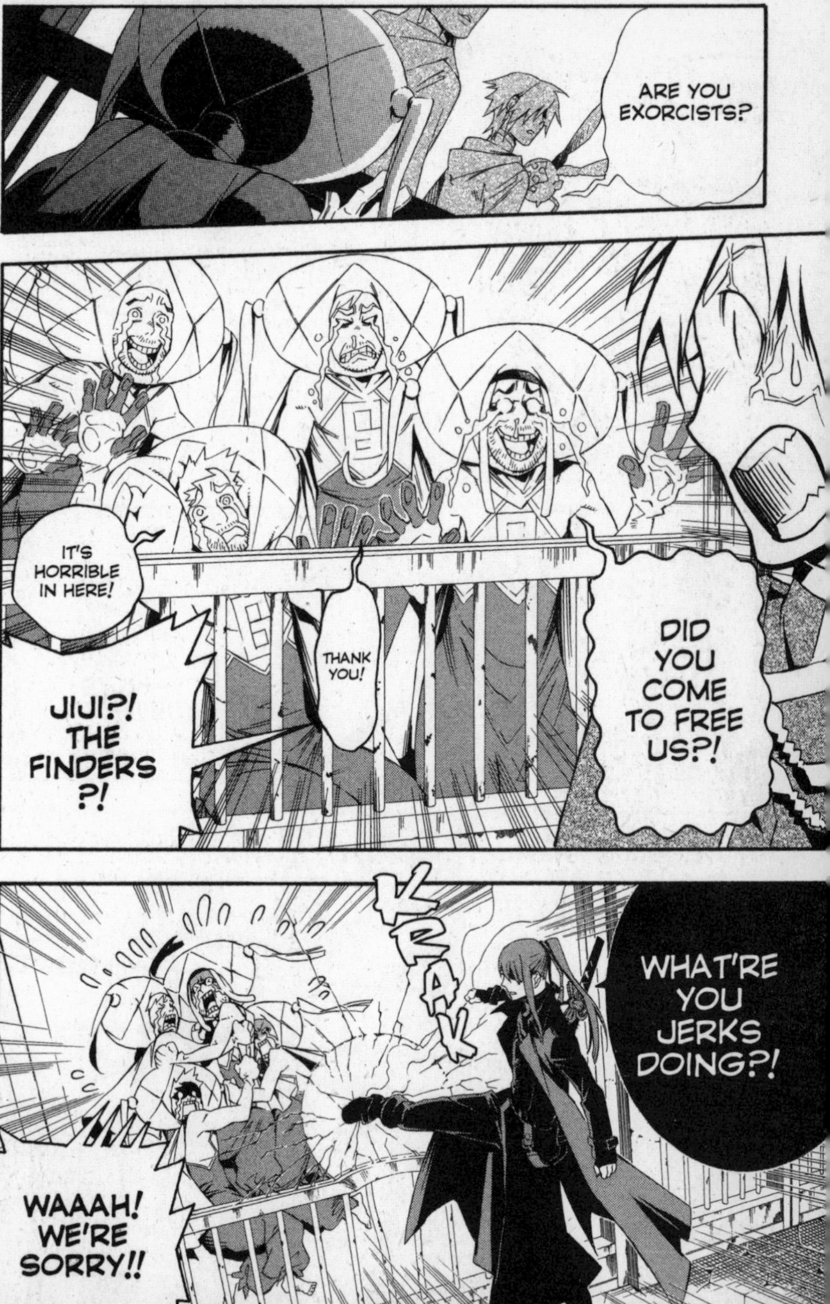
ARE YOU EXORCISTS?
DID YOU COME TO FREE US?!
THANK YOU!
IT'S HORRIBLE IN HERE!
JIJI?! THE FINDERS ?!
WHAT'RE YOU JERKS DOING?!
KRAK
WAAAH! WE'RE SORRY!!

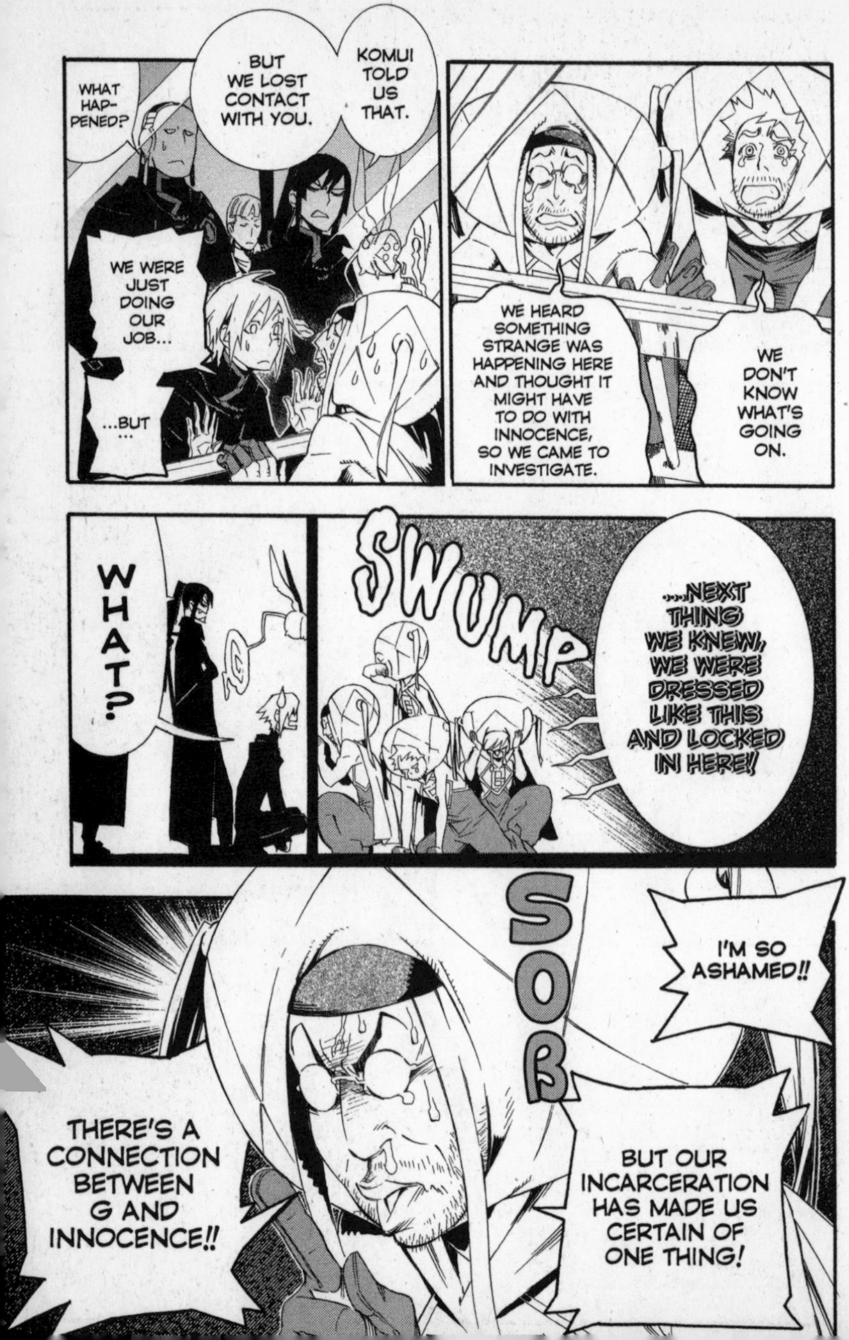
WE DON'T KNOW WHAT'S GOING ON.
WE HEARD SOMETHING STRANGE WAS HAPPENING HERE AND THOUGHT IT MIGHT HAVE TO DO WITH INNOCENCE, SO WE CAME TO INVESTIGATE.
KOMUI TOLD US THAT.
BUT WE LOST CONTACT WITH YOU.
WHAT HAP-PENED?
WE WERE JUST DOING OUR JOB...
...BUT...
...NEXT THING WE KNEW, WE WERE DRESSED LIKE THIS AND LOCKED IN HERE!
SWUMP
WHAT?
I'M SO ASHAMED!!
SOB
BUT OUR INCARCERATION HAS MADE US CERTAIN OF ONE THING!
THERE'S A CONNECTION BETWEEN G AND INNOCENCE!!

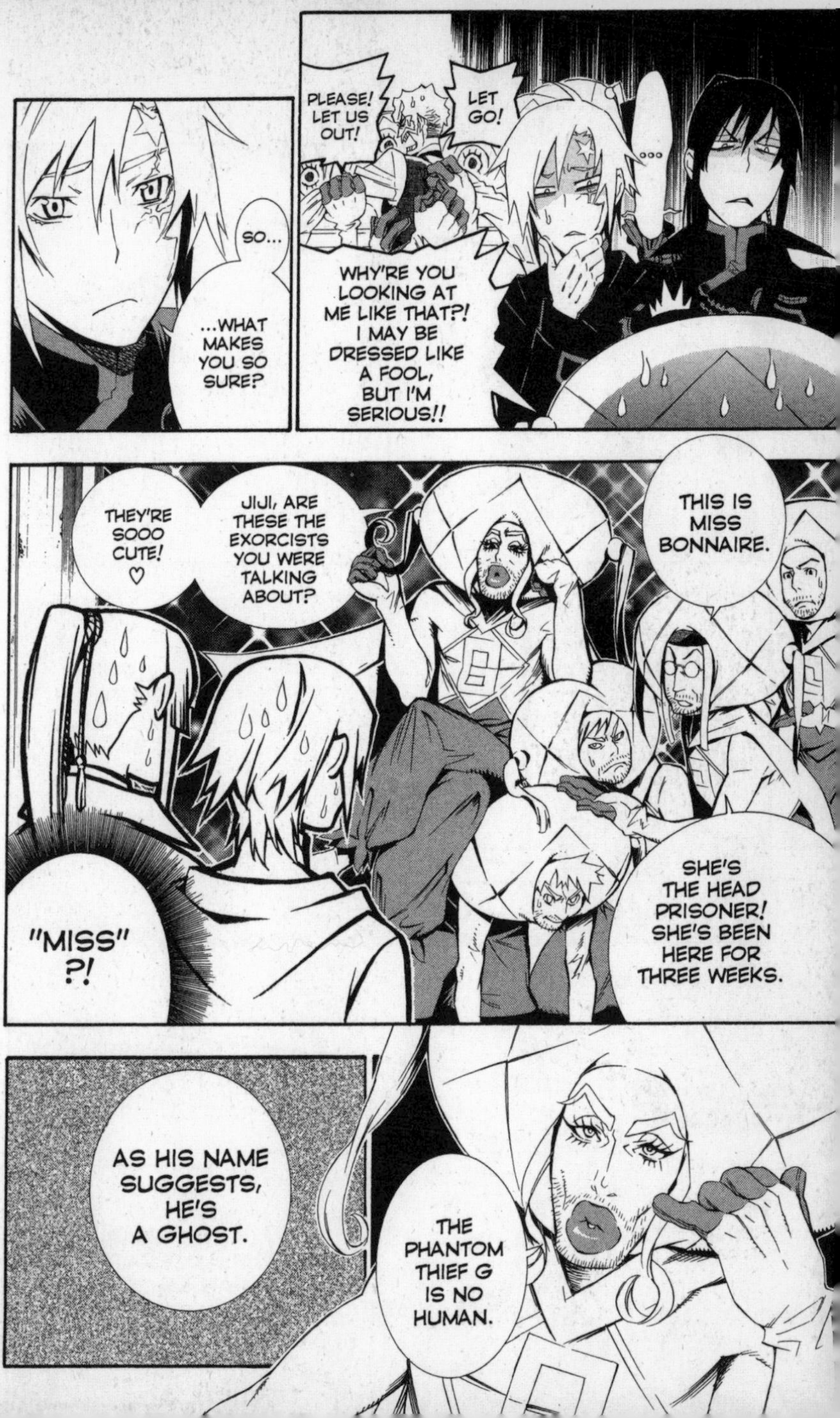
...
LET GO!
PLEASE! LET US OUT!
WHY'RE YOU LOOKING AT ME LIKE THAT?! I MAY BE DRESSED LIKE A FOOL, BUT I'M SERIOUS!!
SO...
...WHAT MAKES YOU SO SURE?
THIS IS MISS BONNAIRE.
JIJI, ARE THESE THE EXORCISTS YOU WERE TALKING ABOUT?
THEY'RE SOOO CUTE! ♡
SHE'S THE HEAD PRISONER! SHE'S BEEN HERE FOR THREE WEEKS.
"MISS" ?!
THE PHANTOM THIEF G IS NO HUMAN.
AS HIS NAME SUGGESTS, HE'S A GHOST.

READ THIS WAY

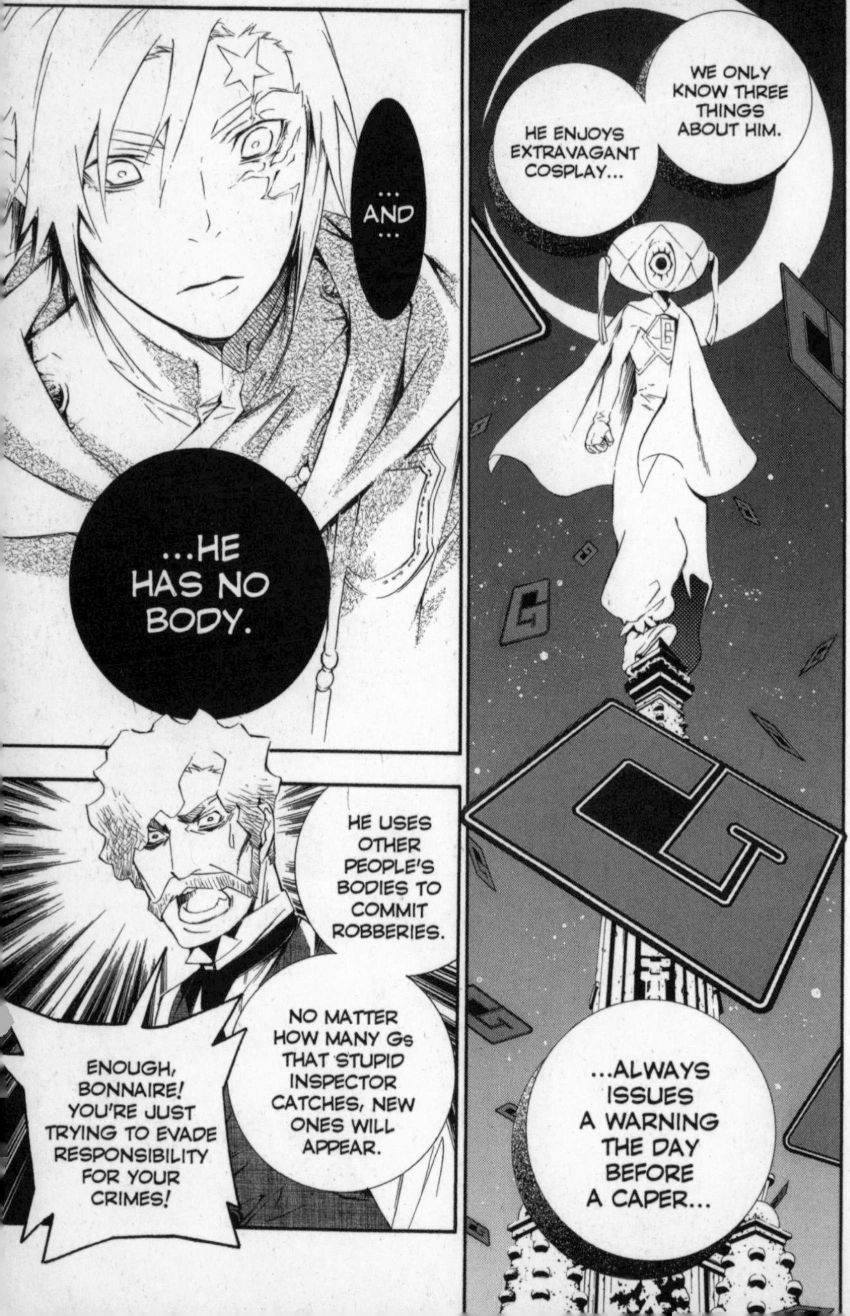
WE ONLY KNOW THREE THINGS ABOUT HIM.
HE ENJOYS EXTRAVAGANT COSPLAY...
...ALWAYS ISSUES A WARNING THE DAY BEFORE A CAPER...
...AND...
...HE HAS NO BODY.
HE USES OTHER PEOPLE'S BODIES TO COMMIT ROBBERIES.
NO MATTER HOW MANY Gs THAT STUPID INSPECTOR CATCHES, NEW ONES WILL APPEAR.
ENOUGH, BONNAIRE! YOU'RE JUST TRYING TO EVADE RESPONSIBILITY FOR YOUR CRIMES!

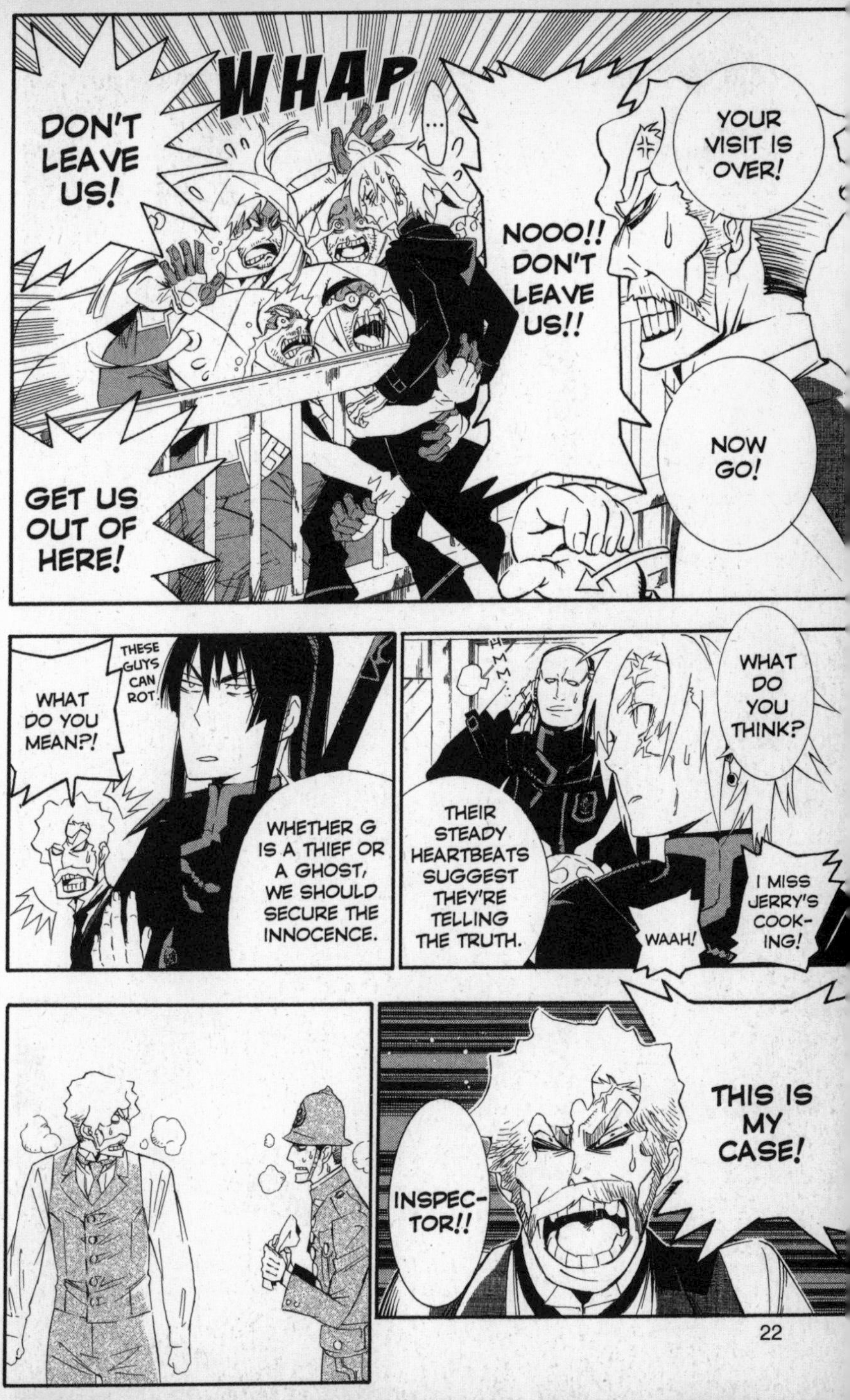
YOUR VISIT IS OVER!
...
NOOO!! DON'T LEAVE US!!
WHAP
DON'T LEAVE US!
NOW GO!
GET US OUT OF HERE!
WHAT DO YOU THINK?
HMM..
I MISS JERRY'S COOK-ING!
WAAH!
THEIR STEADY HEARTBEATS SUGGEST THEY'RE TELLING THE TRUTH.
THESE GUYS CAN ROT.
WHAT DO YOU MEAN?!
WHETHER G IS A THIEF OR A GHOST, WE SHOULD SECURE THE INNOCENCE.
THIS IS MY CASE!
INSPEC-TOR!!

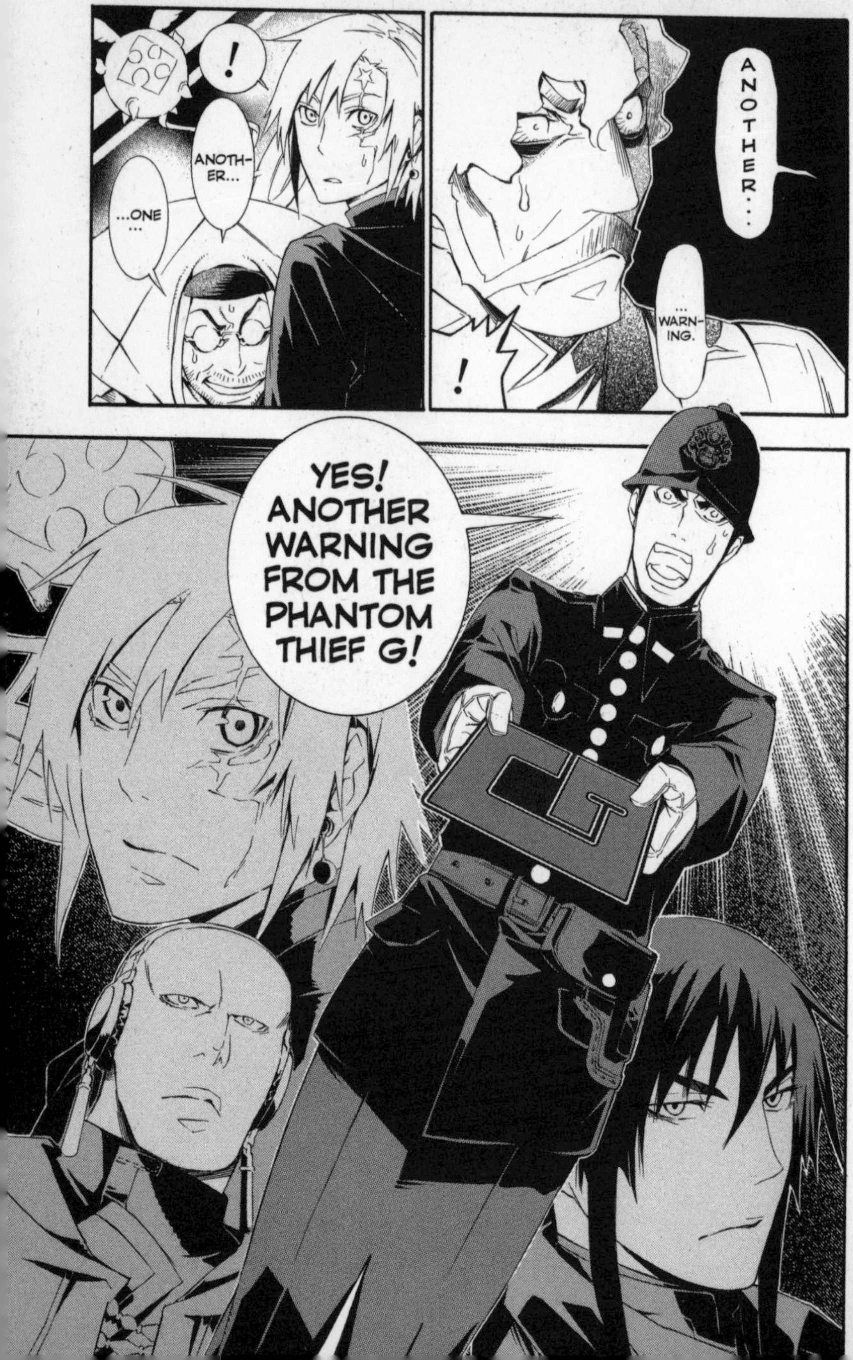
ANOTHER...
...WARNING.
!
!
ANOTHER...
...ONE...
YES! ANOTHER WARNING FROM THE PHANTOM THIEF G!

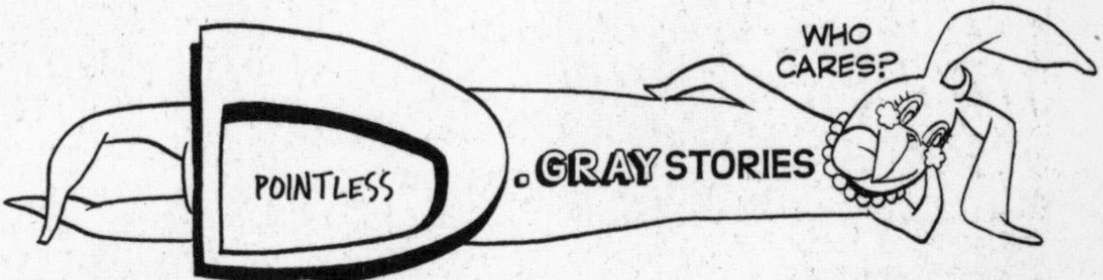
WHO CARES?
POINTLESS D.GRAY STORIES

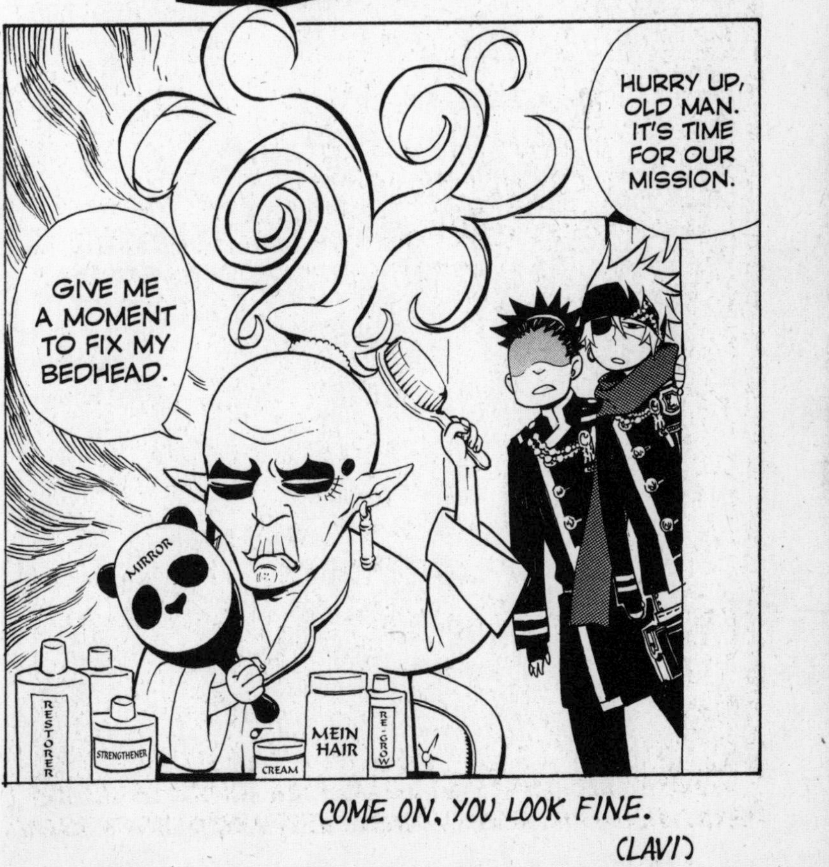
HURRY UP, OLD MAN. IT'S TIME FOR OUR MISSION.
GIVE ME A MOMENT TO FIX MY BEDHEAD.
MIRROR
RESTORER
STRENGTHENER
CREAM
MEIN HAIR
RE-GROW

COME ON, YOU LOOK FINE.

(LAVI)

THE 173RD NIGHT:

THIEF? GHOST? INNOCENCE?

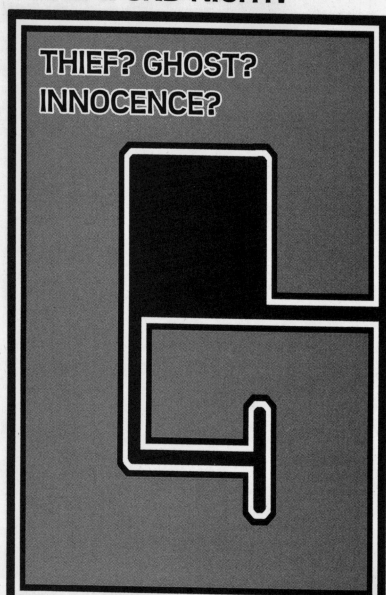

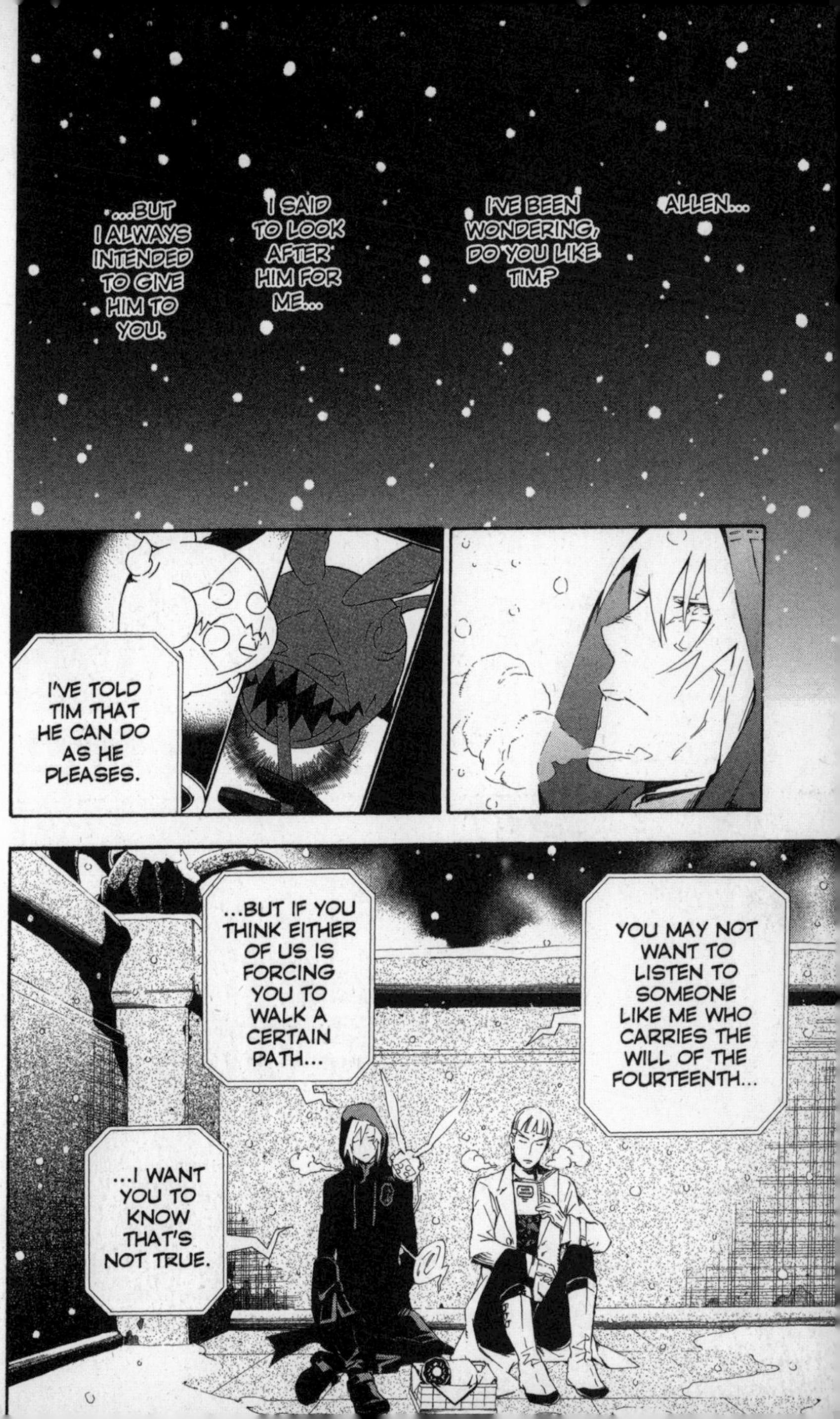
ALLEN...
I'VE BEEN WONDERING, DO YOU LIKE TIM?
I SAID TO LOOK AFTER HIM FOR ME...
...BUT I ALWAYS INTENDED TO GIVE HIM TO YOU.
I'VE TOLD TIM THAT HE CAN DO AS HE PLEASES.
YOU MAY NOT WANT TO LISTEN TO SOMEONE LIKE ME WHO CARRIES THE WILL OF THE FOURTEENTH...
...BUT IF YOU THINK EITHER OF US IS FORCING YOU TO WALK A CERTAIN PATH...
...I WANT YOU TO KNOW THAT'S NOT TRUE.

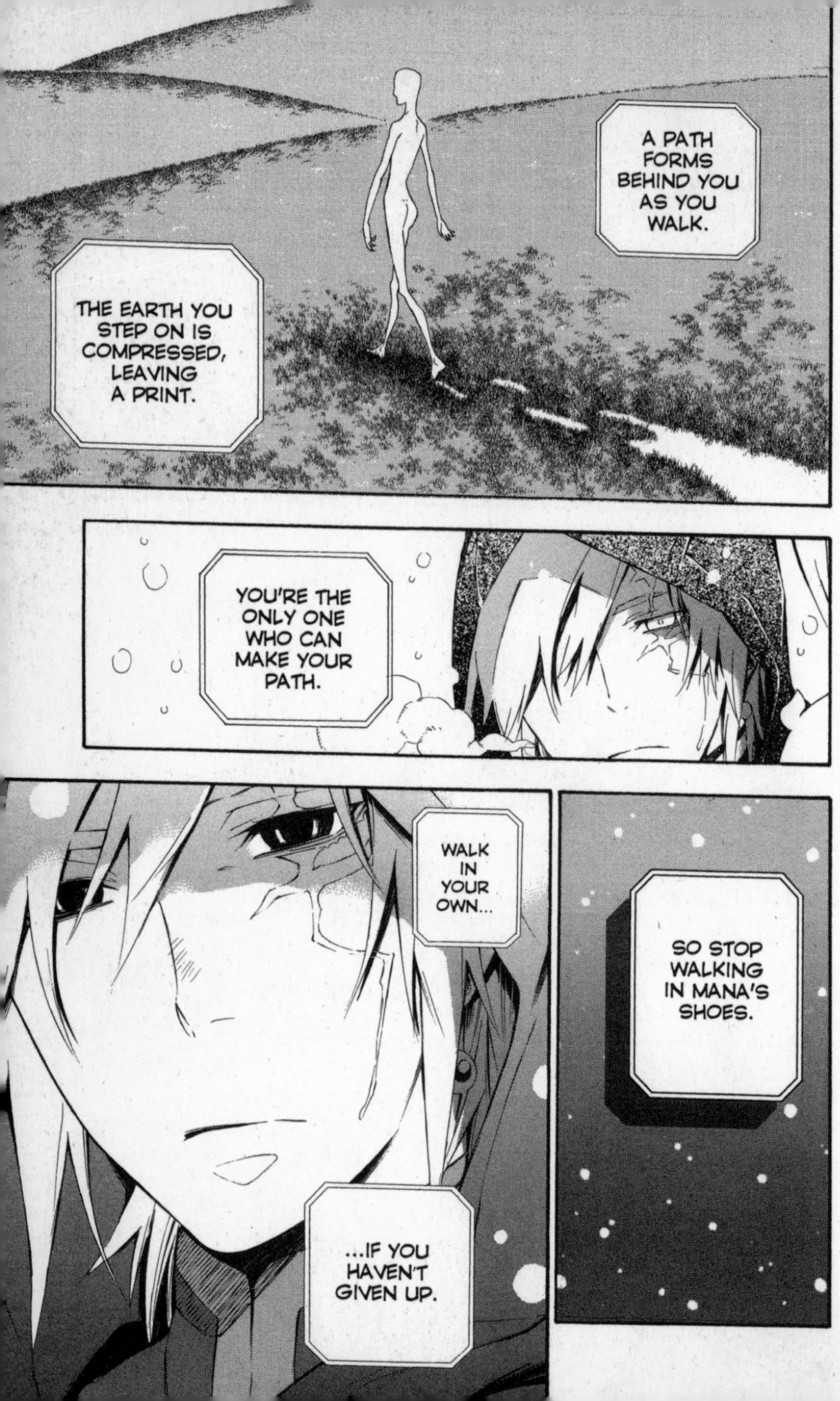
A PATH FORMS BEHIND YOU AS YOU WALK.
THE EARTH YOU STEP ON IS COMPRESSED, LEAVING A PRINT.
YOU'RE THE ONLY ONE WHO CAN MAKE YOUR PATH.
SO STOP WALKING IN MANA'S SHOES.
WALK IN YOUR OWN...
...IF YOU HAVEN'T GIVEN UP.

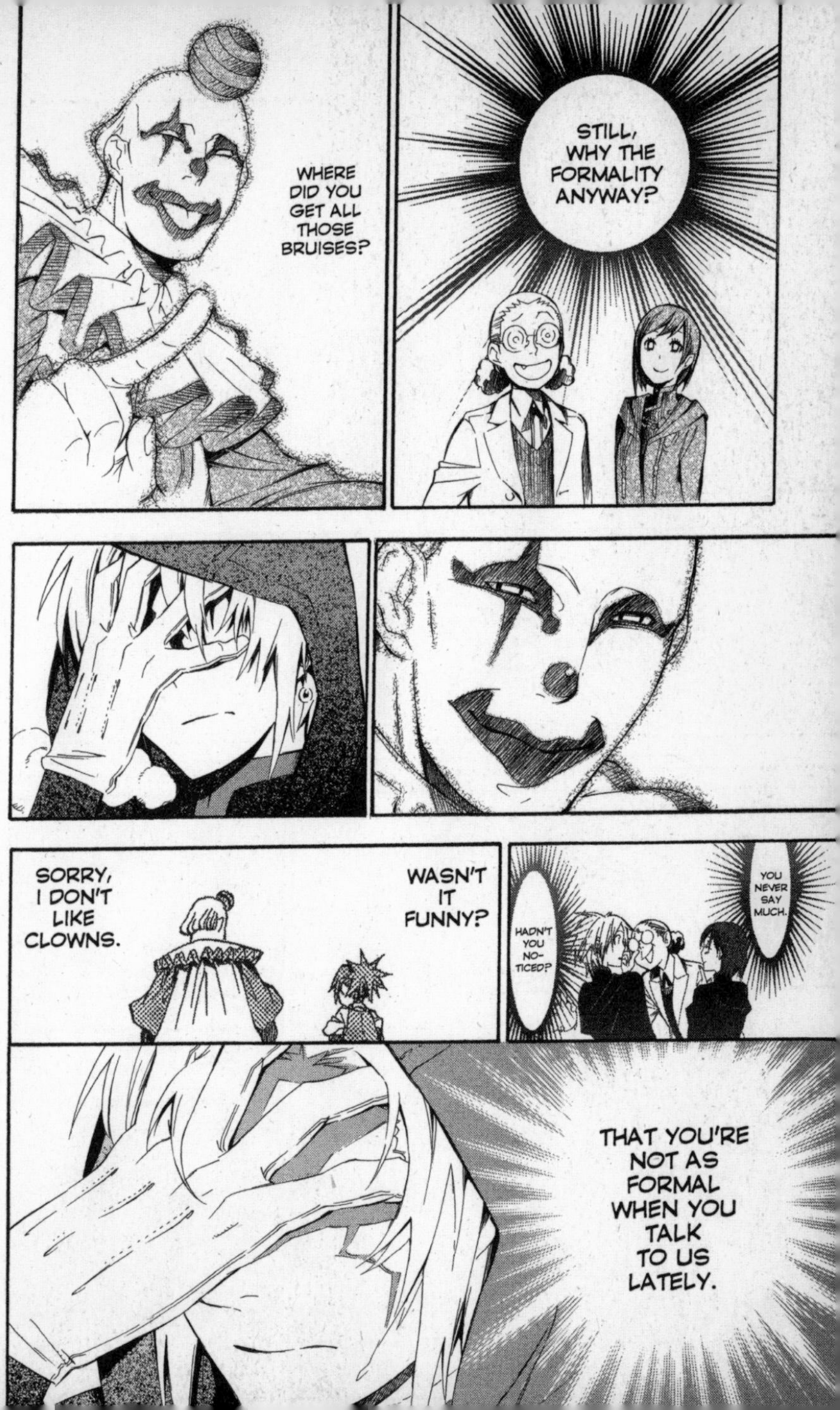
STILL, WHY THE FORMALITY ANYWAY?
WHERE DID YOU GET ALL THOSE BRUISES?
YOU NEVER SAY MUCH.
HADN'T YOU NO-TICED?
WASN'T IT FUNNY?
SORRY, I DON'T LIKE CLOWNS.
THAT YOU'RE NOT AS FORMAL WHEN YOU TALK TO US LATELY.

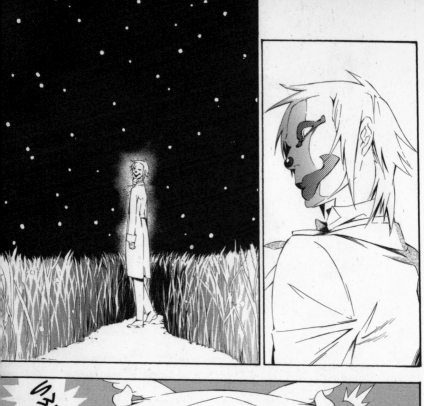

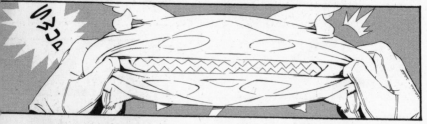

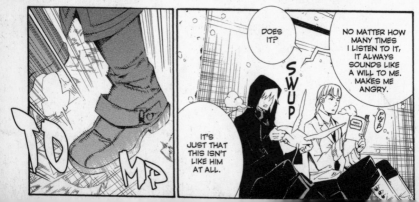

DOES IT?

NO MATTER HOW MANY TIMES I LISTEN TO IT, IT ALWAYS SOUNDS LIKE A WILL TO ME. MAKES ME ANGRY.

IT'S JUST THAT THIS ISN'T LIKE HIM AT ALL.

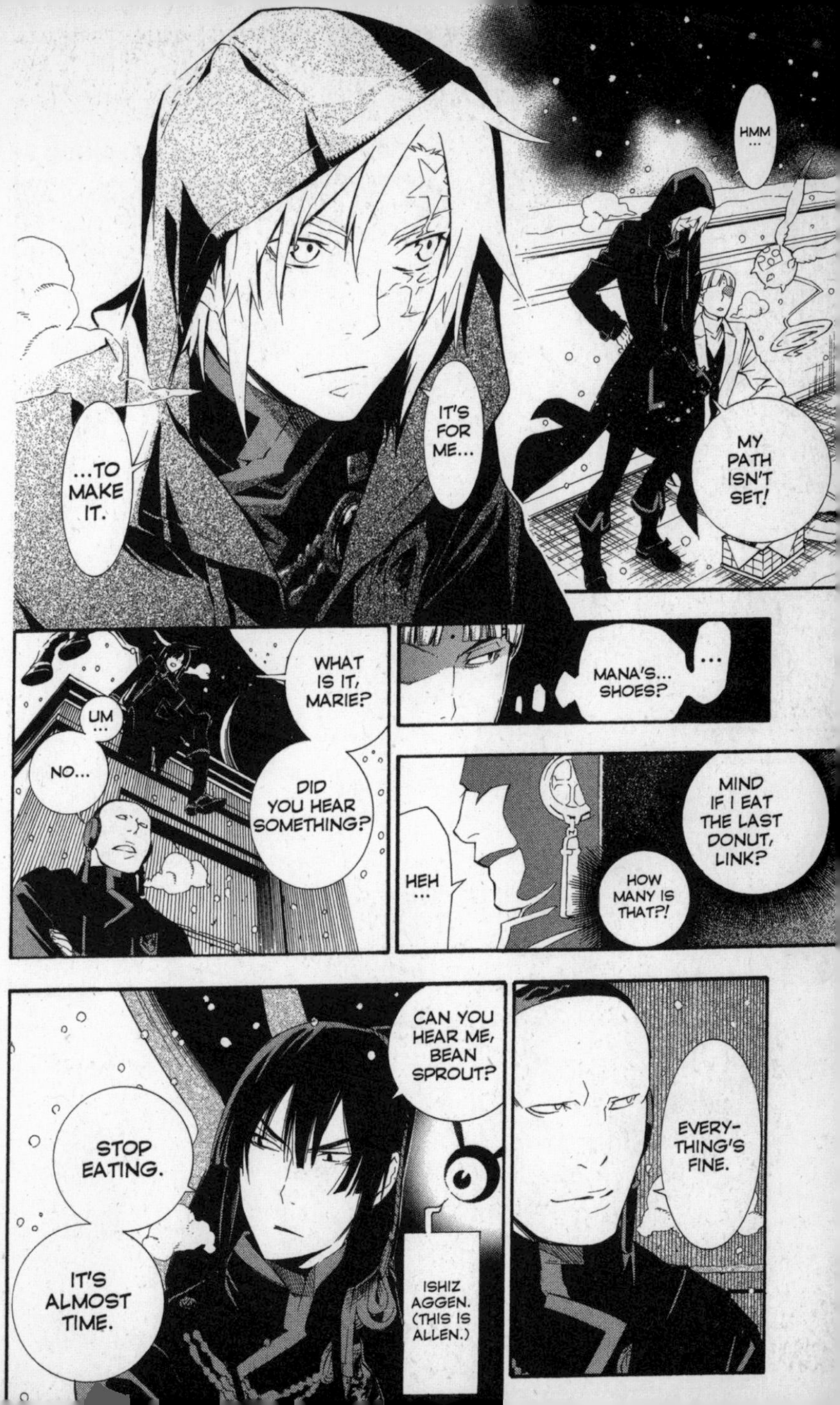
HMM...
MY PATH ISN'T SET!
IT'S FOR ME...
...TO MAKE IT.
...
MANA'S... SHOES?
MIND IF I EAT THE LAST DONUT, LINK?
HOW MANY IS THAT?!
HEH...
WHAT IS IT, MARIE?
DID YOU HEAR SOMETHING?
UM...
NO...
EVERY-THING'S FINE.
CAN YOU HEAR ME, BEAN SPROUT?
STOP EATING.
ISHIZ AGGEN. (THIS IS ALLEN.)
IT'S ALMOST TIME.

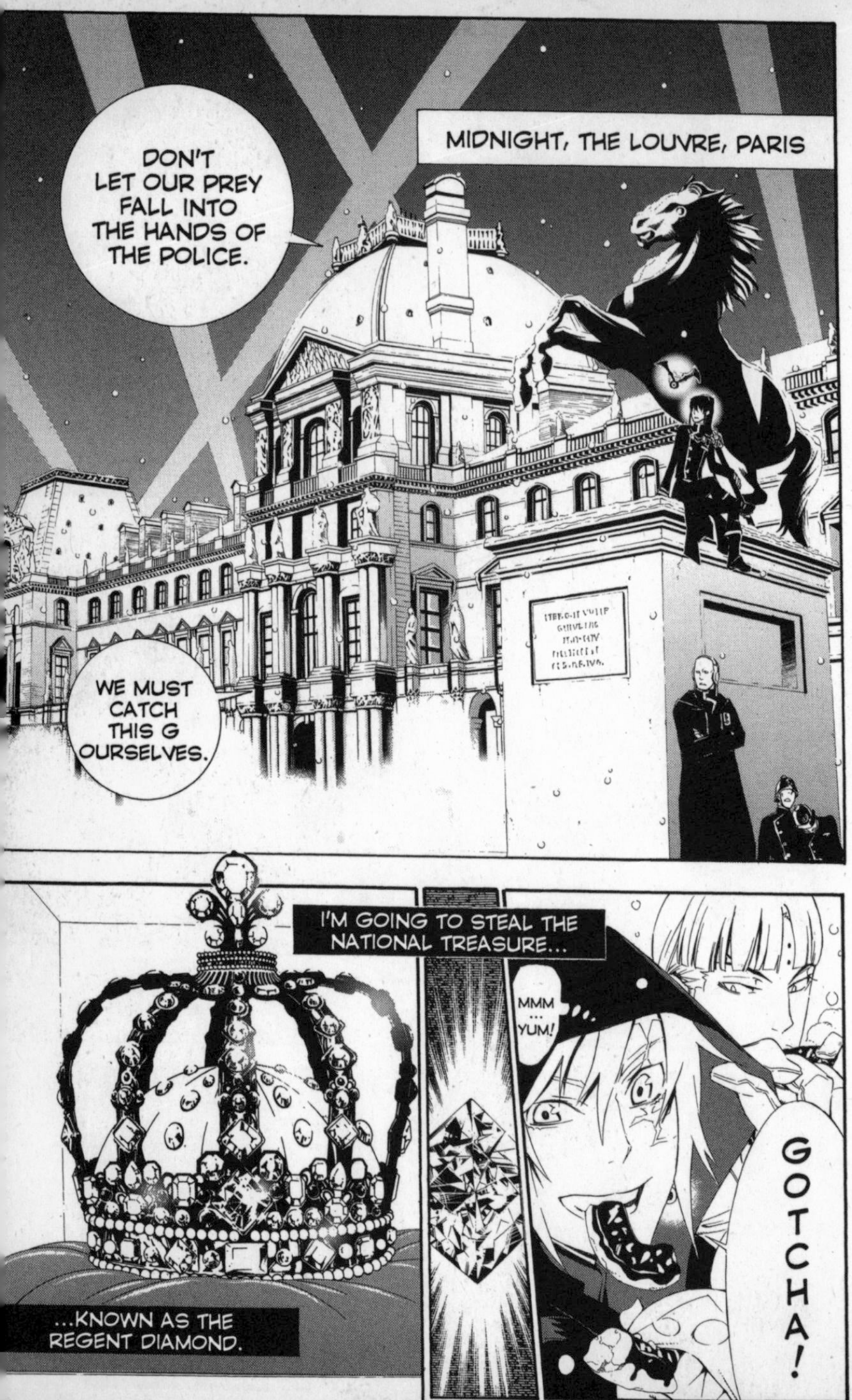
MIDNIGHT, THE LOUVRE, PARIS
DON'T LET OUR PREY FALL INTO THE HANDS OF THE POLICE.
WE MUST CATCH THIS G OURSELVES.
MMM... YUM!
GOTCHA!
I'M GOING TO STEAL THE NATIONAL TREASURE...
...KNOWN AS THE REGENT DIAMOND.

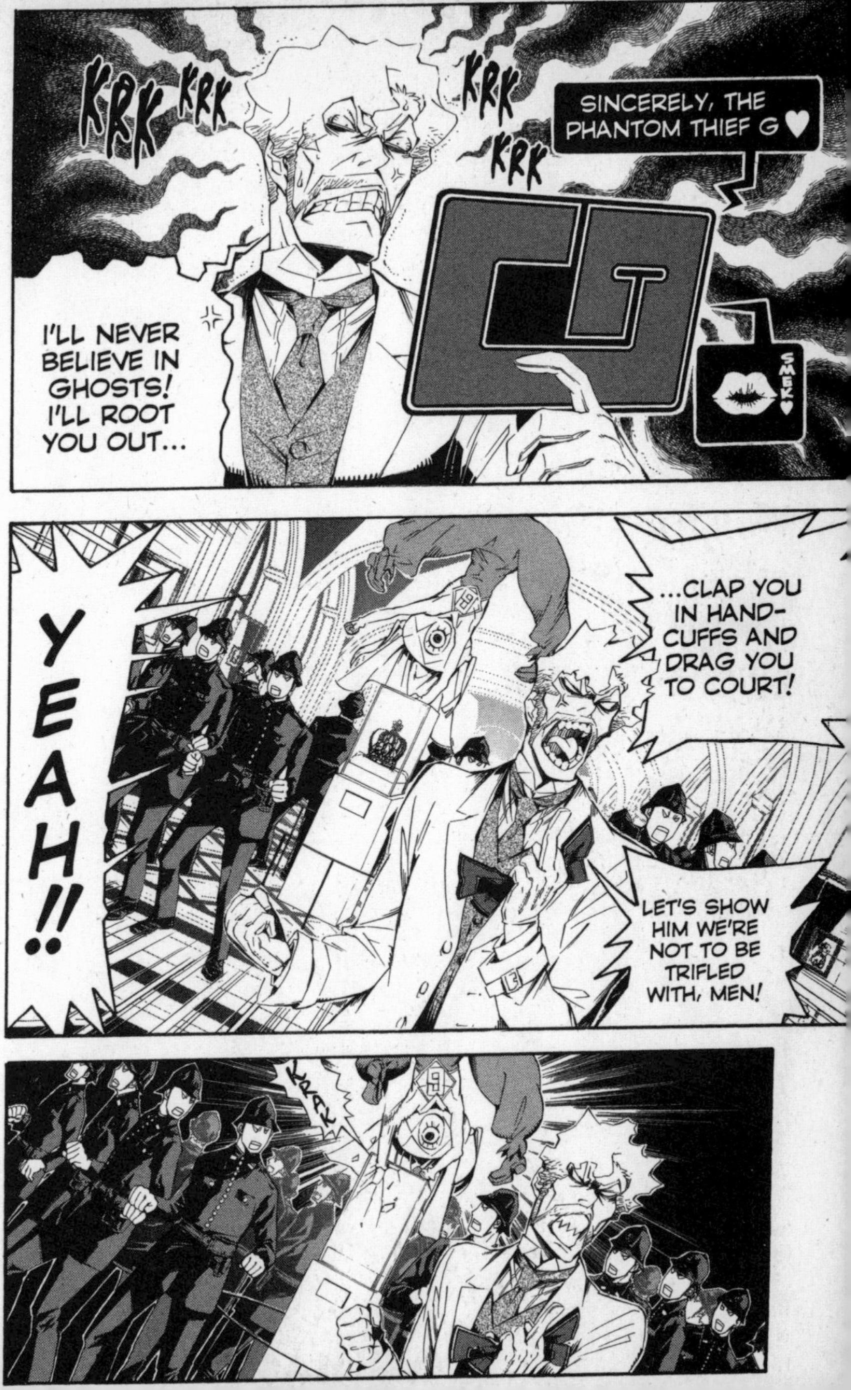
SINCERELY, THE PHANTOM THIEF G ♥
SMEK ♥
KRK
KRK
KRK
KRK
I'LL NEVER BELIEVE IN GHOSTS! I'LL ROOT YOU OUT...
...CLAP YOU IN HAND-CUFFS AND DRAG YOU TO COURT!
LET'S SHOW HIM WE'RE NOT TO BE TRIFLED WITH, MEN!
YEAH!!
KRAK

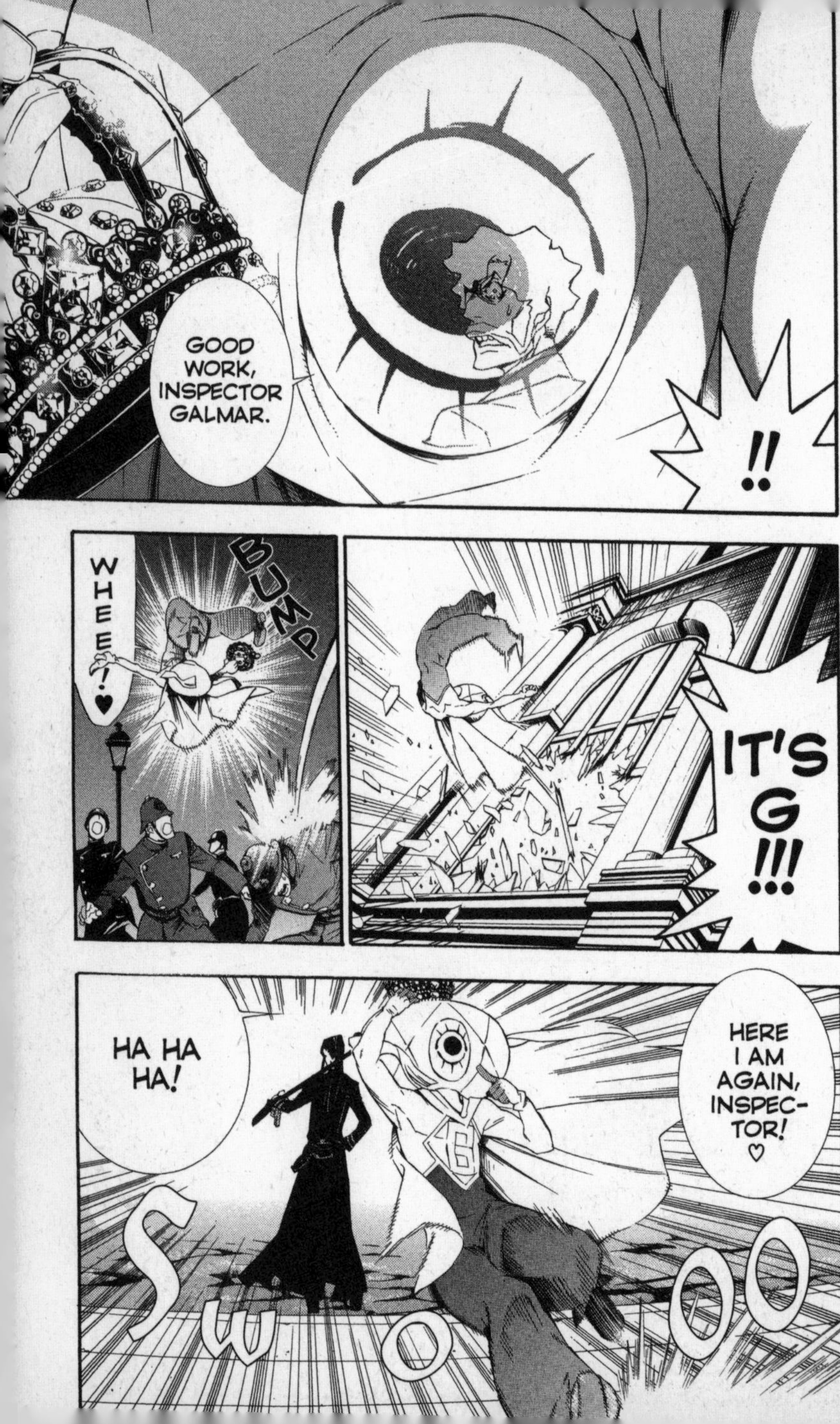

!!
GOOD WORK, INSPECTOR GALMAR.
IT'S G!!!
BUMP
WHEEE!♥
HERE I AM AGAIN, INSPECTOR! ♡
HA HA HA!
SWOOOO

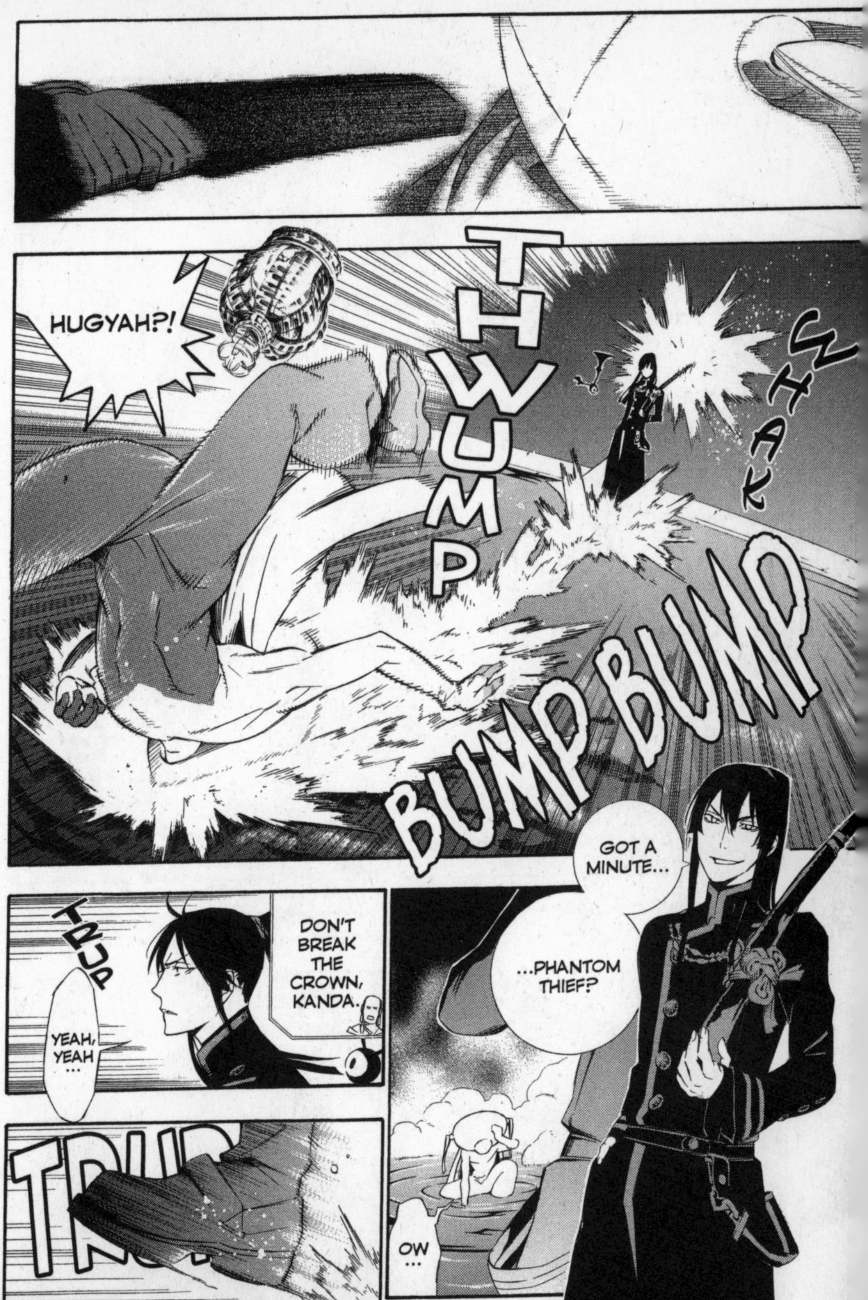
WHAK
THWUMP
HUGYAH?!
BUMP BUMP
GOT A MINUTE...
...PHANTOM THIEF?
OW ...
TRUP
DON'T BREAK THE CROWN, KANDA.
YEAH, YEAH ...
TRUP

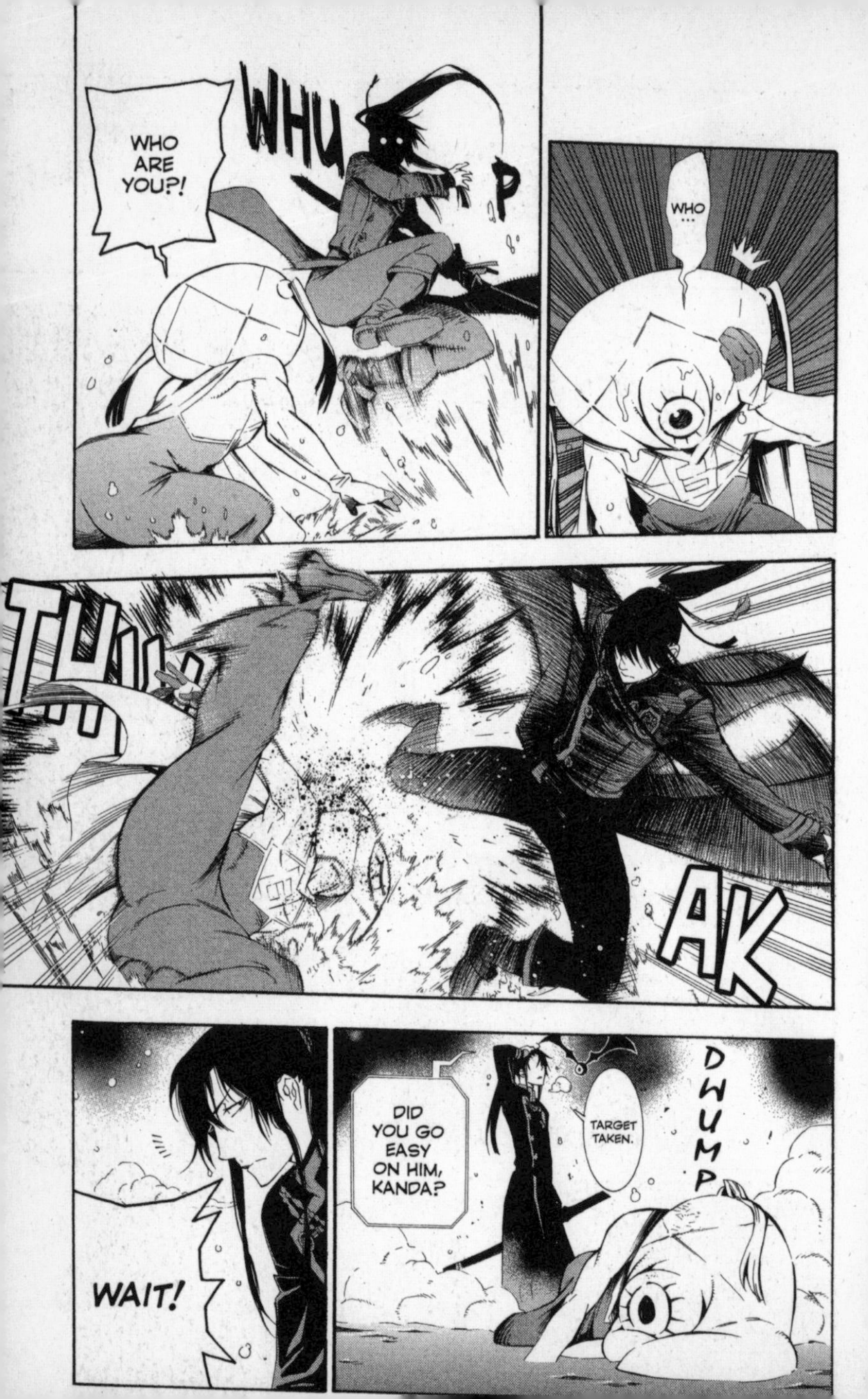
WHO ...
WHUP
WHO ARE YOU?!
TH
AK
DWUMP
TARGET TAKEN.
DID YOU GO EASY ON HIM, KANDA?
WAIT!

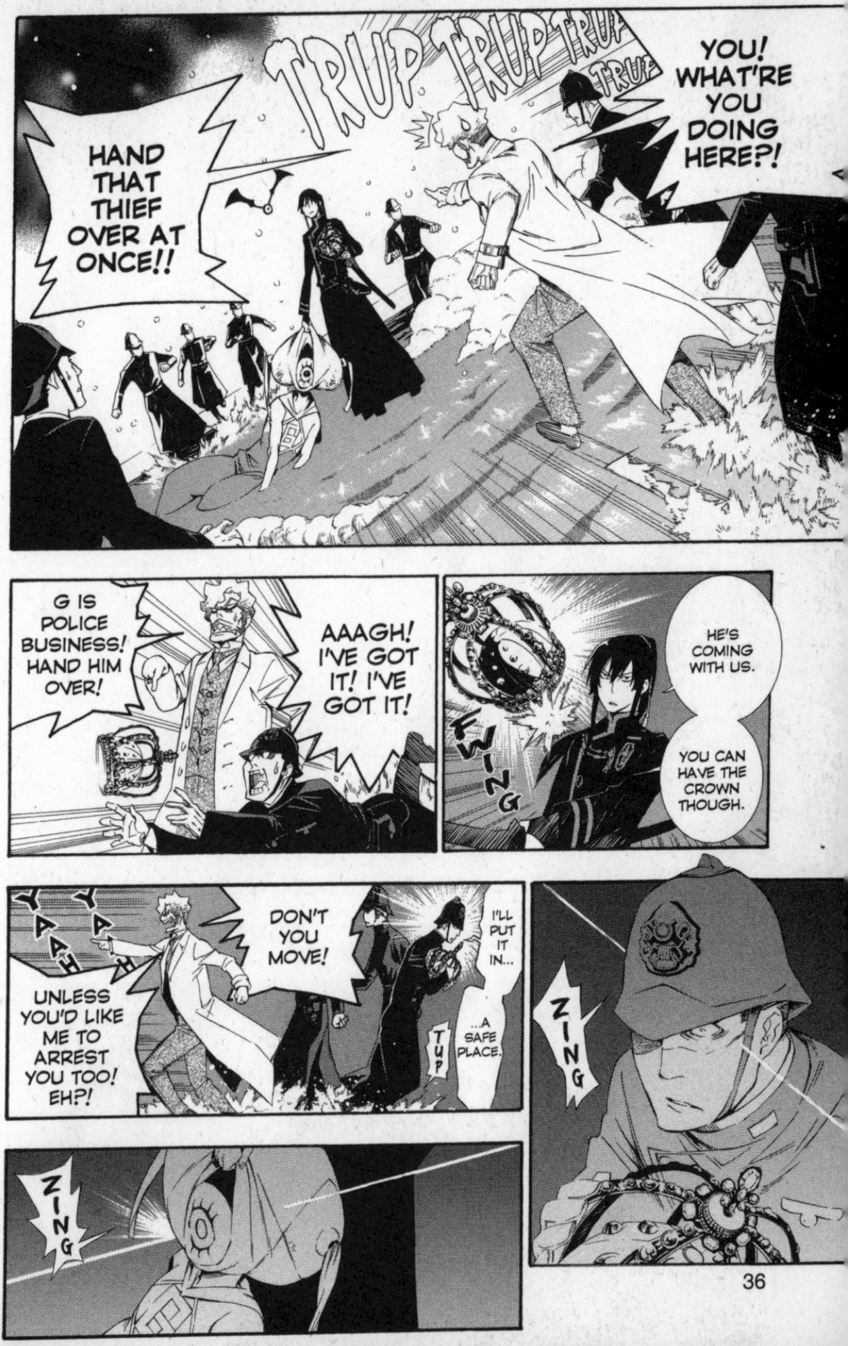
YOU! WHAT'RE YOU DOING HERE?!
TRUP TRUP TRUP TRUP
HAND THAT THIEF OVER AT ONCE!!
HE'S COMING WITH US.
YOU CAN HAVE THE CROWN THOUGH.
FWING
AAAGH! I'VE GOT IT! I'VE GOT IT!
G IS POLICE BUSINESS! HAND HIM OVER!
ZING
I'LL PUT IT IN...
...A SAFE PLACE.
TUP
DON'T YOU MOVE!
YAAAH
UNLESS YOU'D LIKE ME TO ARREST YOU TOO! EH?!
ZING

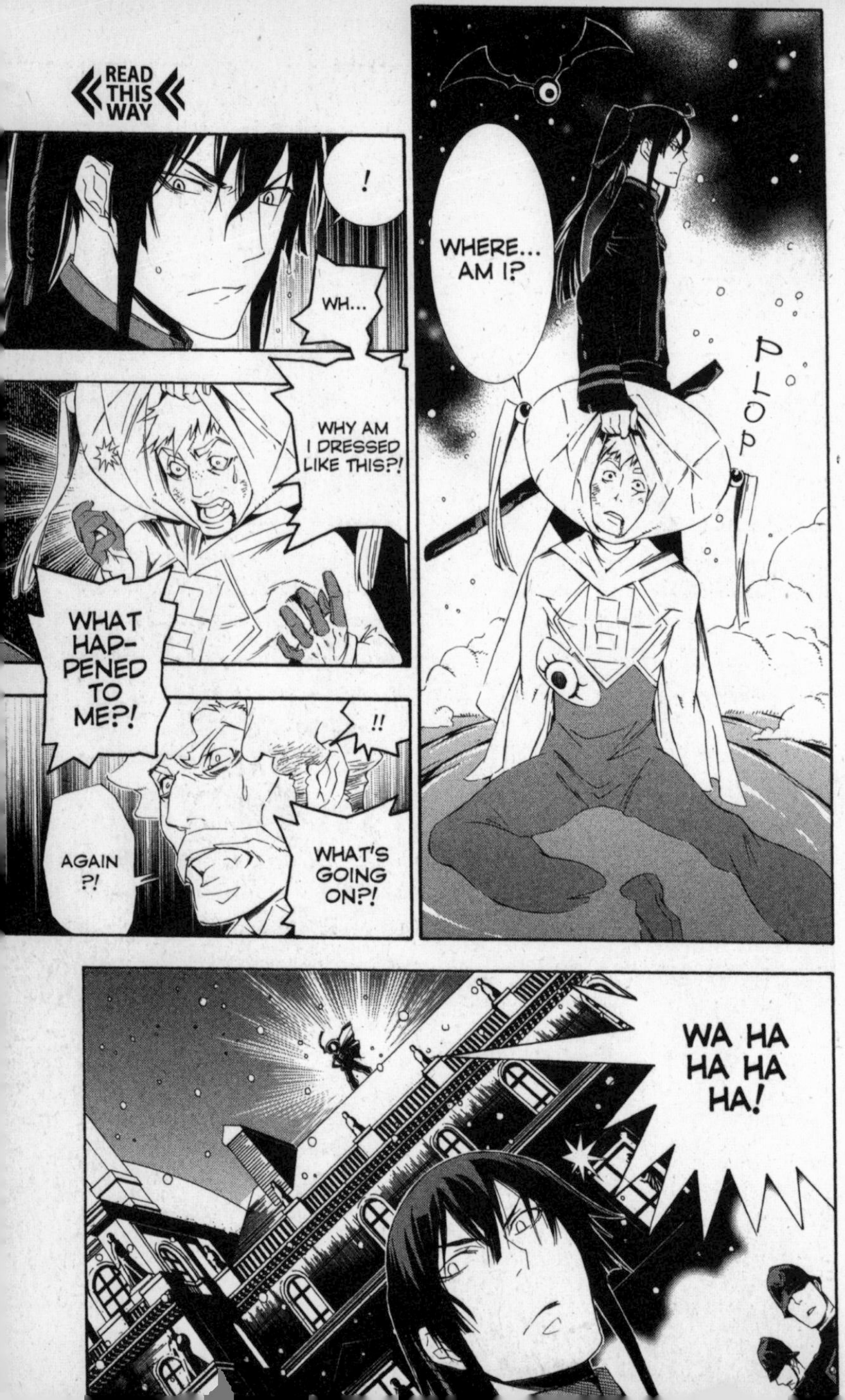
READ THIS WAY
WHERE... AM I?
PLOP
!
WH...
WHY AM I DRESSED LIKE THIS?!
WHAT HAP-PENED TO ME?!
!!
WHAT'S GOING ON?!
AGAIN ?!
WA HA HA HA HA!

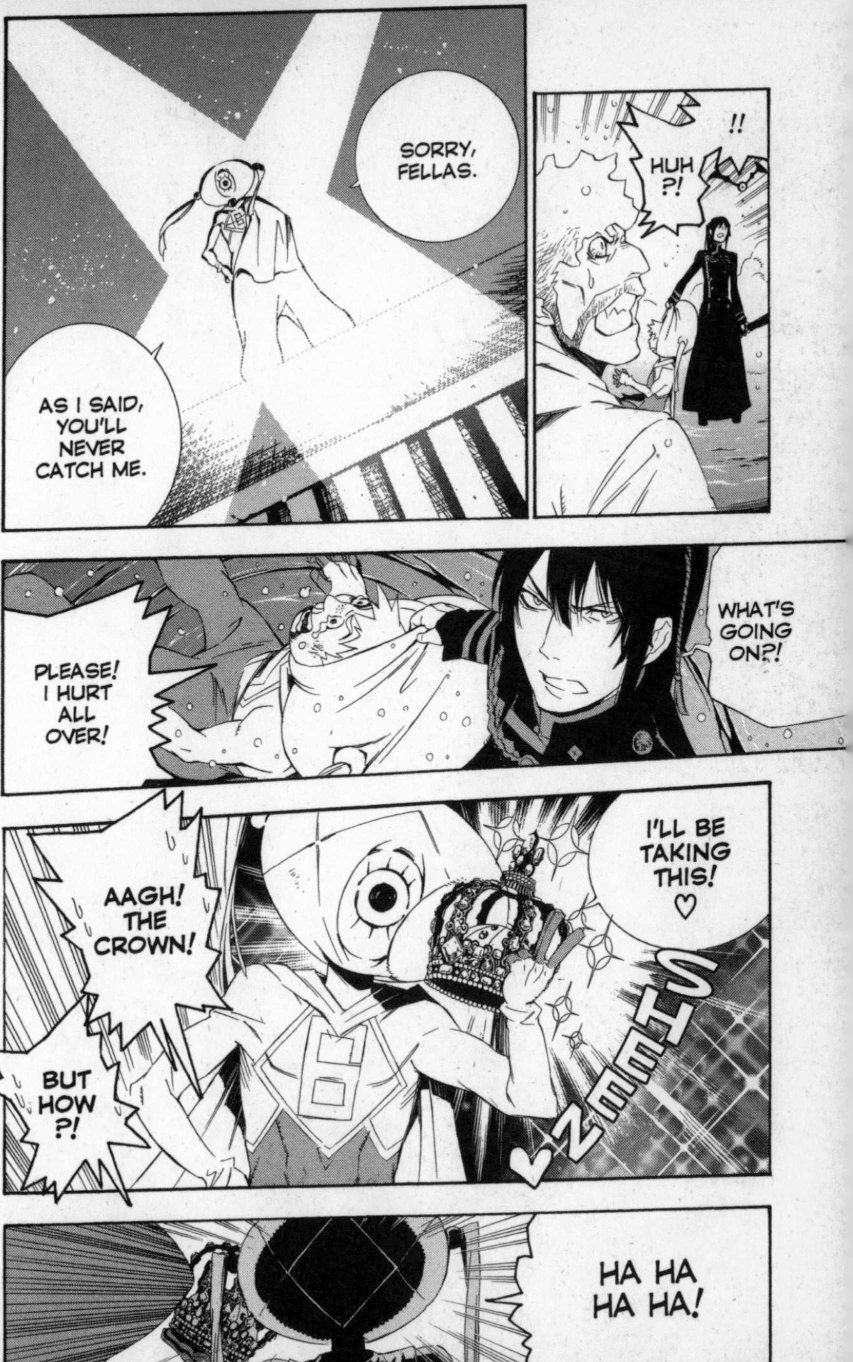
!!
HUH ?!
SORRY, FELLAS.
AS I SAID, YOU'LL NEVER CATCH ME.
WHAT'S GOING ON?!
PLEASE! I HURT ALL OVER!
I'LL BE TAKING THIS! ♡
SHEEN
AAGH! THE CROWN!
BUT HOW ?!
HA HA HA HA!

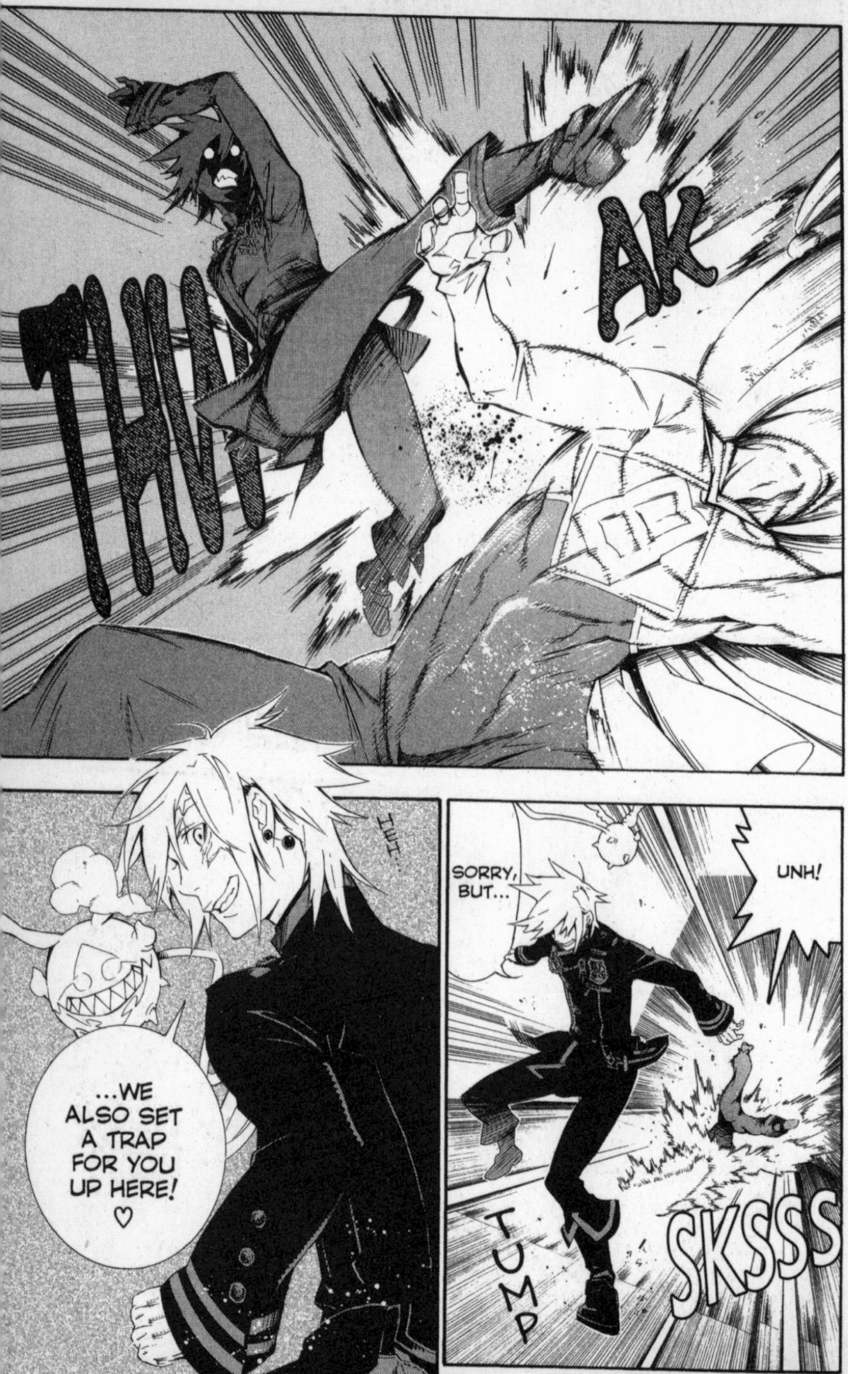
THW
AK
UNH!
SORRY, BUT...
SKSSS
TUMP
HEH...
...WE ALSO SET A TRAP FOR YOU UP HERE! ♡

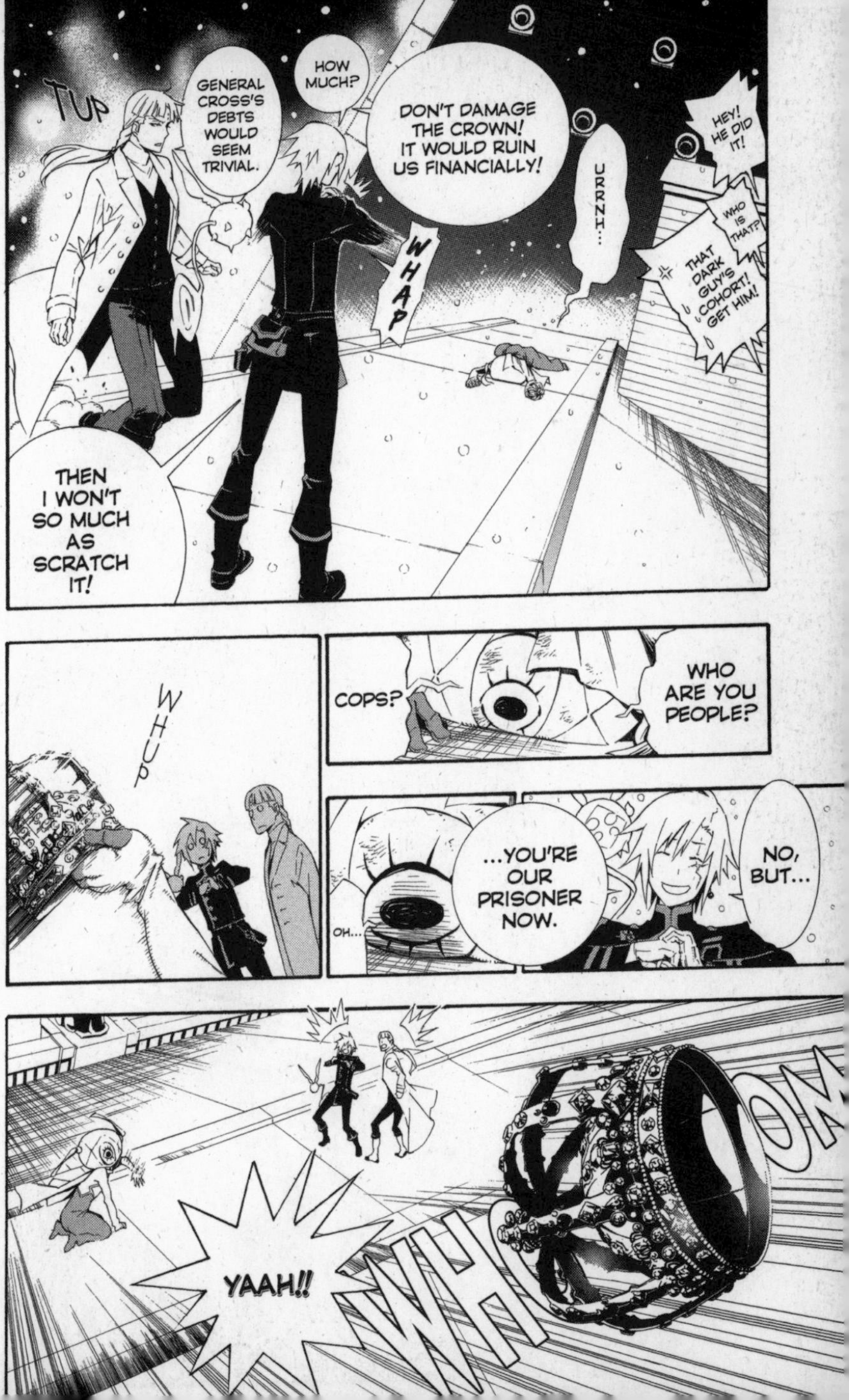
HEY! HE DID IT!
WHO IS THAT?
THAT DARK GUY'S COHORT! GET HIM!
URRNH...
DON'T DAMAGE THE CROWN! IT WOULD RUIN US FINANCIALLY!
HOW MUCH?
GENERAL CROSS'S DEBTS WOULD SEEM TRIVIAL.
TUP
WHAP
THEN I WON'T SO MUCH AS SCRATCH IT!
WHO ARE YOU PEOPLE?
COPS?
NO, BUT...
...YOU'RE OUR PRISONER NOW.
OH...
WHUP
YAAH!!

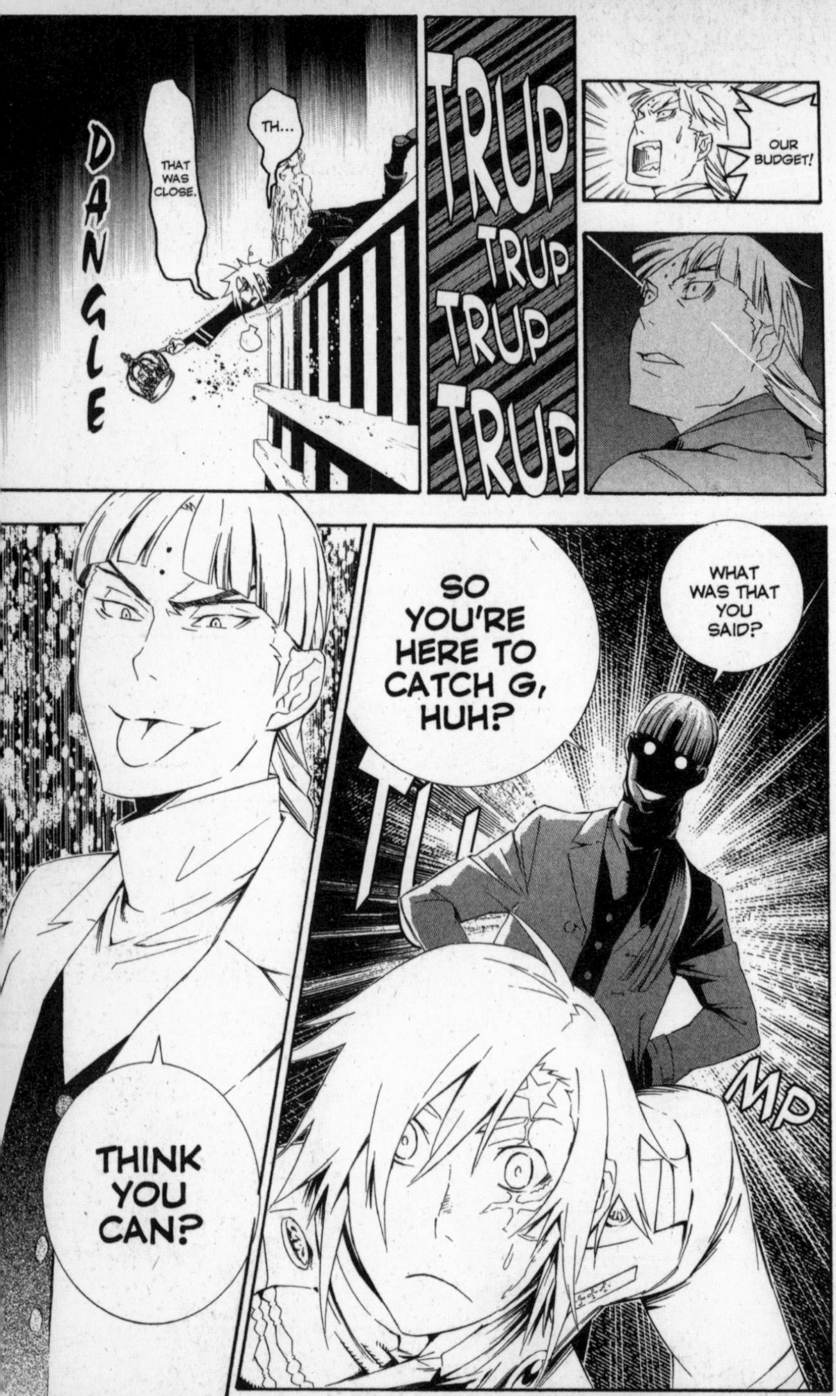
OUR BUDGET!
TRUP
TRUP
TRUP
TRUP
TH...
THAT WAS CLOSE.
DANGLE
WHAT WAS THAT YOU SAID?
SO YOU'RE HERE TO CATCH G, HUH?
MP
THINK YOU CAN?

POINTLESS D.GRAY STORIES

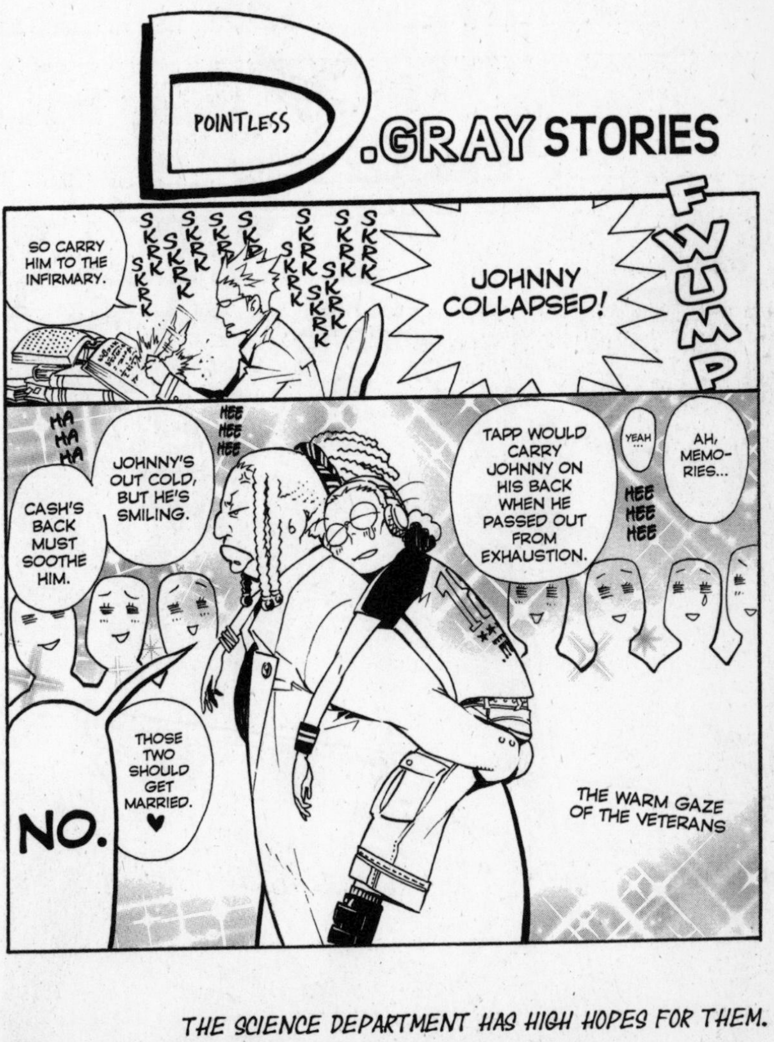
FWUMP
JOHNNY COLLAPSED!
SKRK SKRK SKRK SKRK SKRK SKRK SKRK SKRK SKRK SKRK SKRK SKRK
SO CARRY HIM TO THE INFIRMARY.
AH, MEMORIES...
YEAH...
HEE HEE HEE
TAPP WOULD CARRY JOHNNY ON HIS BACK WHEN HE PASSED OUT FROM EXHAUSTION.
HEE HEE HEE
JOHNNY'S OUT COLD, BUT HE'S SMILING.
HA HA HA
CASH'S BACK MUST SOOTHE HIM.
THE WARM GAZE OF THE VETERANS
THOSE TWO SHOULD GET MARRIED. ♥
NO.

THE SCIENCE DEPARTMENT HAS HIGH HOPES FOR THEM.

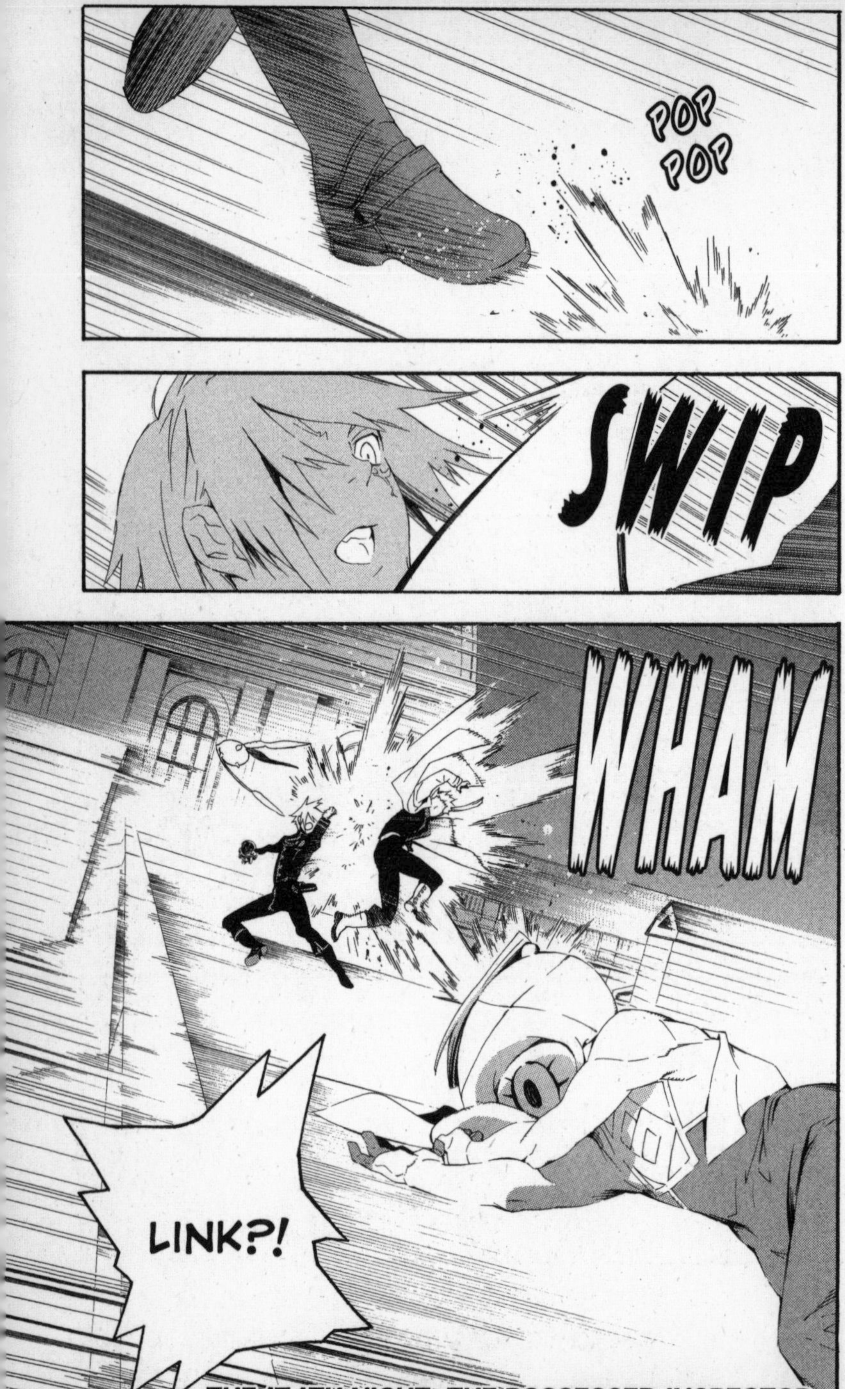
POP POP
SWIP
WHAM
LINK?!

THE 174TH NIGHT: THE POSSESSED INSPECTOR

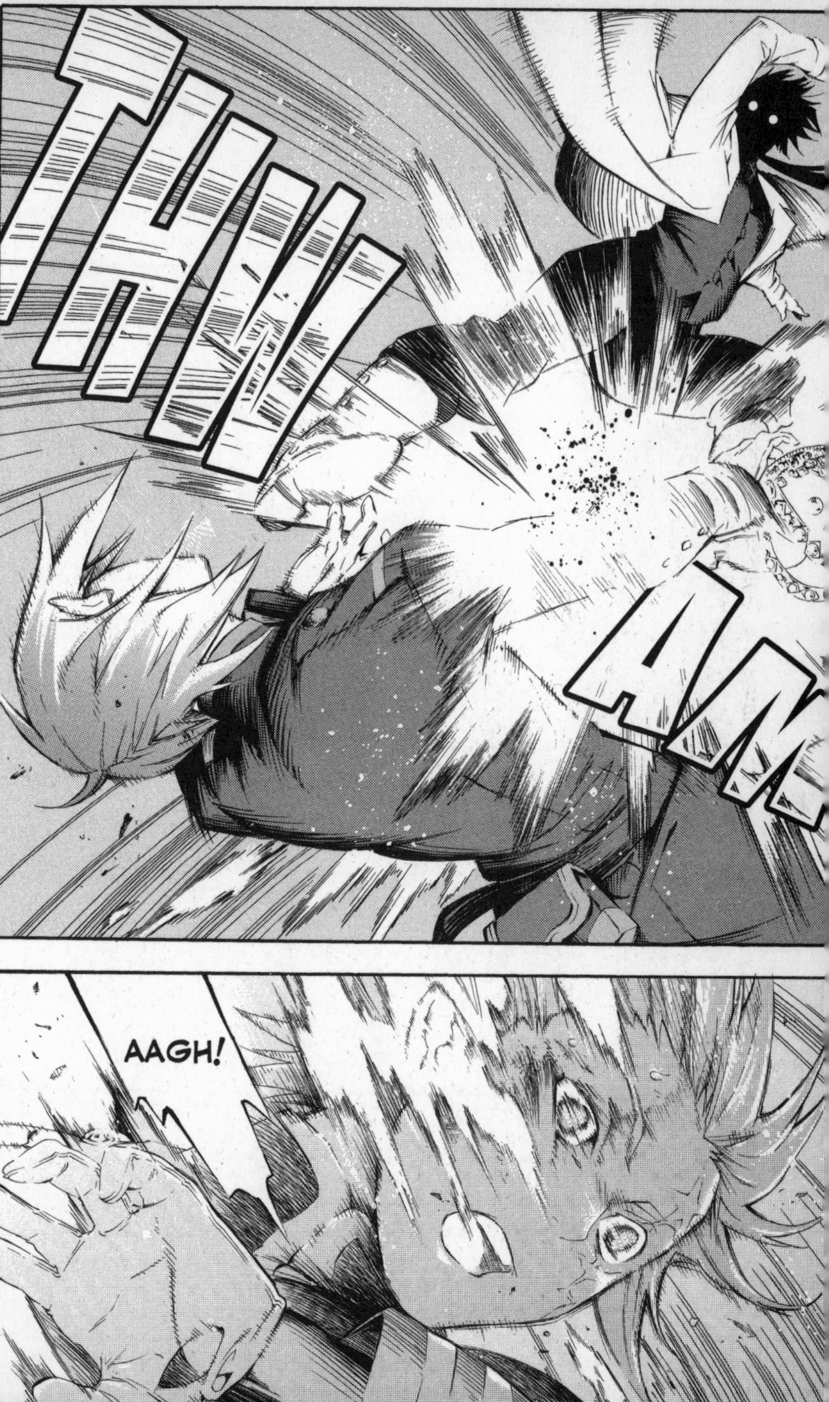
THW
AM
AAGH!

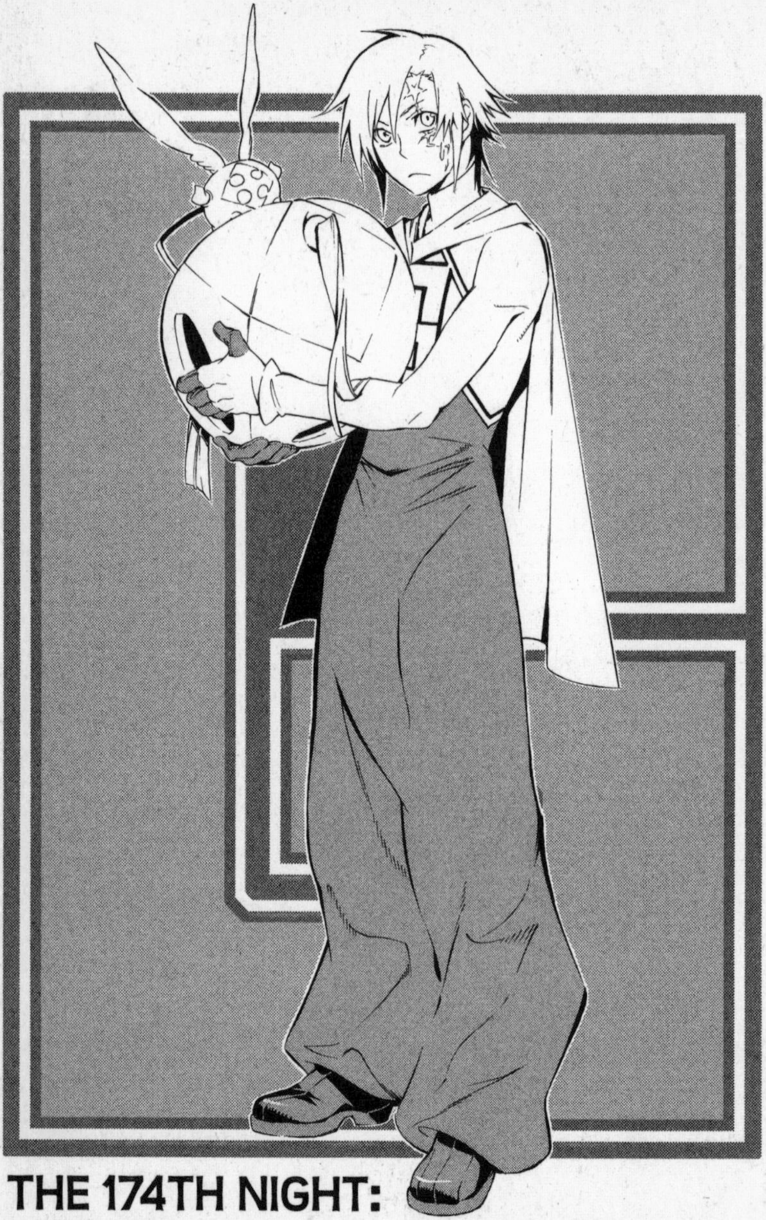

THE 174TH NIGHT: THE POSSESSED INSPECTOR

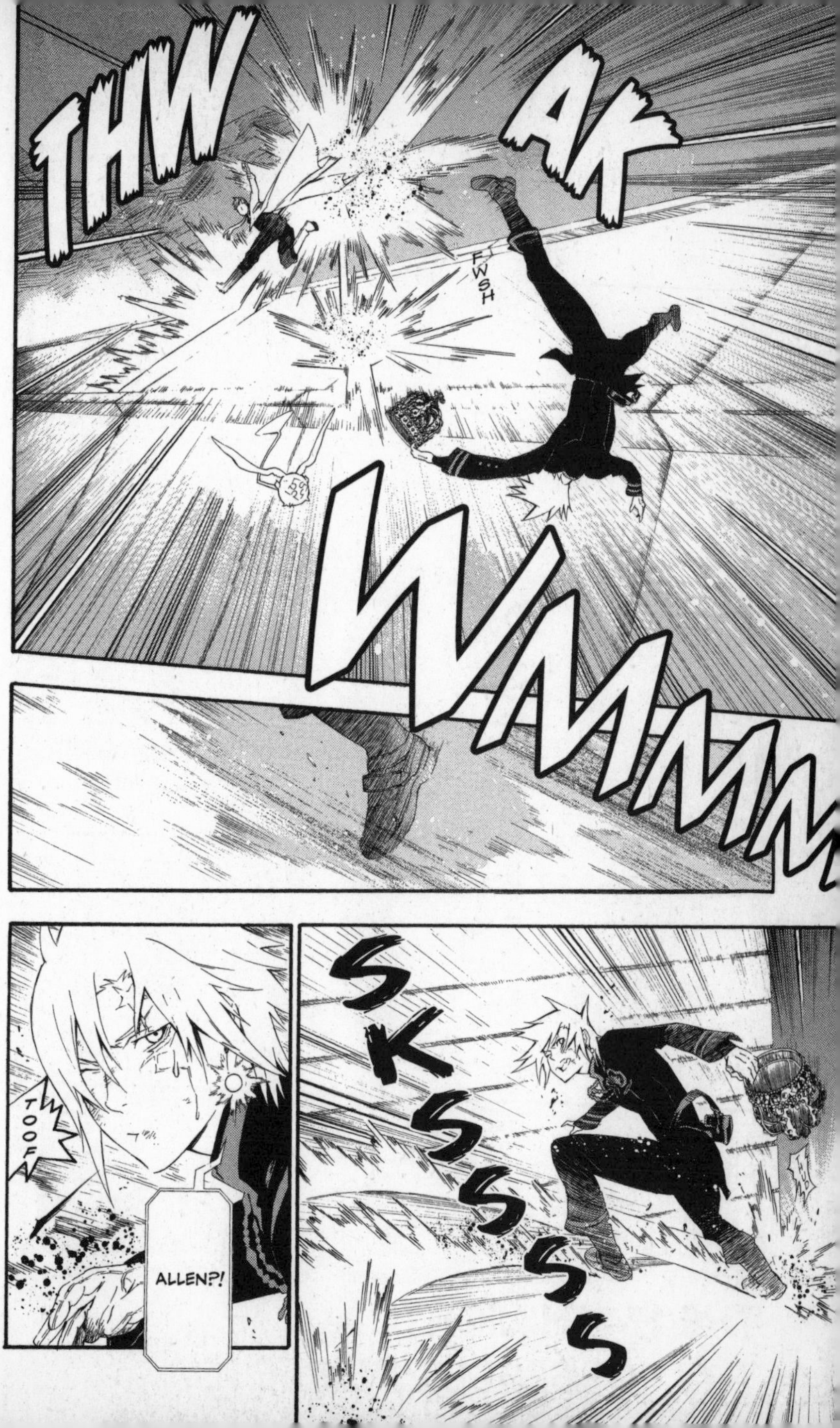
THWAK
FWSH
WMMMM
SKSSSSS
THUD
TOOF
ALLEN?!

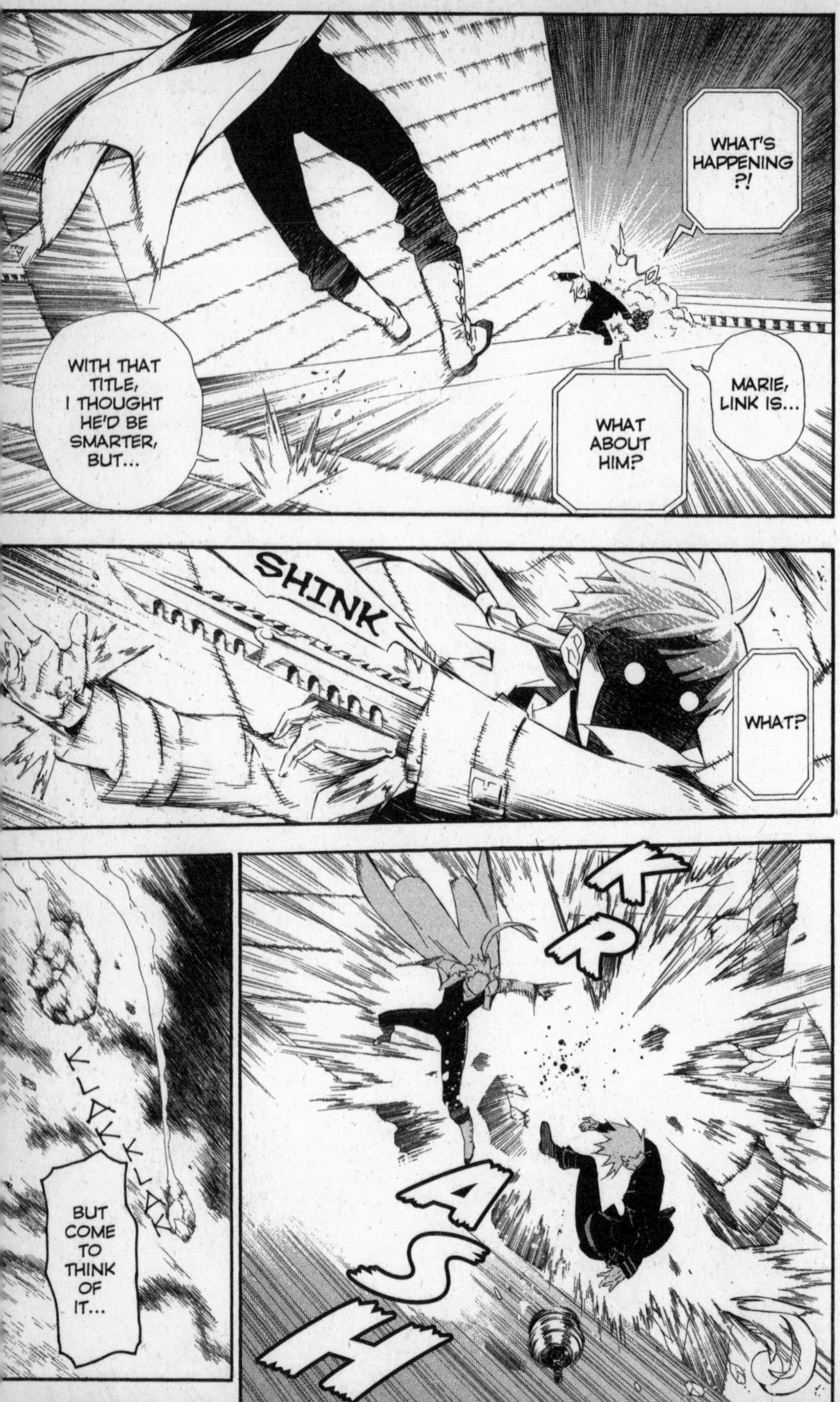
WHAT'S HAPPENING ?!
MARIE, LINK IS...
WHAT ABOUT HIM?
WITH THAT TITLE, I THOUGHT HE'D BE SMARTER, BUT...
SHINK
WHAT?
KRASH
KLAK KLAK
BUT COME TO THINK OF IT...

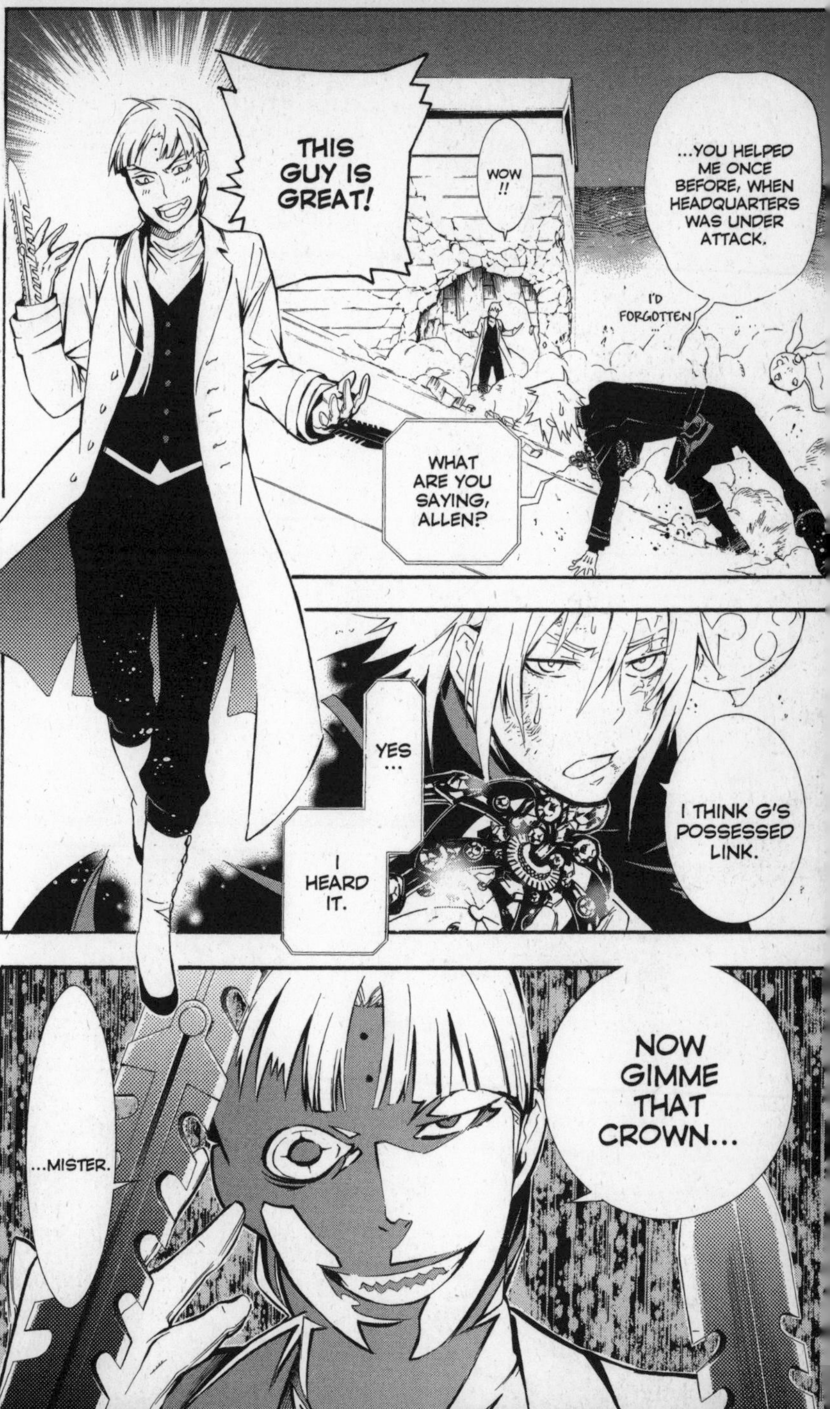
...YOU HELPED ME ONCE BEFORE, WHEN HEADQUARTERS WAS UNDER ATTACK.
I'D FORGOTTEN...
WOW!!
THIS GUY IS GREAT!
WHAT ARE YOU SAYING, ALLEN?
I THINK G'S POSSESSED LINK.
YES... I HEARD IT.
NOW GIMME THAT CROWN...
...MISTER.

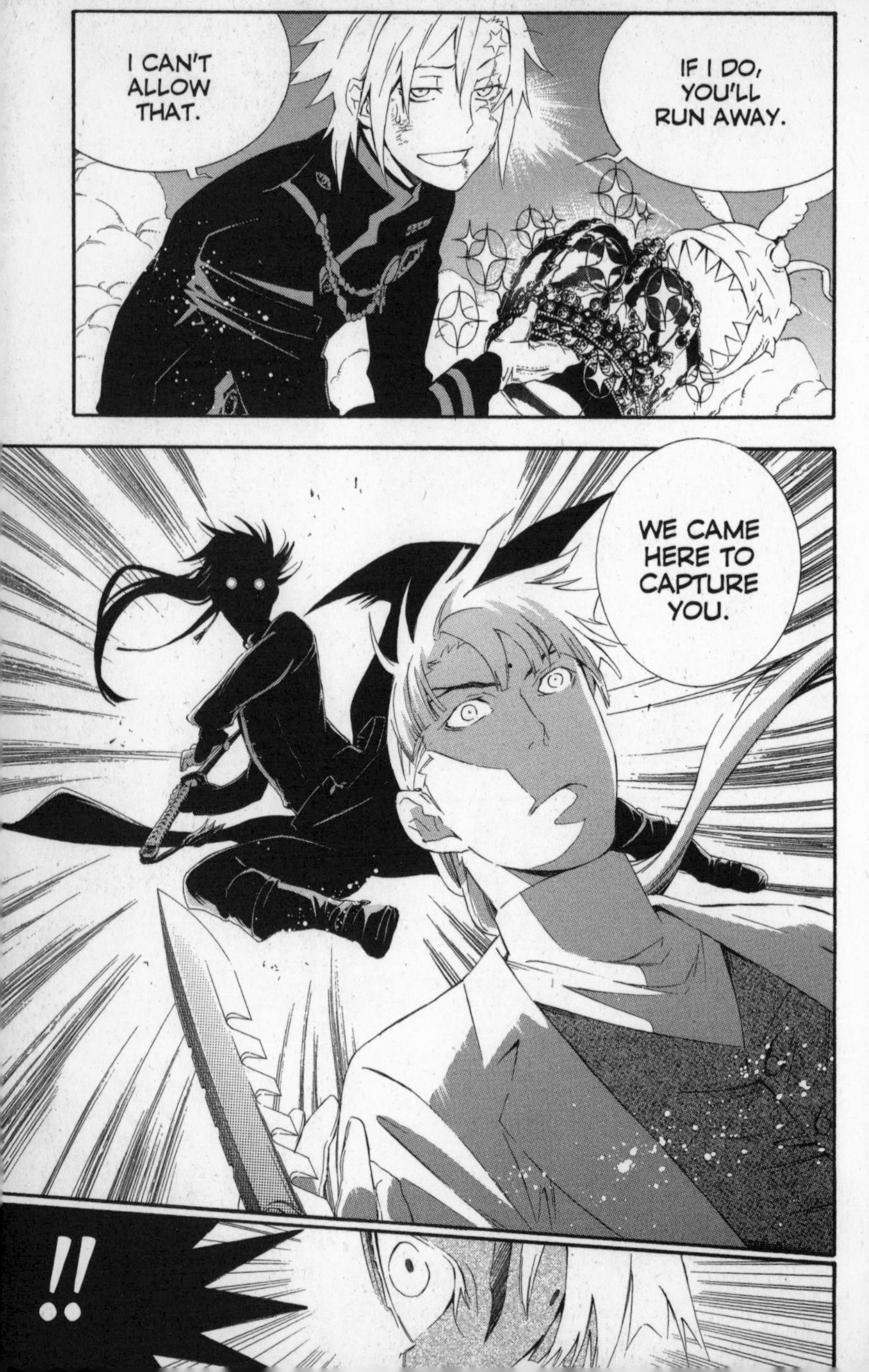
IF I DO, YOU'LL RUN AWAY.
I CAN'T ALLOW THAT.
WE CAME HERE TO CAPTURE YOU.
!!

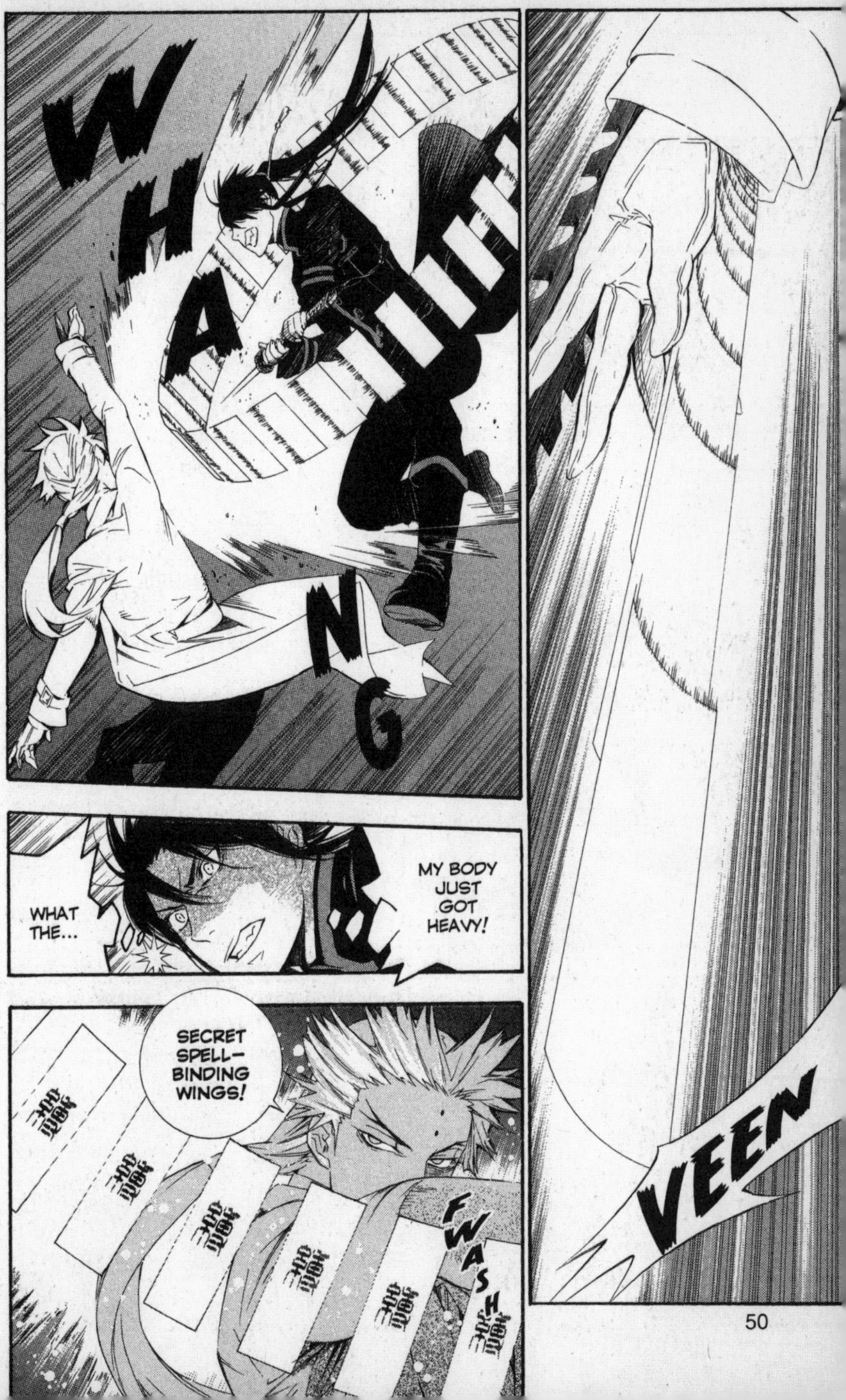
VEEN
WHANG
MY BODY JUST GOT HEAVY!
WHAT THE...
SECRET SPELL-BINDING WINGS!
FWASH

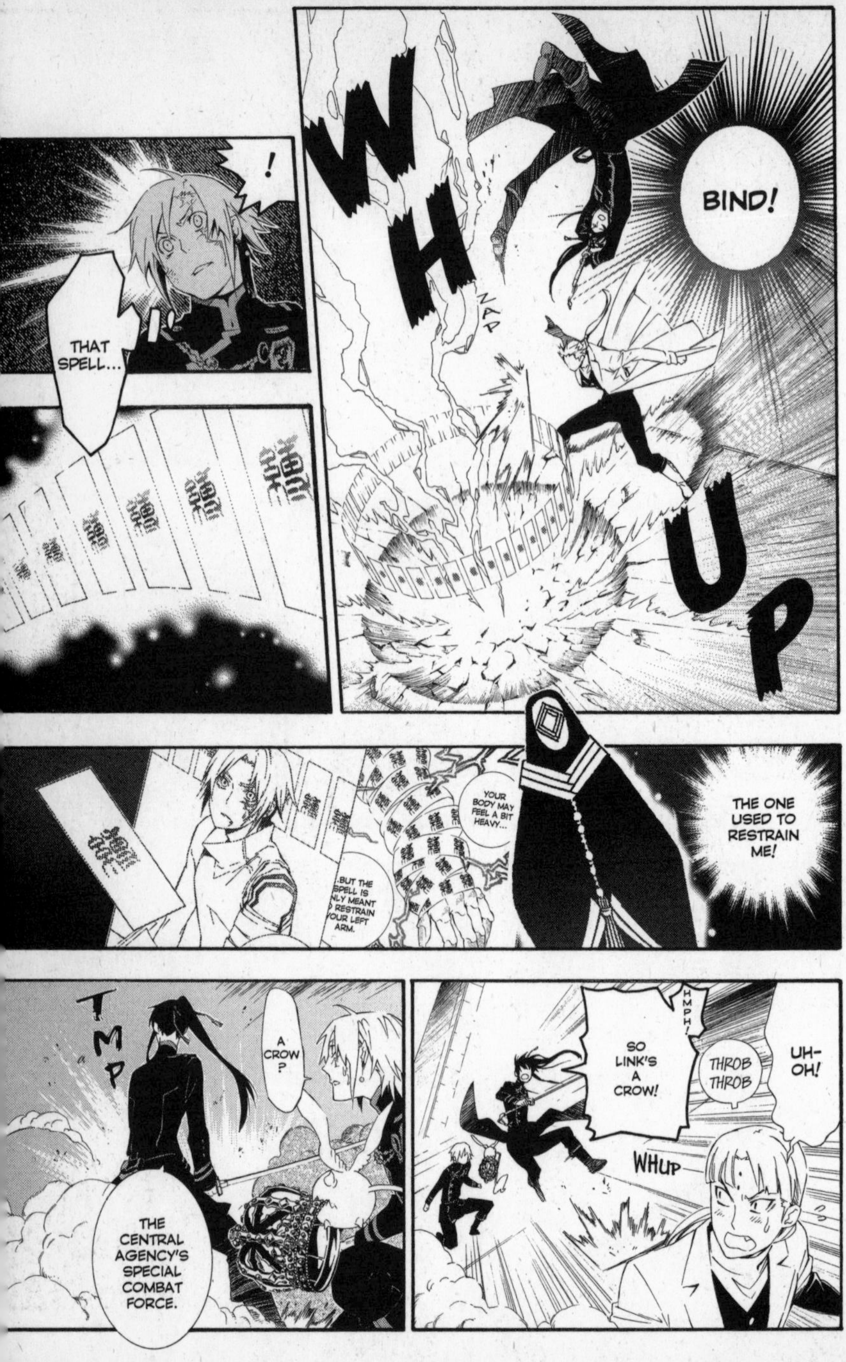
BIND!
WH UP
ZAP
!
THAT SPELL...
THE ONE USED TO RESTRAIN ME!
YOUR BODY MAY FEEL A BIT HEAVY...
.BUT THE SPELL IS NLY MEANT O RESTRAIN OUR LEFT ARM.
UH-OH!
THROB THROB
HMPH!
SO LINK'S A CROW!
WHUP
A CROW?
TMP
THE CENTRAL AGENCY'S SPECIAL COMBAT FORCE.

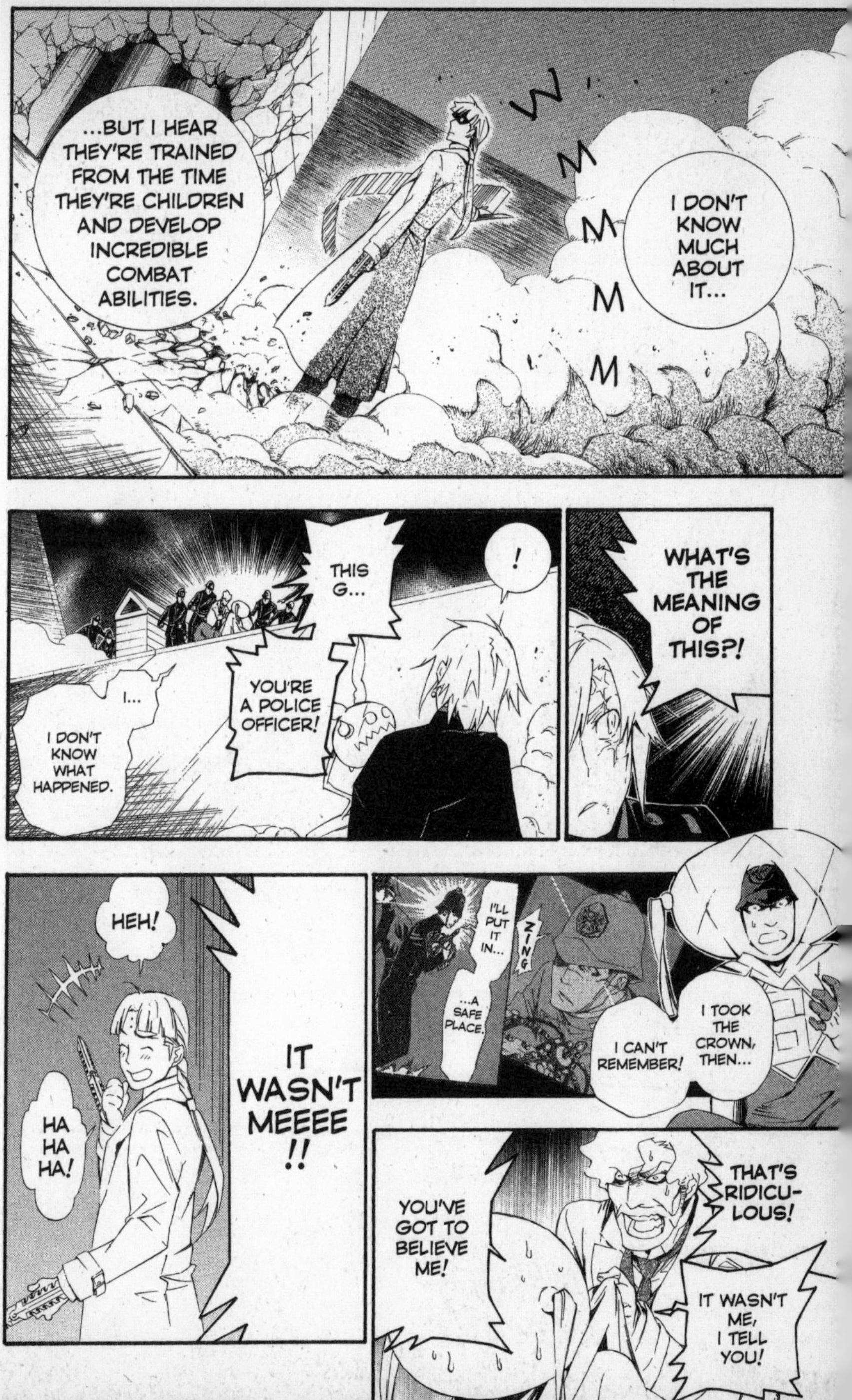
I DON'T KNOW MUCH ABOUT IT...
WMMMM
...BUT I HEAR THEY'RE TRAINED FROM THE TIME THEY'RE CHILDREN AND DEVELOP INCREDIBLE COMBAT ABILITIES.
WHAT'S THE MEANING OF THIS?!
!
THIS G...
YOU'RE A POLICE OFFICER!
I...
I DON'T KNOW WHAT HAPPENED.
I TOOK THE CROWN, THEN...
I CAN'T REMEMBER!
I'LL PUT IT IN...
ZING
...A SAFE PLACE.
THAT'S RIDICU-LOUS!
IT WASN'T ME, I TELL YOU!
YOU'VE GOT TO BELIEVE ME!
IT WASN'T MEEEE!!
HEH!
HA HA HA!

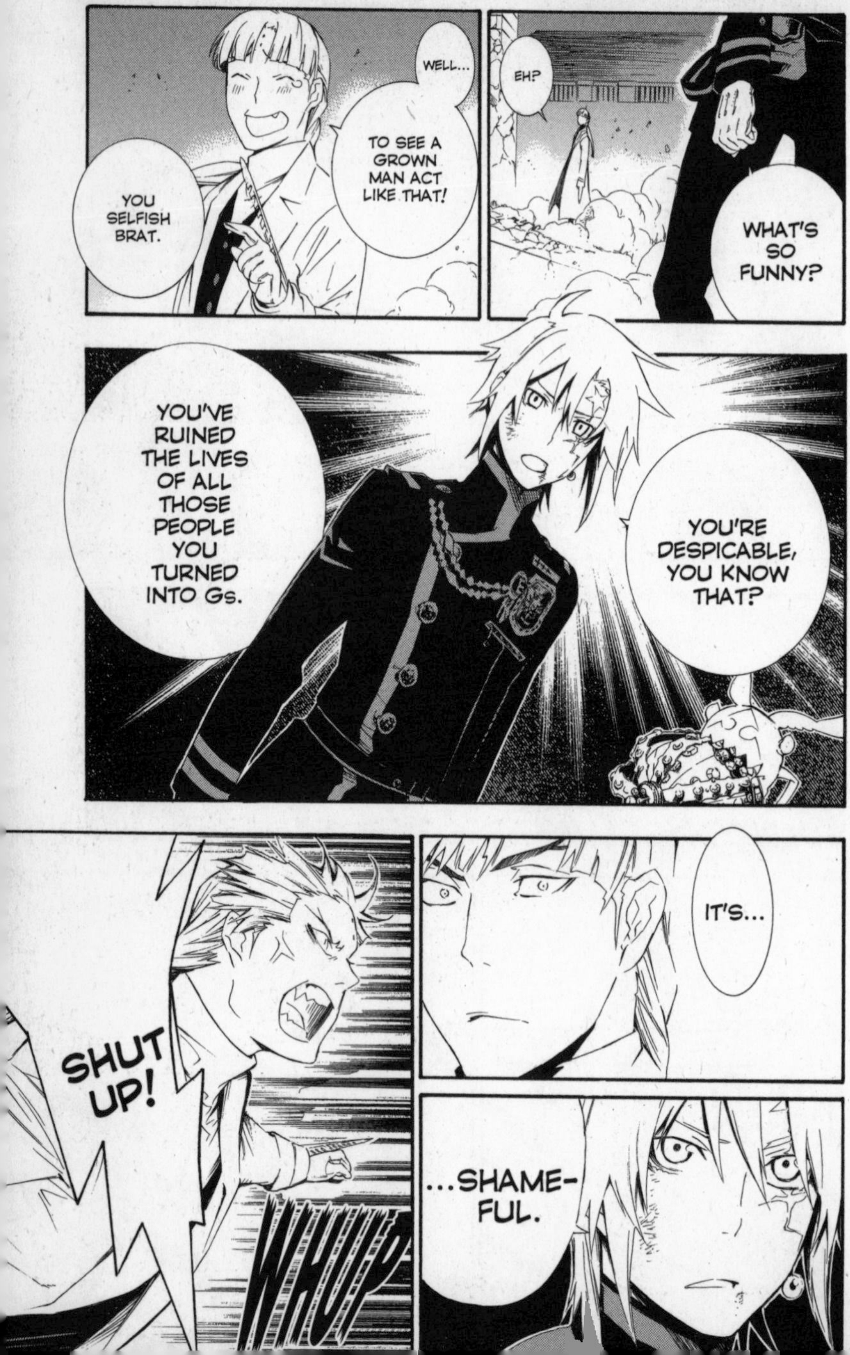
WHAT'S SO FUNNY?
EH?
WELL...
TO SEE A GROWN MAN ACT LIKE THAT!
YOU SELFISH BRAT.
YOU'RE DESPICABLE, YOU KNOW THAT?
YOU'VE RUINED THE LIVES OF ALL THOSE PEOPLE YOU TURNED INTO Gs.
IT'S...
...SHAME-FUL.
SHUT UP!
WHUP

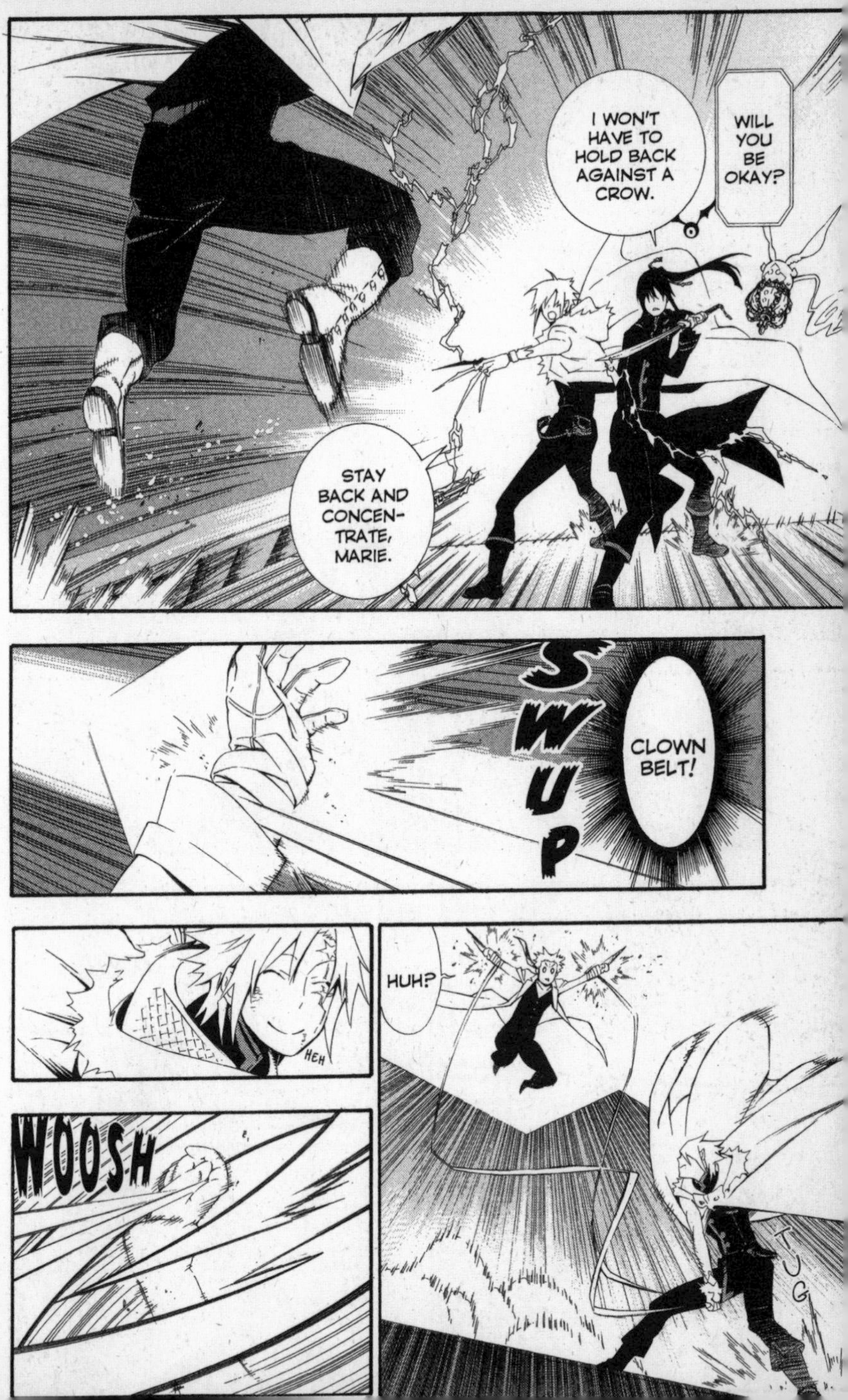
WILL YOU BE OKAY?
I WON'T HAVE TO HOLD BACK AGAINST A CROW.
STAY BACK AND CONCEN-TRATE, MARIE.
CLOWN BELT!
SWUP
HUH?
TUG
HEH
WOOSH

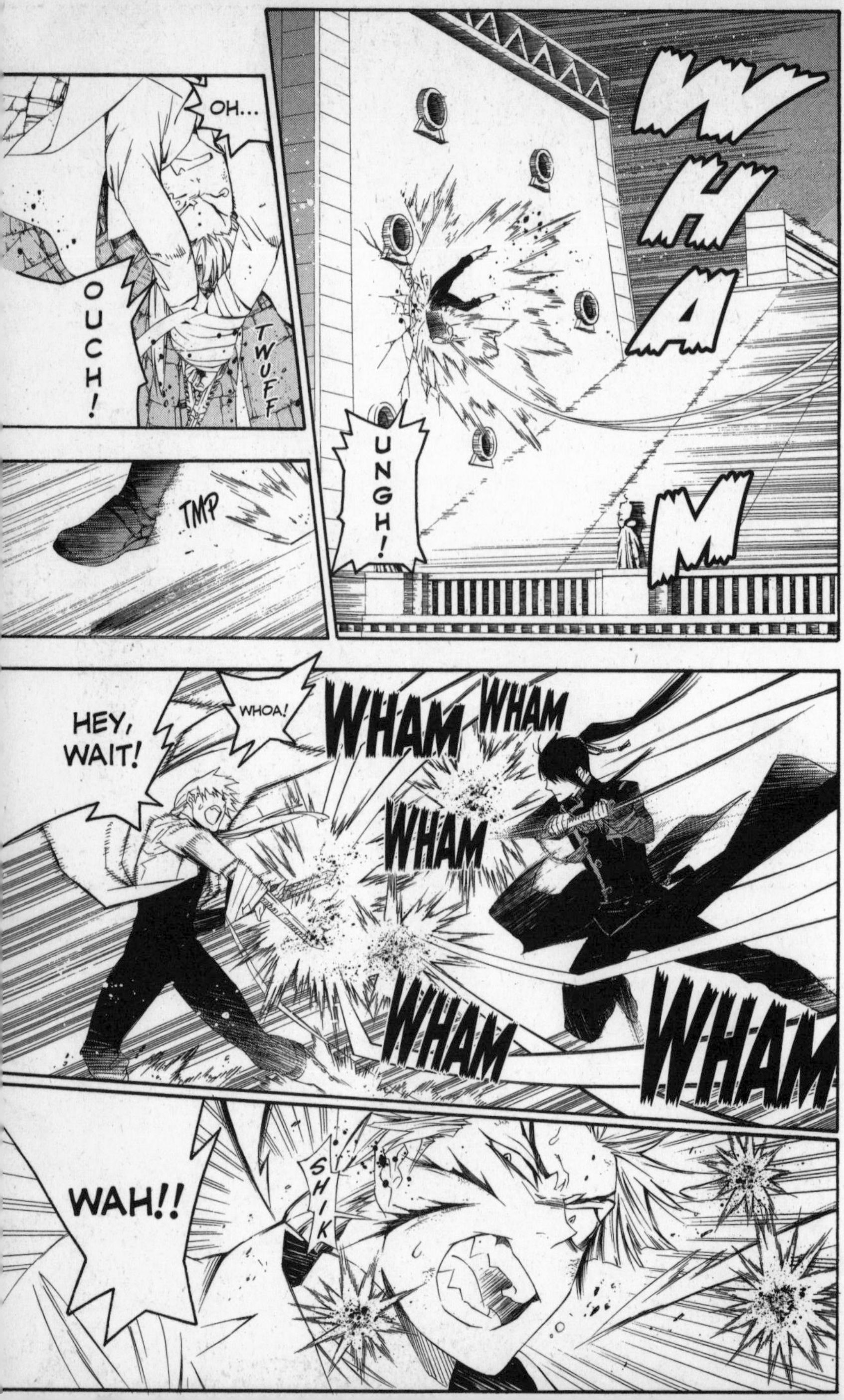
WHAM
UNGH!
OH...
TWUFF
OUCH!
TMP
WHAM
WHAM
WHOA!
HEY, WAIT!
WHAM
WHAM
WHAM
SHIK
WAH!!

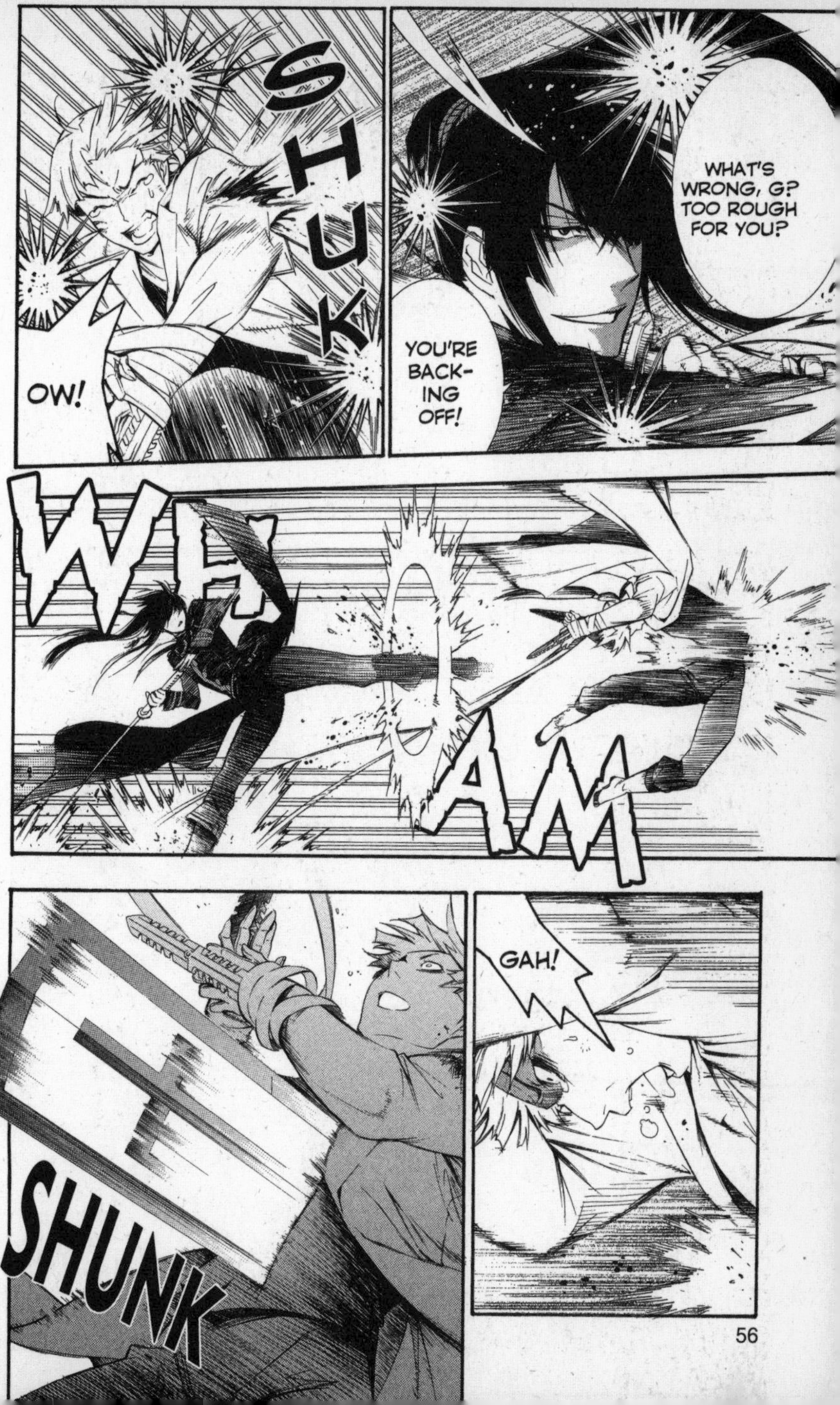
WHAT'S WRONG, G? TOO ROUGH FOR YOU?
YOU'RE BACK-ING OFF!
SHUK
OW!
WHAM
GAH!
SHUNK

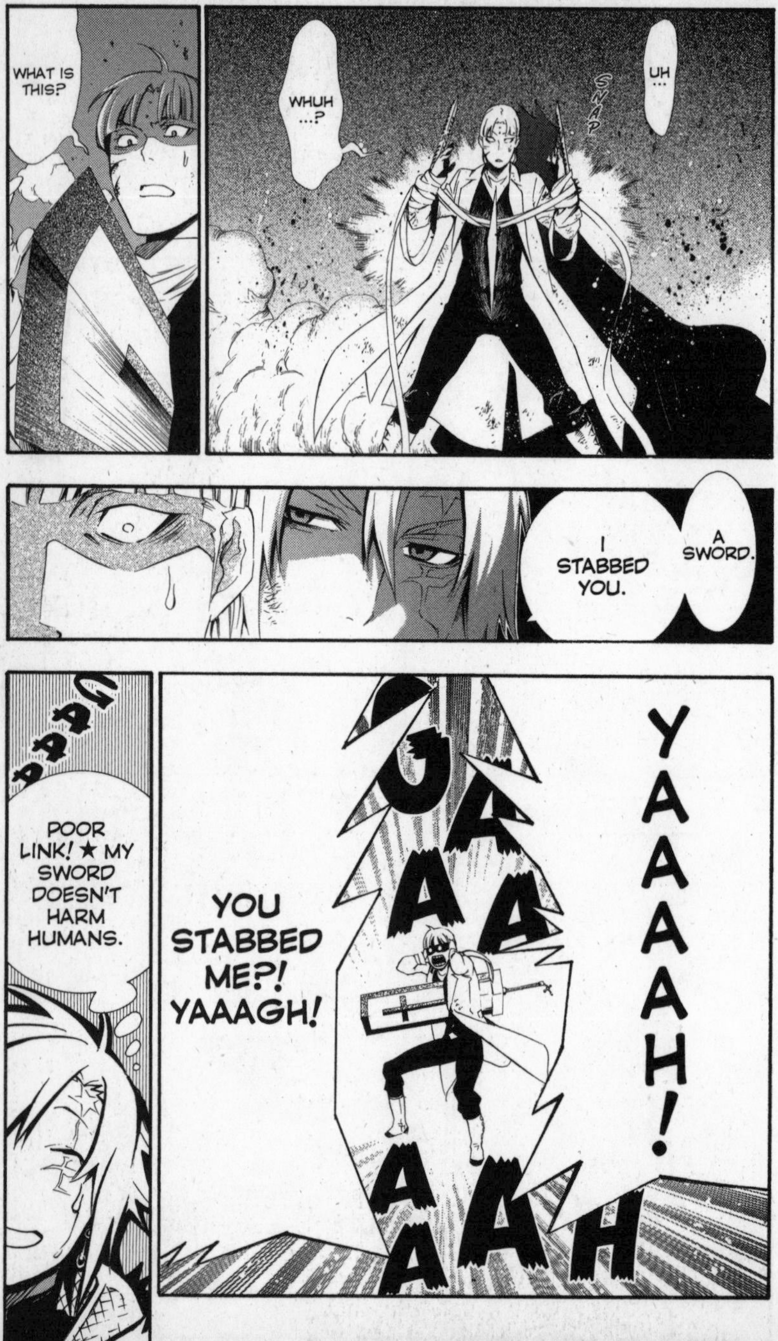
UH ...
SNAP
WHUH ...?
WHAT IS THIS?
A SWORD.
I STABBED YOU.
YAAAAH!
GAAAAAAH
YOU STABBED ME?! YAAAGH!
GAAAA
POOR LINK! ★ MY SWORD DOESN'T HARM HUMANS.

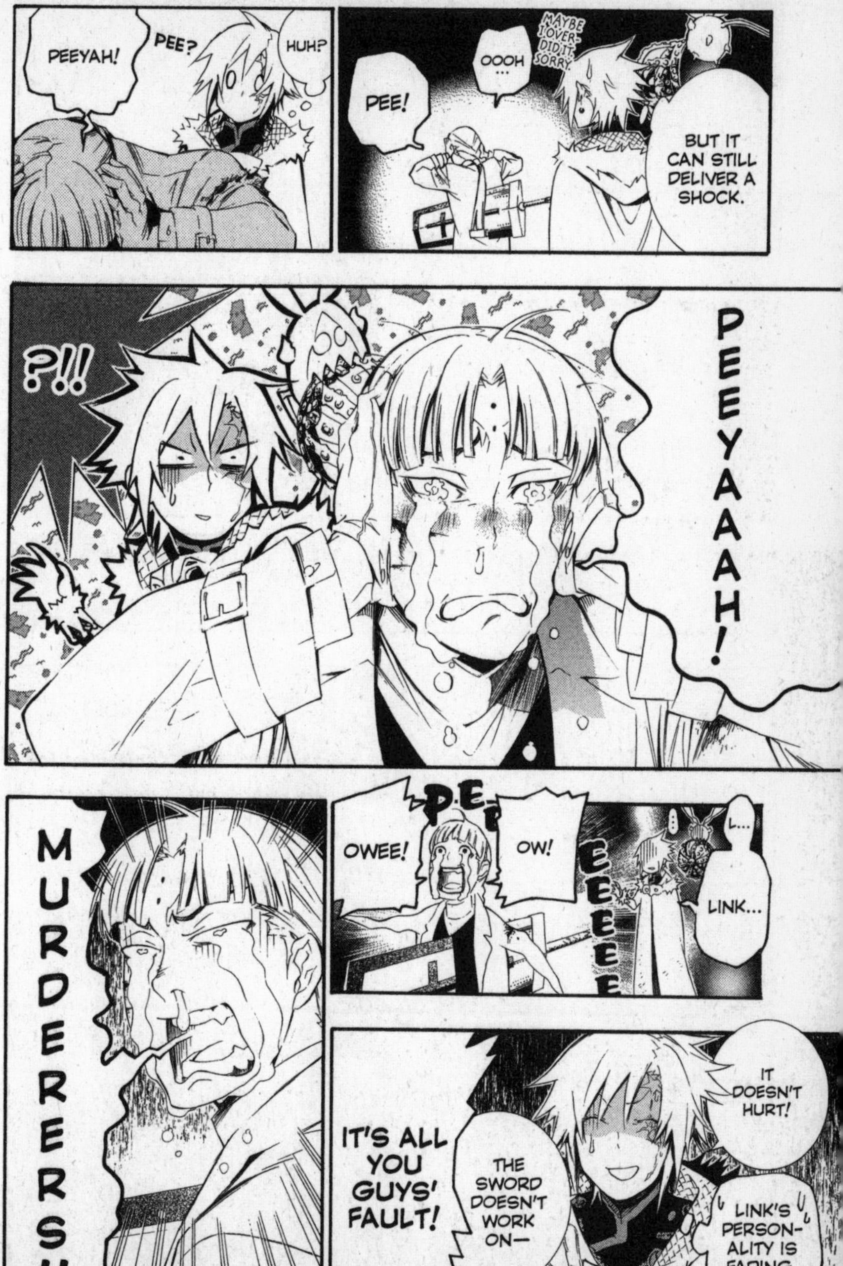
MAYBE I OVER-DID IT. SORRY.
BUT IT CAN STILL DELIVER A SHOCK.
OOOH ...
PEE!
HUH?
PEE?
PEEYAH!
PEEYAAAH!
?!!
L...
LINK...
P-E-EEEEE
OW!
OWEE!
IT DOESN'T HURT!
LINK'S PERSON-ALITY IS FADING.
THE SWORD DOESN'T WORK ON—
IT'S ALL YOU GUYS' FAULT!
MURDERERS!!

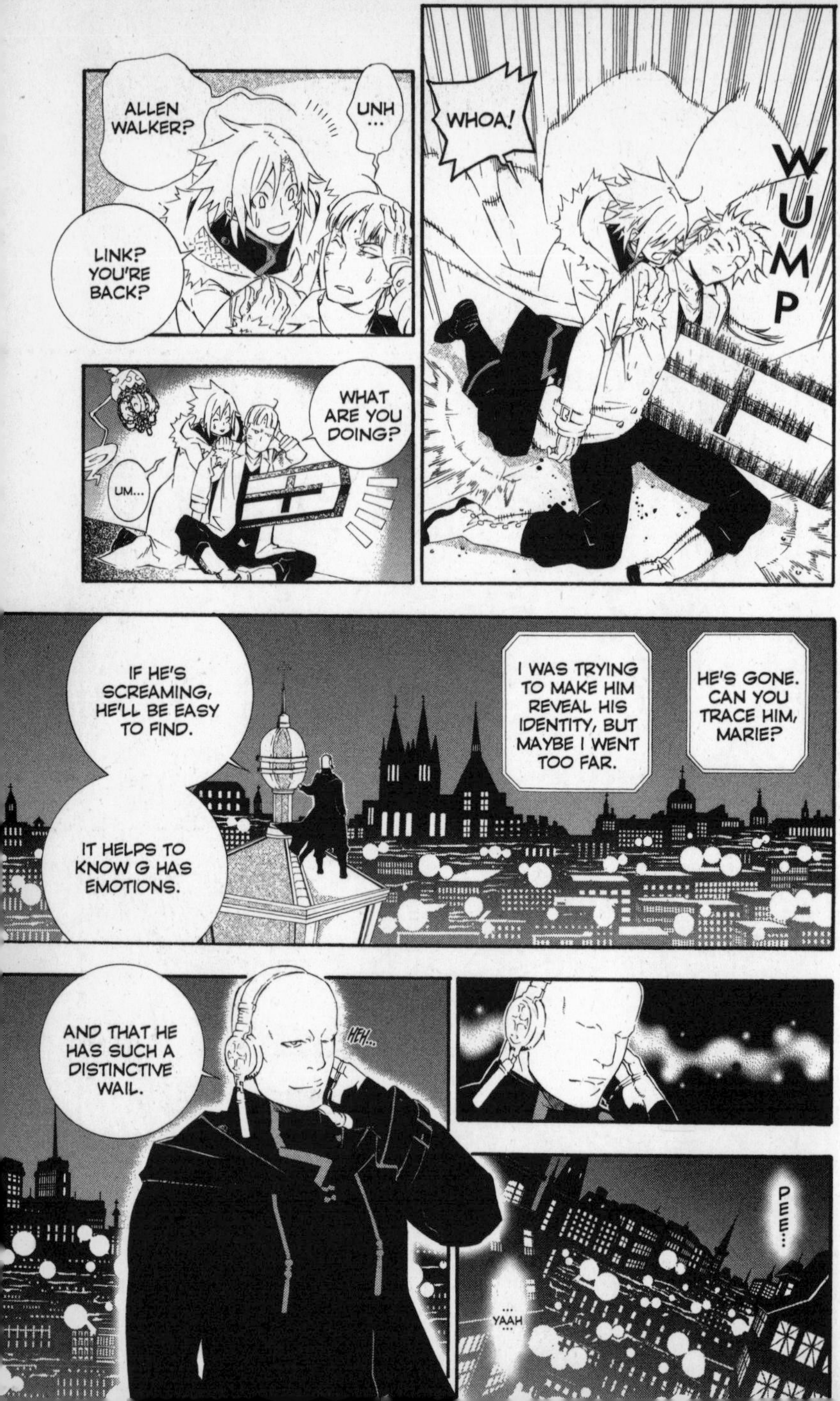
WHOA!
WUMP
UNH...
ALLEN WALKER?
LINK? YOU'RE BACK?
WHAT ARE YOU DOING?
UM...
HE'S GONE. CAN YOU TRACE HIM, MARIE?
I WAS TRYING TO MAKE HIM REVEAL HIS IDENTITY, BUT MAYBE I WENT TOO FAR.
IF HE'S SCREAMING, HE'LL BE EASY TO FIND.
IT HELPS TO KNOW G HAS EMOTIONS.
PEE...
...YAAH...
HEH...
AND THAT HE HAS SUCH A DISTINCTIVE WAIL.

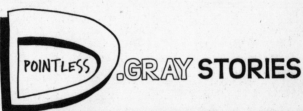

POINTLESS D.GRAY STORIES

SHAKE SHAKE SHAKE
WHAT DID I DO ?!!
PEEYA-AAAH!
OWEE! OWEE!

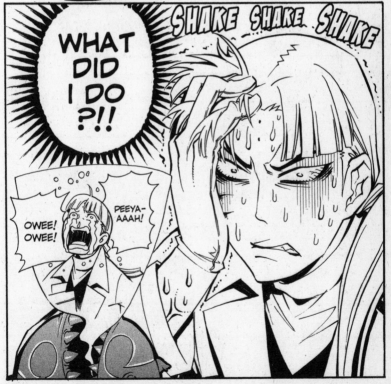

HOW MUCH WOULD YOU PAY FOR THIS VIDEO?

WALKER, YOU JERK!!

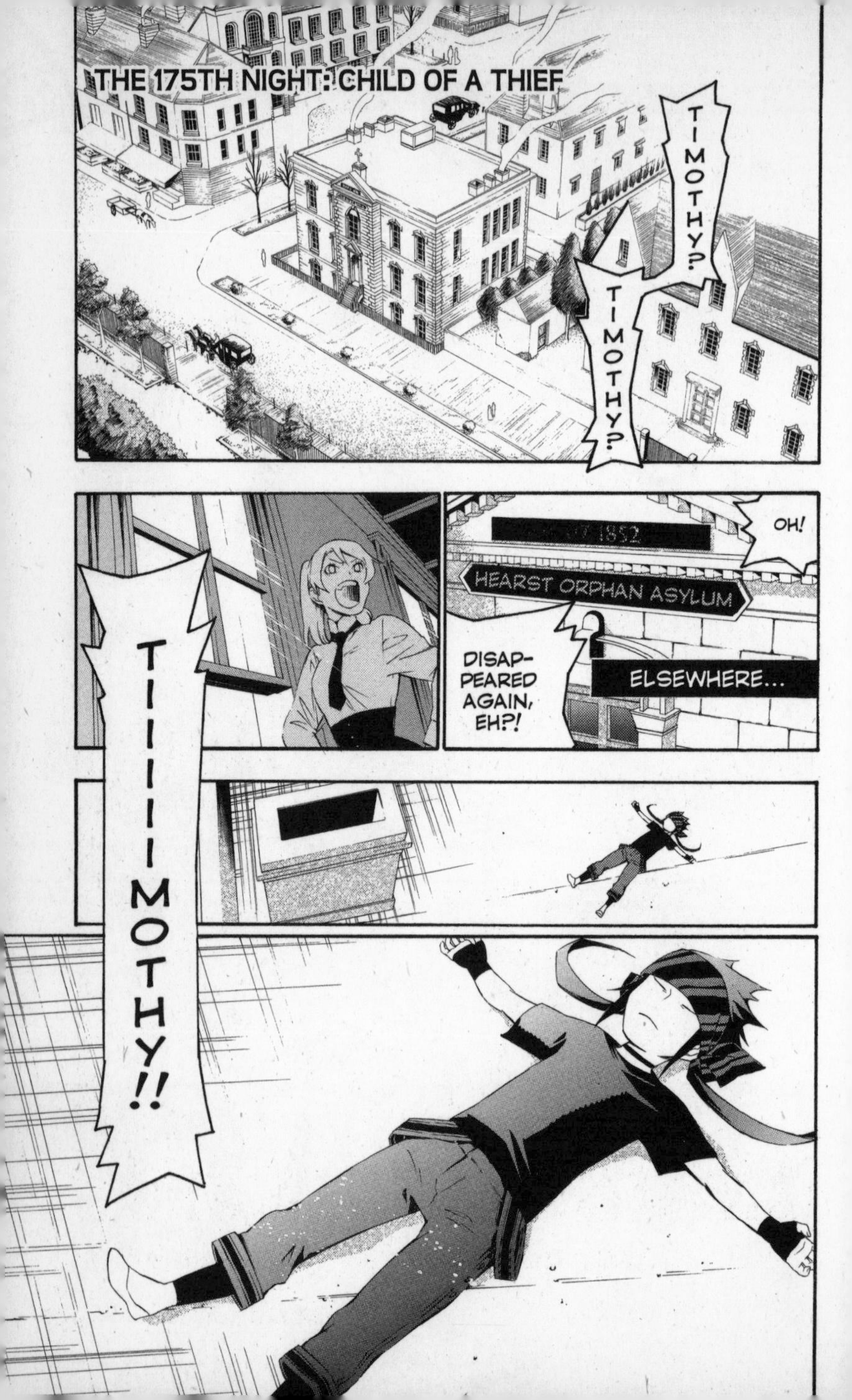
THE 175TH NIGHT: CHILD OF A THIEF
TIMOTHY?
TIMOTHY?
OH!
HEARST ORPHAN ASYLUM
ELSEWHERE...
DISAPPEARED AGAIN, EH?!
TIIIIIMOTHY!!

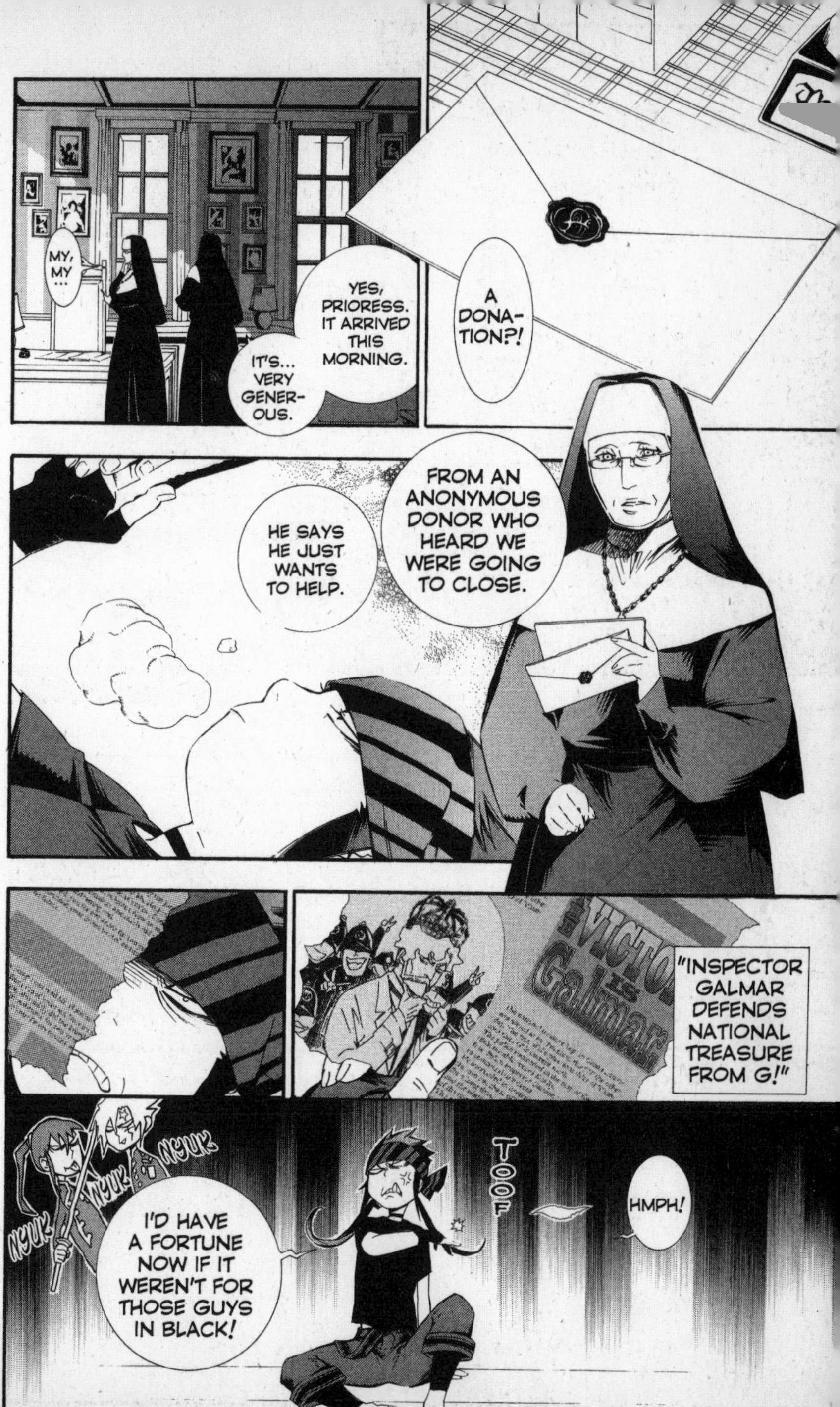
A DONA-TION?!
YES, PRIORESS. IT ARRIVED THIS MORNING.
MY, MY...
IT'S... VERY GENER-OUS.
FROM AN ANONYMOUS DONOR WHO HEARD WE WERE GOING TO CLOSE.
HE SAYS HE JUST WANTS TO HELP.
"INSPECTOR GALMAR DEFENDS NATIONAL TREASURE FROM G!"
HMPH!
TOOF
I'D HAVE A FORTUNE NOW IF IT WEREN'T FOR THOSE GUYS IN BLACK!
NYUK
NYUK
NYUK
NYUK

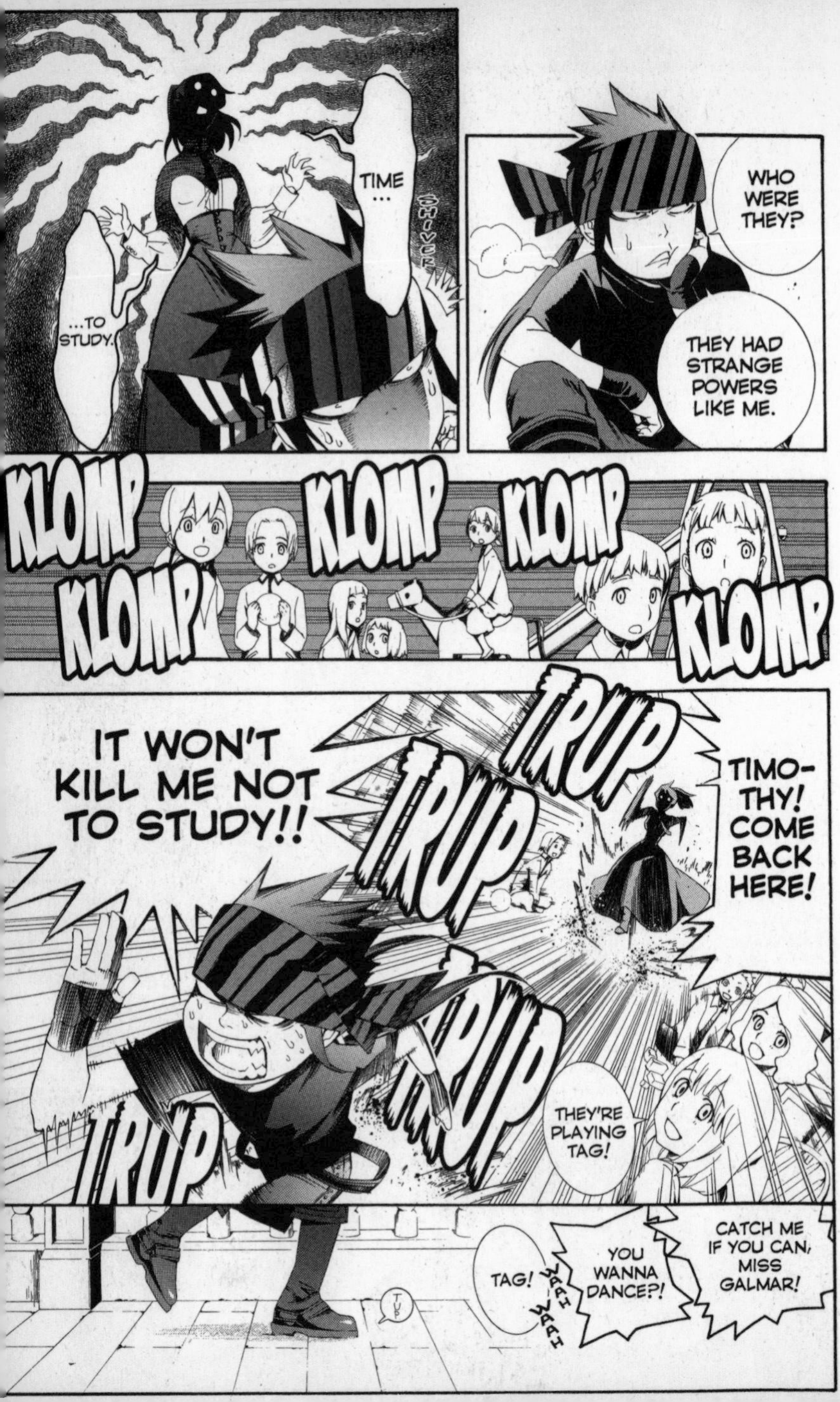
WHO WERE THEY?
THEY HAD STRANGE POWERS LIKE ME.
TIME...
SHIVER
...TO STUDY.
KLOMP
KLOMP
KLOMP
KLOMP
KLOMP
KLOMP
TIMO-THY! COME BACK HERE!
TRUP
TRUP
IT WON'T KILL ME NOT TO STUDY!!
TRUP
THEY'RE PLAYING TAG!
TRUP
CATCH ME IF YOU CAN, MISS GALMAR!
YOU WANNA DANCE?!
WAAH WAAH
TAG!
TUP

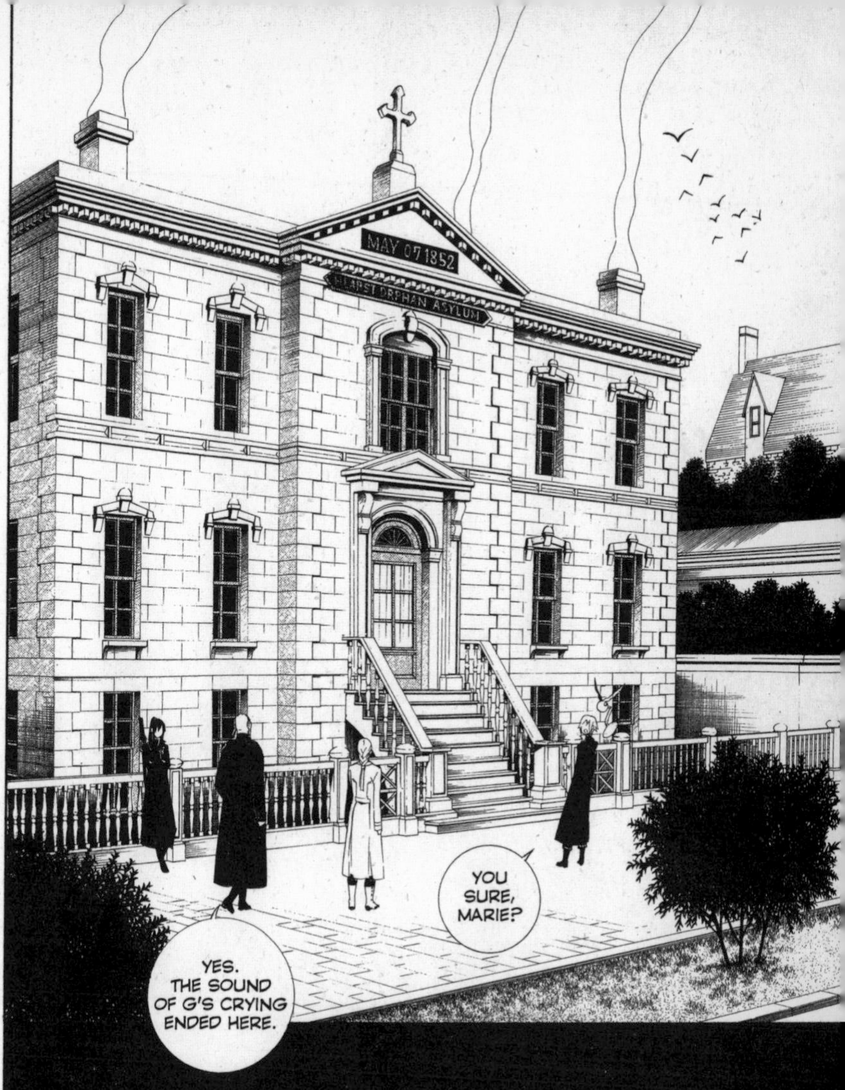
MAY 07 1852
HEARST ORPHAN ASYLUM
YOU SURE, MARIE?
YES. THE SOUND OF G'S CRYING ENDED HERE.

THE 175TH NIGHT: CHILD OF A THIEF

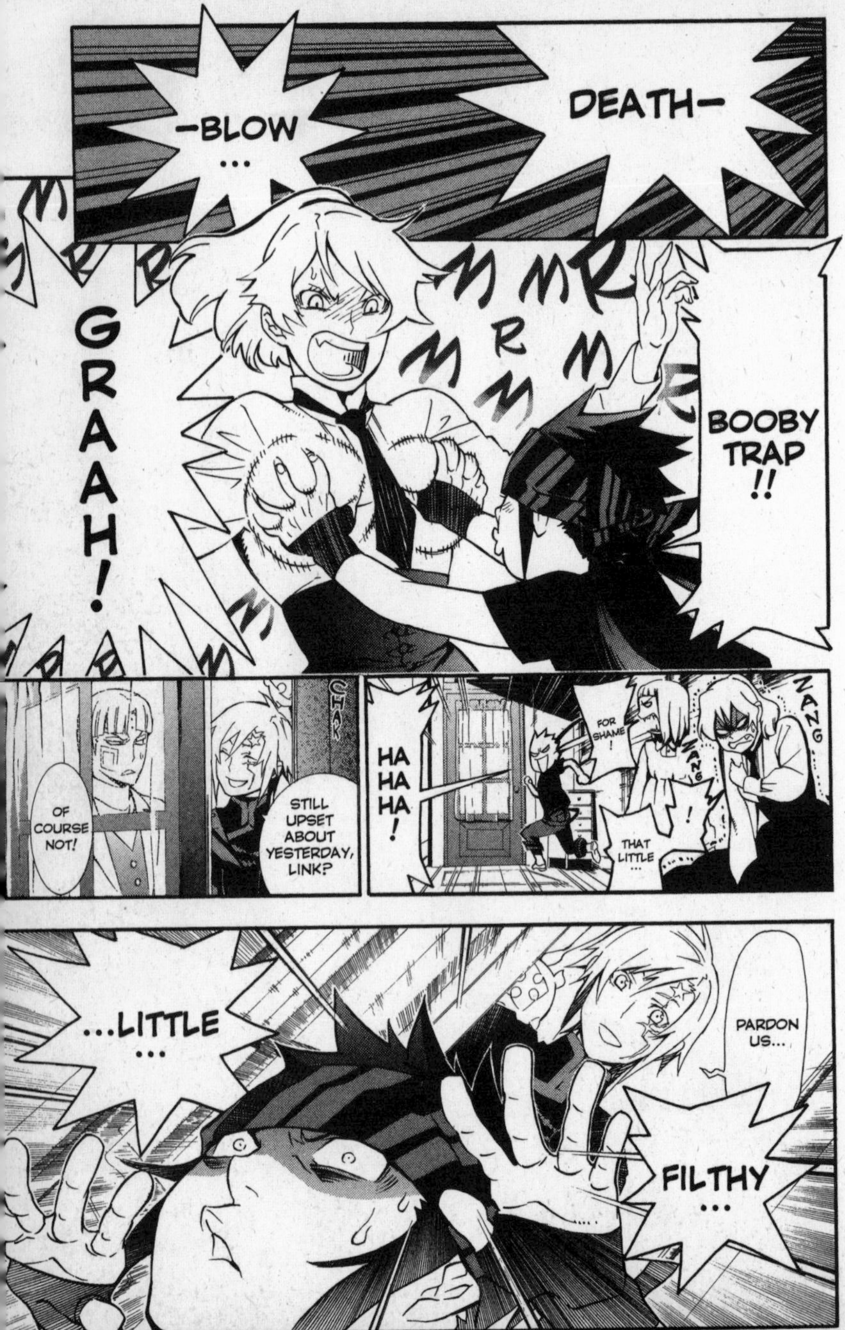

DEATH-
-BLOW ...
BOOBY TRAP !!
GRAAH!
ZANG
FOR SHAME!
ZANG
!
THAT LITTLE ...
HA HA HA!
CHAK
STILL UPSET ABOUT YESTERDAY, LINK?
OF COURSE NOT!
PARDON US...
FILTHY ...
...LITTLE ...

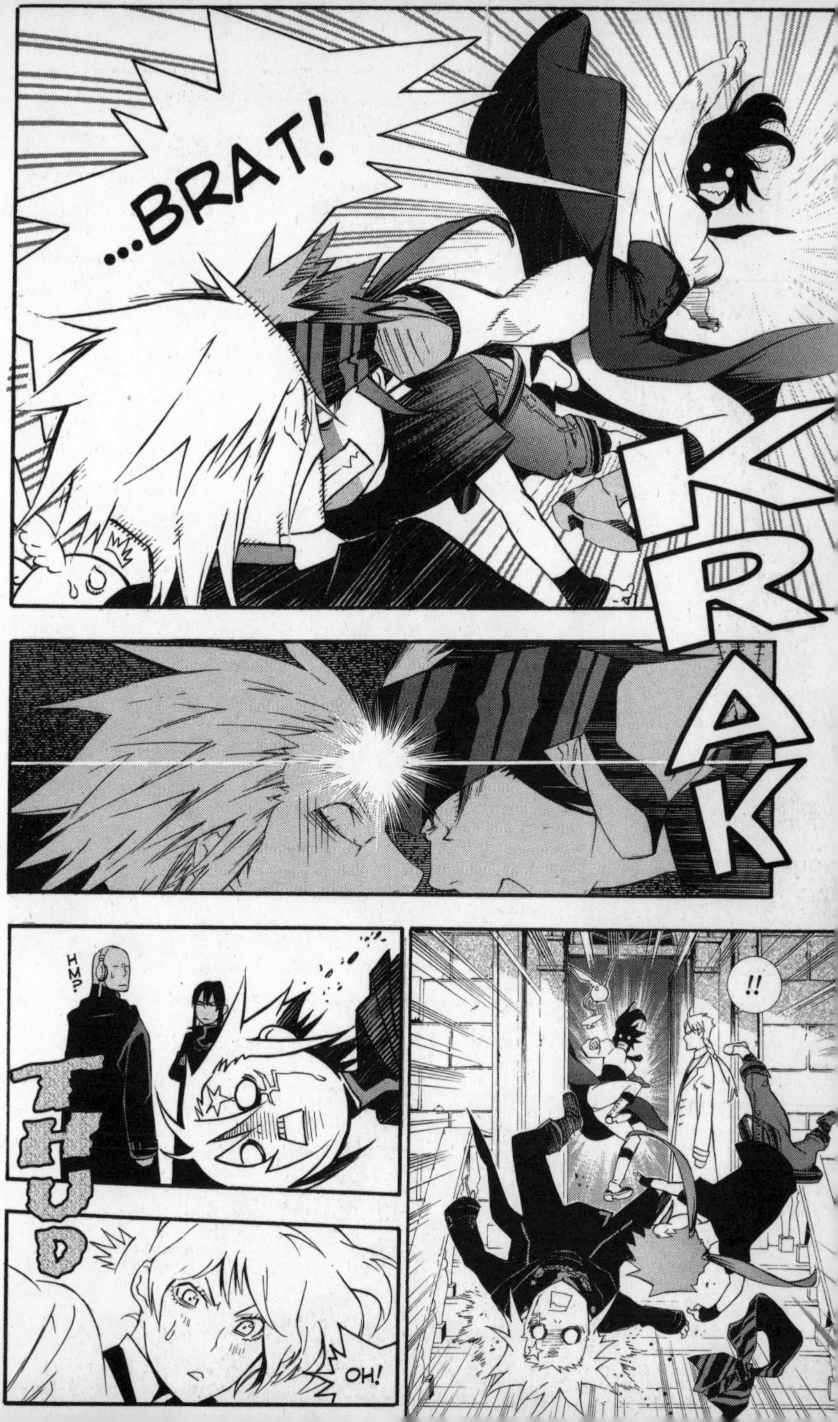
...BRAT!
KRAK
!!
HM?
THUD
OH!

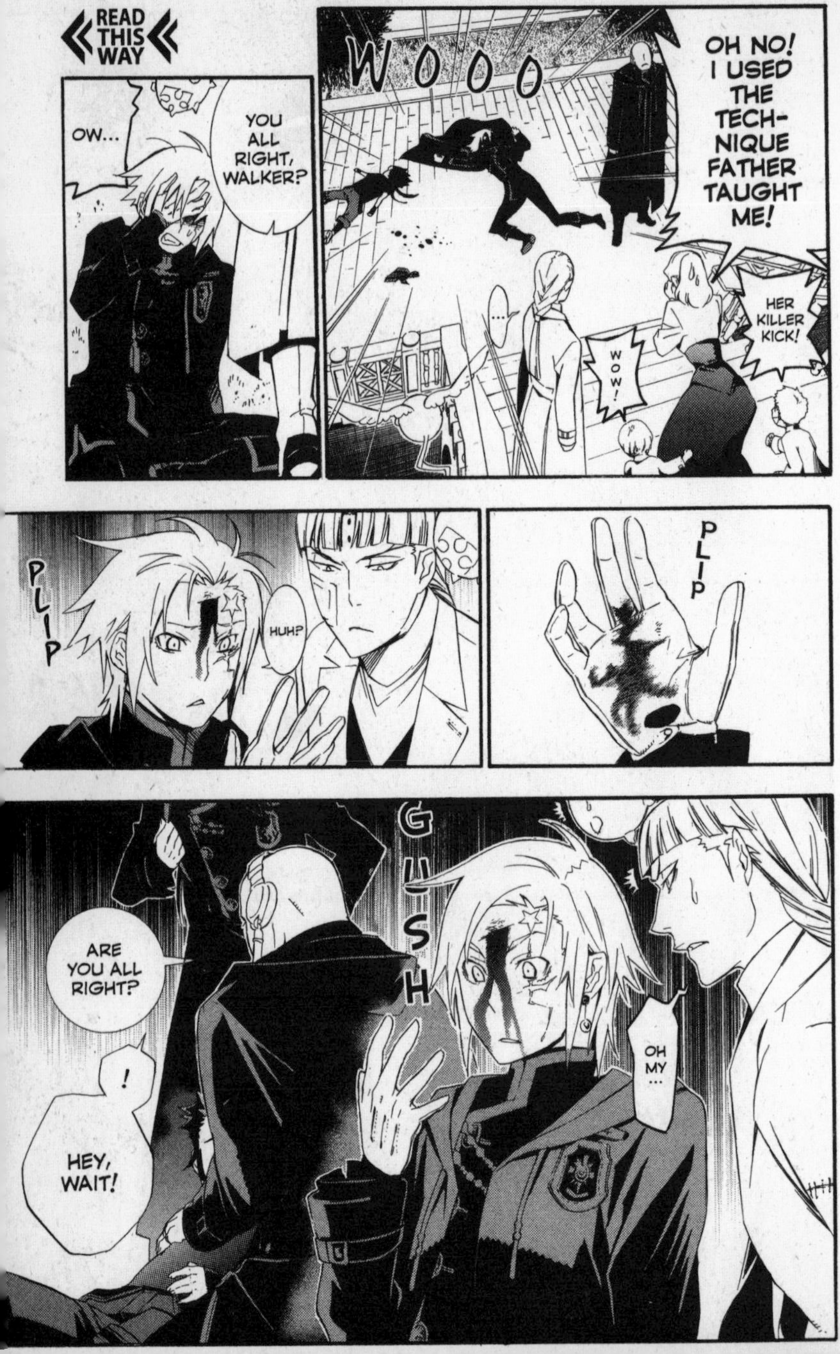
READ THIS WAY
WOOO
OH NO! I USED THE TECH-NIQUE FATHER TAUGHT ME!
HER KILLER KICK!
WOW!
...
YOU ALL RIGHT, WALKER?
OW...
PLIP
HUH?
PLIP
GUSH
OH MY ...
ARE YOU ALL RIGHT?
!
HEY, WAIT!

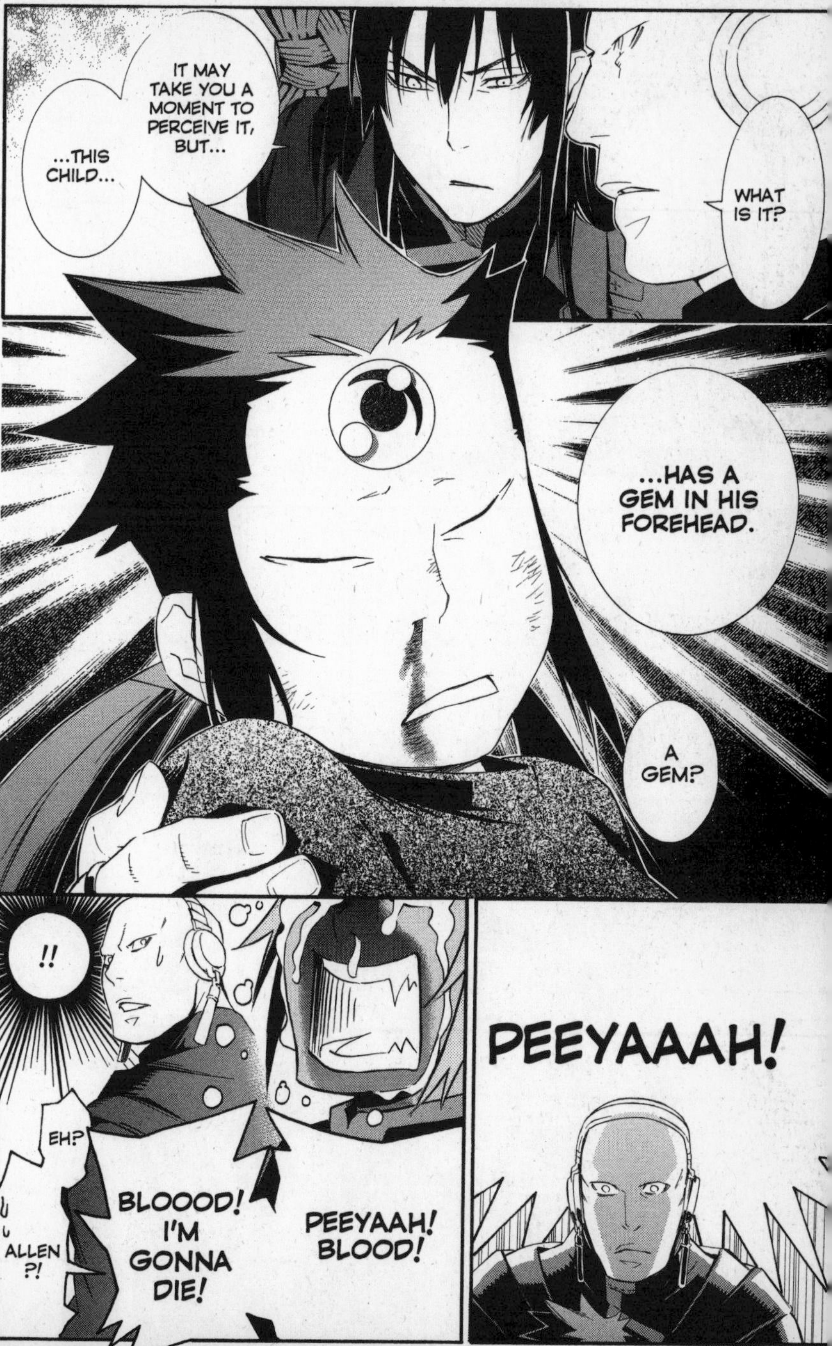
IT MAY TAKE YOU A MOMENT TO PERCEIVE IT, BUT...
...THIS CHILD...
WHAT IS IT?
...HAS A GEM IN HIS FOREHEAD.
A GEM?
PEEYAAAH!
PEEYAAH! BLOOD!
BLOOOD! I'M GONNA DIE!
!!
EH?
ALLEN ?!

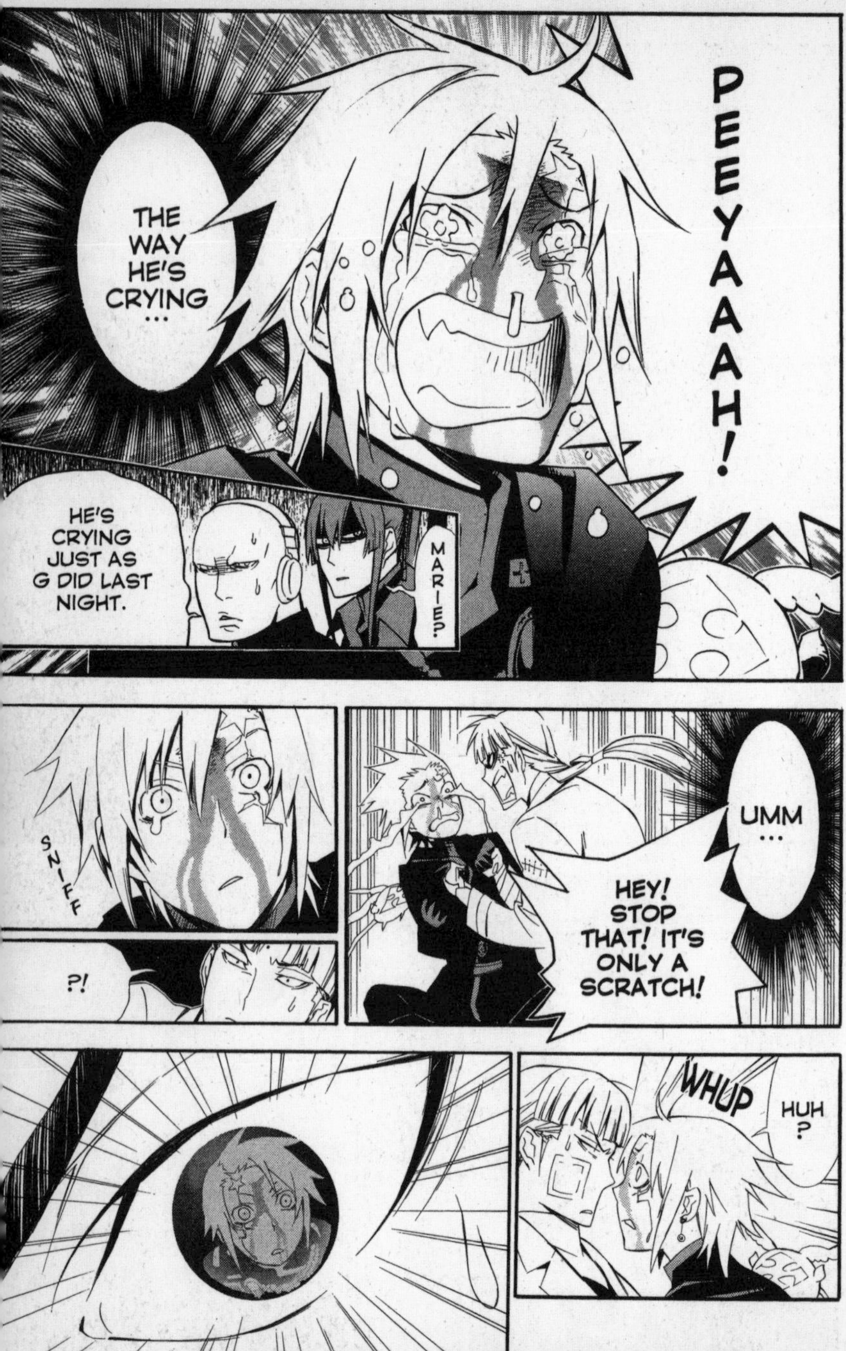
PEEYAAAH!
THE WAY HE'S CRYING...
MARIE?
HE'S CRYING JUST AS G DID LAST NIGHT.
UMM...
HEY! STOP THAT! IT'S ONLY A SCRATCH!
SNIFF
?!
HUH?
WHUP

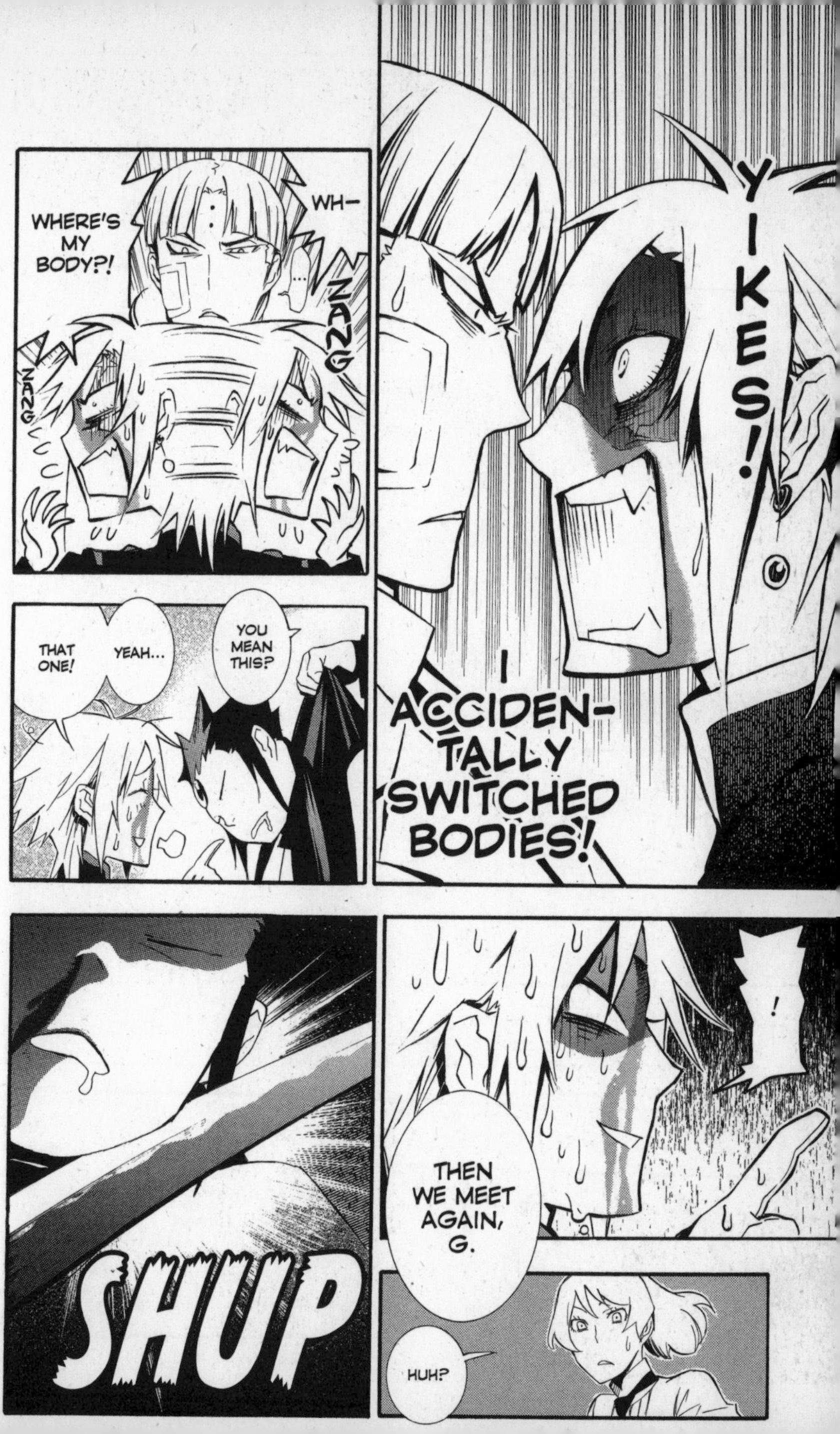
YIKES!
I ACCIDEN-TALLY SWITCHED BODIES!
WH—
ZANG
...
WHERE'S MY BODY?!
ZANG
YOU MEAN THIS?
YEAH...
THAT ONE!
!
THEN WE MEET AGAIN, G.
HUH?
SHUP

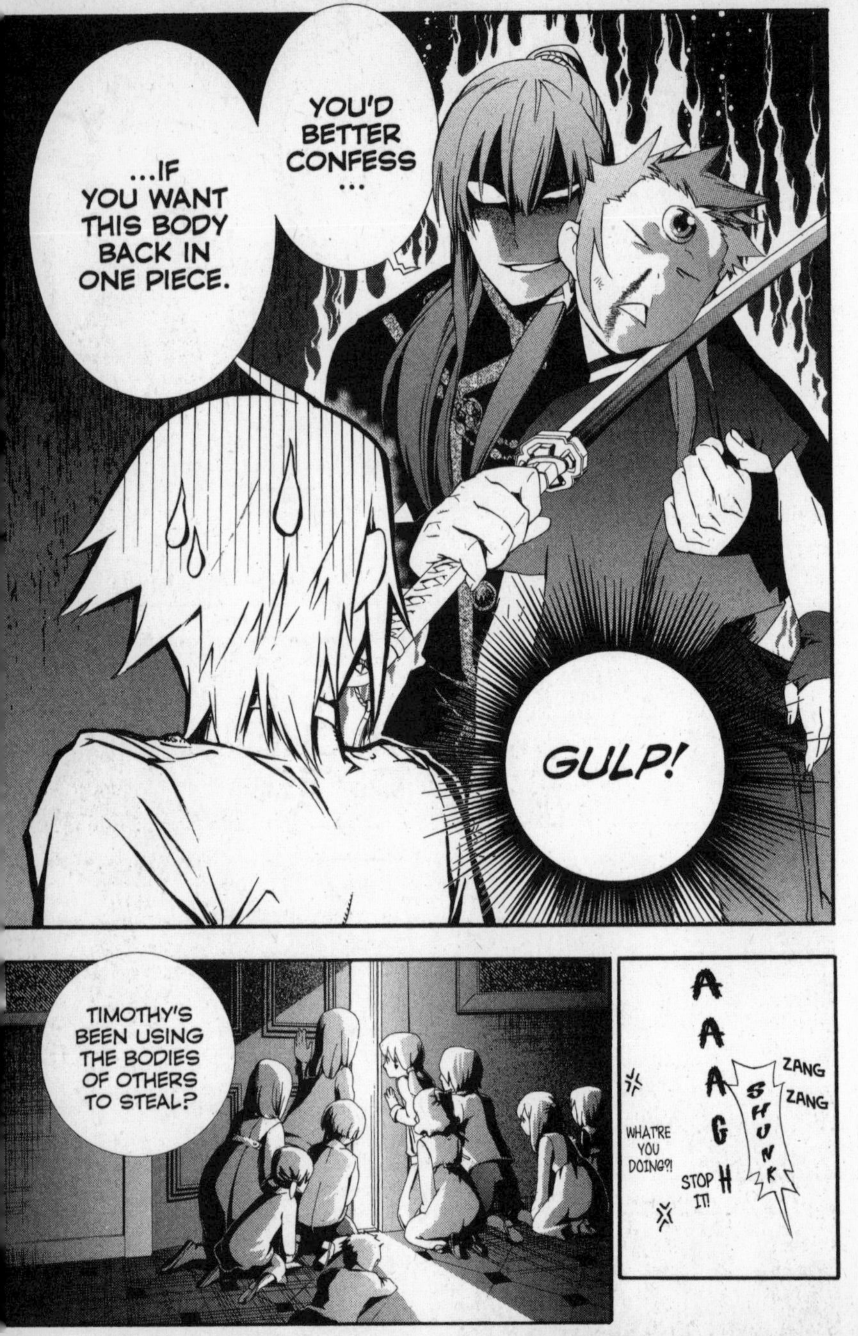
YOU'D BETTER CONFESS ...
...IF YOU WANT THIS BODY BACK IN ONE PIECE.
GULP!
AAAGH
ZANG ZANG
SHUNK
WHAT'RE YOU DOING?!
STOP IT!
TIMOTHY'S BEEN USING THE BODIES OF OTHERS TO STEAL?

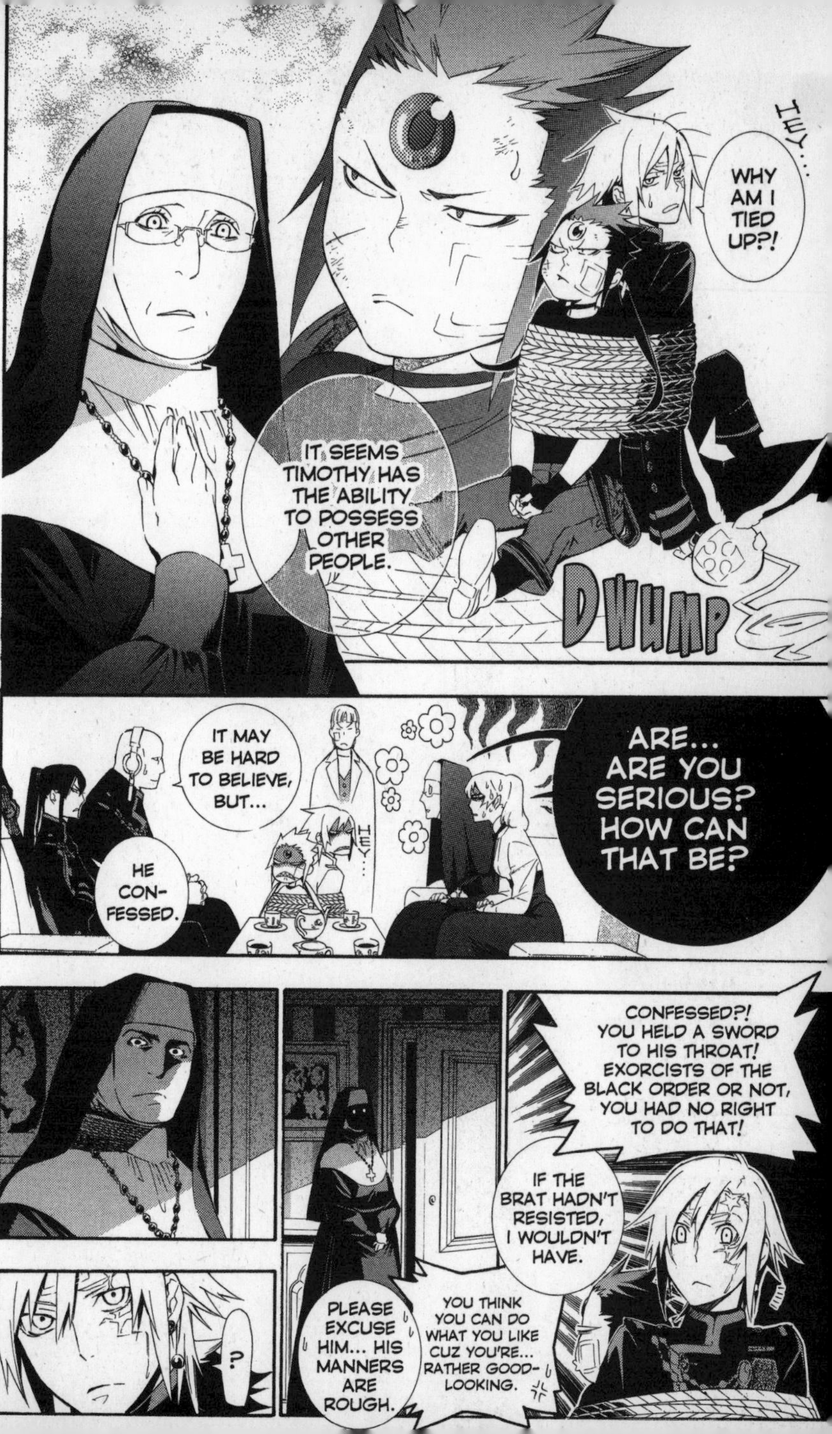
HEY...
WHY AM I TIED UP?!
IT SEEMS TIMOTHY HAS THE ABILITY TO POSSESS OTHER PEOPLE.
DWUMP
ARE... ARE YOU SERIOUS? HOW CAN THAT BE?
HEY...
IT MAY BE HARD TO BELIEVE, BUT...
HE CON-FESSED.
CONFESSED?! YOU HELD A SWORD TO HIS THROAT! EXORCISTS OF THE BLACK ORDER OR NOT, YOU HAD NO RIGHT TO DO THAT!
IF THE BRAT HADN'T RESISTED, I WOULDN'T HAVE.
YOU THINK YOU CAN DO WHAT YOU LIKE CUZ YOU'RE... RATHER GOOD-LOOKING.
PLEASE EXCUSE HIM... HIS MANNERS ARE ROUGH.
?

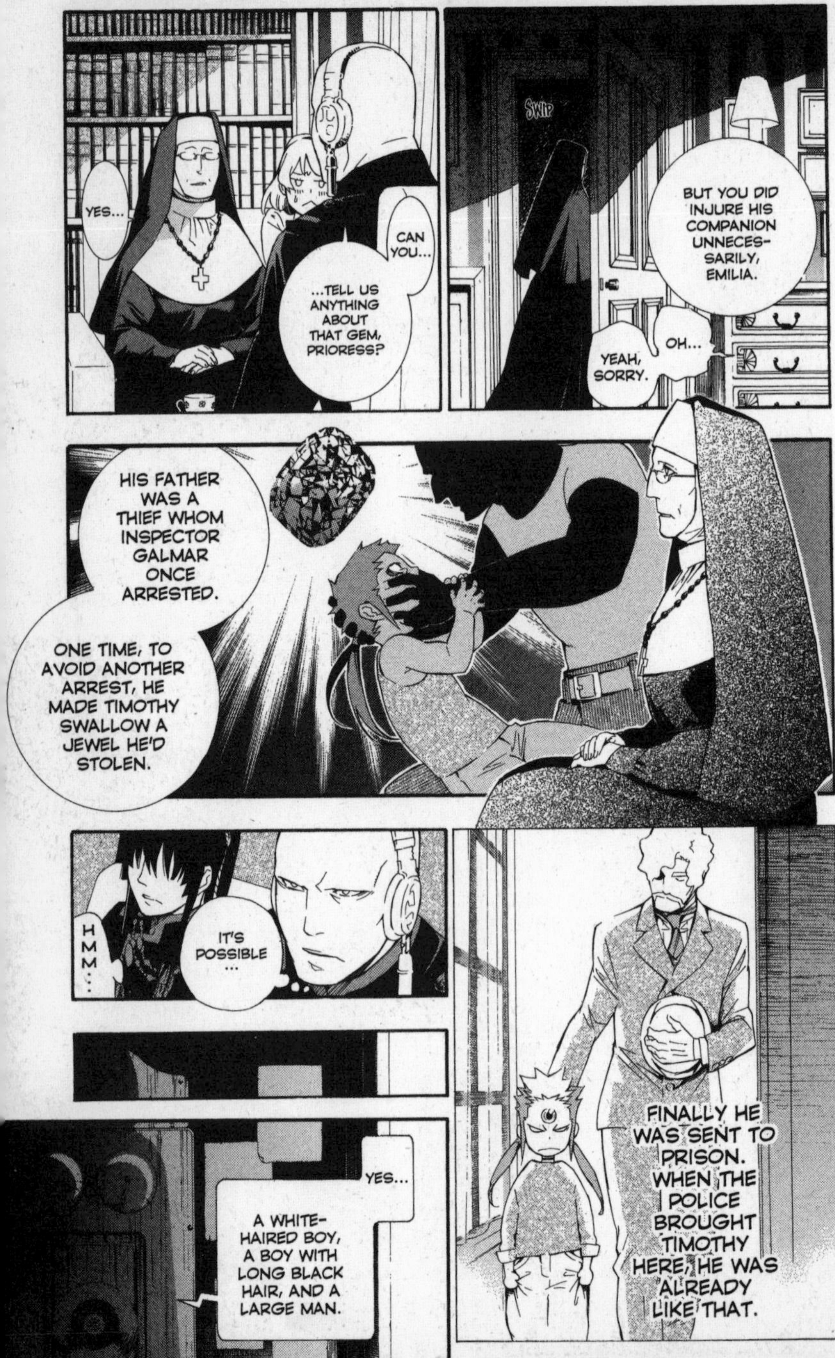
SWIP
BUT YOU DID INJURE HIS COMPANION UNNECES-SARILY, EMILIA.
OH...
YEAH, SORRY.
CAN YOU...
...TELL US ANYTHING ABOUT THAT GEM, PRIORESS?
YES...
HIS FATHER WAS A THIEF WHOM INSPECTOR GALMAR ONCE ARRESTED.
ONE TIME, TO AVOID ANOTHER ARREST, HE MADE TIMOTHY SWALLOW A JEWEL HE'D STOLEN.
FINALLY HE WAS SENT TO PRISON. WHEN THE POLICE BROUGHT TIMOTHY HERE, HE WAS ALREADY LIKE THAT.
IT'S POSSIBLE ...
HMM...
YES...
A WHITE-HAIRED BOY, A BOY WITH LONG BLACK HAIR, AND A LARGE MAN.

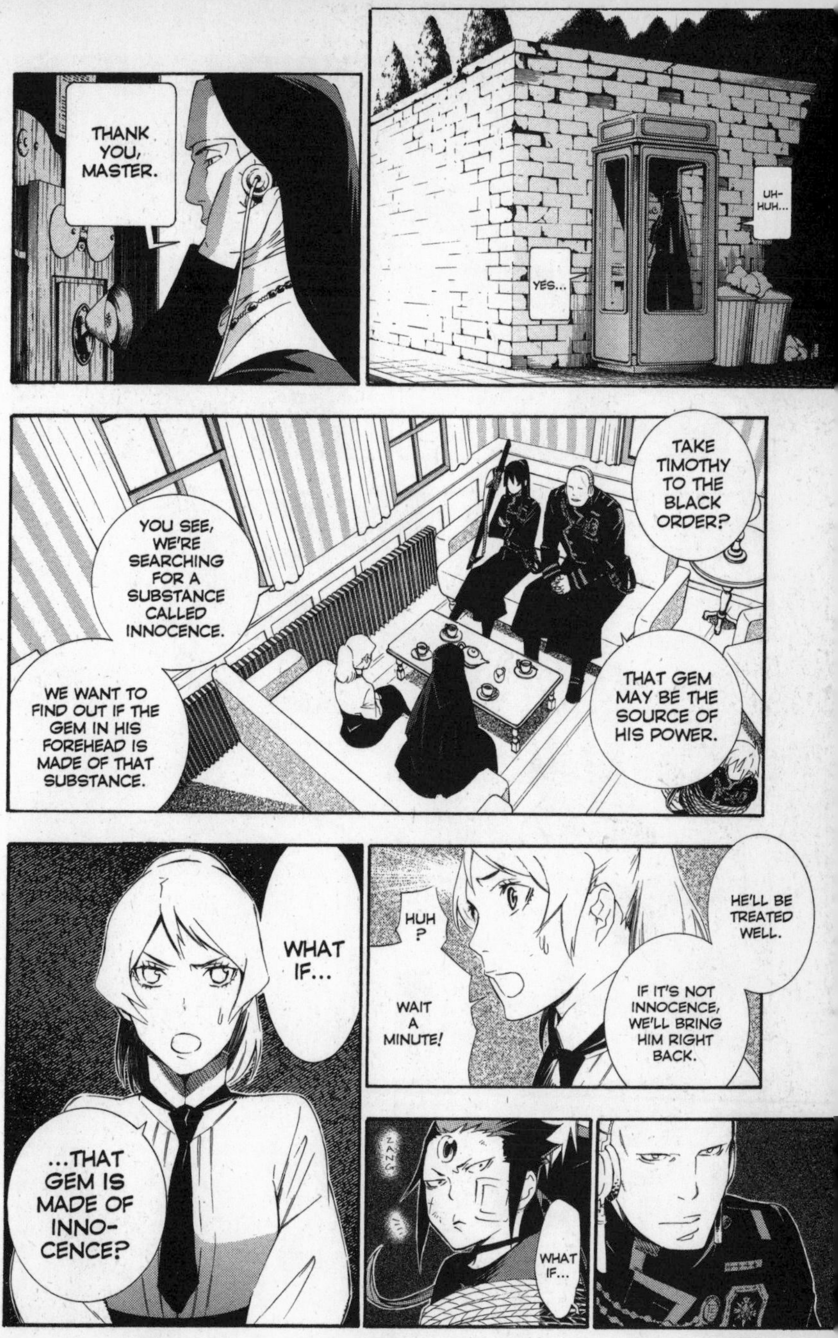
UH-HUH...
YES...
THANK YOU, MASTER.
TAKE TIMOTHY TO THE BLACK ORDER?
YOU SEE, WE'RE SEARCHING FOR A SUBSTANCE CALLED INNOCENCE.
WE WANT TO FIND OUT IF THE GEM IN HIS FOREHEAD IS MADE OF THAT SUBSTANCE.
THAT GEM MAY BE THE SOURCE OF HIS POWER.
HE'LL BE TREATED WELL.
HUH?
IF IT'S NOT INNOCENCE, WE'LL BRING HIM RIGHT BACK.
WAIT A MINUTE!
ZANG
WHAT IF...
WHAT IF...
...THAT GEM IS MADE OF INNO-CENCE?

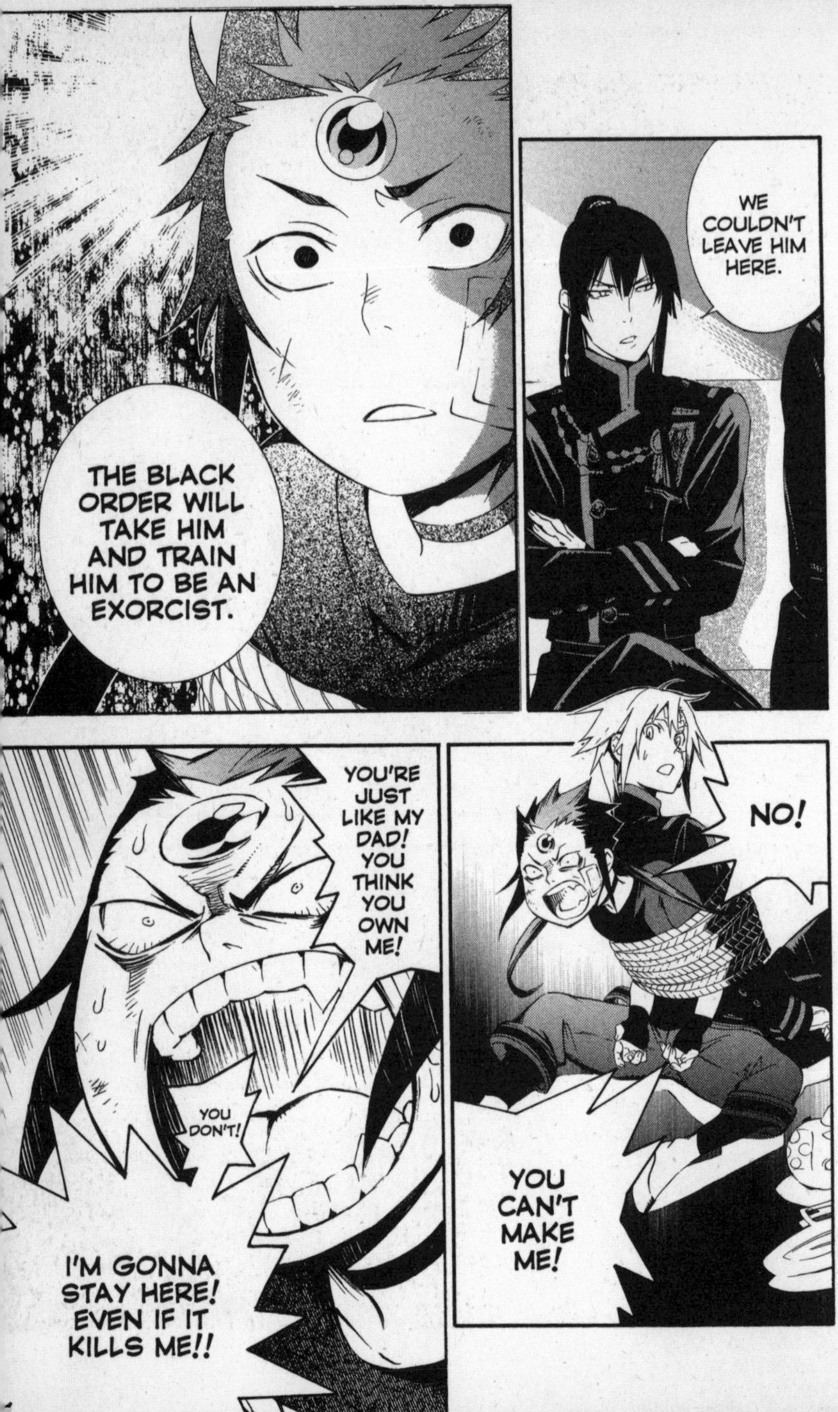
WE COULDN'T LEAVE HIM HERE.
THE BLACK ORDER WILL TAKE HIM AND TRAIN HIM TO BE AN EXORCIST.
NO!
YOU CAN'T MAKE ME!
YOU'RE JUST LIKE MY DAD! YOU THINK YOU OWN ME!
YOU DON'T!
I'M GONNA STAY HERE! EVEN IF IT KILLS ME!!

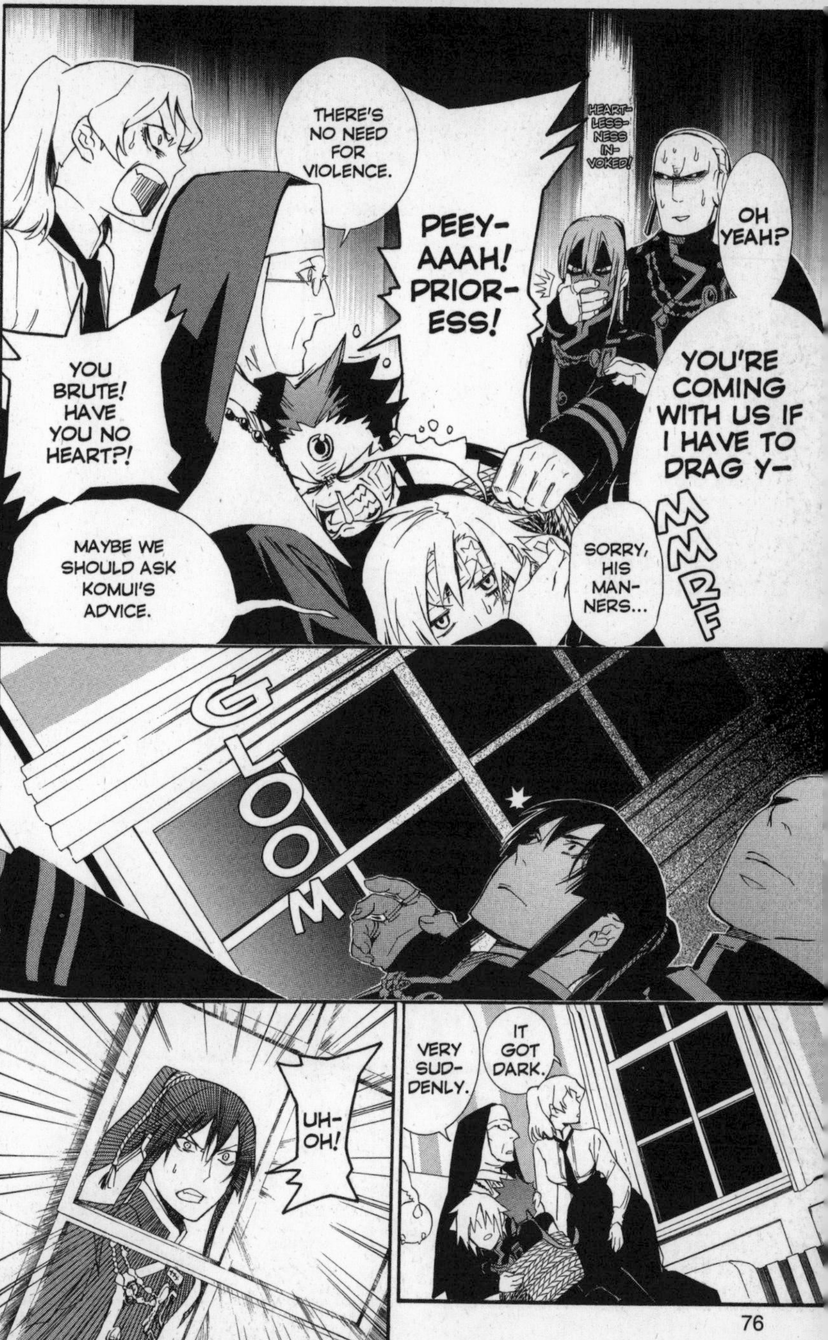
OH YEAH?
HEART-LESSNESS IN-VOKED!
YOU'RE COMING WITH US IF I HAVE TO DRAG Y—
MMRF
PEEY-AAAH! PRIOR-ESS!
THERE'S NO NEED FOR VIOLENCE.
SORRY, HIS MAN-NERS...
YOU BRUTE! HAVE YOU NO HEART?!
MAYBE WE SHOULD ASK KOMUI'S ADVICE.
GLOOM
IT GOT DARK.
VERY SUD-DENLY.
UH-OH!

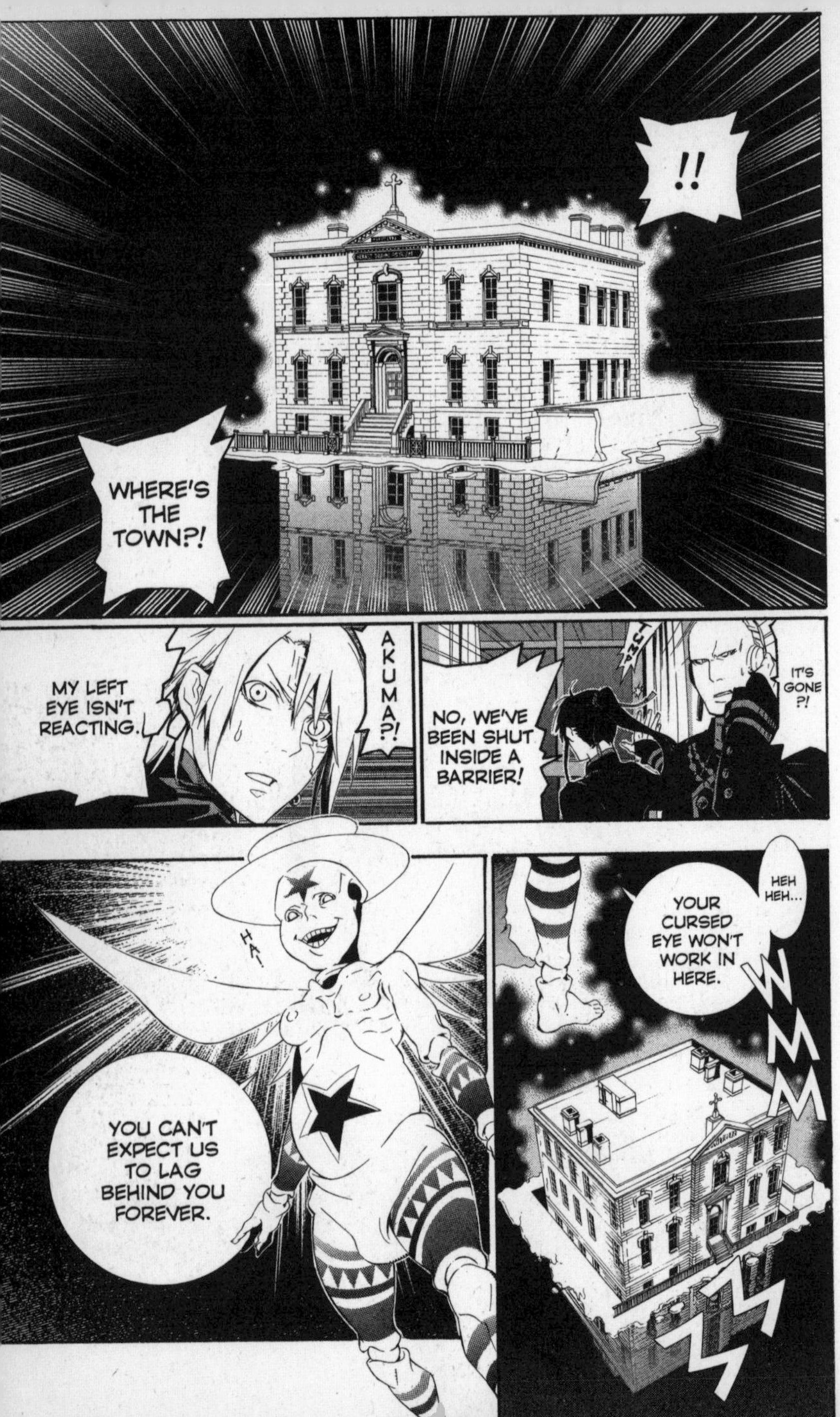
!!
WHERE'S THE TOWN?!
IT'S GONE?!
NO, WE'VE BEEN SHUT INSIDE A BARRIER!
AKUMA?!
MY LEFT EYE ISN'T REACTING.
HEH HEH...
YOUR CURSED EYE WON'T WORK IN HERE.
HA!
YOU CAN'T EXPECT US TO LAG BEHIND YOU FOREVER.

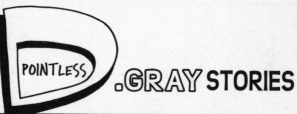

POINTLESS D.GRAY STORIES

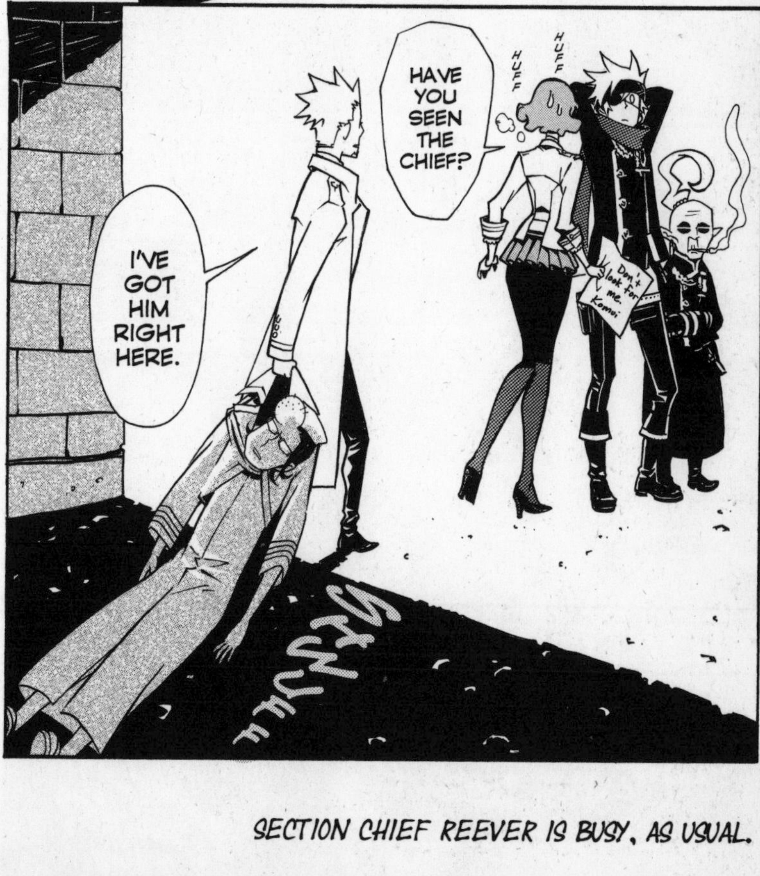
HUFF
HUFF
Don't look for me. Komui
HAVE YOU SEEN THE CHIEF?
I'VE GOT HIM RIGHT HERE.
SHUFF

SECTION CHIEF REEVER IS BUSY, AS USUAL.

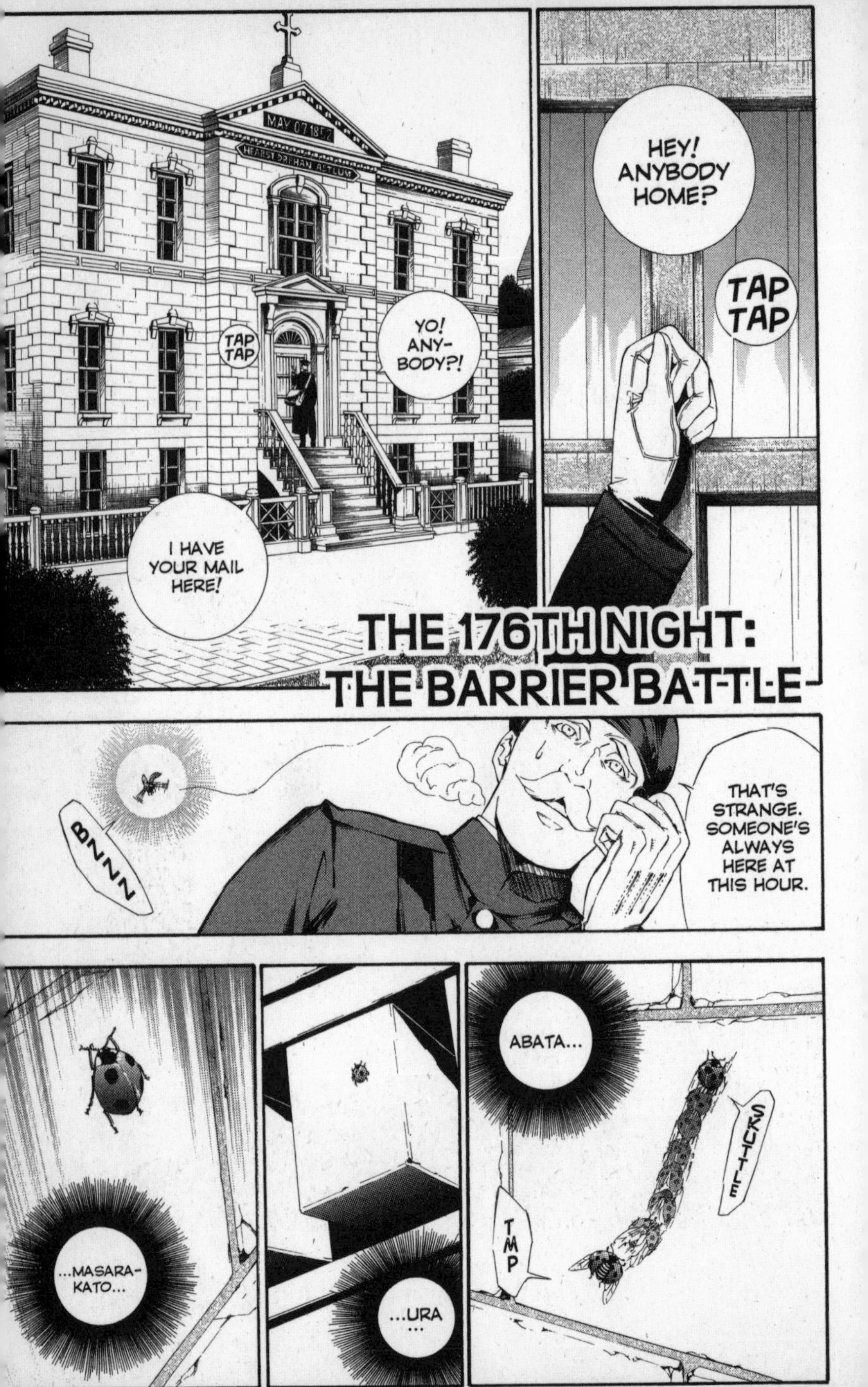
HEY! ANYBODY HOME?
TAP TAP
MAY 07 1852
HEARST ORPHAN ASYLUM
YO! ANY-BODY?!
TAP TAP
I HAVE YOUR MAIL HERE!
THE 176TH NIGHT: THE BARRIER BATTLE
THAT'S STRANGE. SOMEONE'S ALWAYS HERE AT THIS HOUR.
BNNN
ABATA...
SKUTTLE
TMP
...URA...
...MASARA-KATO...

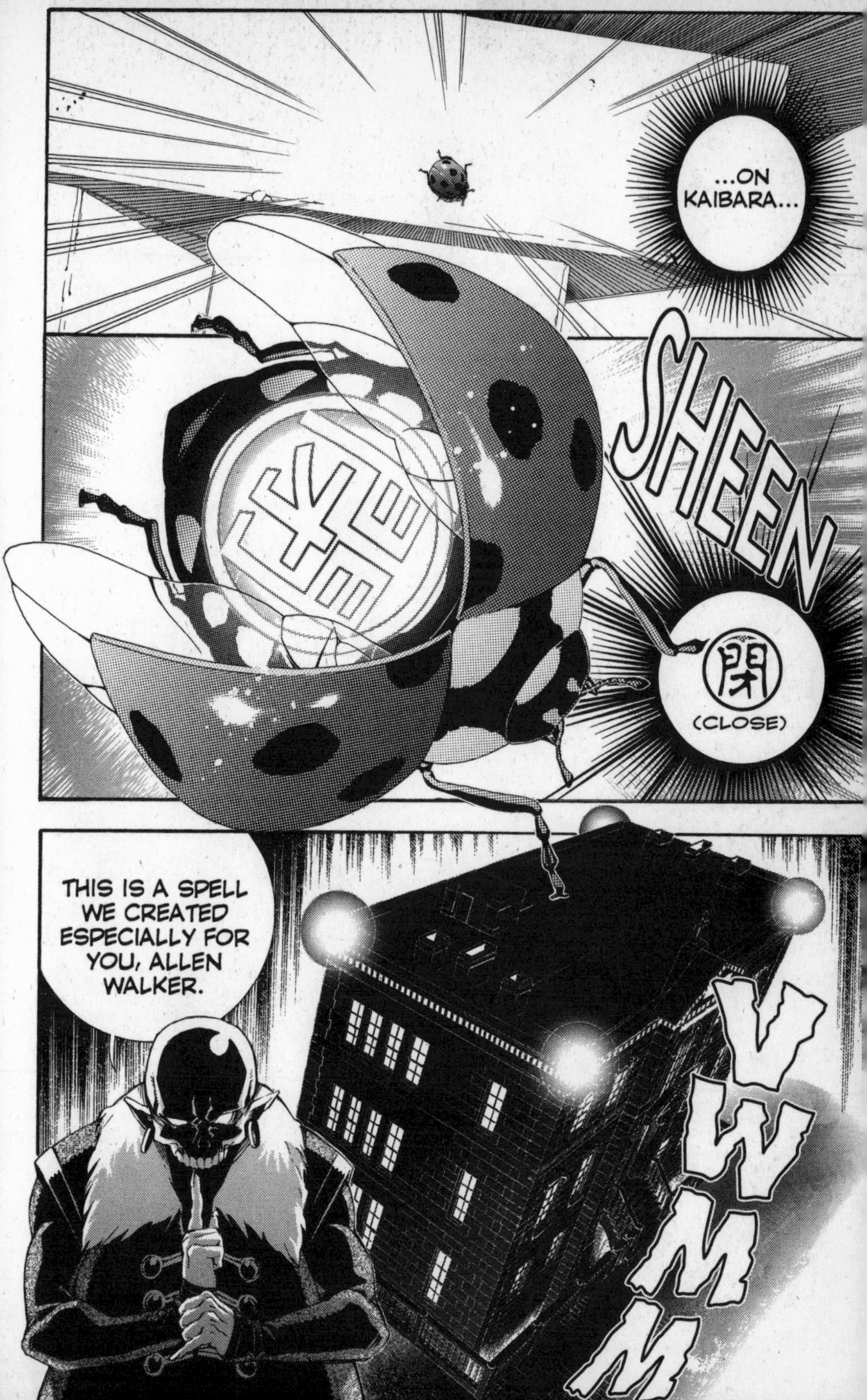
...ON KAIBARA...
SHEEN
閉
(CLOSE)
VWMMM
THIS IS A SPELL WE CREATED ESPECIALLY FOR YOU, ALLEN WALKER.

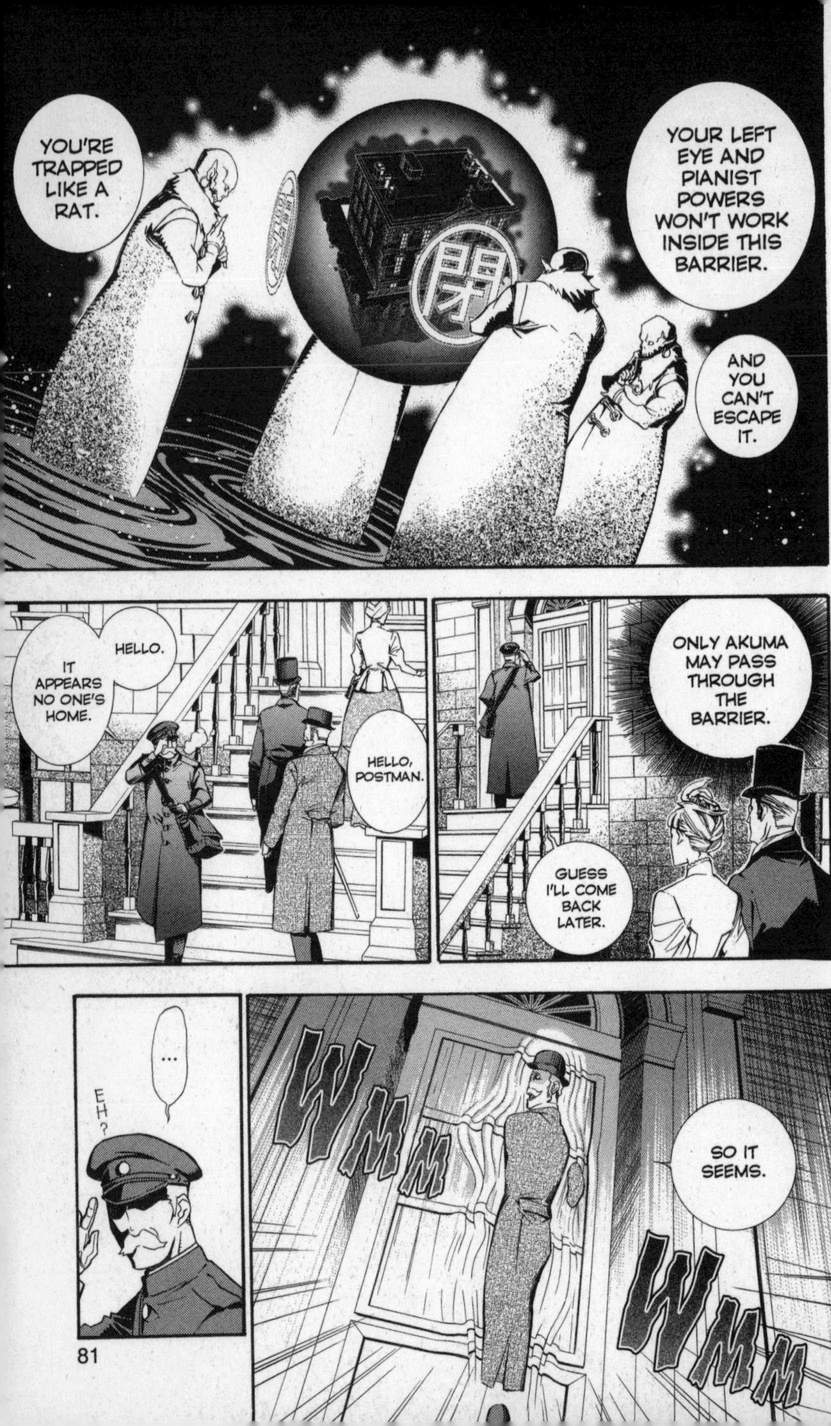
YOUR LEFT EYE AND PIANIST POWERS WON'T WORK INSIDE THIS BARRIER.
YOU'RE TRAPPED LIKE A RAT.
AND YOU CAN'T ESCAPE IT.
ONLY AKUMA MAY PASS THROUGH THE BARRIER.
GUESS I'LL COME BACK LATER.
HELLO.
IT APPEARS NO ONE'S HOME.
HELLO, POSTMAN.
WMM
SO IT SEEMS.
WMM
...
EH?

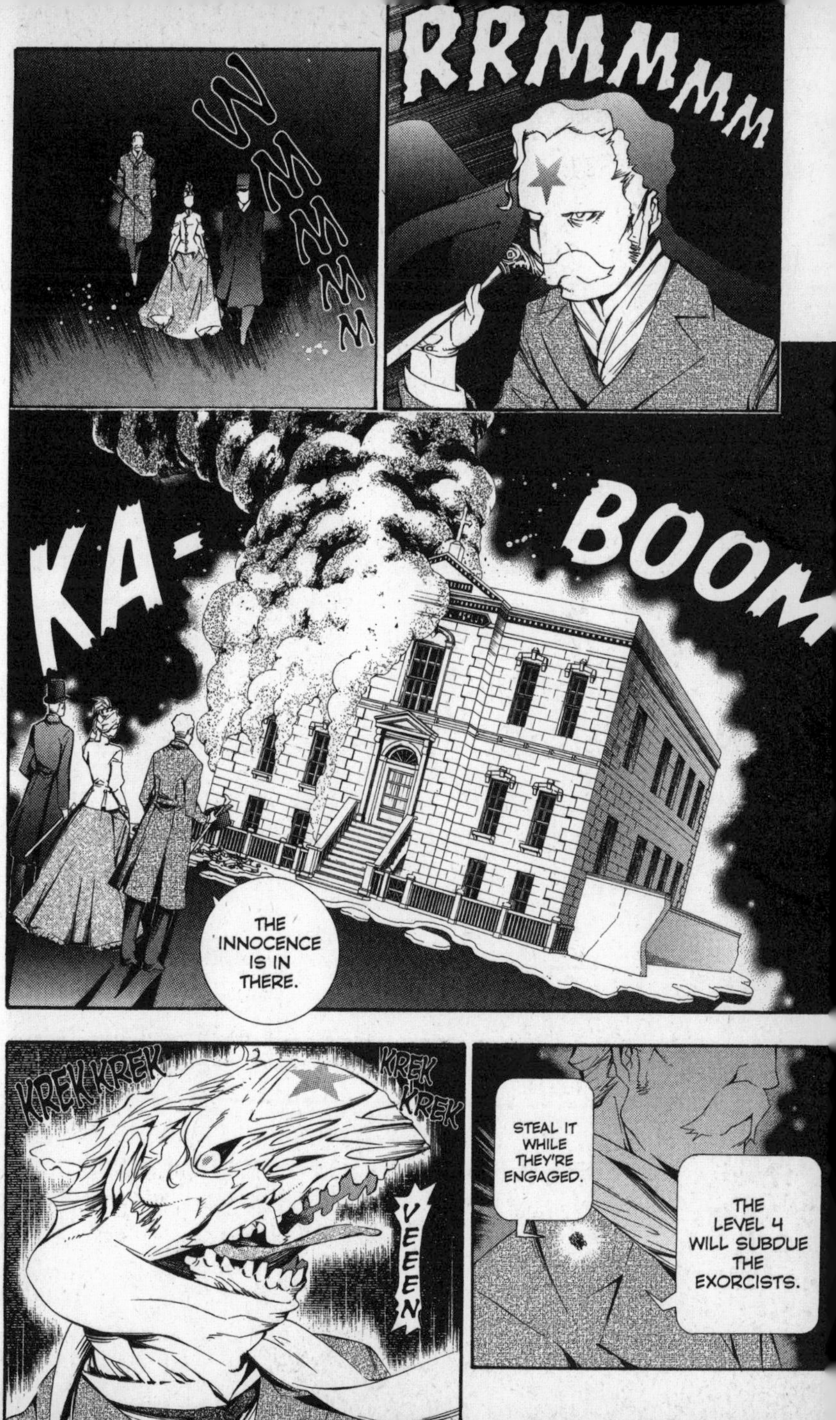
RRMMMMMM
WMMMMM
KA-BOOM
THE INNOCENCE IS IN THERE.
THE LEVEL 4 WILL SUBDUE THE EXORCISTS.
STEAL IT WHILE THEY'RE ENGAGED.
KREK KREK
KREK KREK
VEEEN

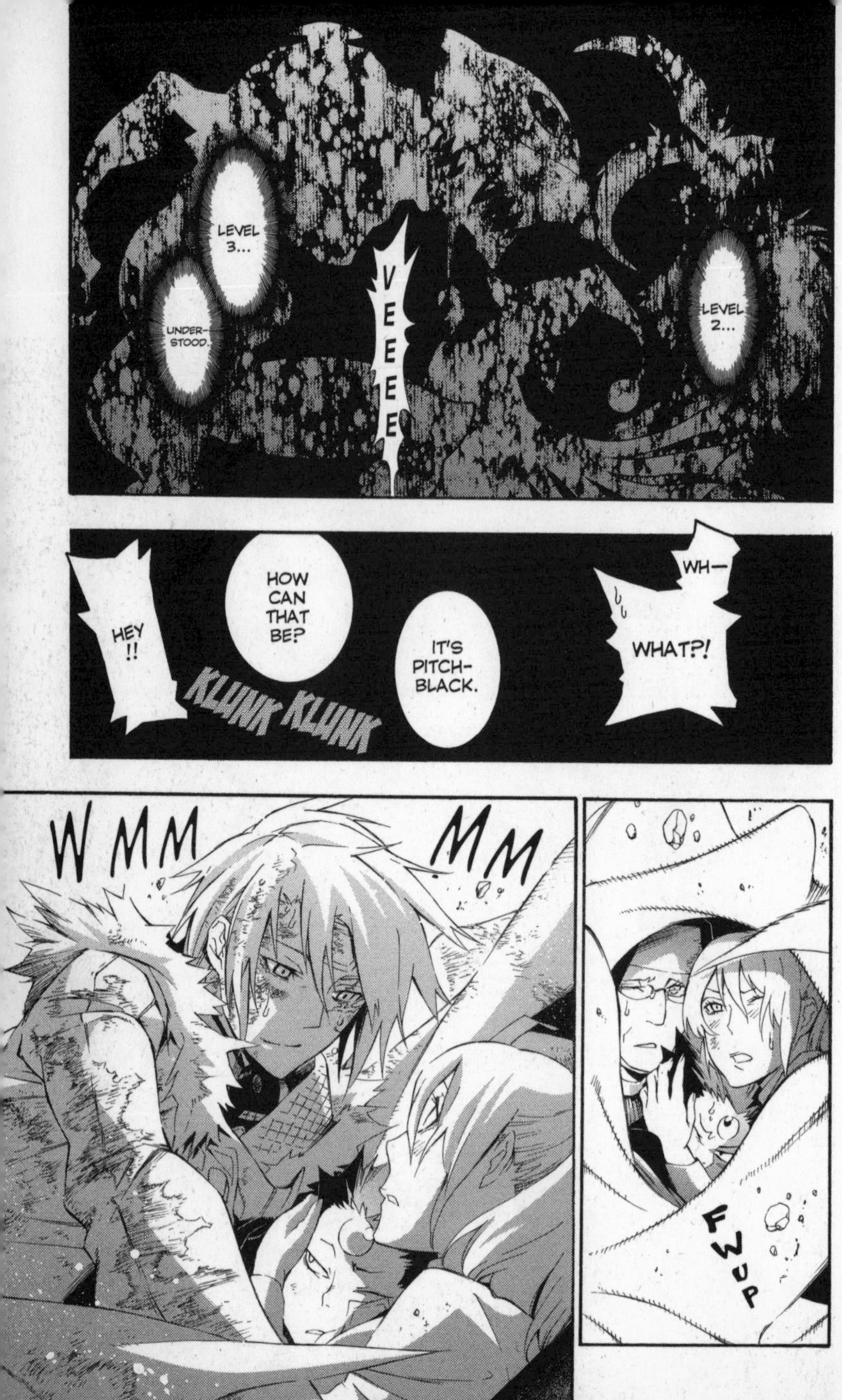
LEVEL 2...
VEEEE
LEVEL 3...
UNDER-STOOD.
WH— WHAT?!
IT'S PITCH-BLACK.
HOW CAN THAT BE?
KLUNK KLUNK
HEY!!
FWUP
WMM MM

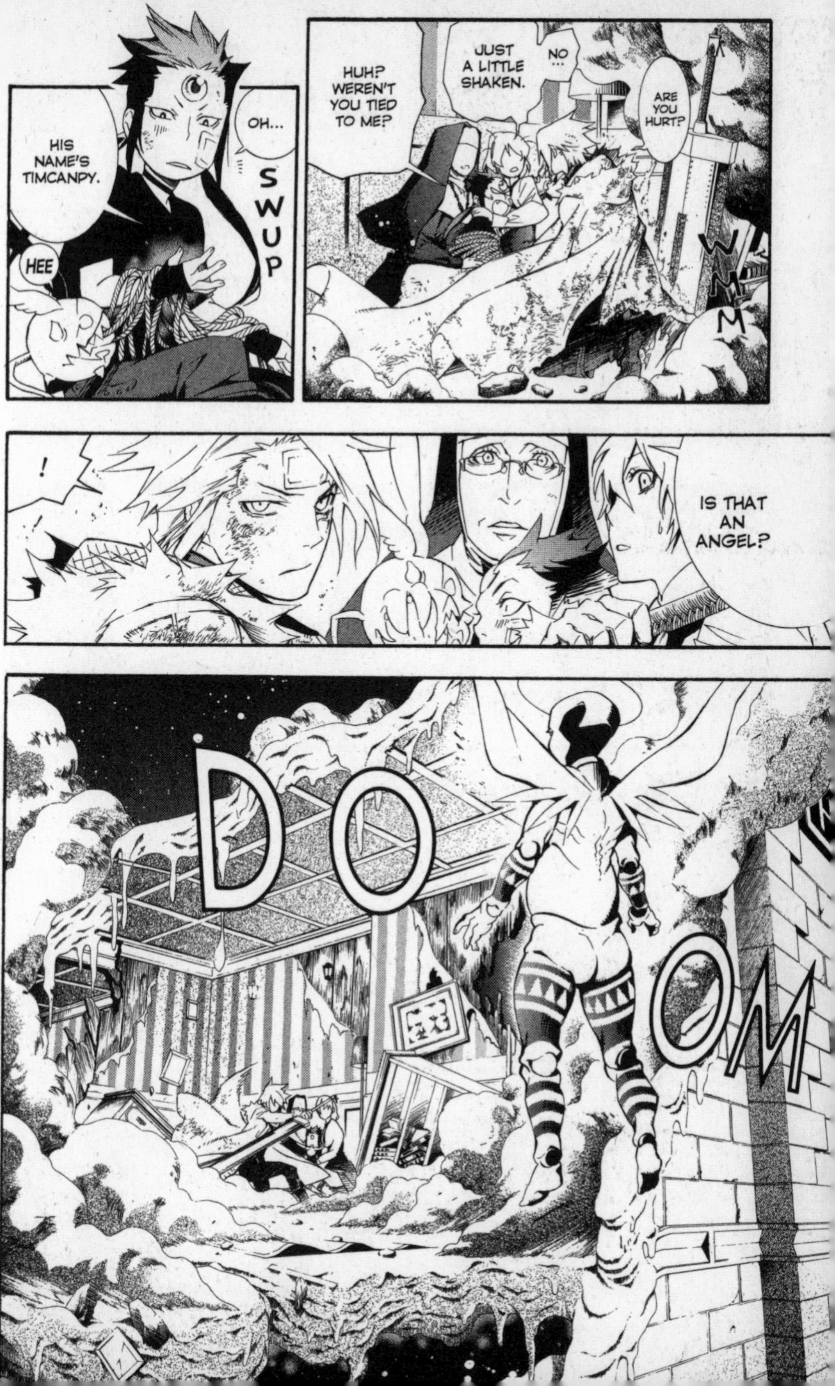
ARE YOU HURT?
WMM
NO...
JUST A LITTLE SHAKEN.
HUH? WEREN'T YOU TIED TO ME?
OH...
SWUP
HIS NAME'S TIMCANPY.
HEE
IS THAT AN ANGEL?
!
DOOM

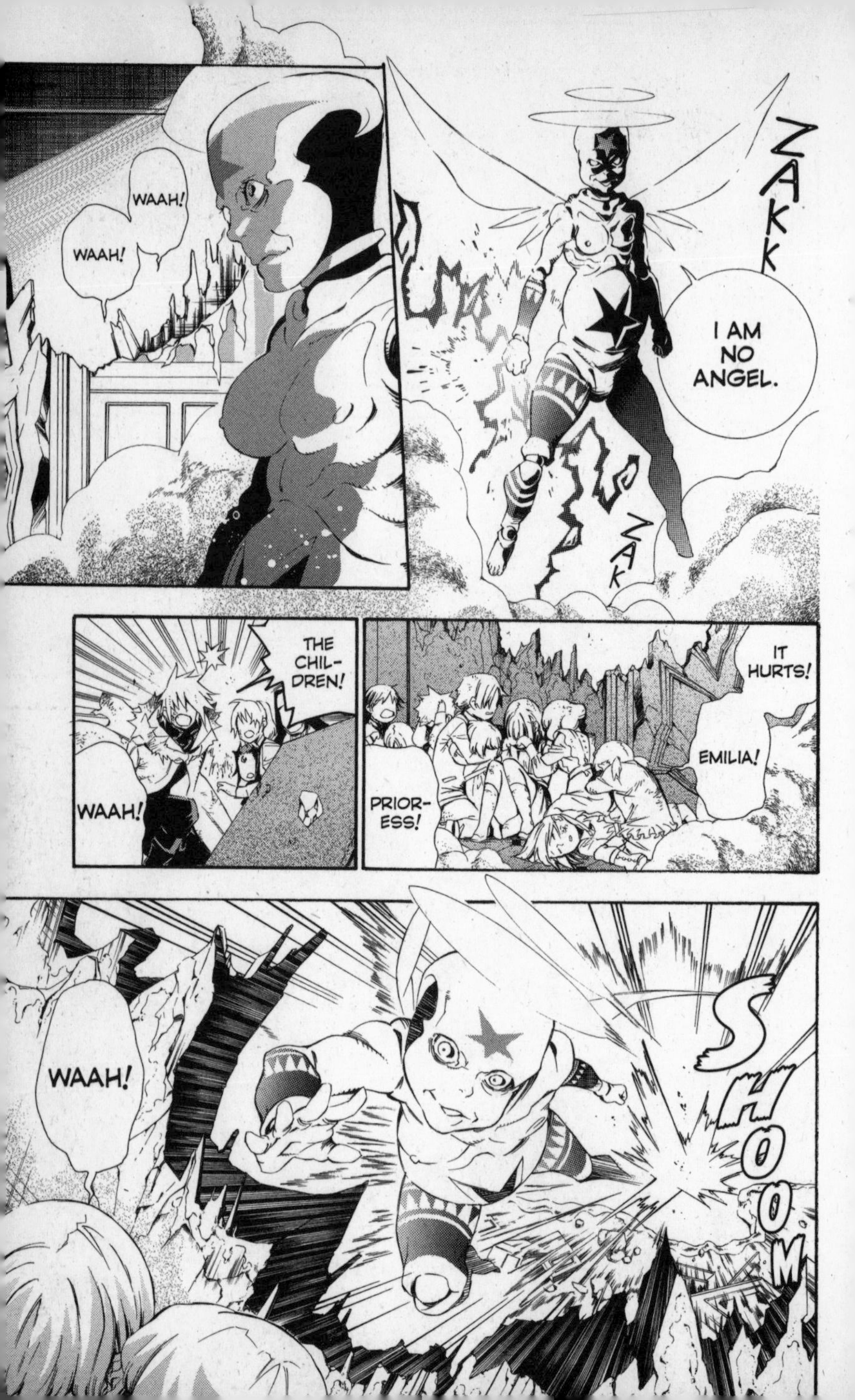
ZAKK
I AM NO ANGEL.
ZAK
WAAH!
WAAH!
IT HURTS!
EMILIA!
PRIOR-ESS!
THE CHIL-DREN!
WAAH!
SHOOM
WAAH!

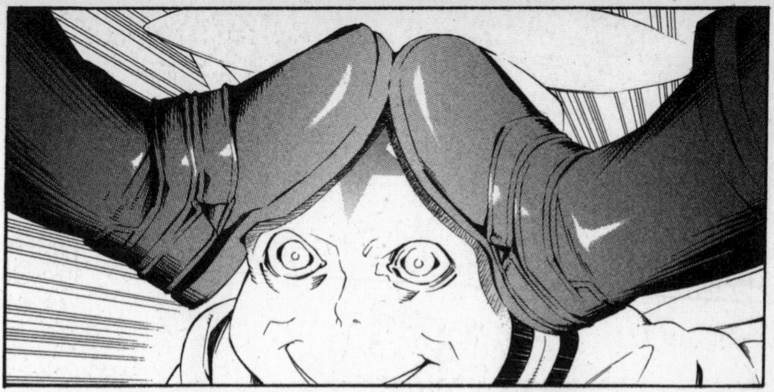

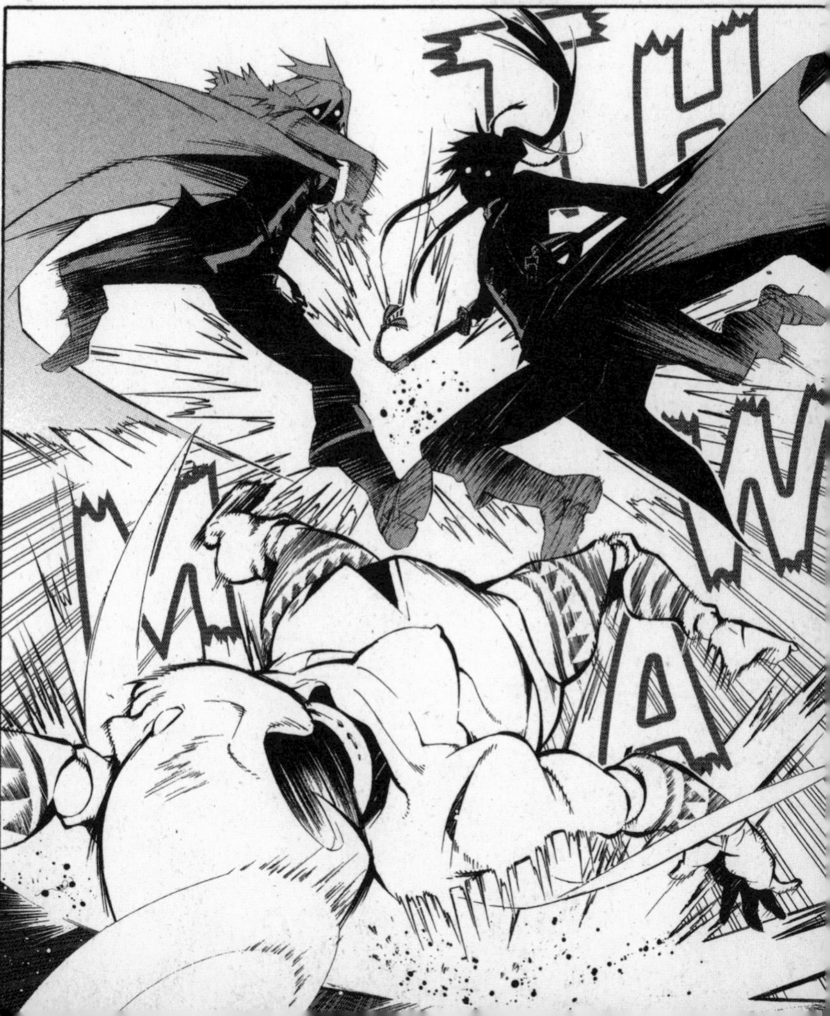

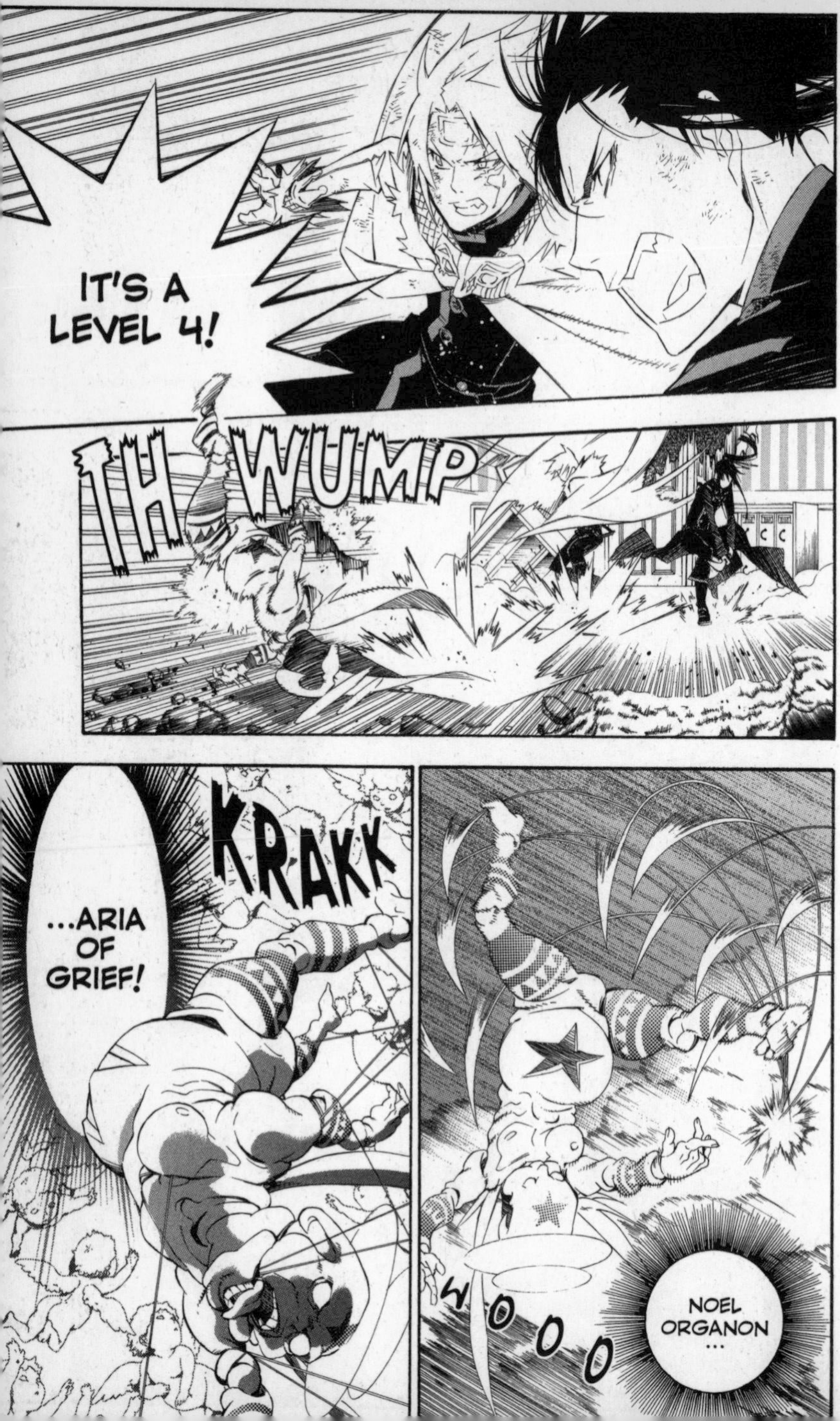
IT'S A LEVEL 4!
THWUMP
NOEL ORGANON ...
WOOOO
KRAKK
...ARIA OF GRIEF!

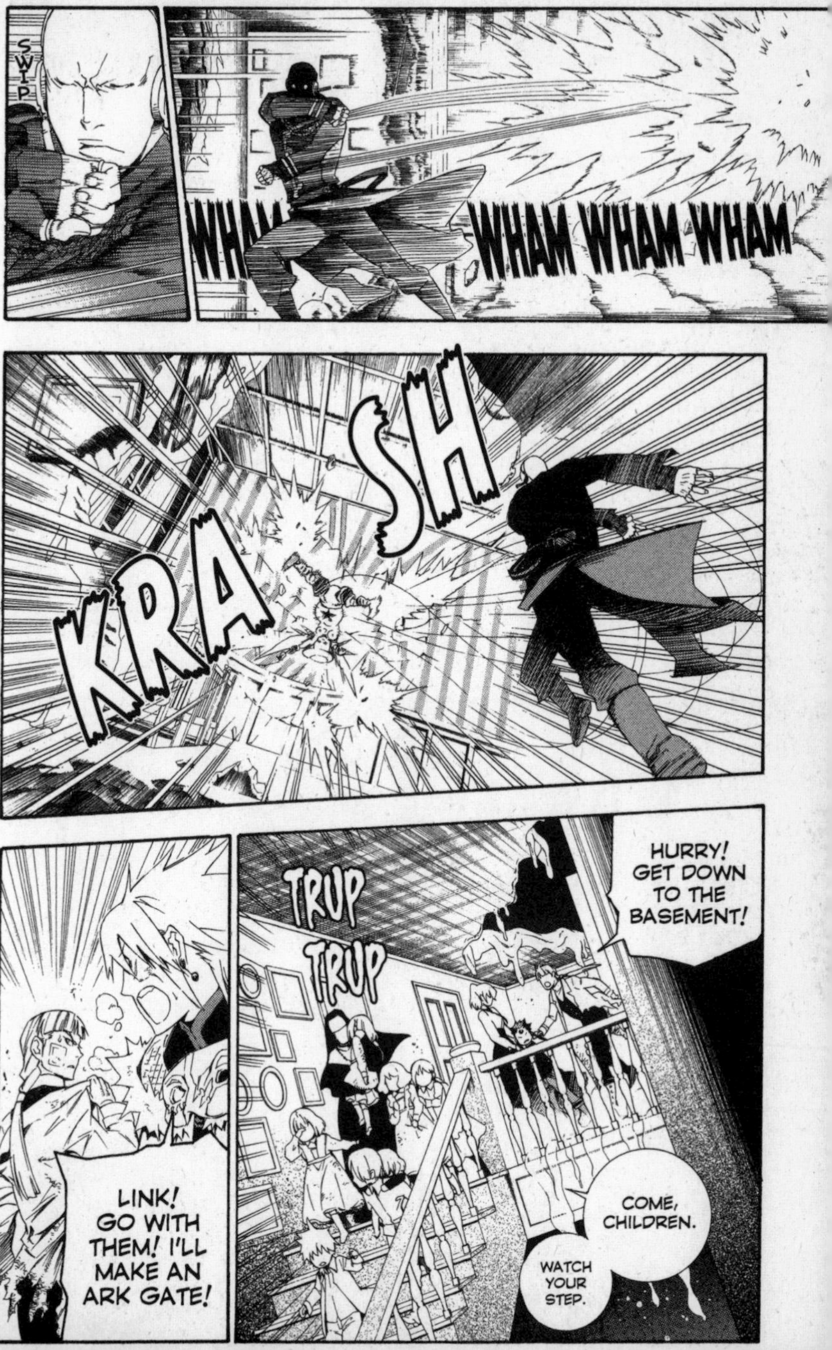
WHAM
WHAM WHAM WHAM
SWIP
KRASH
HURRY! GET DOWN TO THE BASEMENT!
TRUP
TRUP
COME, CHILDREN.
WATCH YOUR STEP.
LINK! GO WITH THEM! I'LL MAKE AN ARK GATE!

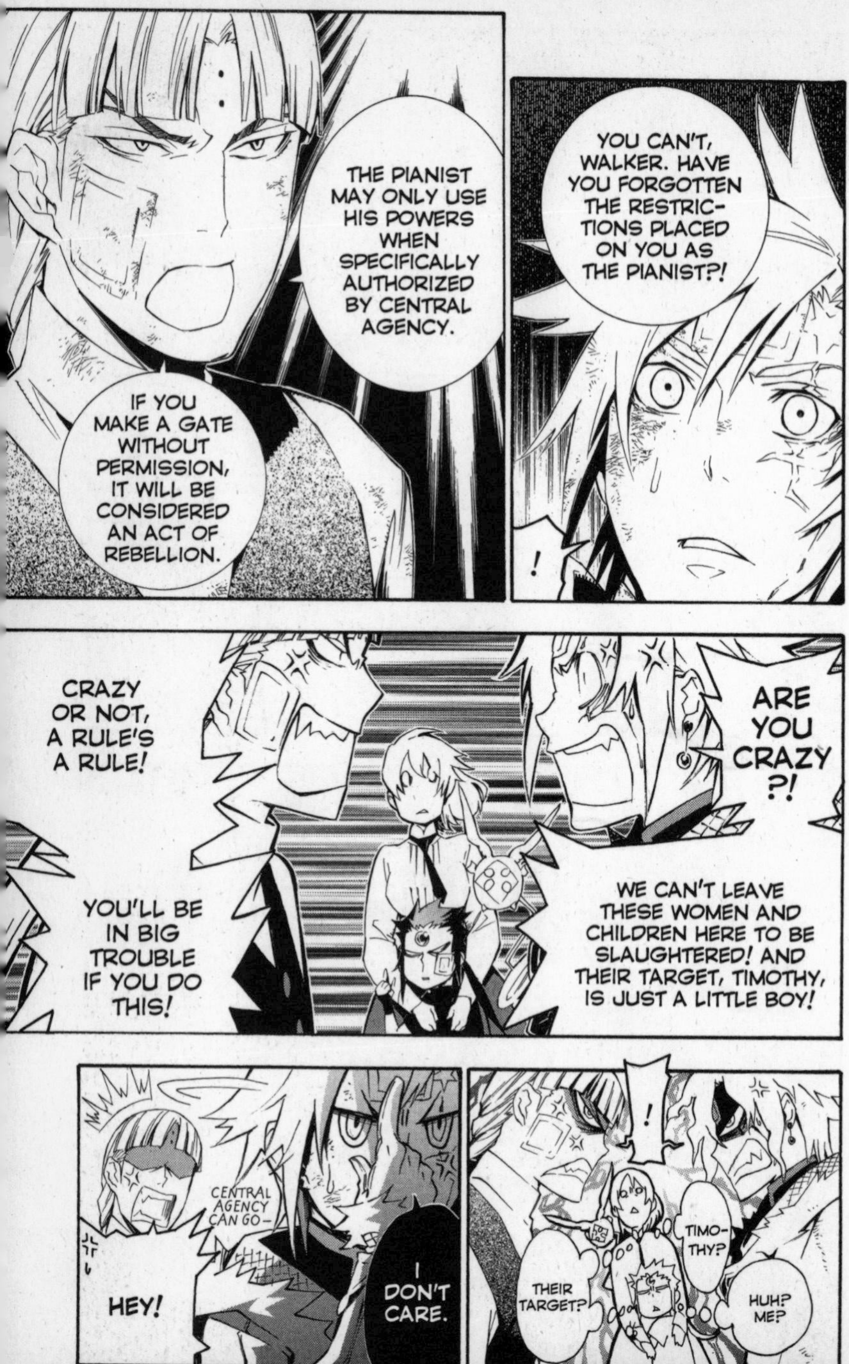
YOU CAN'T, WALKER. HAVE YOU FORGOTTEN THE RESTRICTIONS PLACED ON YOU AS THE PIANIST?!
!
THE PIANIST MAY ONLY USE HIS POWERS WHEN SPECIFICALLY AUTHORIZED BY CENTRAL AGENCY.
IF YOU MAKE A GATE WITHOUT PERMISSION, IT WILL BE CONSIDERED AN ACT OF REBELLION.
ARE YOU CRAZY?!
CRAZY OR NOT, A RULE'S A RULE!
WE CAN'T LEAVE THESE WOMEN AND CHILDREN HERE TO BE SLAUGHTERED! AND THEIR TARGET, TIMOTHY, IS JUST A LITTLE BOY!
YOU'LL BE IN BIG TROUBLE IF YOU DO THIS!
!
TIMOTHY?
HUH? ME?
THEIR TARGET?
I DON'T CARE.
CENTRAL AGENCY CAN GO—
HEY!

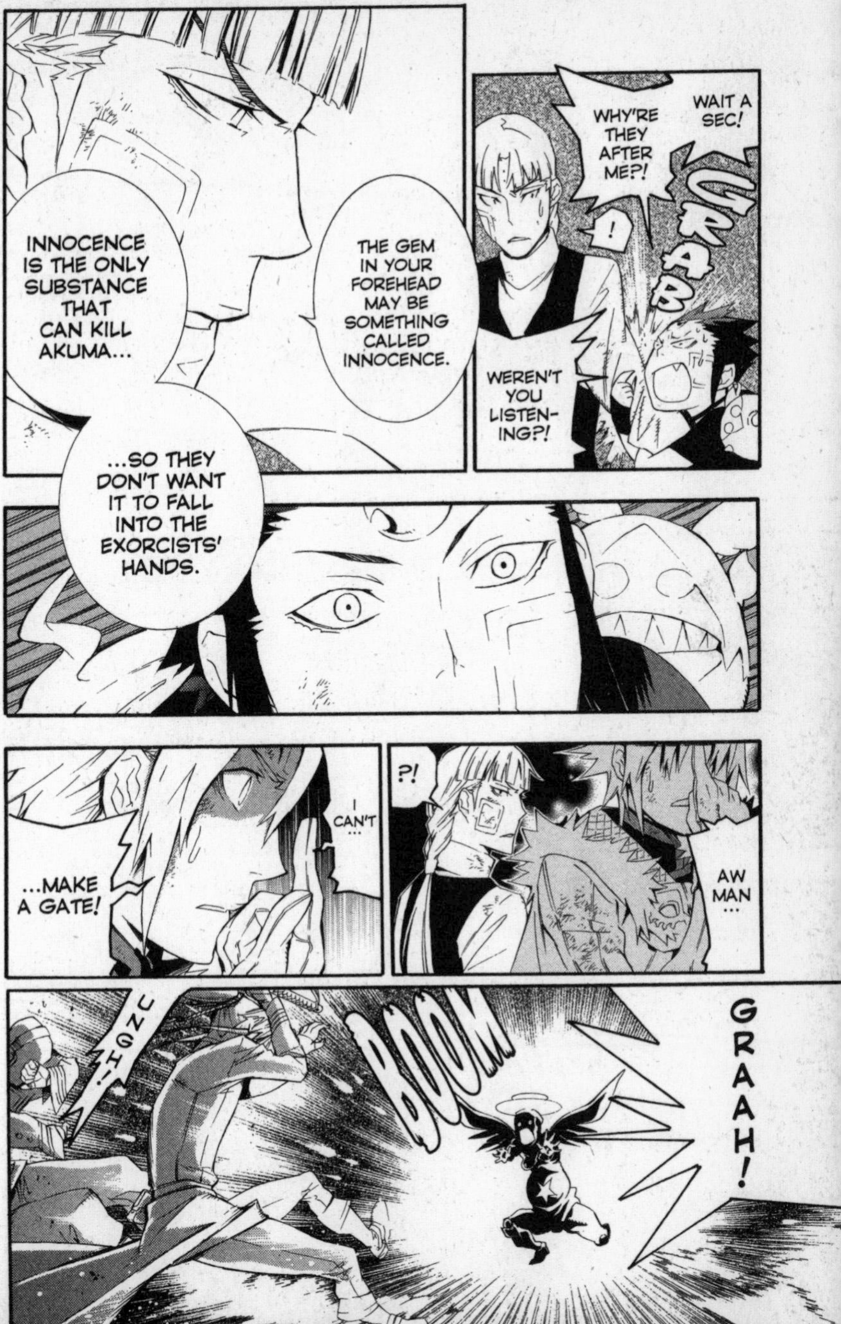
WAIT A SEC!
WHY'RE THEY AFTER ME?!
GRAB
!
WEREN'T YOU LISTENING?!
THE GEM IN YOUR FOREHEAD MAY BE SOMETHING CALLED INNOCENCE.
INNOCENCE IS THE ONLY SUBSTANCE THAT CAN KILL AKUMA...
...SO THEY DON'T WANT IT TO FALL INTO THE EXORCISTS' HANDS.
AW MAN...
?!
I CAN'T...
...MAKE A GATE!
GRAAH!
BOOM
UNGH!

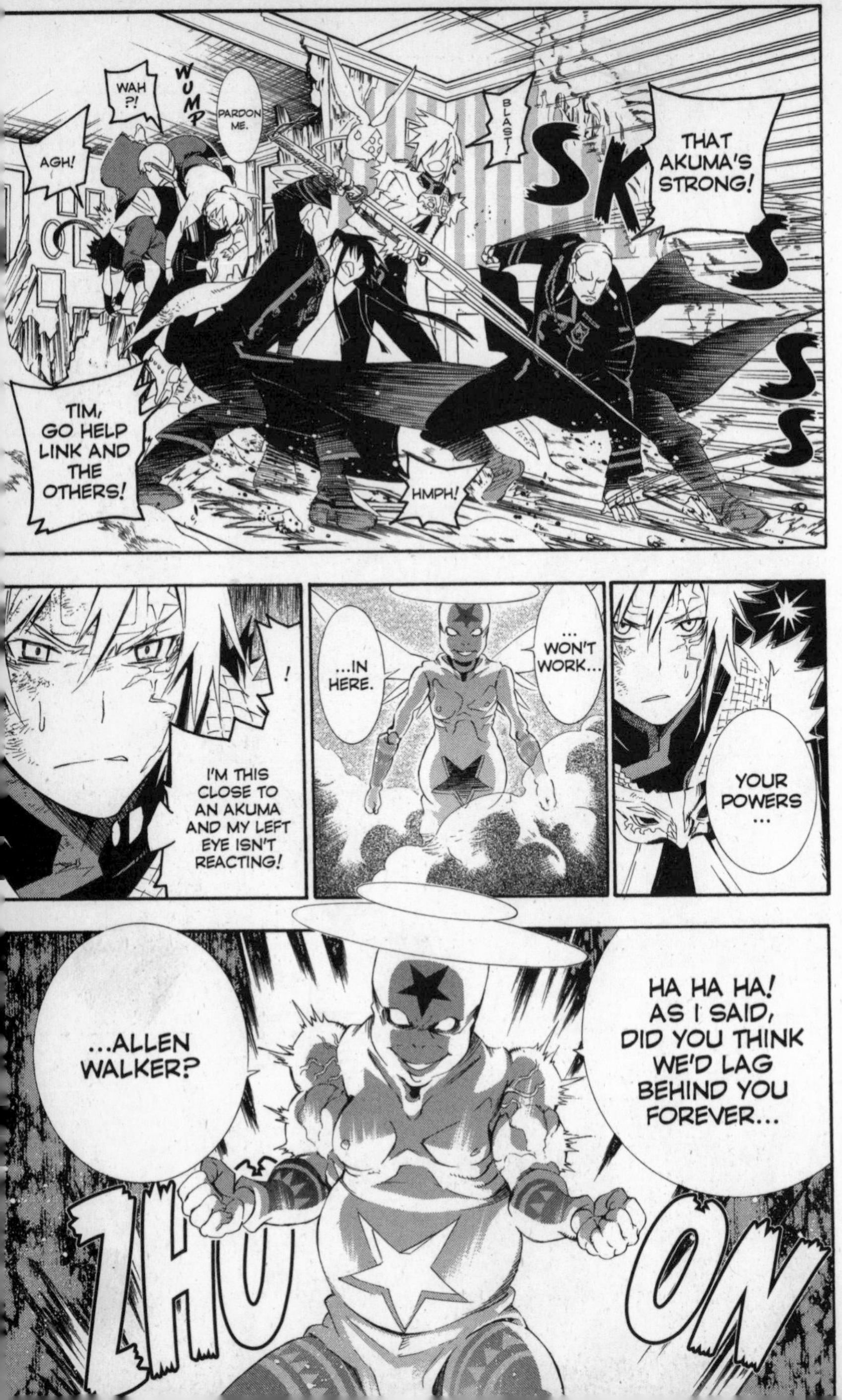
THAT AKUMA'S STRONG!
SKSSS
BLAST!
PARDON ME.
WUMP
WAH ?!
AGH!
TIM, GO HELP LINK AND THE OTHERS!
HMPH!
YOUR POWERS ...
... WON'T WORK...
...IN HERE.
!
I'M THIS CLOSE TO AN AKUMA AND MY LEFT EYE ISN'T REACTING!
HA HA HA! AS I SAID, DID YOU THINK WE'D LAG BEHIND YOU FOREVER...
...ALLEN WALKER?
ZHUON

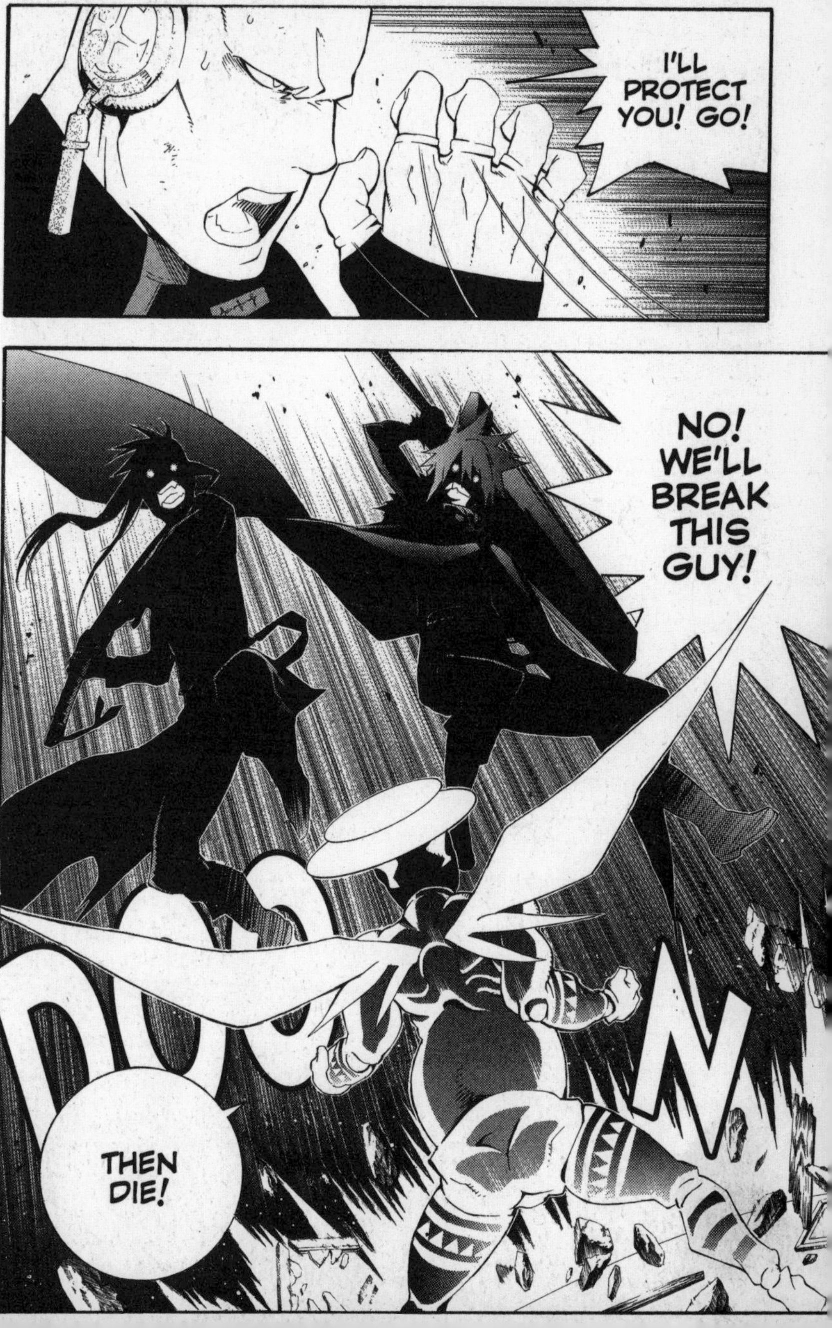
I'LL PROTECT YOU! GO!
NO! WE'LL BREAK THIS GUY!
THEN DIE!

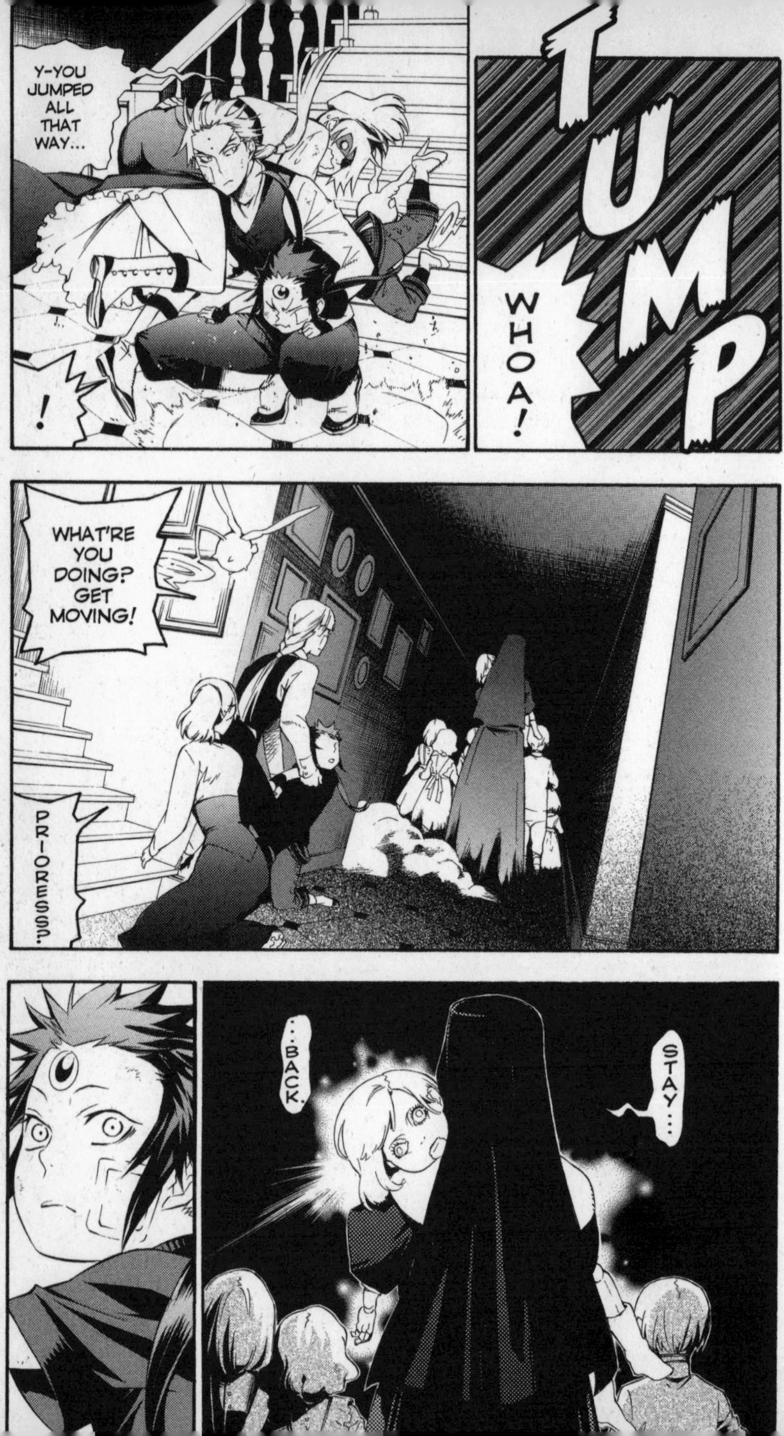
TUMP
WHOA!
Y-YOU JUMPED ALL THAT WAY...
!
WHAT'RE YOU DOING? GET MOVING!
PRIORESS?!
STAY...
...BACK.

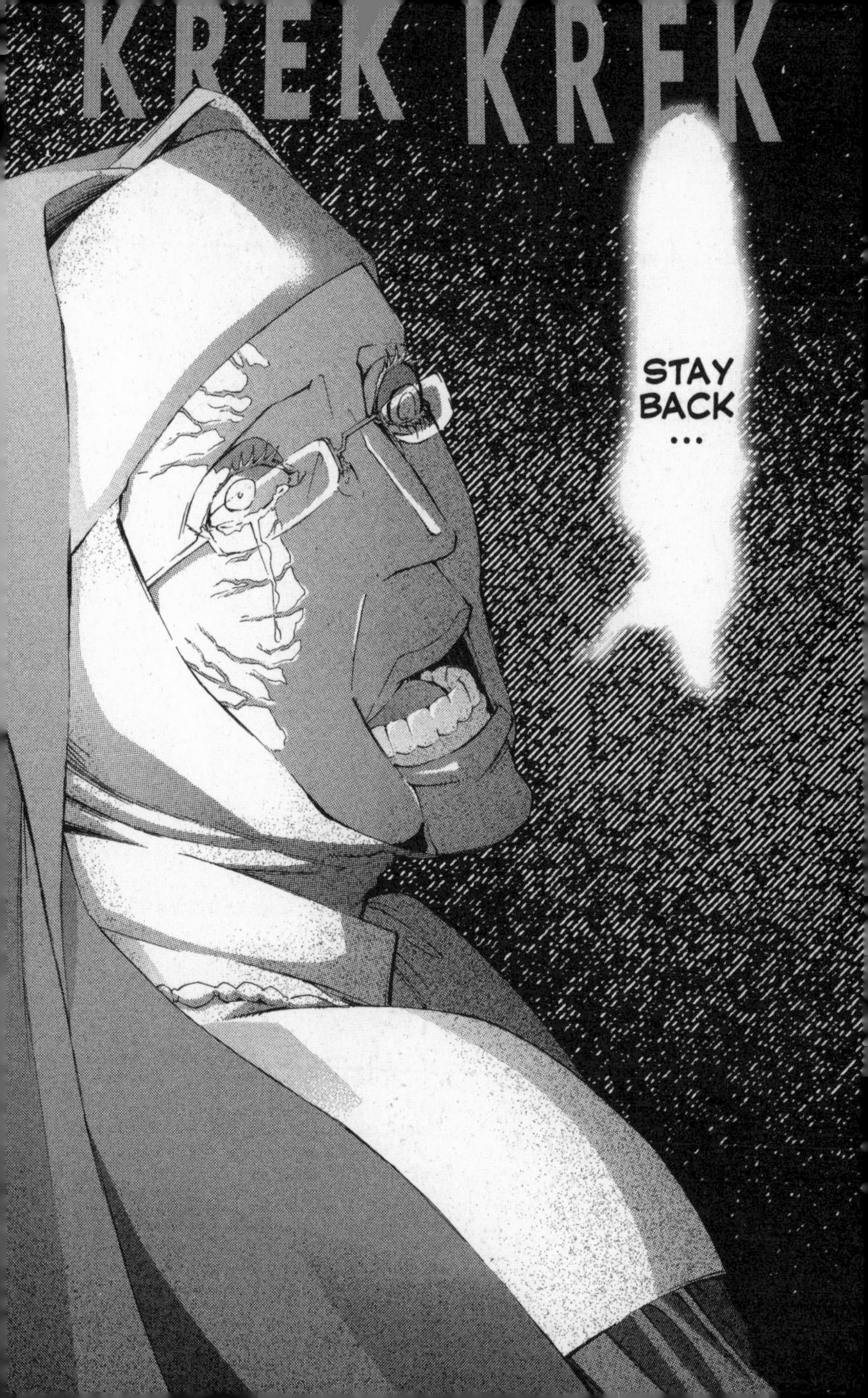
KREK KREK
STAY BACK ...

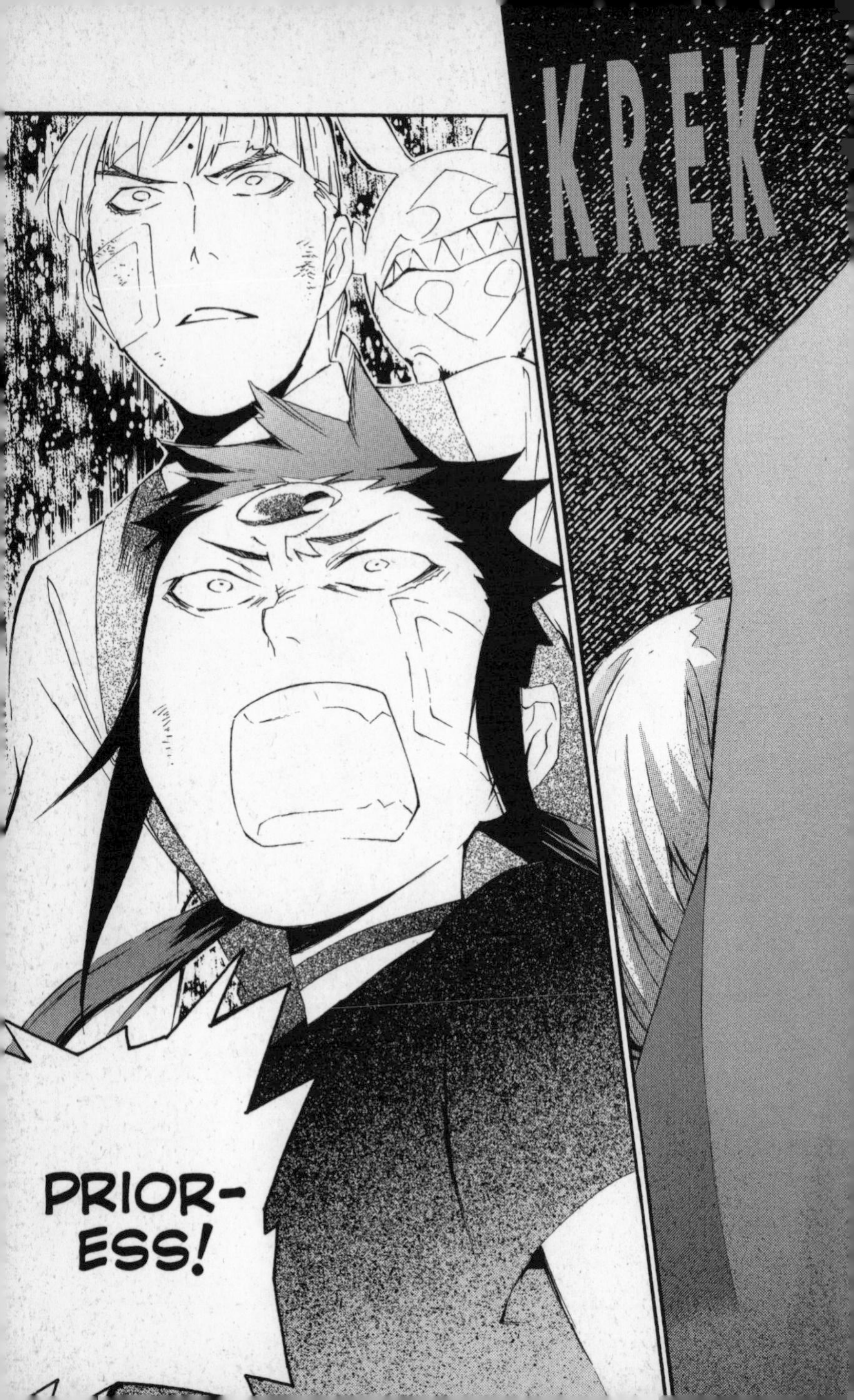
KREK
PRIOR-ESS!

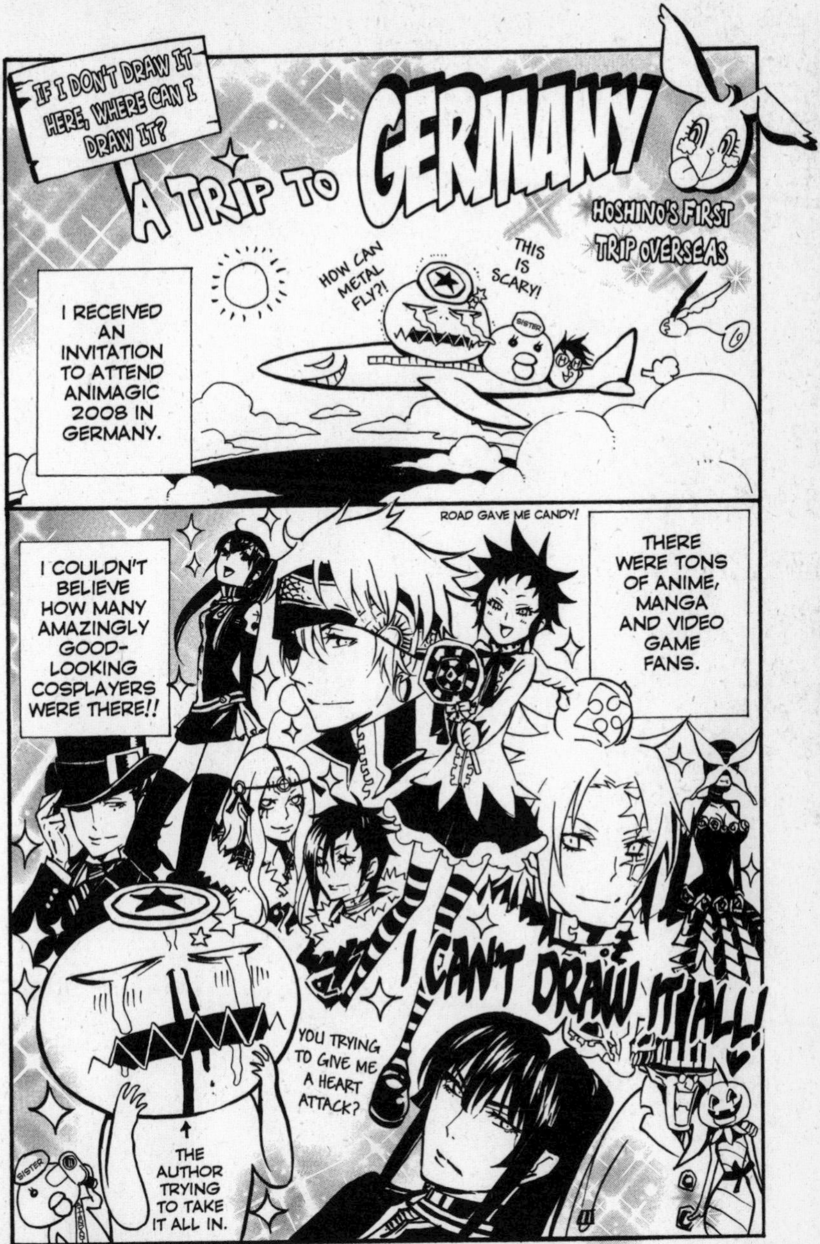
IF I DON'T DRAW IT HERE, WHERE CAN I DRAW IT?
A TRIP TO GERMANY
HOSHINO'S FIRST TRIP OVERSEAS
THIS IS SCARY!
HOW CAN METAL FLY?!
I RECEIVED AN INVITATION TO ATTEND ANIMAGIC 2008 IN GERMANY.
THERE WERE TONS OF ANIME, MANGA AND VIDEO GAME FANS.
ROAD GAVE ME CANDY!
I COULDN'T BELIEVE HOW MANY AMAZINGLY GOOD-LOOKING COSPLAYERS WERE THERE!!
I CAN'T DRAW IT ALL!
YOU TRYING TO GIVE ME A HEART ATTACK?
THE AUTHOR TRYING TO TAKE IT ALL IN.

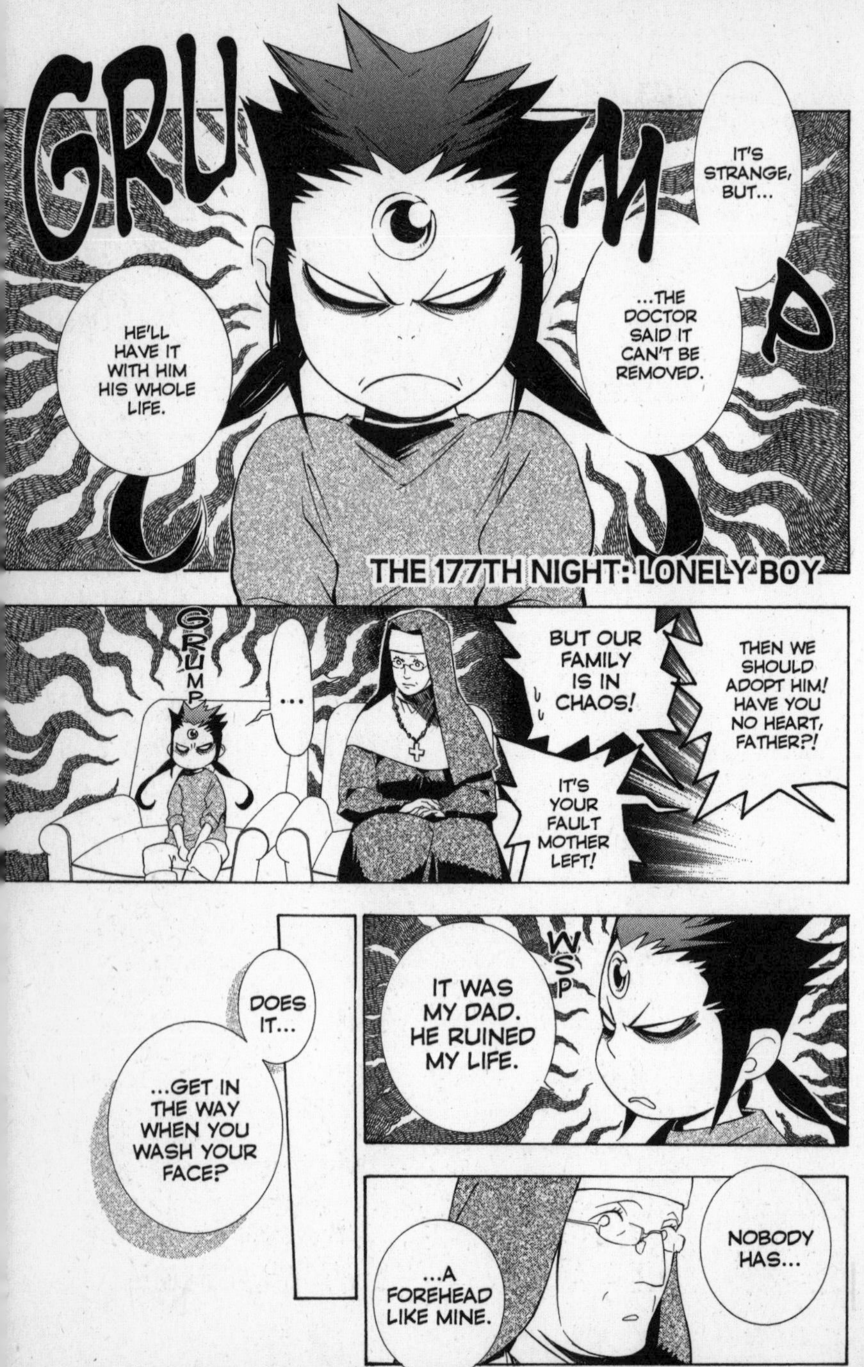
GRUMP
IT'S STRANGE, BUT...
...THE DOCTOR SAID IT CAN'T BE REMOVED.
HE'LL HAVE IT WITH HIM HIS WHOLE LIFE.
THE 177TH NIGHT: LONELY BOY
THEN WE SHOULD ADOPT HIM! HAVE YOU NO HEART, FATHER?!
BUT OUR FAMILY IS IN CHAOS!
IT'S YOUR FAULT MOTHER LEFT!
...
GRUMP
WSP
IT WAS MY DAD. HE RUINED MY LIFE.
NOBODY HAS...
...A FOREHEAD LIKE MINE.
DOES IT...
...GET IN THE WAY WHEN YOU WASH YOUR FACE?

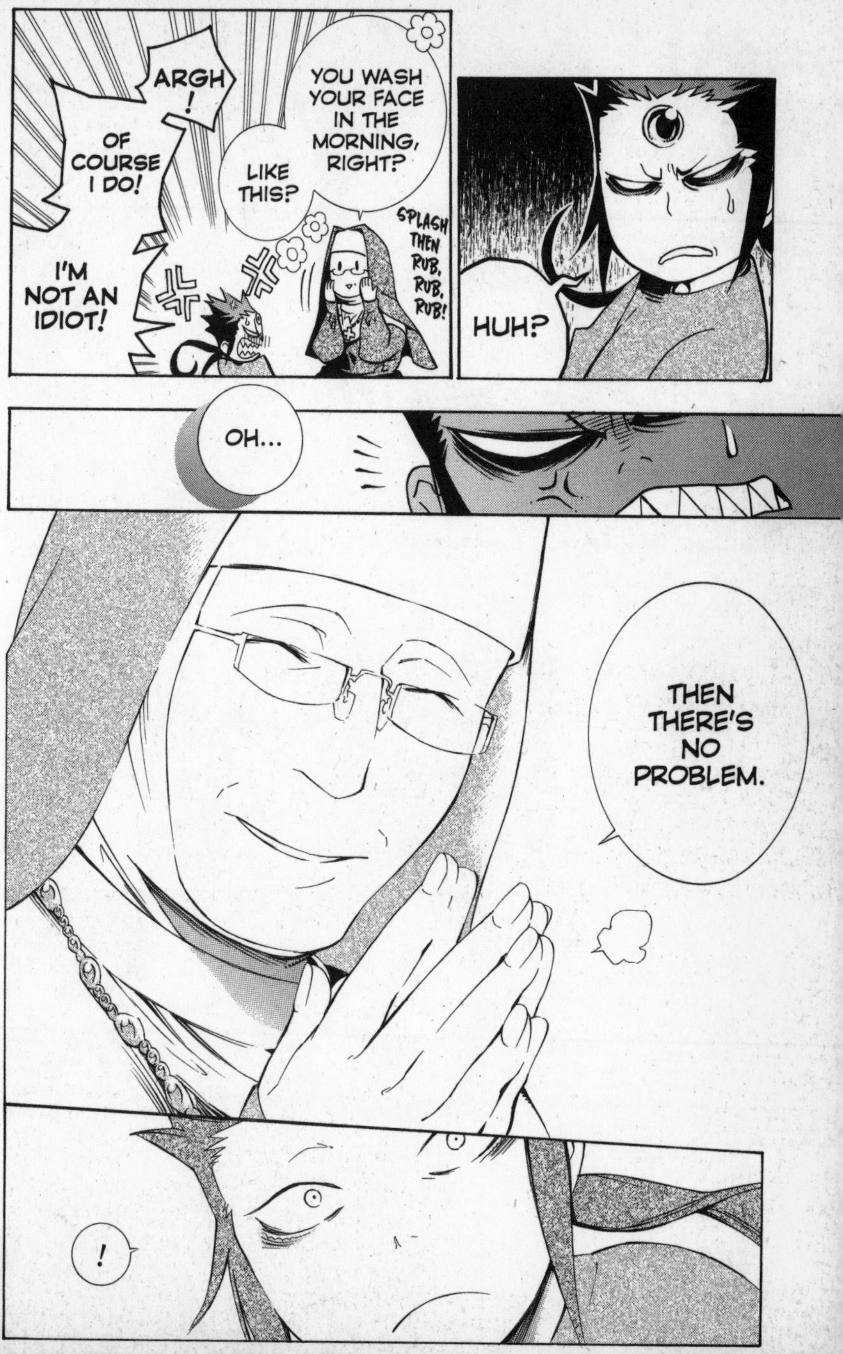
HUH?
YOU WASH YOUR FACE IN THE MORNING, RIGHT?
LIKE THIS?
SPLASH THEN RUB, RUB, RUB!
ARGH!
OF COURSE I DO!
I'M NOT AN IDIOT!
OH...
THEN THERE'S NO PROBLEM.
!

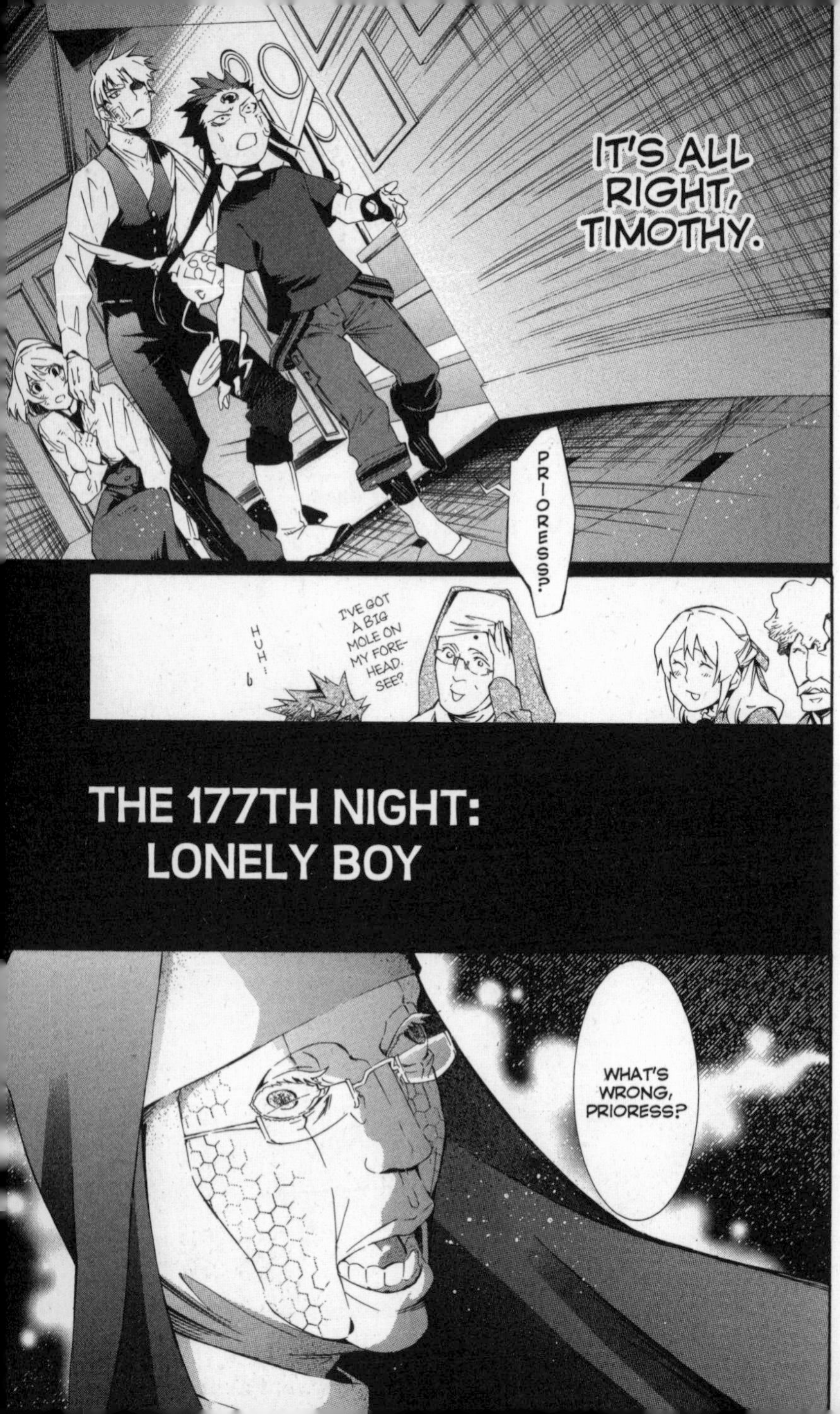
IT'S ALL RIGHT, TIMOTHY.
PRIORESS?
I'VE GOT A BIG MOLE ON MY FORE-HEAD. SEE?
HUH...
THE 177TH NIGHT: LONELY BOY
WHAT'S WRONG, PRIORESS?

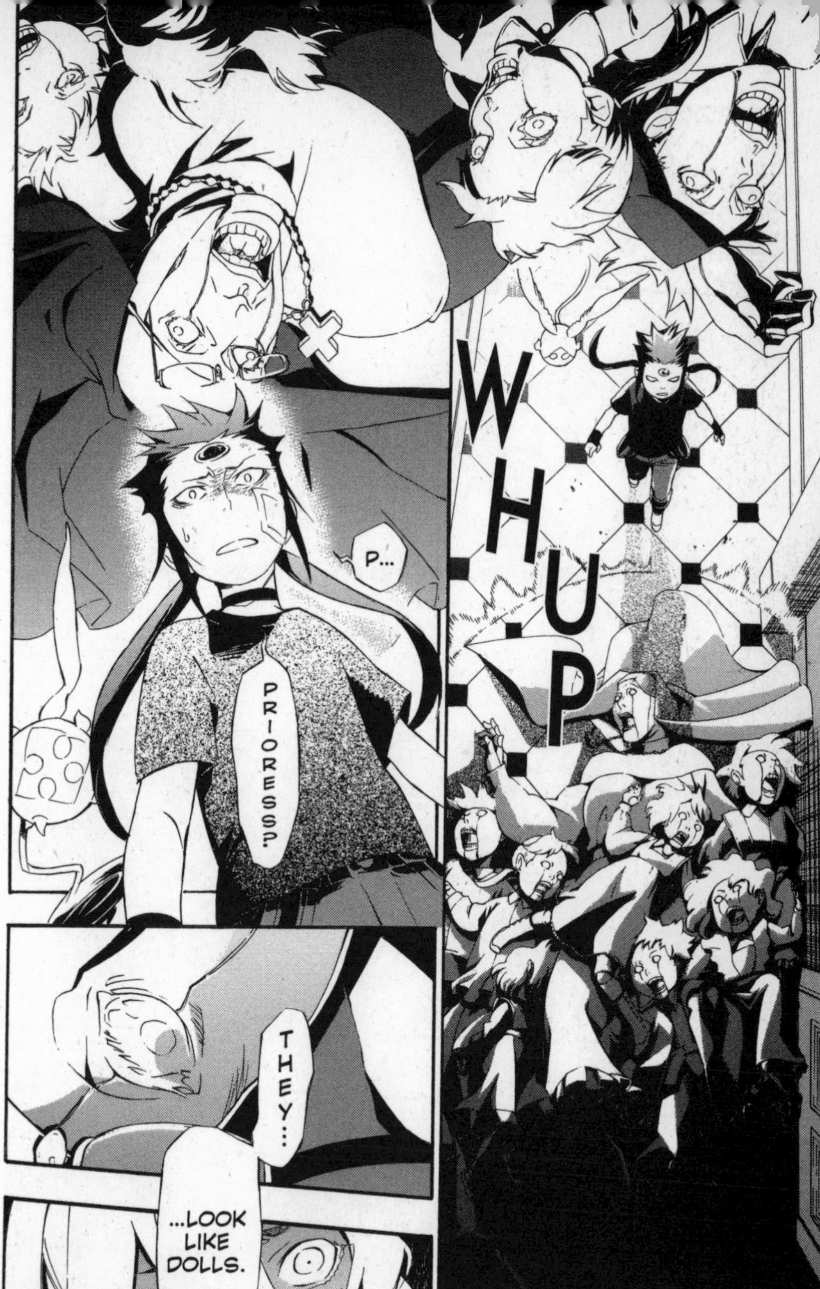
WHUP
P...
PRIORESS?
THEY...
...LOOK LIKE DOLLS.

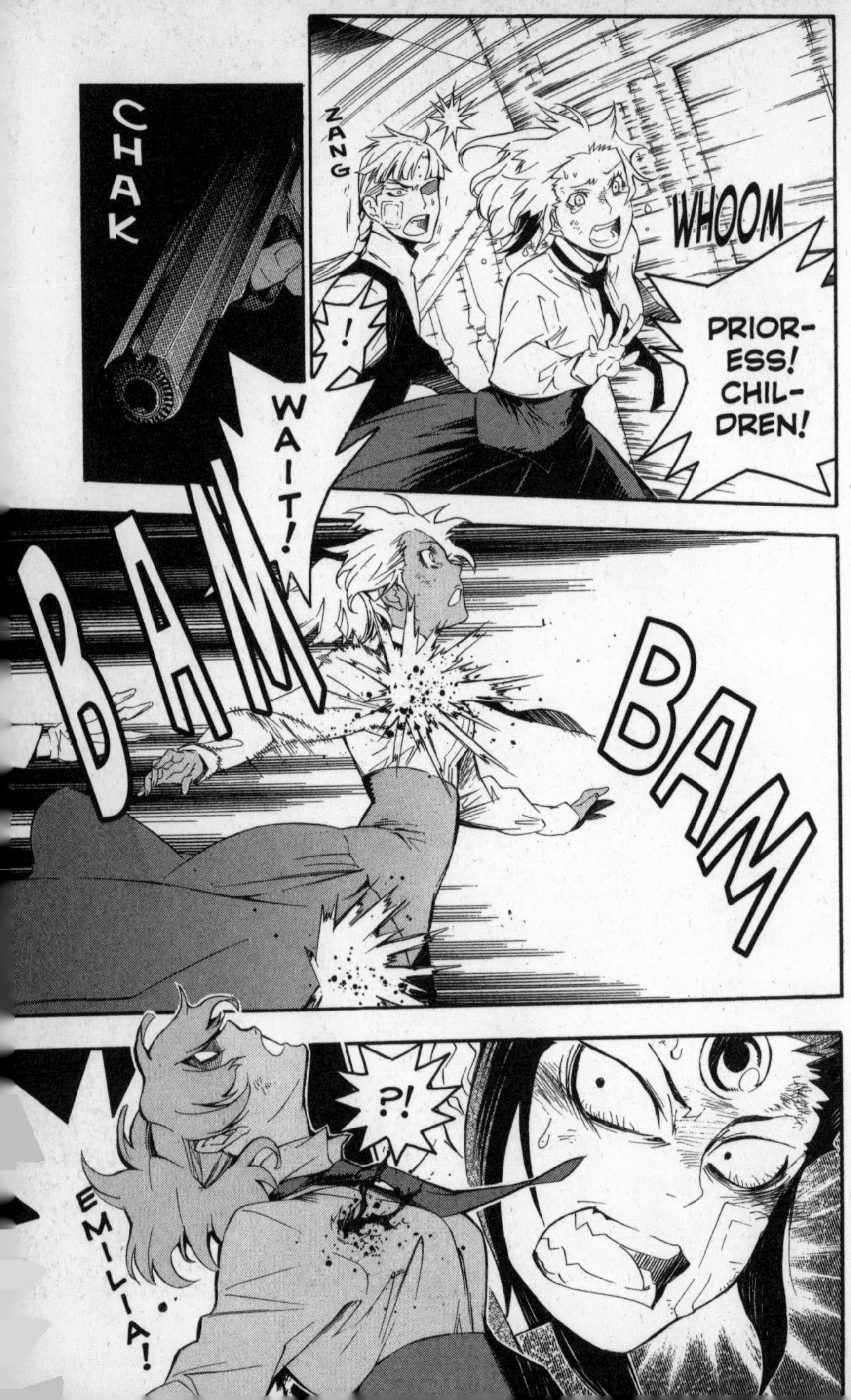
ZANG
WHOOM
PRIOR-ESS! CHIL-DREN!
!
CHAK
WAIT!
BAM
BAM
?!
EMILIA!

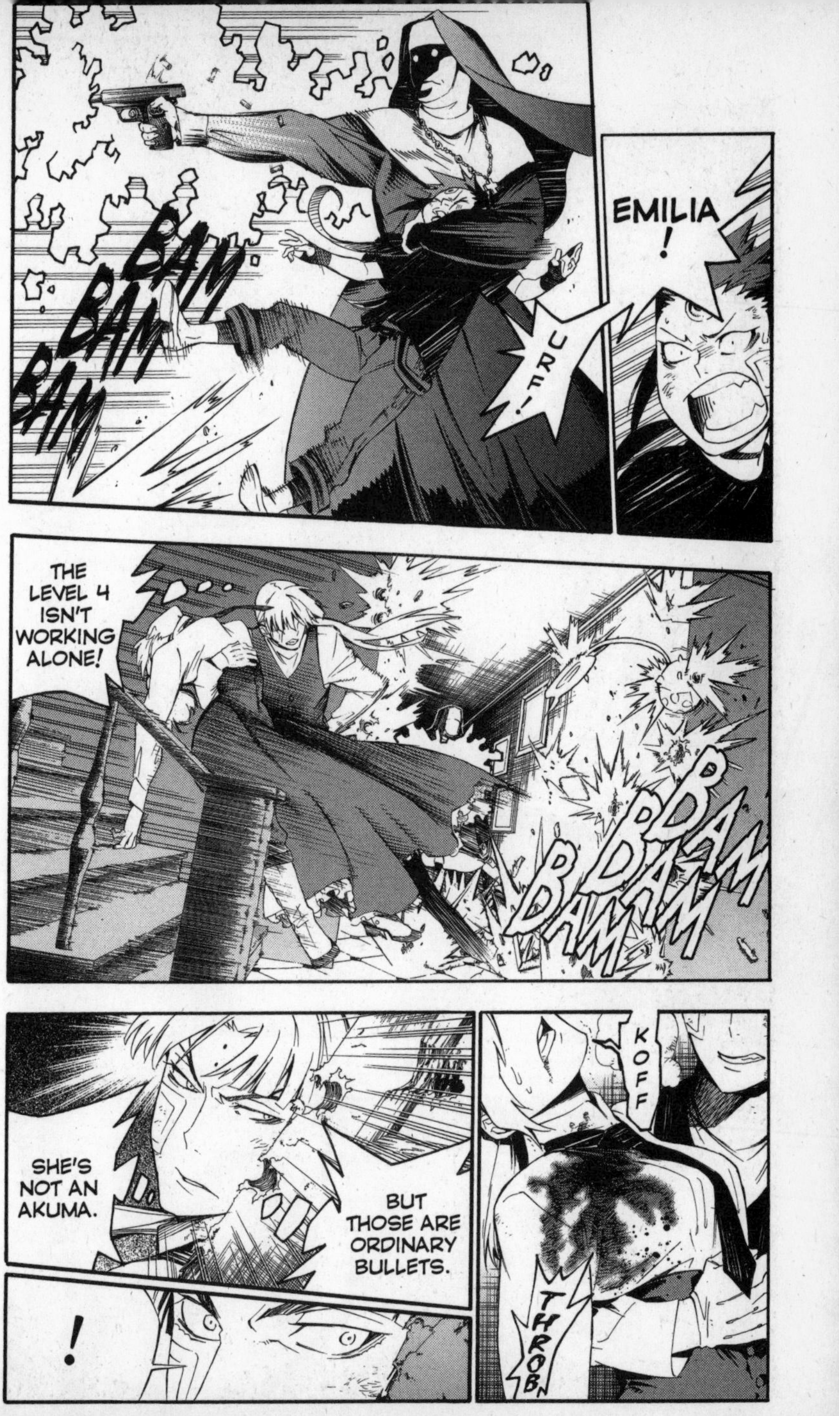
EMILIA !
URF!
BAM BAM BAM
THE LEVEL 4 ISN'T WORKING ALONE!
BAM DAM DAM
KOFF
THROB
SHE'S NOT AN AKUMA.
BUT THOSE ARE ORDINARY BULLETS.
!

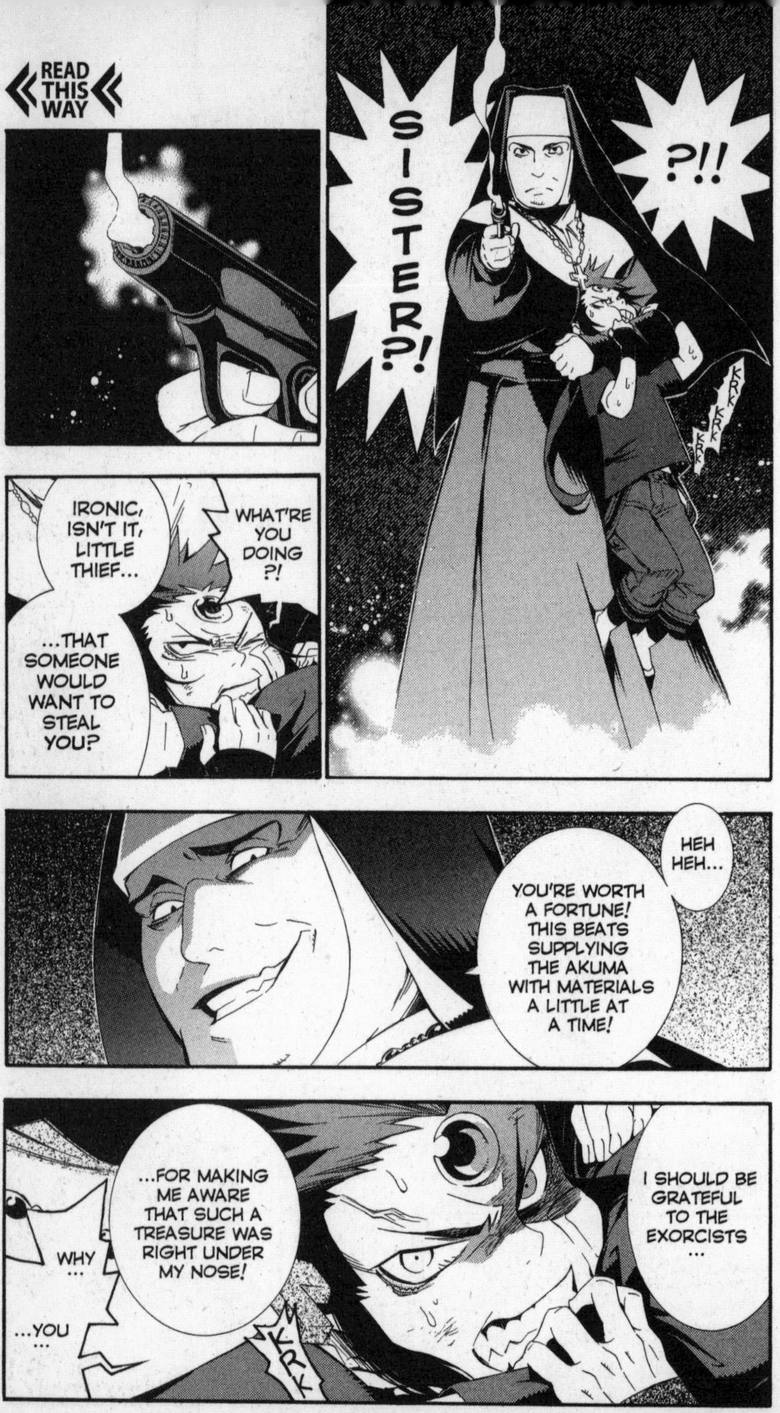
READ THIS WAY
?!!
SISTER?!
KRK KRK KRK
WHAT'RE YOU DOING?!
IRONIC, ISN'T IT, LITTLE THIEF...
...THAT SOMEONE WOULD WANT TO STEAL YOU?
HEH HEH...
YOU'RE WORTH A FORTUNE! THIS BEATS SUPPLYING THE AKUMA WITH MATERIALS A LITTLE AT A TIME!
I SHOULD BE GRATEFUL TO THE EXORCISTS...
...FOR MAKING ME AWARE THAT SUCH A TREASURE WAS RIGHT UNDER MY NOSE!
KRK
WHY...
...YOU...

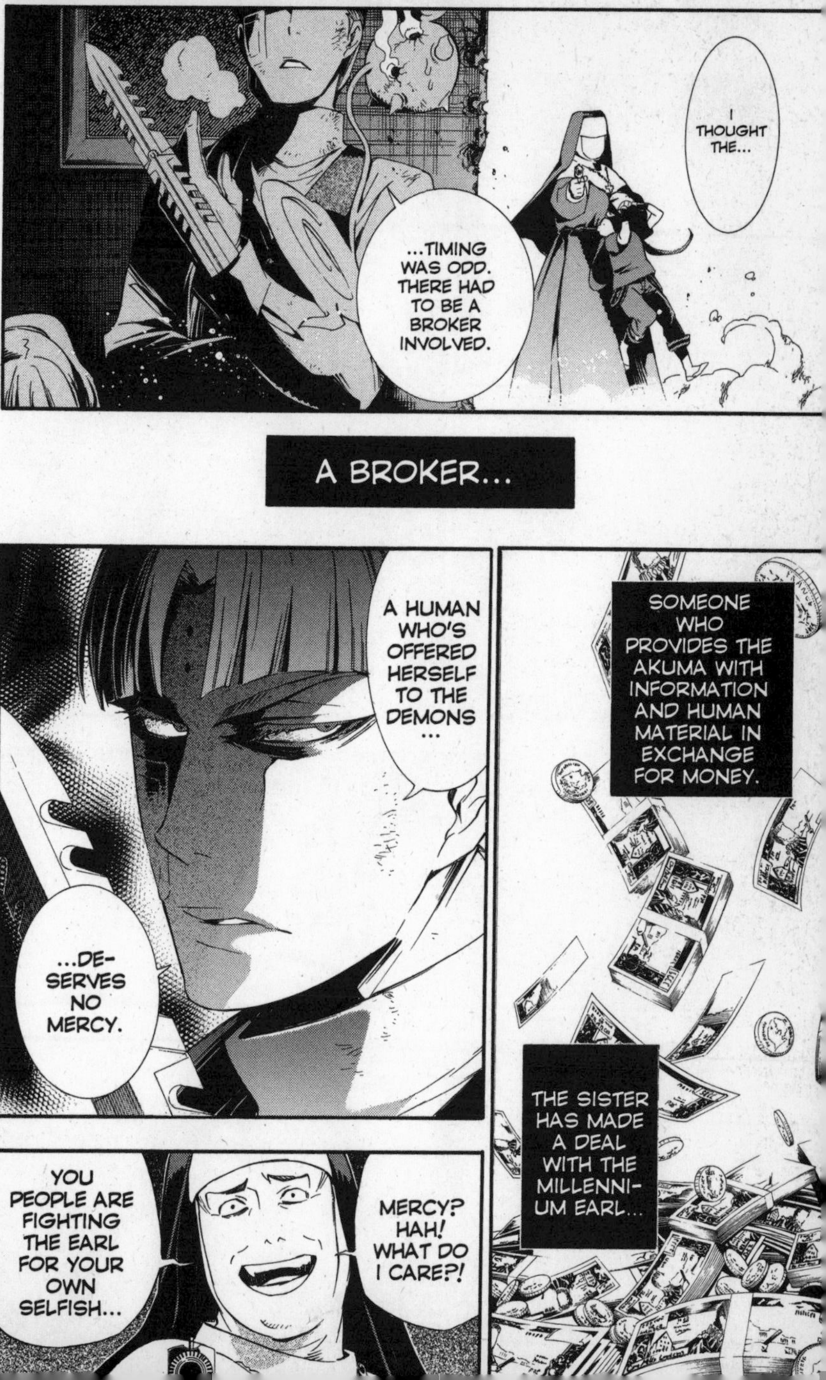
I THOUGHT THE...
...TIMING WAS ODD. THERE HAD TO BE A BROKER INVOLVED.
A BROKER...
SOMEONE WHO PROVIDES THE AKUMA WITH INFORMATION AND HUMAN MATERIAL IN EXCHANGE FOR MONEY.
THE SISTER HAS MADE A DEAL WITH THE MILLENNI-UM EARL...
A HUMAN WHO'S OFFERED HERSELF TO THE DEMONS...
...DE-SERVES NO MERCY.
MERCY? HAH! WHAT DO I CARE?!
YOU PEOPLE ARE FIGHTING THE EARL FOR YOUR OWN SELFISH...

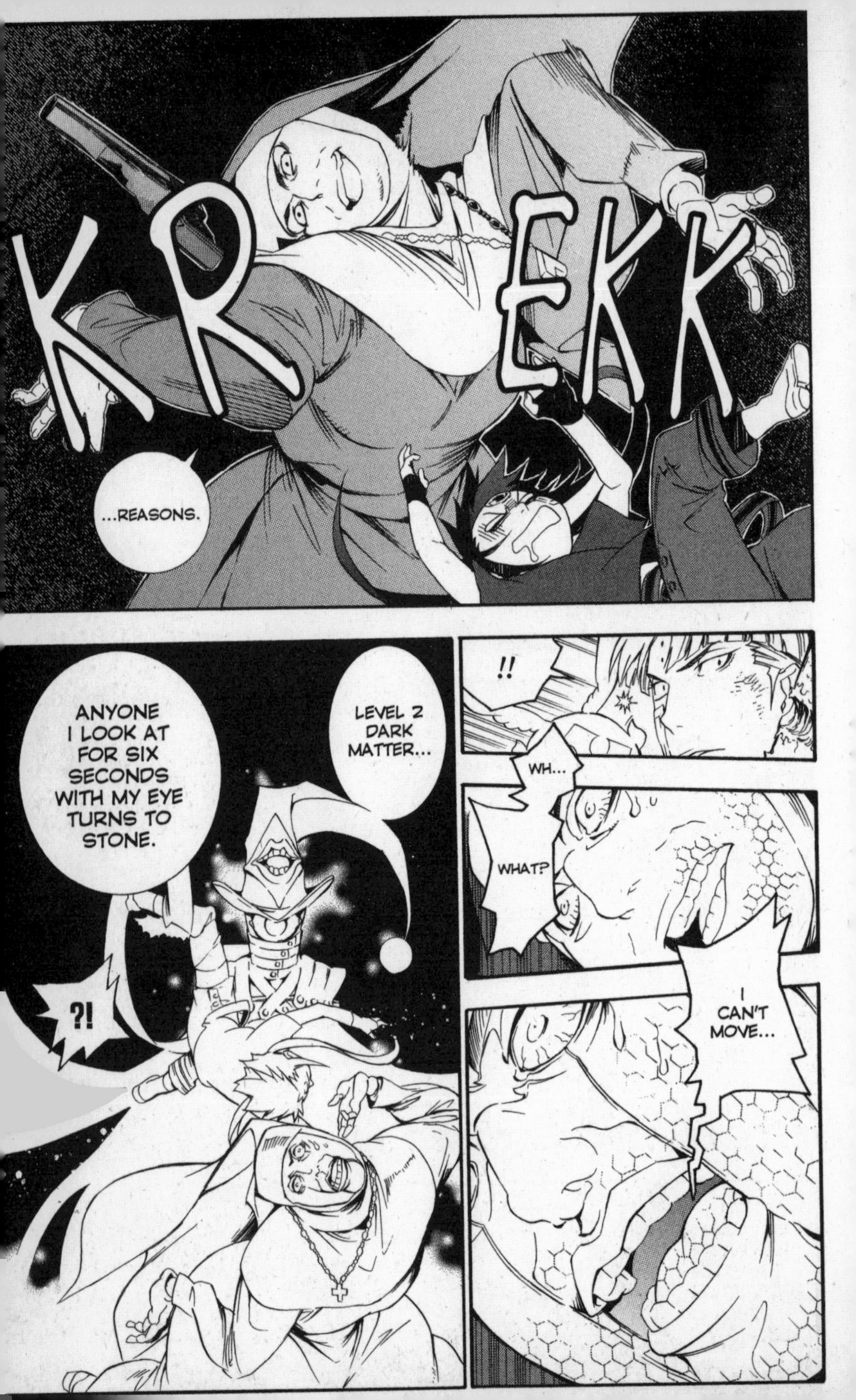
KREKK
...REASONS.
!!
WH...
WHAT?
I CAN'T MOVE...
LEVEL 2 DARK MATTER...
ANYONE I LOOK AT FOR SIX SECONDS WITH MY EYE TURNS TO STONE.
?!

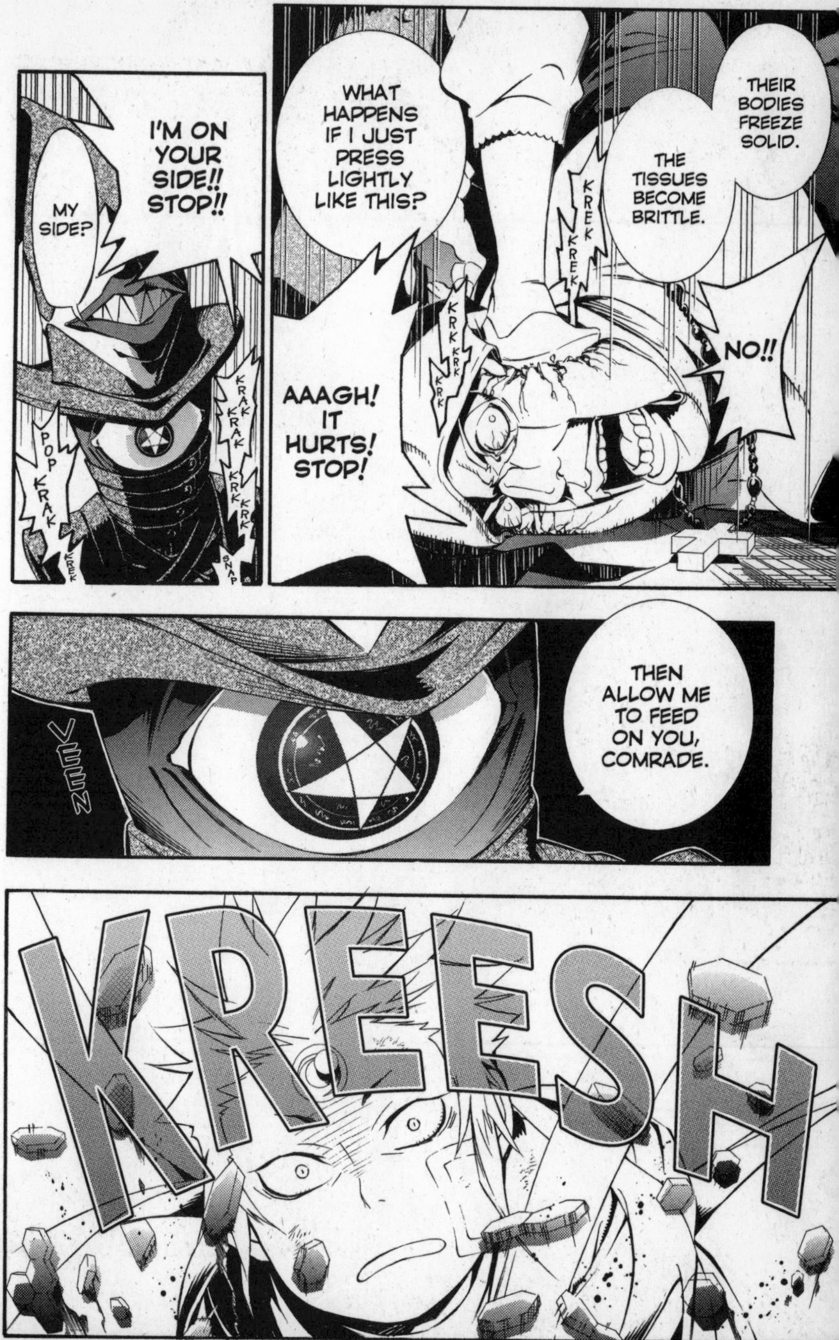
THEIR BODIES FREEZE SOLID.
THE TISSUES BECOME BRITTLE.
WHAT HAPPENS IF I JUST PRESS LIGHTLY LIKE THIS?
KREK KREK
NO!!
KRK KRK KRK
AAAGH! IT HURTS! STOP!
I'M ON YOUR SIDE!! STOP!!
MY SIDE?
KRAK KRAK
KRK KRK
SNAP
POP KRAK KRAK
KREK
THEN ALLOW ME TO FEED ON YOU, COMRADE.
VEEN
KREESH

READ THIS WAY

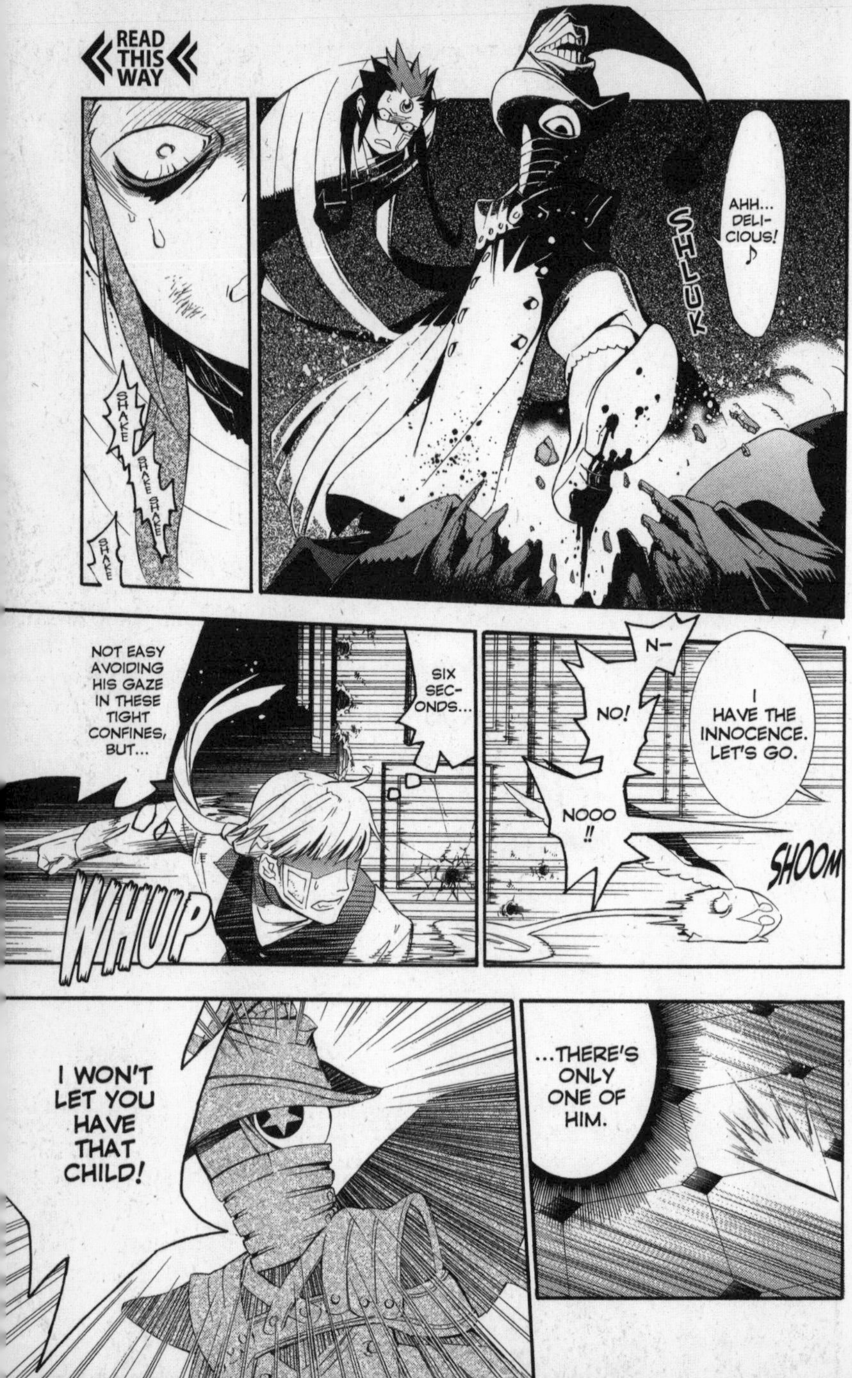
SHLUK
AHH... DELICIOUS! ♪
SHAKE
SHAKE SHAKE
SHAKE
I HAVE THE INNOCENCE. LET'S GO.
N-
NO!
NOOO!!
SHOOM
SIX SECONDS...
NOT EASY AVOIDING HIS GAZE IN THESE TIGHT CONFINES, BUT...
WHUIP
...THERE'S ONLY ONE OF HIM.
I WON'T LET YOU HAVE THAT CHILD!

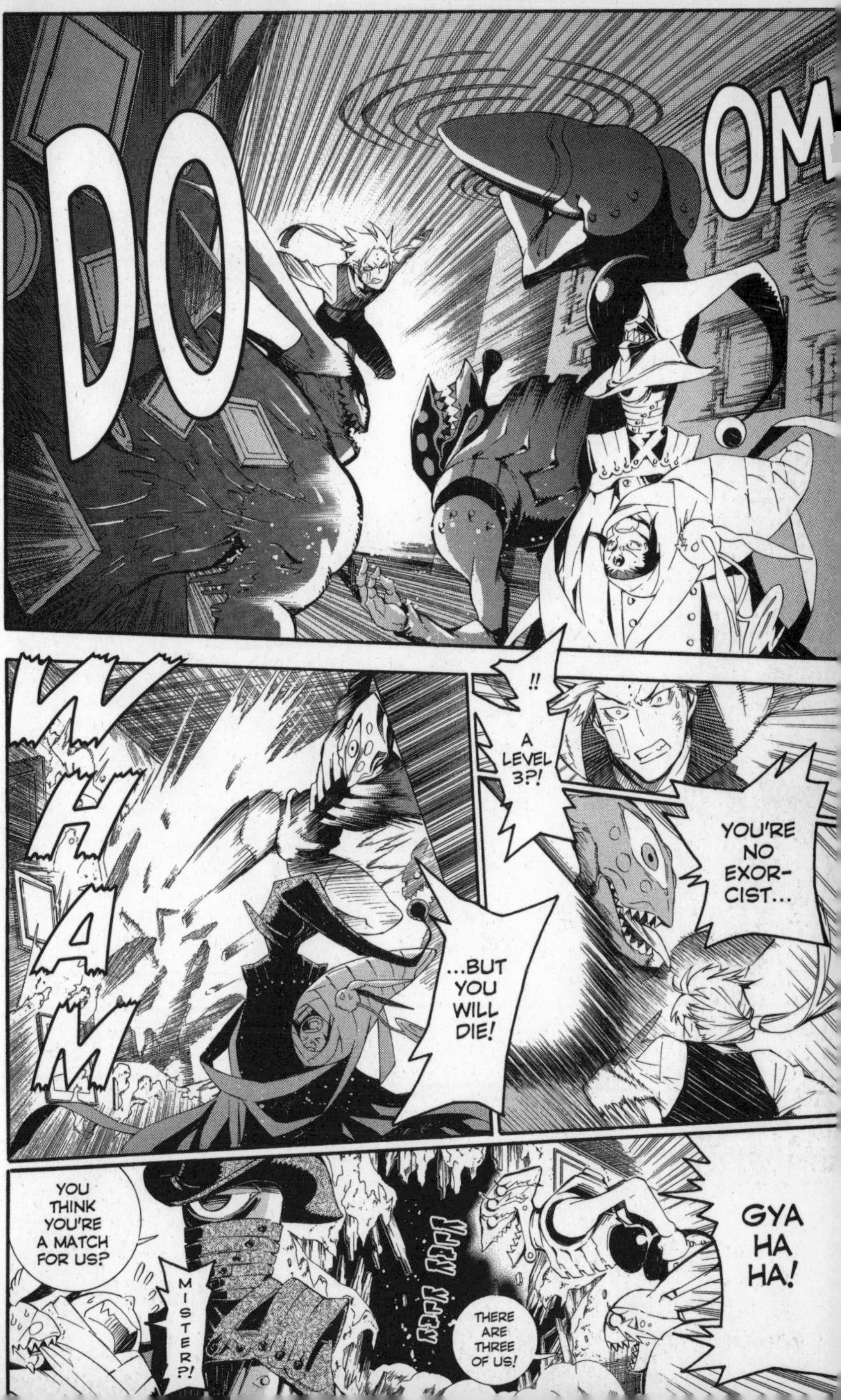
DOOM
!!
A LEVEL 3?!
YOU'RE NO EXORCIST...
...BUT YOU WILL DIE!
WHAM
GYA HA HA!
THERE ARE THREE OF US!
YOU THINK YOU'RE A MATCH FOR US?
MISTER?!

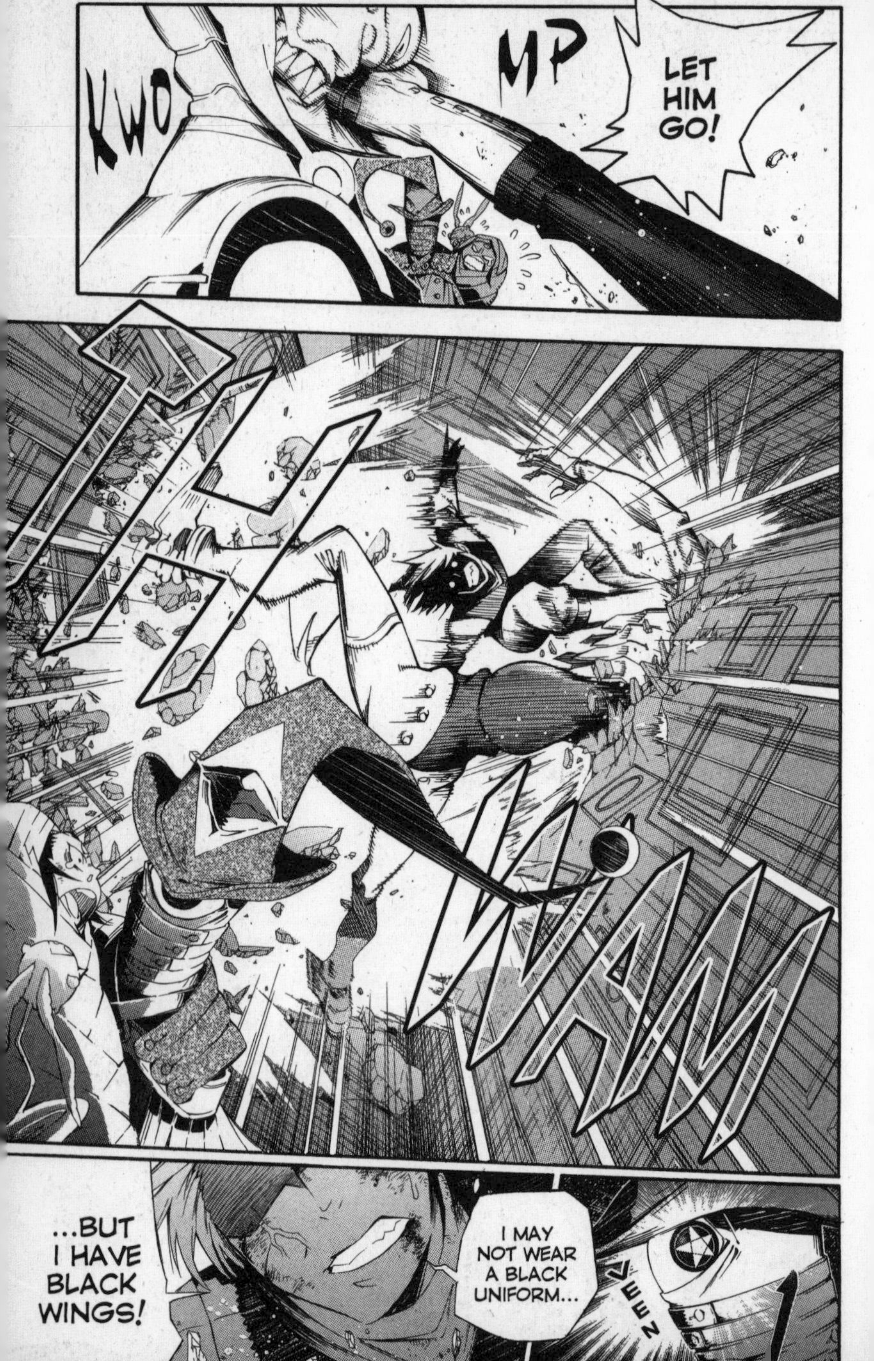
LET HIM GO!
KWOMP
THWAM
VEEN
I MAY NOT WEAR A BLACK UNIFORM...
...BUT I HAVE BLACK WINGS!

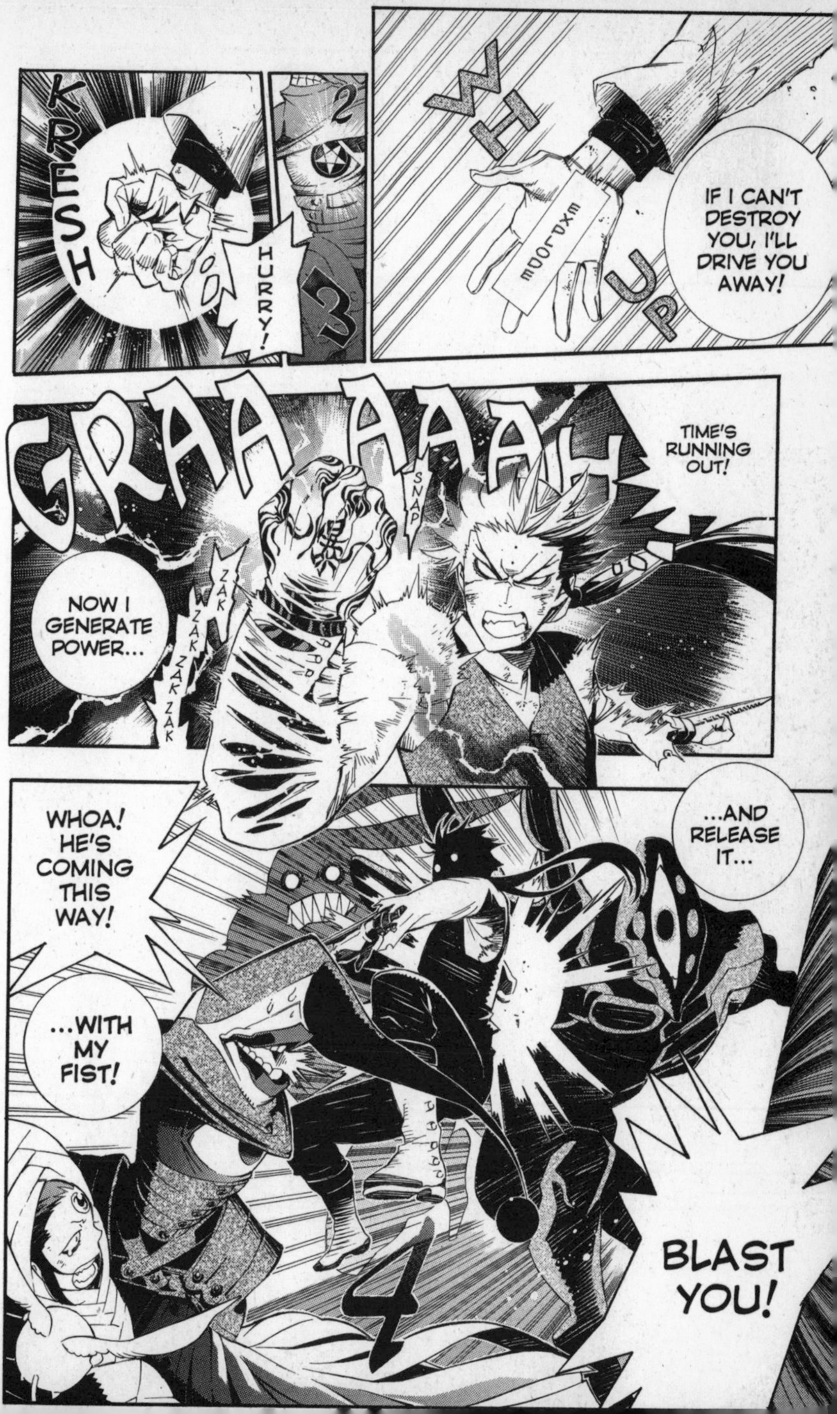
IF I CAN'T DESTROY YOU, I'LL DRIVE YOU AWAY!
WHUP
2
3
HURRY!
KRESH
TIME'S RUNNING OUT!
GRAAAAAH
SNAP
NOW I GENERATE POWER...
ZAK ZAK ZAK ZAK ZAK
...AND RELEASE IT...
WHOA! HE'S COMING THIS WAY!
...WITH MY FIST!
BLAST YOU!
4

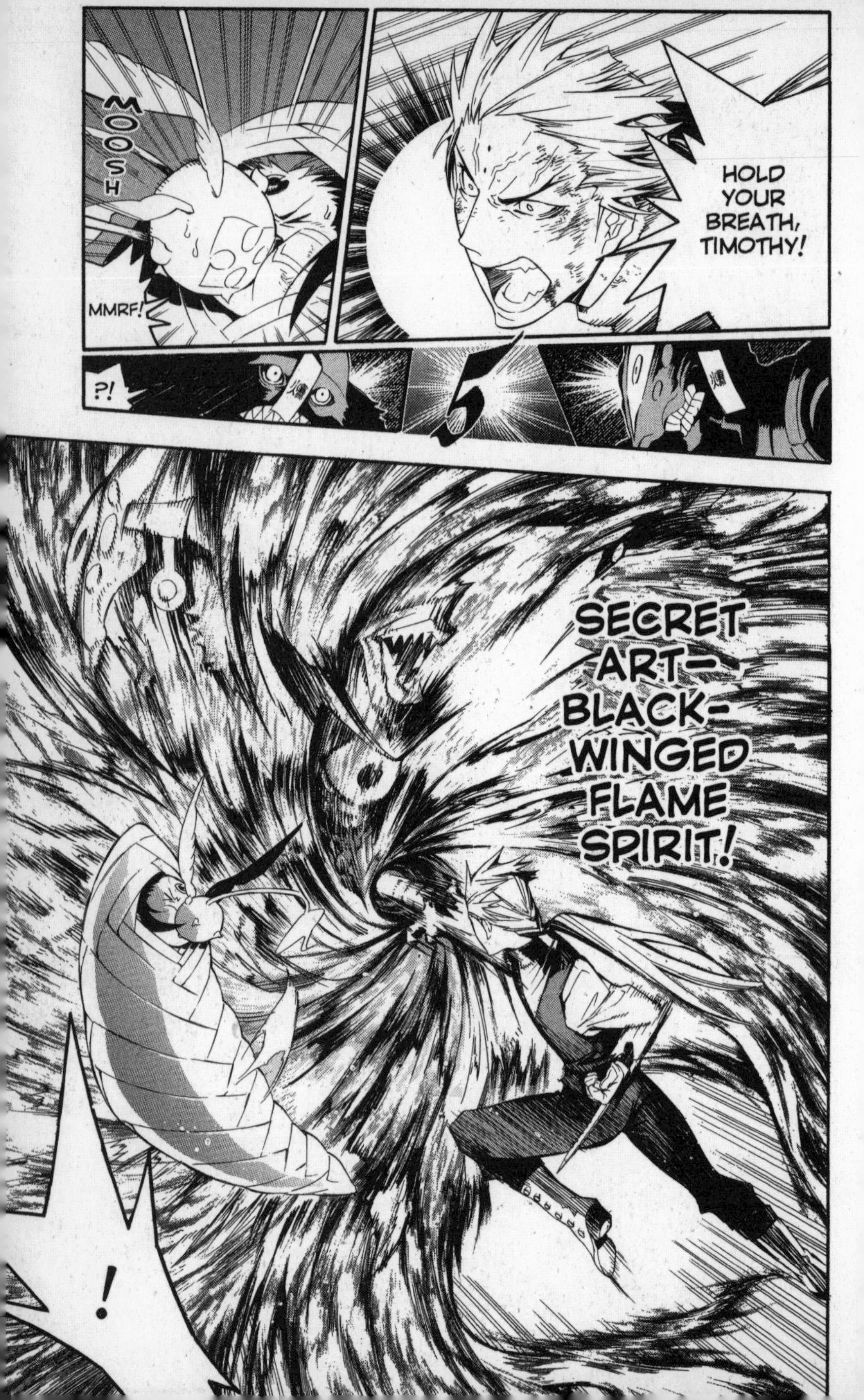
HOLD YOUR BREATH, TIMOTHY!
MOOSH
MMRF!
?!
SECRET ART— BLACK-WINGED FLAME SPIRIT!
!

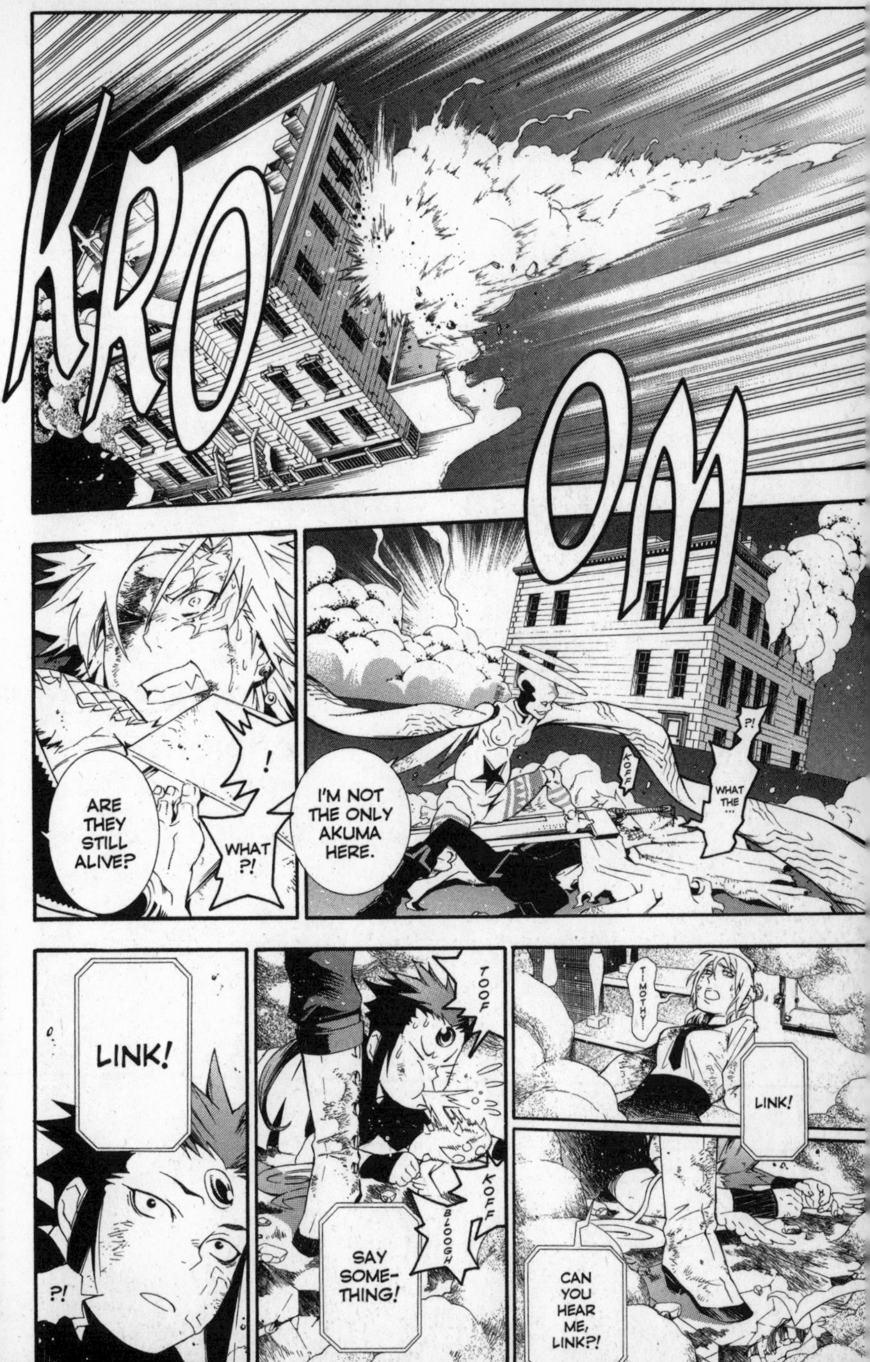
KROOM
?!
WHAT THE...
KOFF
I'M NOT THE ONLY AKUMA HERE.
!
WHAT ?!
ARE THEY STILL ALIVE?
TIMOTHY...
LINK!
CAN YOU HEAR ME, LINK?!
TOOF
KOFF
BLOOGH
SAY SOME-THING!
LINK!
?!

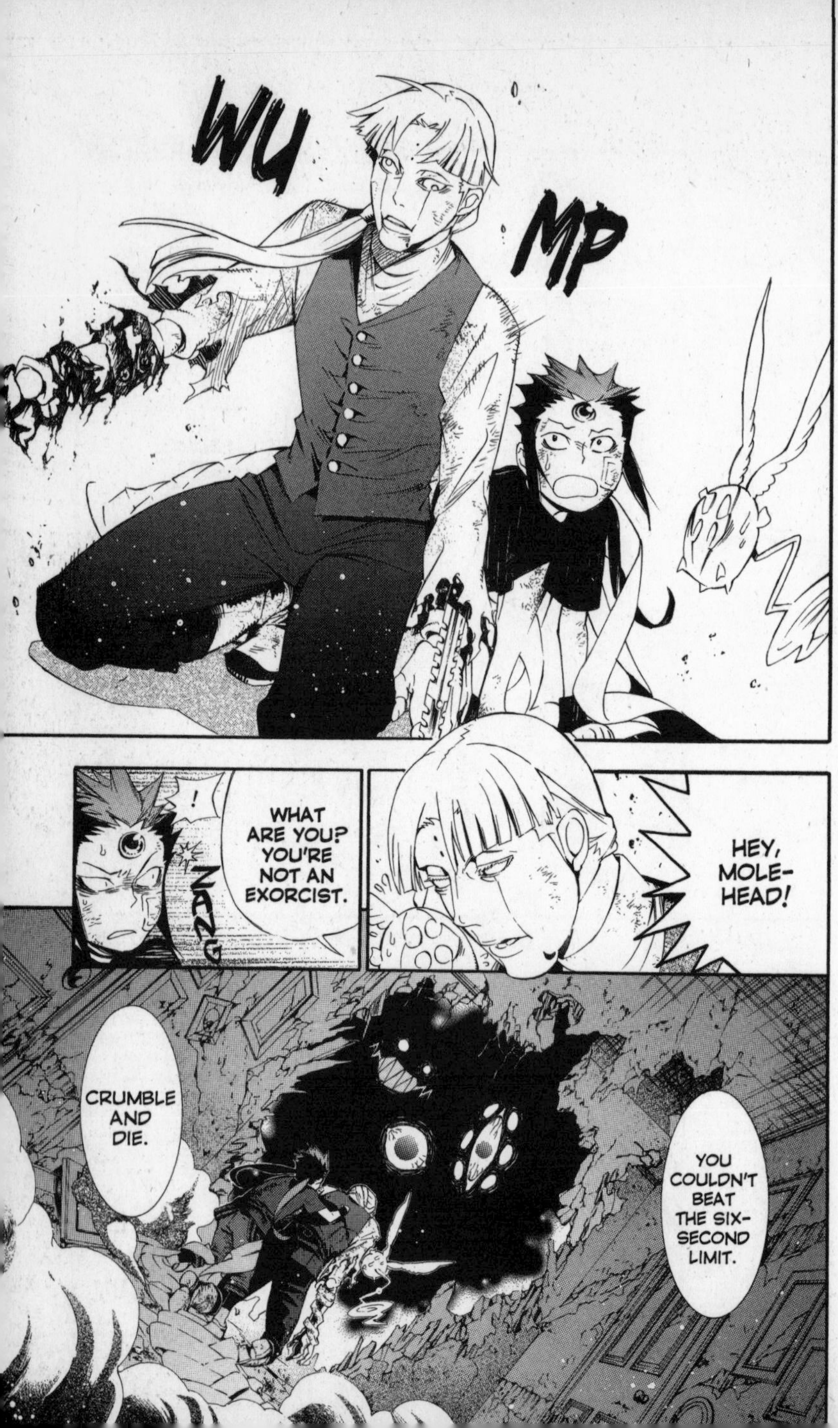
WUMP
HEY, MOLE-HEAD!
WHAT ARE YOU? YOU'RE NOT AN EXORCIST.
!
ZANG
YOU COULDN'T BEAT THE SIX-SECOND LIMIT.
CRUMBLE AND DIE.

MEMORIES OF GERMANY

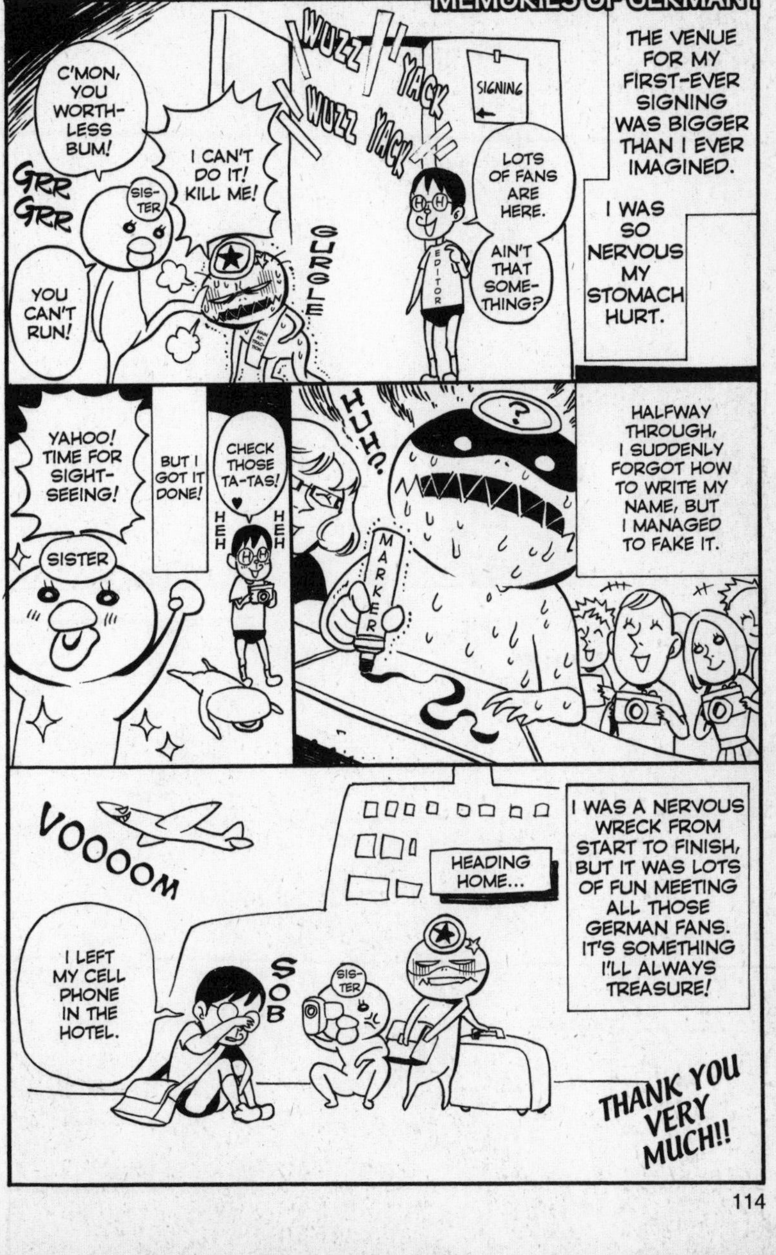
THE VENUE FOR MY FIRST-EVER SIGNING WAS BIGGER THAN I EVER IMAGINED.
I WAS SO NERVOUS MY STOMACH HURT.
SIGNING
LOTS OF FANS ARE HERE.
AIN'T THAT SOMETHING?
EDITOR
WUZZ YACK WUZZ YACK
GURGLE
I CAN'T DO IT! KILL ME!
C'MON, YOU WORTHLESS BUM!
GRR GRR
SISTER
YOU CAN'T RUN!
HALFWAY THROUGH, I SUDDENLY FORGOT HOW TO WRITE MY NAME, BUT I MANAGED TO FAKE IT.
?
HUH?
MARKER
CHECK THOSE TA-TAS!
HEH HEH
BUT I GOT IT DONE!
YAHOO! TIME FOR SIGHT-SEEING!
SISTER
I WAS A NERVOUS WRECK FROM START TO FINISH, BUT IT WAS LOTS OF FUN MEETING ALL THOSE GERMAN FANS. IT'S SOMETHING I'LL ALWAYS TREASURE!
HEADING HOME...
VOOOOM
SOB
SISTER
I LEFT MY CELL PHONE IN THE HOTEL.
THANK YOU VERY MUCH!!

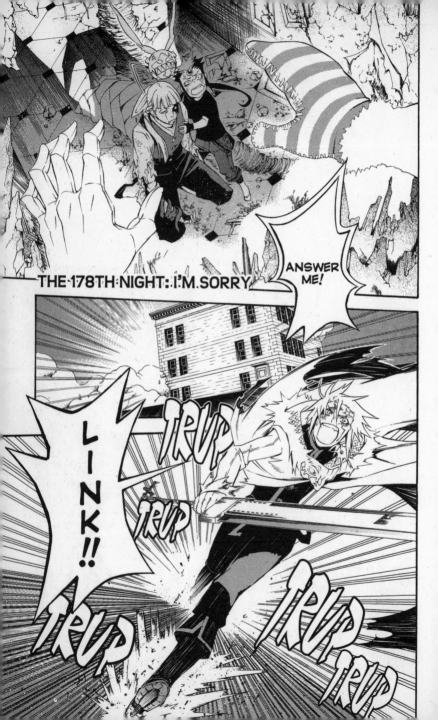

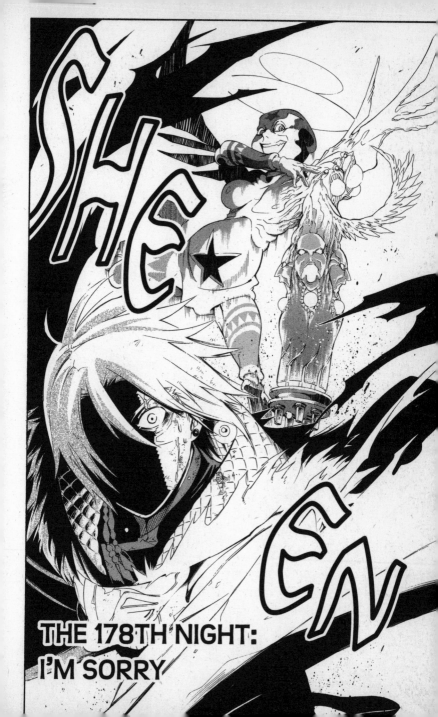

THE 178TH NIGHT: I'M SORRY

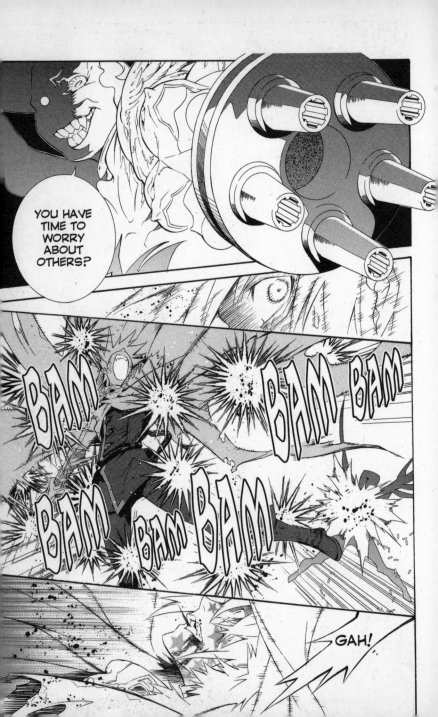

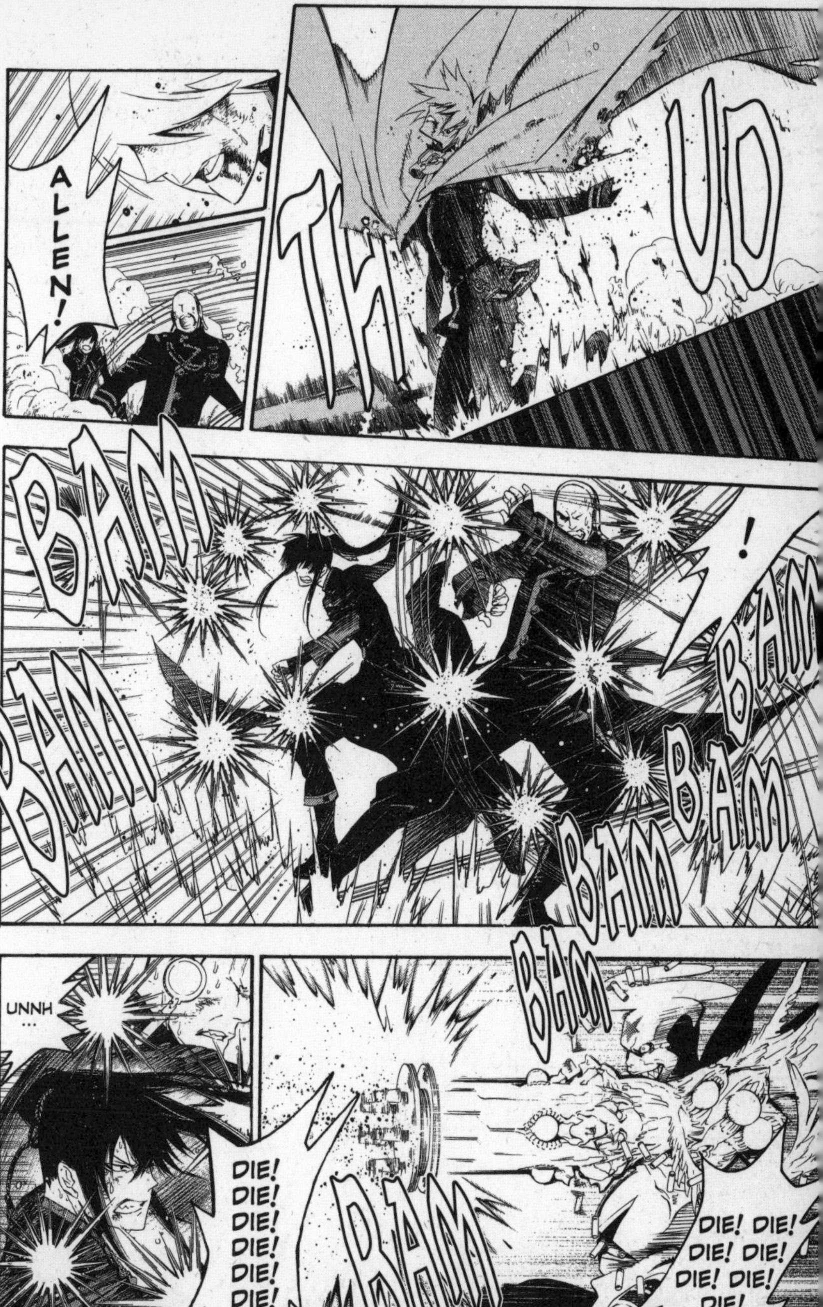
THUD
ALLEN!
!
BAM
BAM
BAM
BAM
BAM
BAM
BAM
DIE! DIE! DIE! DIE! DIE! DIE! DIE!
BAM
DIE! DIE! DIE! DIE! DIE! DIE! DIE!
UNNH ...

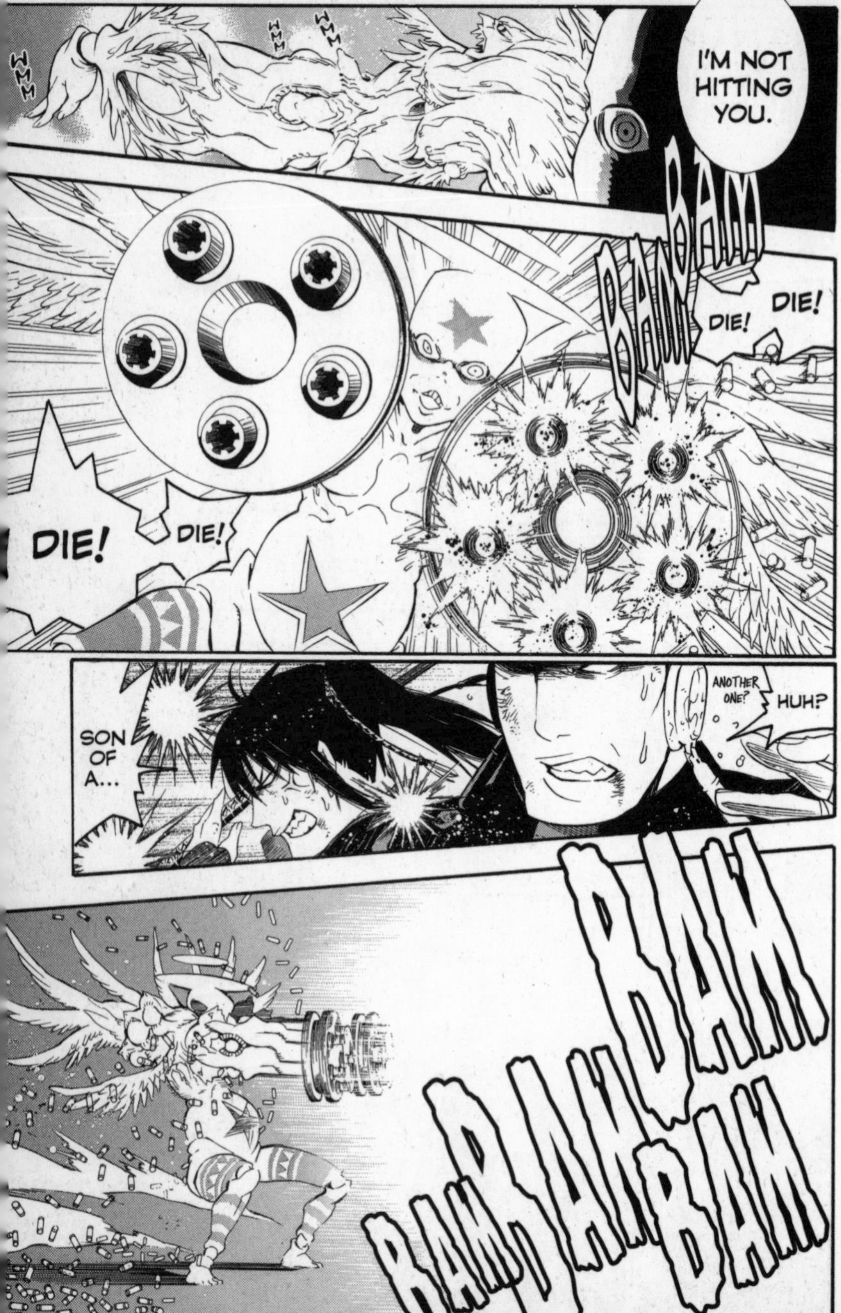

I'M NOT HITTING YOU.
BAM
WMM
WMM
WMM
BAM
DIE!
DIE!
DIE!
DIE!
HUH?
ANOTHER ONE?
SON OF A...
BAM
BAM
BAM,
BAM

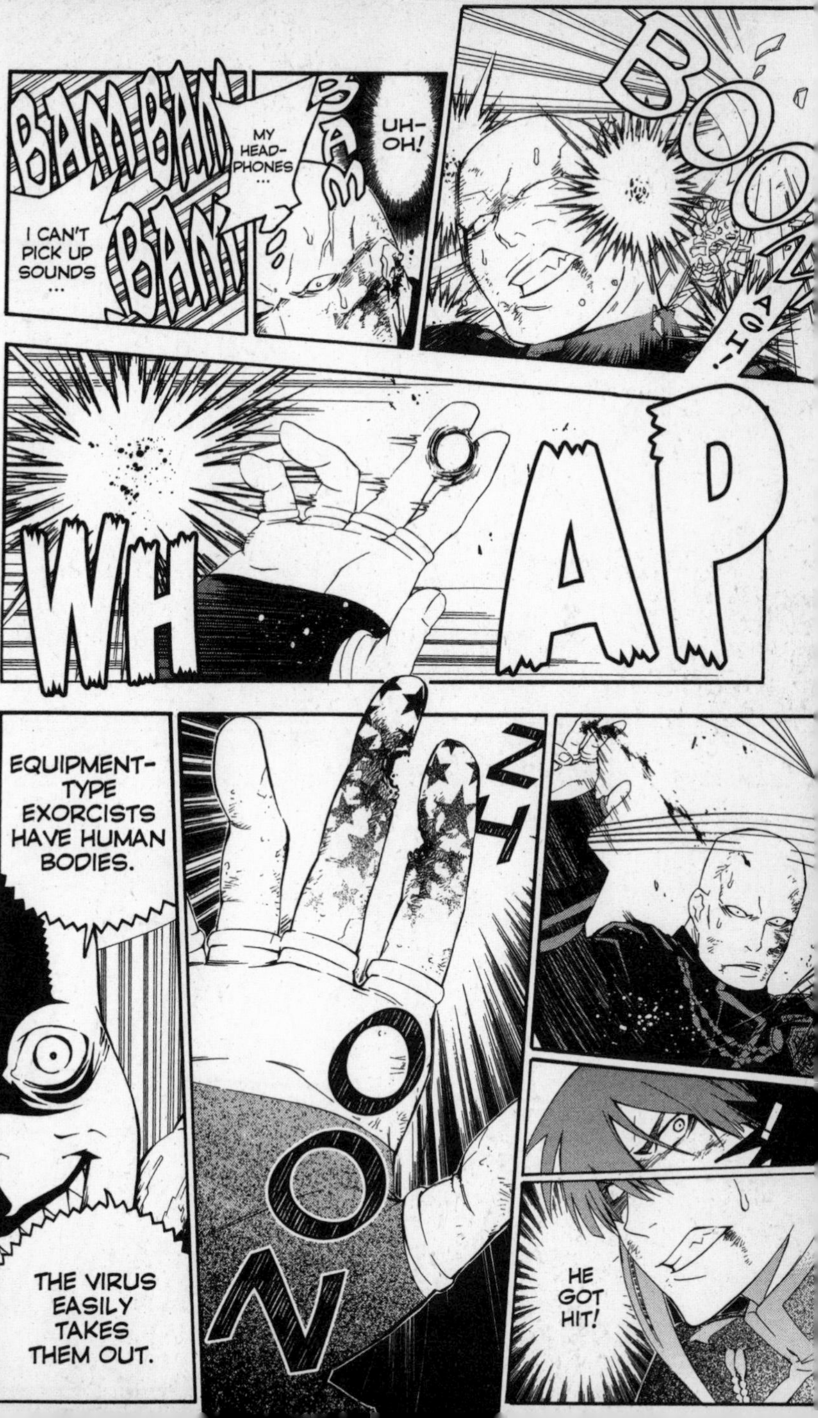
BOOM
AGH!
UH-OH!
BAM
MY HEADPHONES...
BAM BAN BAN
I CAN'T PICK UP SOUNDS...
WHAP
HE GOT HIT!
ZHOON
EQUIPMENT-TYPE EXORCISTS HAVE HUMAN BODIES.
THE VIRUS EASILY TAKES THEM OUT.

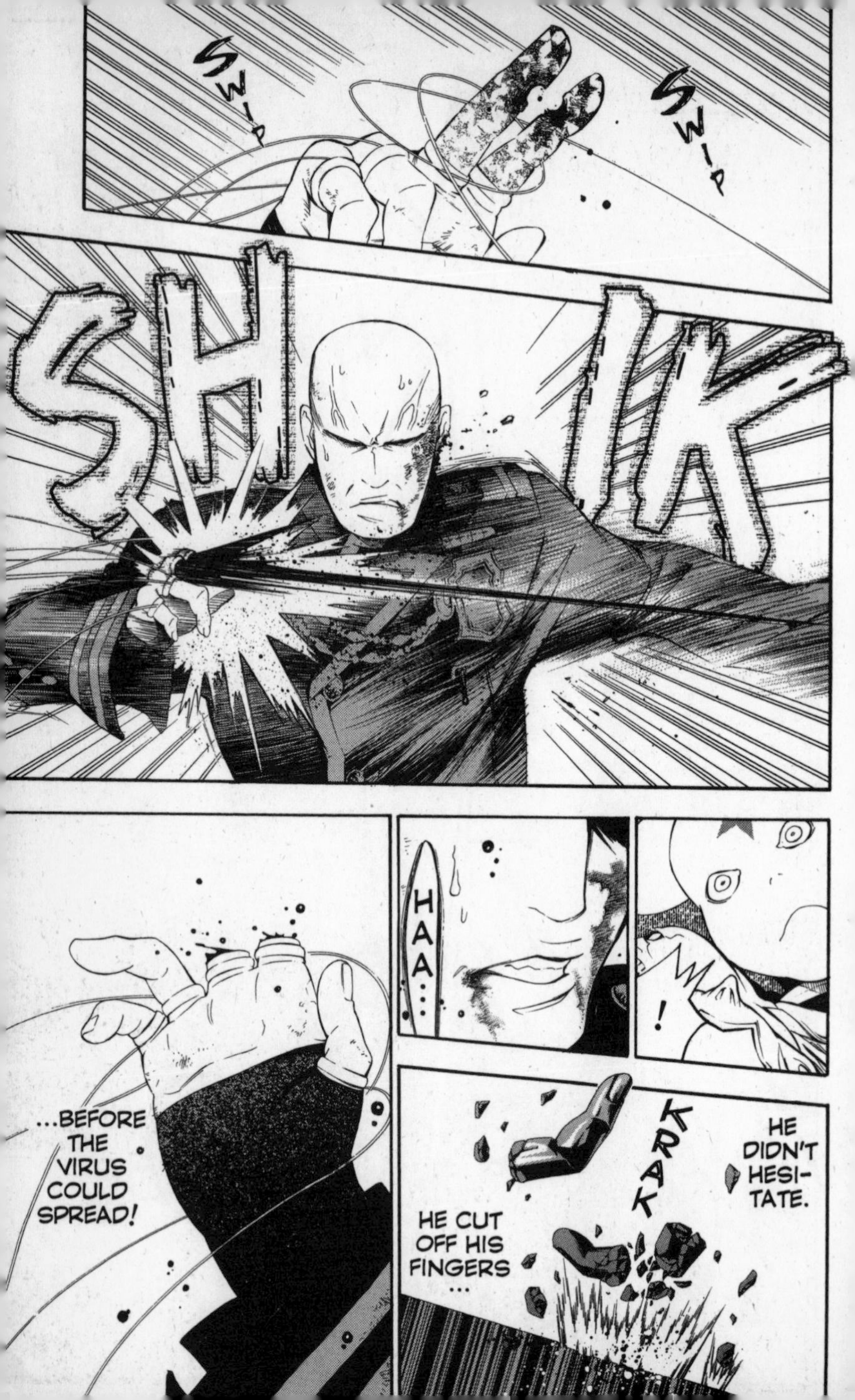
SWIP
SWIP
SHHAK
!
HAA...
HE DIDN'T HESITATE.
KRAK
HE CUT OFF HIS FINGERS...
...BEFORE THE VIRUS COULD SPREAD!

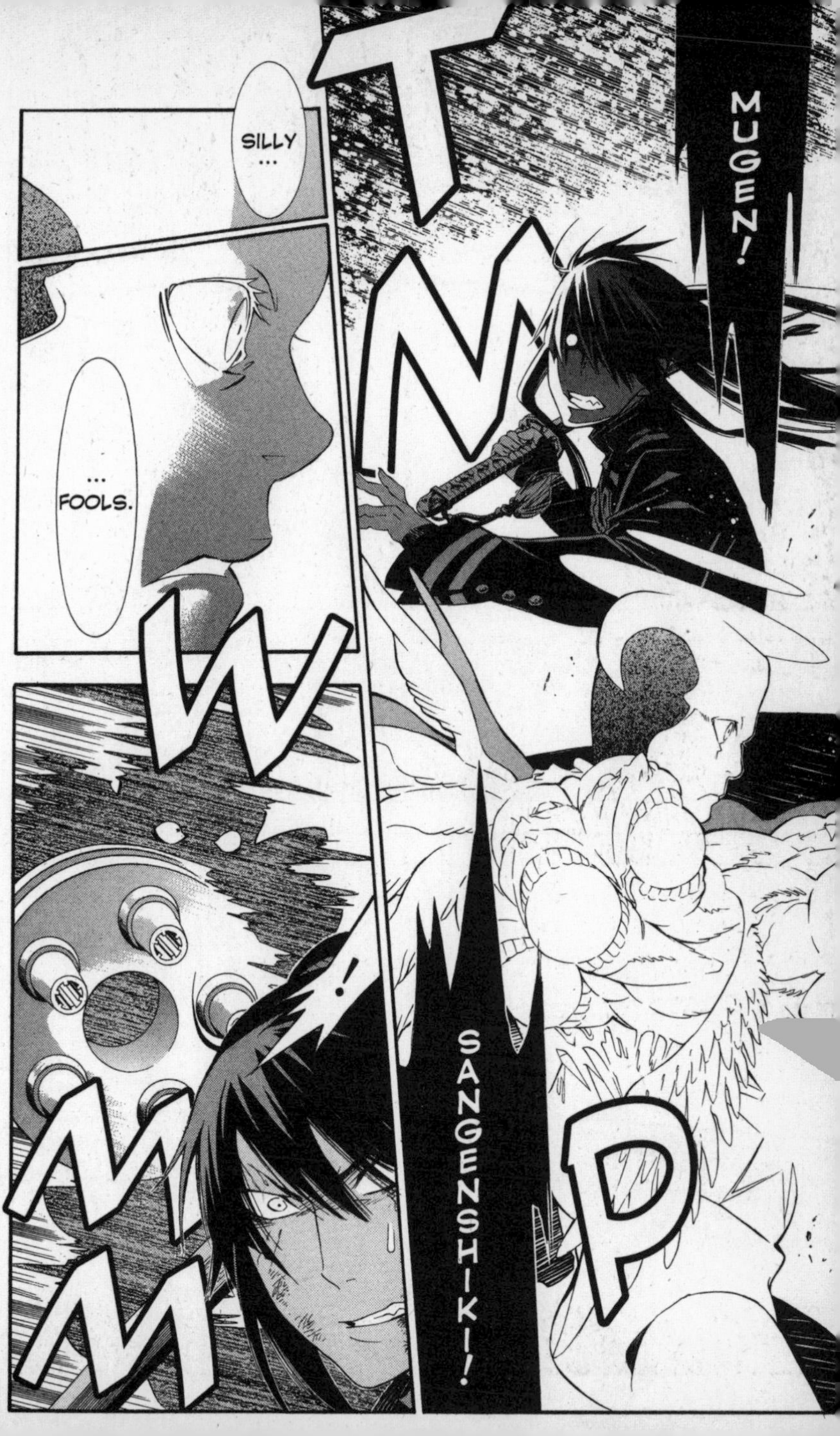
MUGEN!
SANGENSHIKI!
SILLY...
...FOOLS.

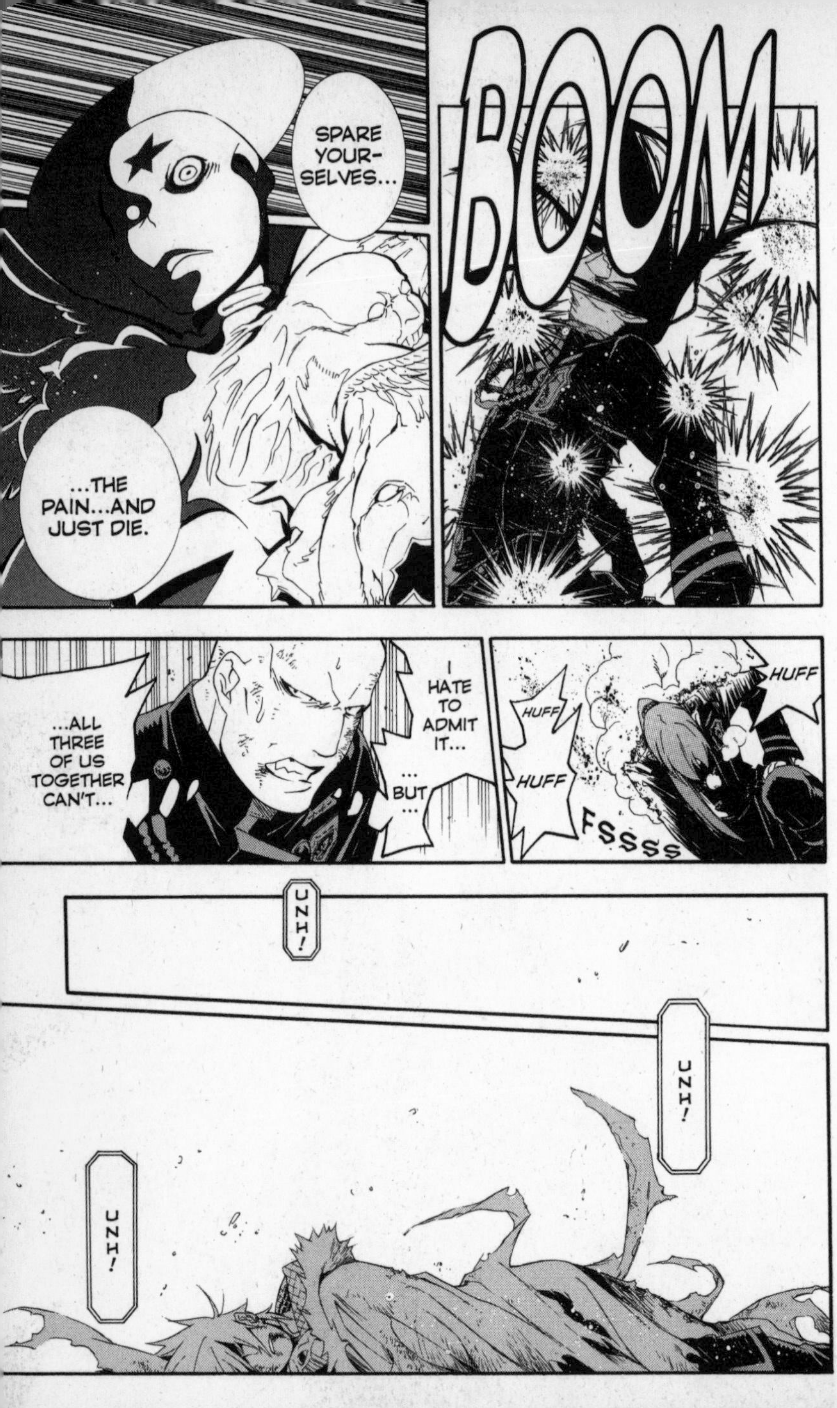
BOOM
SPARE YOUR-SELVES...
...THE PAIN...AND JUST DIE.
HUFF
HUFF
HUFF
FSSSS
I HATE TO ADMIT IT...
...BUT...
...ALL THREE OF US TOGETHER CAN'T...
UNH!
UNH!
UNH!

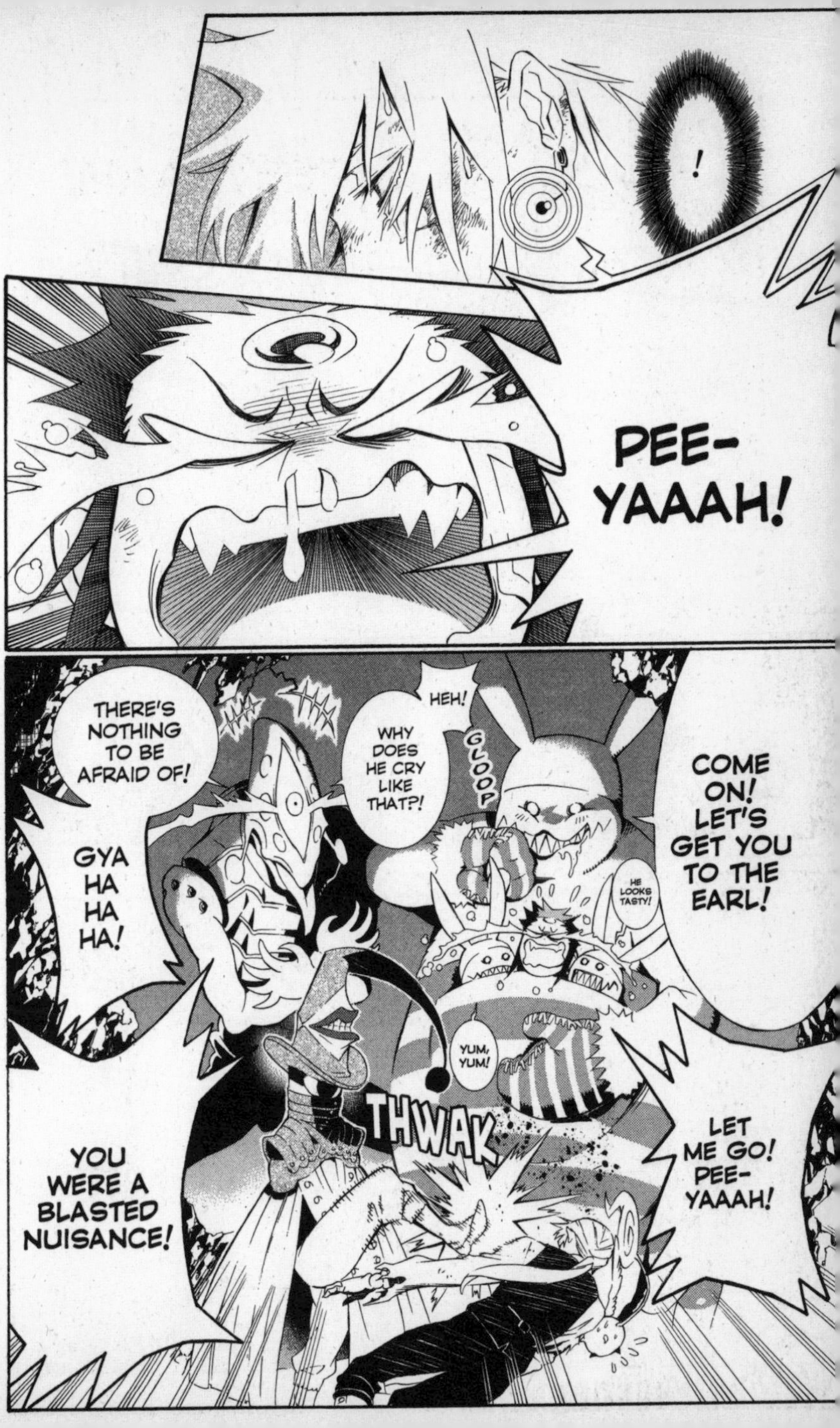
!
PEE-YAAAH!
COME ON! LET'S GET YOU TO THE EARL!
HEH!
WHY DOES HE CRY LIKE THAT?!
GLOOP
THERE'S NOTHING TO BE AFRAID OF!
HE LOOKS TASTY!
GYA HA HA HA!
YUM, YUM!
LET ME GO! PEE-YAAAH!
THWAK
YOU WERE A BLASTED NUISANCE!

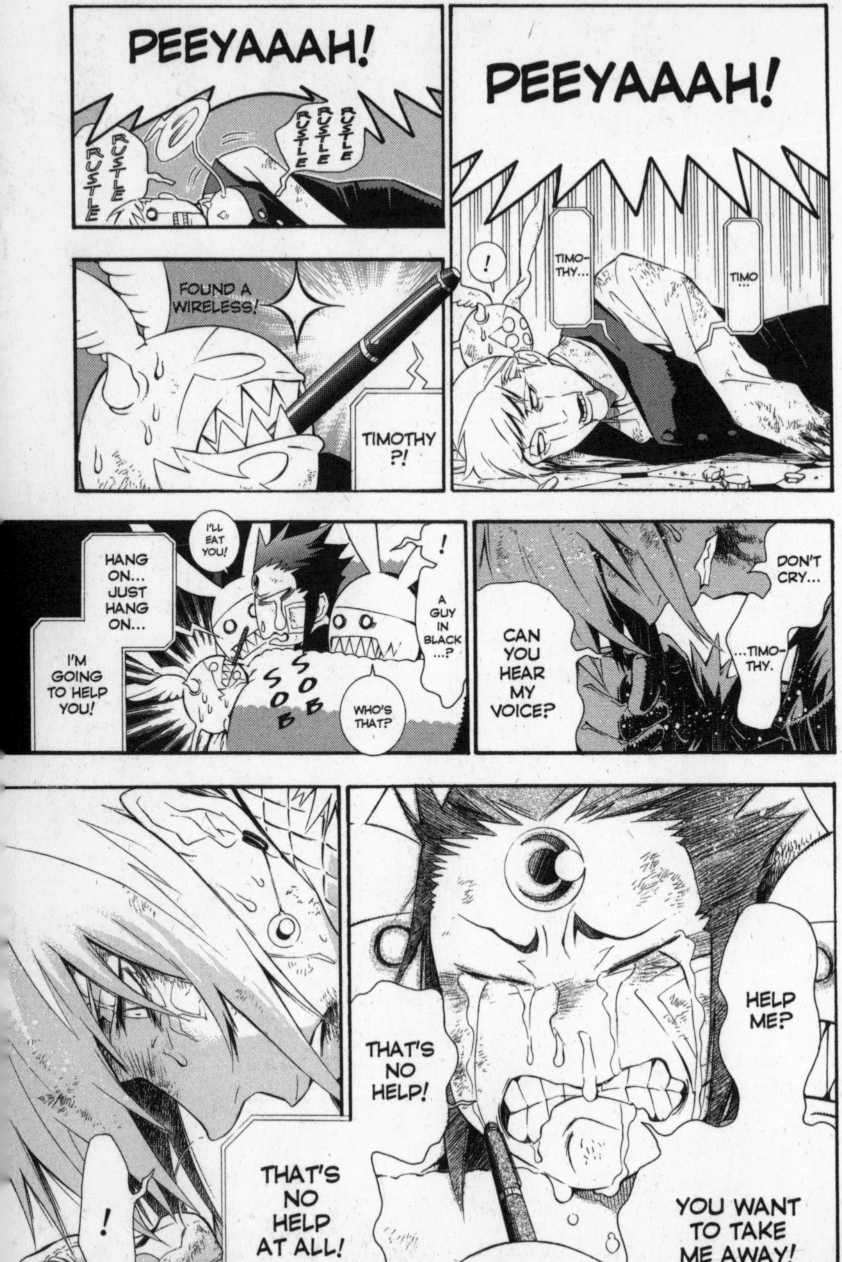
PEEYAAAH!
!
TIMO...
TIMOTHY...
PEEYAAAH!
RUSTLE RUSTLE RUSTLE
RUSTLE RUSTLE
FOUND A WIRELESS!
TIMOTHY?!
DON'T CRY...
...TIMOTHY.
CAN YOU HEAR MY VOICE?
!
A GUY IN BLACK...?
WHO'S THAT?
I'LL EAT YOU!
HANG ON... JUST HANG ON...
I'M GOING TO HELP YOU!
SOB SOB
HELP ME?
YOU WANT TO TAKE ME AWAY!
THAT'S NO HELP!
THAT'S NO HELP AT ALL!
!

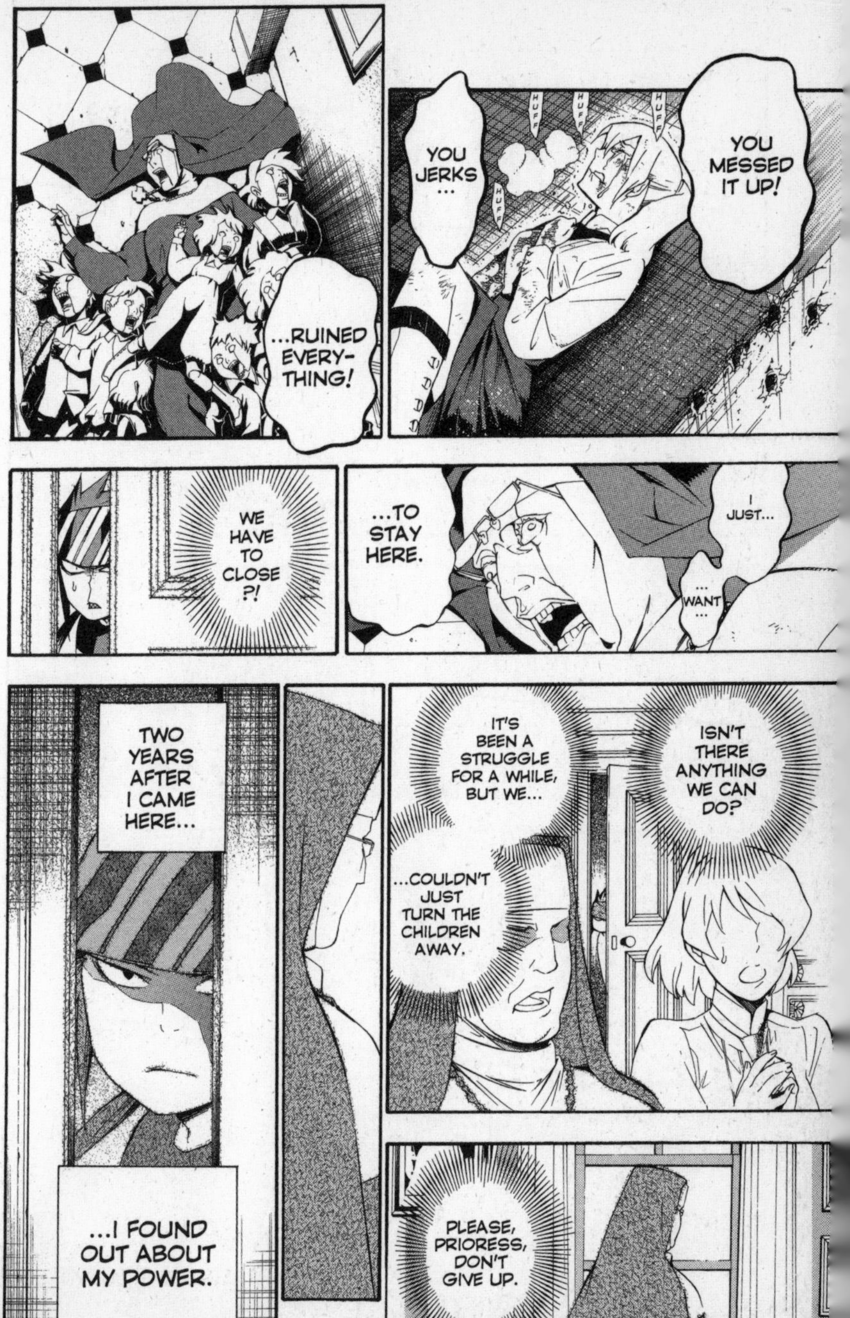
YOU MESSED IT UP!
HUFF
HUFF
HUFF
HUFF
YOU JERKS ...
...RUINED EVERY-THING!
I JUST...
...WANT ...
...TO STAY HERE.
WE HAVE TO CLOSE ?!
ISN'T THERE ANYTHING WE CAN DO?
IT'S BEEN A STRUGGLE FOR A WHILE, BUT WE...
...COULDN'T JUST TURN THE CHILDREN AWAY.
PLEASE, PRIORESS, DON'T GIVE UP.
TWO YEARS AFTER I CAME HERE...
...I FOUND OUT ABOUT MY POWER.

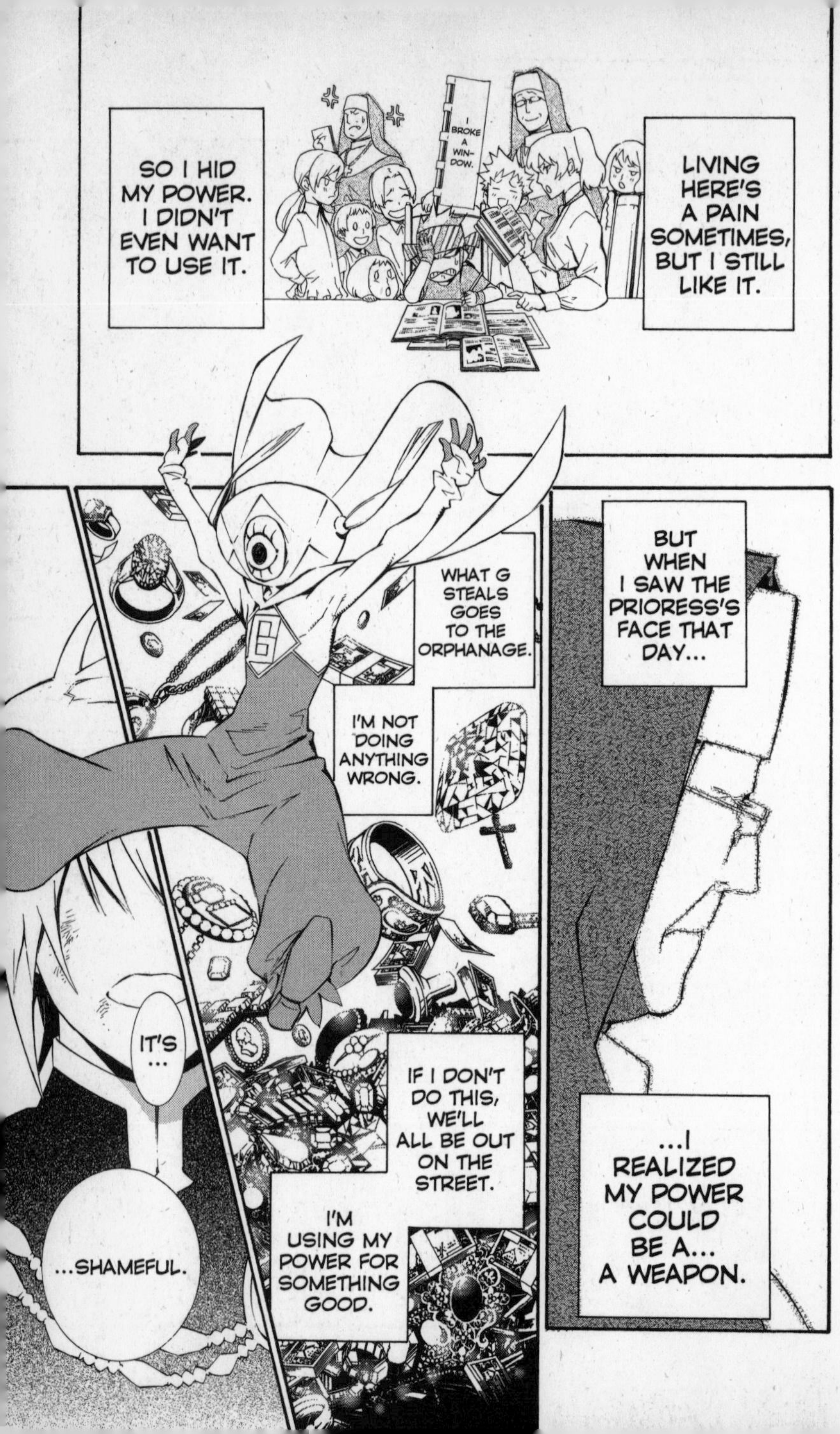
LIVING HERE'S A PAIN SOMETIMES, BUT I STILL LIKE IT.
I BROKE A WIN-DOW.
SO I HID MY POWER. I DIDN'T EVEN WANT TO USE IT.
BUT WHEN I SAW THE PRIORESS'S FACE THAT DAY...
...I REALIZED MY POWER COULD BE A... A WEAPON.
WHAT G STEALS GOES TO THE ORPHANAGE.
I'M NOT DOING ANYTHING WRONG.
IF I DON'T DO THIS, WE'LL ALL BE OUT ON THE STREET.
I'M USING MY POWER FOR SOMETHING GOOD.
IT'S...
...SHAMEFUL.

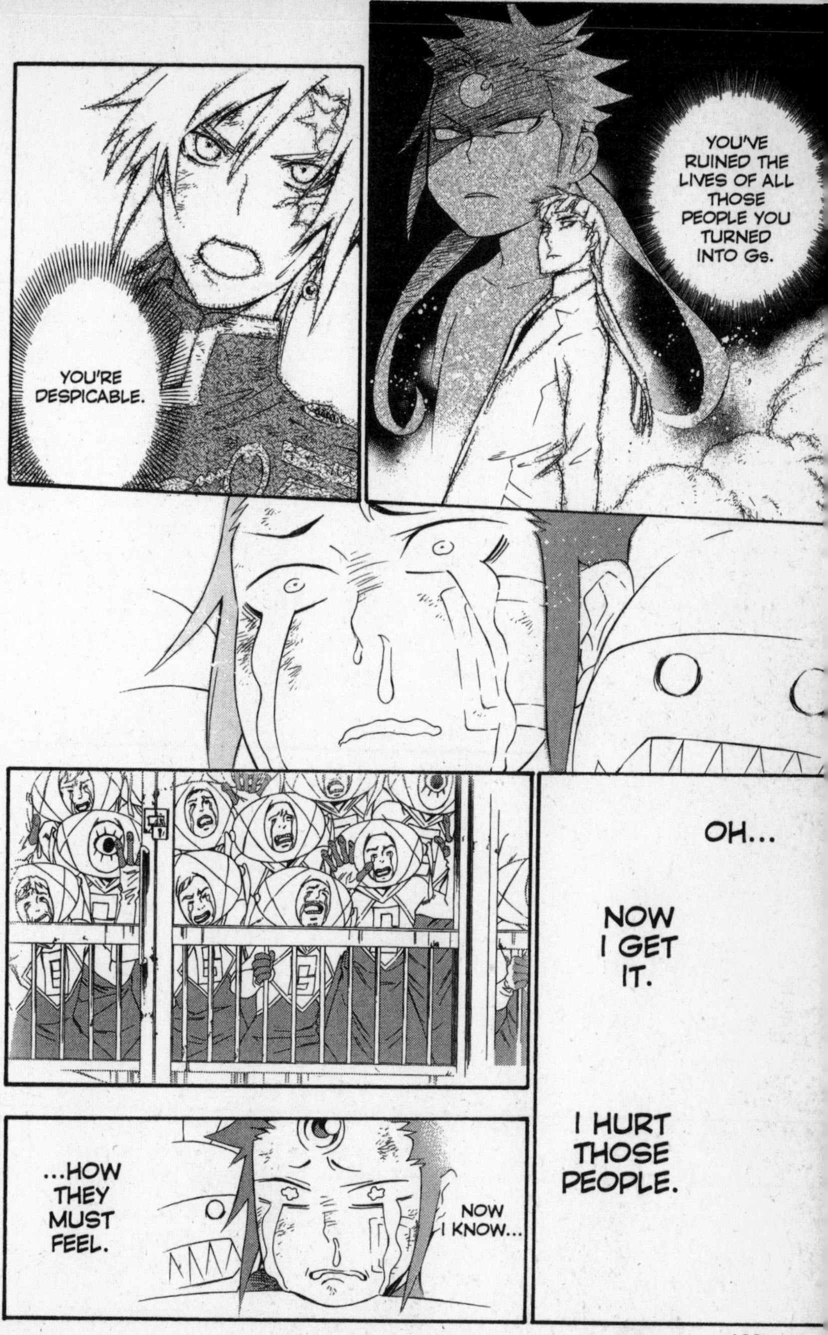
YOU'VE RUINED THE LIVES OF ALL THOSE PEOPLE YOU TURNED INTO Gs.
YOU'RE DESPICABLE.
OH...
NOW I GET IT.
I HURT THOSE PEOPLE.
NOW I KNOW...
...HOW THEY MUST FEEL.

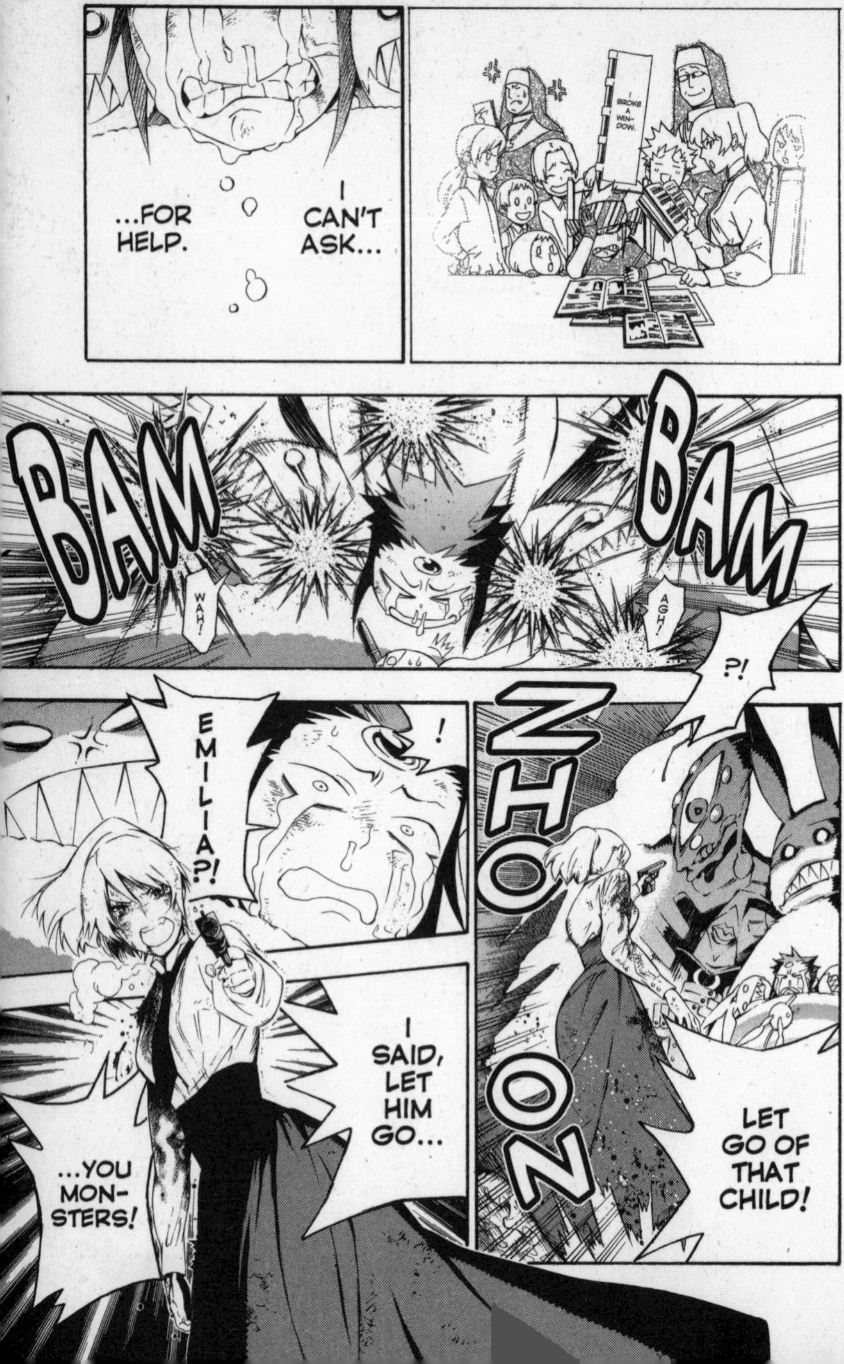
I BROKE A WIN-DOW.
I CAN'T ASK...
...FOR HELP.
BAM
AGH!
WAH!
BAM
?!
ZHOON
LET GO OF THAT CHILD!
!
EMILIA?!
I SAID, LET HIM GO...
...YOU MONSTERS!

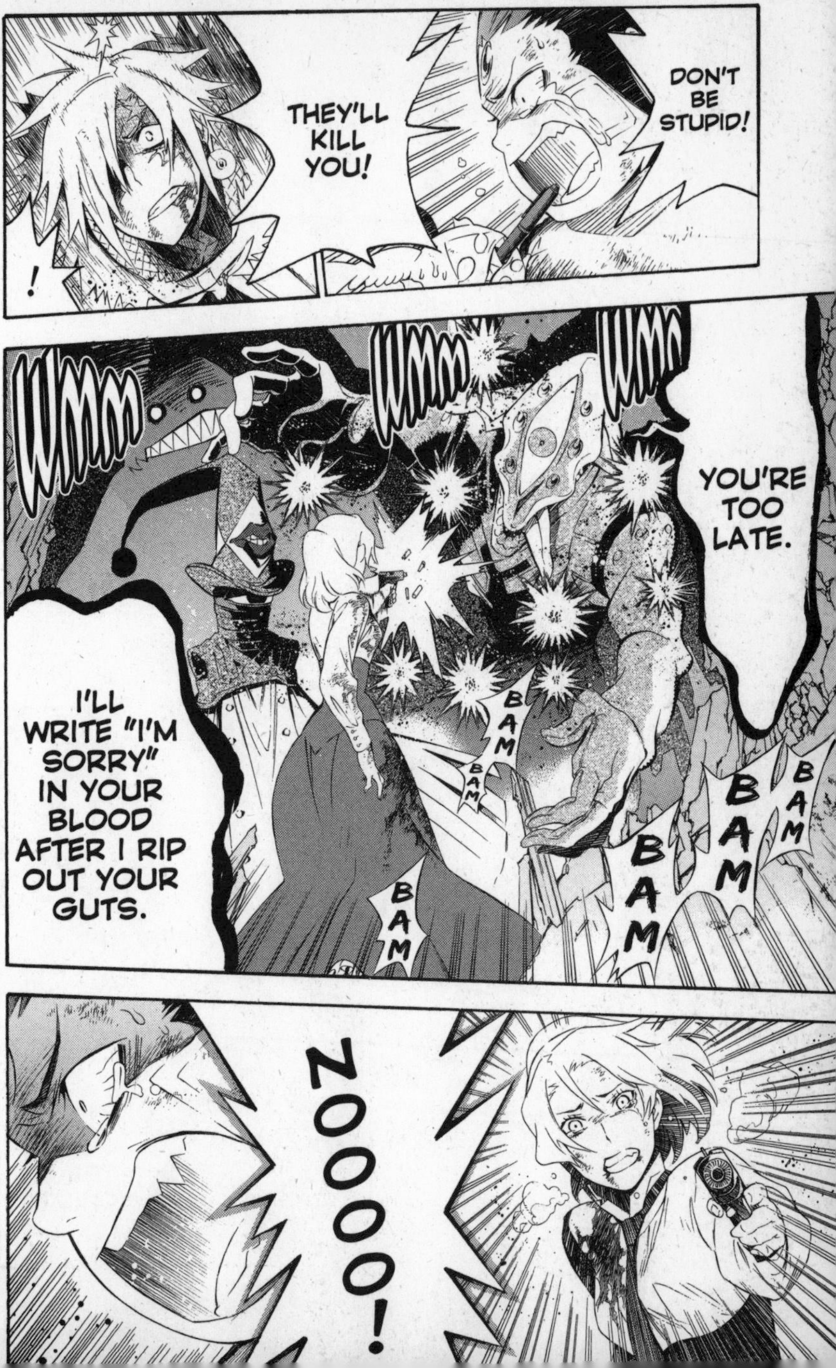
DON'T BE STUPID!
THEY'LL KILL YOU!
!
WMM
WMM
WMM
YOU'RE TOO LATE.
BAM
BAM
BAM
BAM
BAM
I'LL WRITE "I'M SORRY" IN YOUR BLOOD AFTER I RIP OUT YOUR GUTS.
BAM
NOOOO!

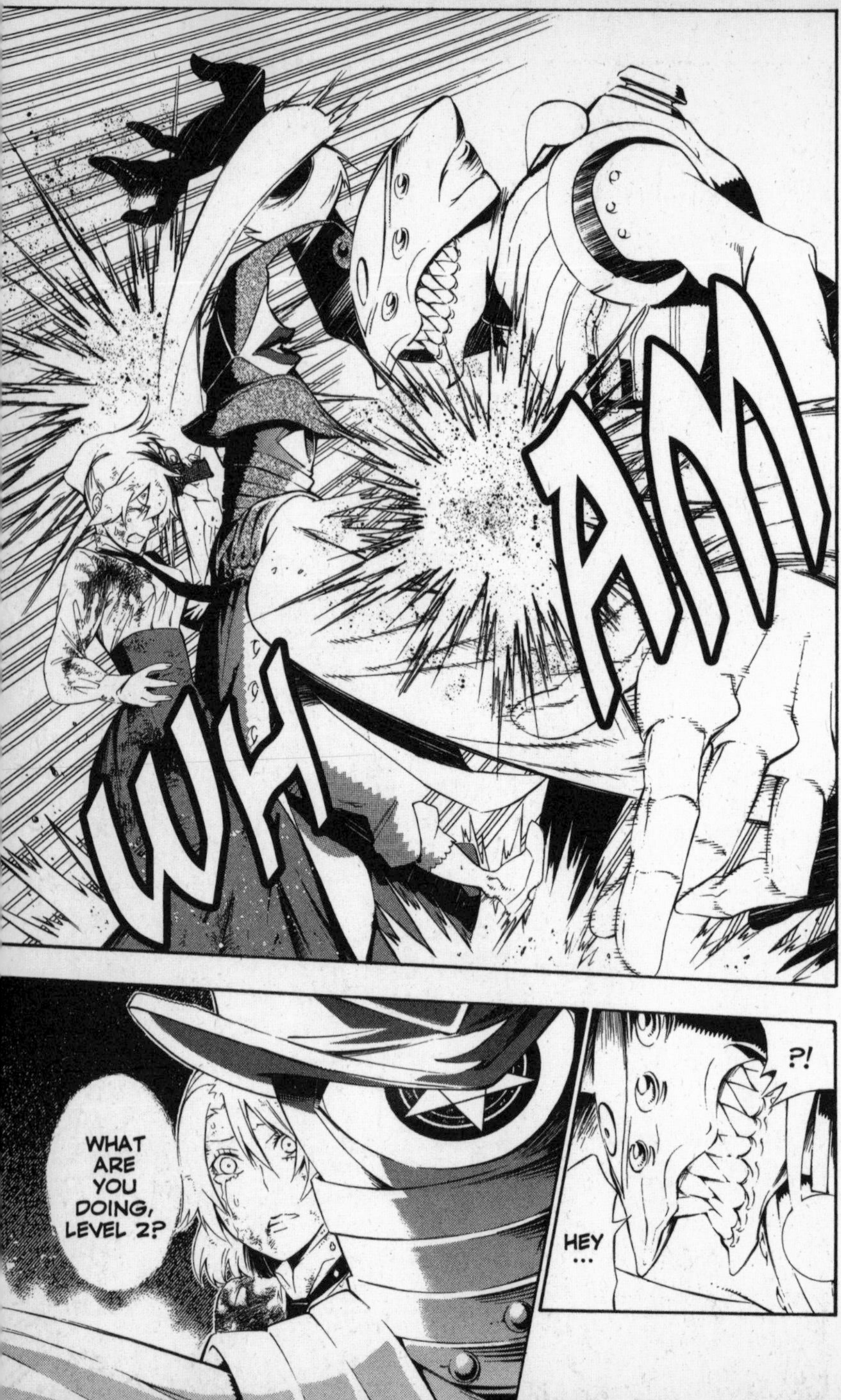
WHAM
?!
HEY...
WHAT ARE YOU DOING, LEVEL 2?

MEANWHILE, INSPECTOR GALMAR...

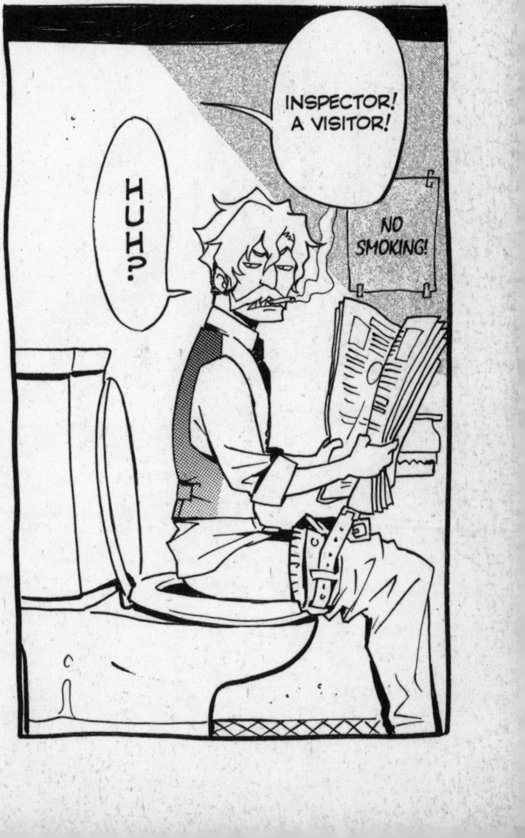
INSPECTOR! A VISITOR!
NO SMOKING!
HUH?

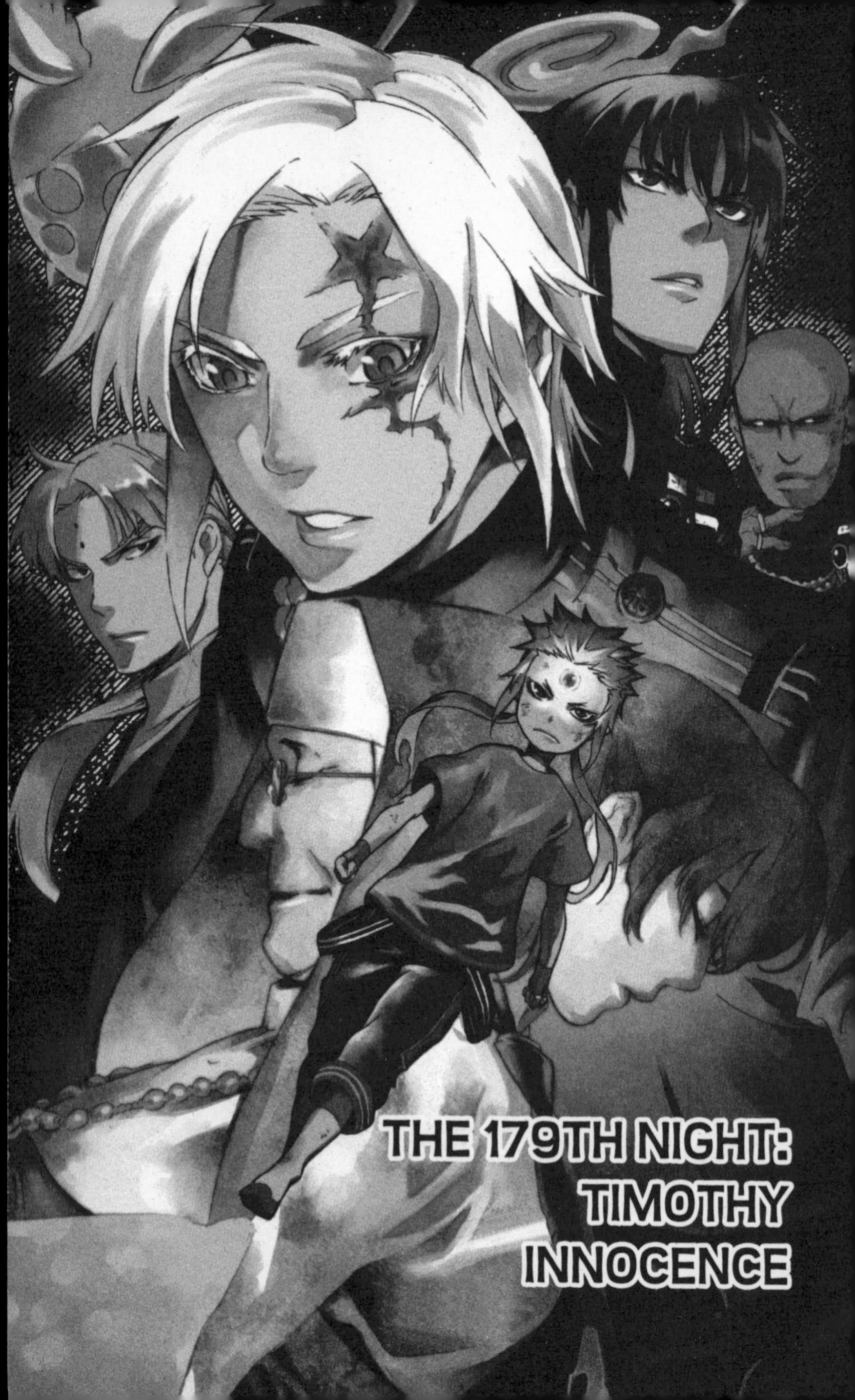
THE 179TH NIGHT:
TIMOTHY
INNOCENCE

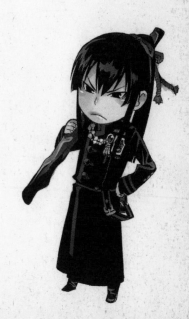

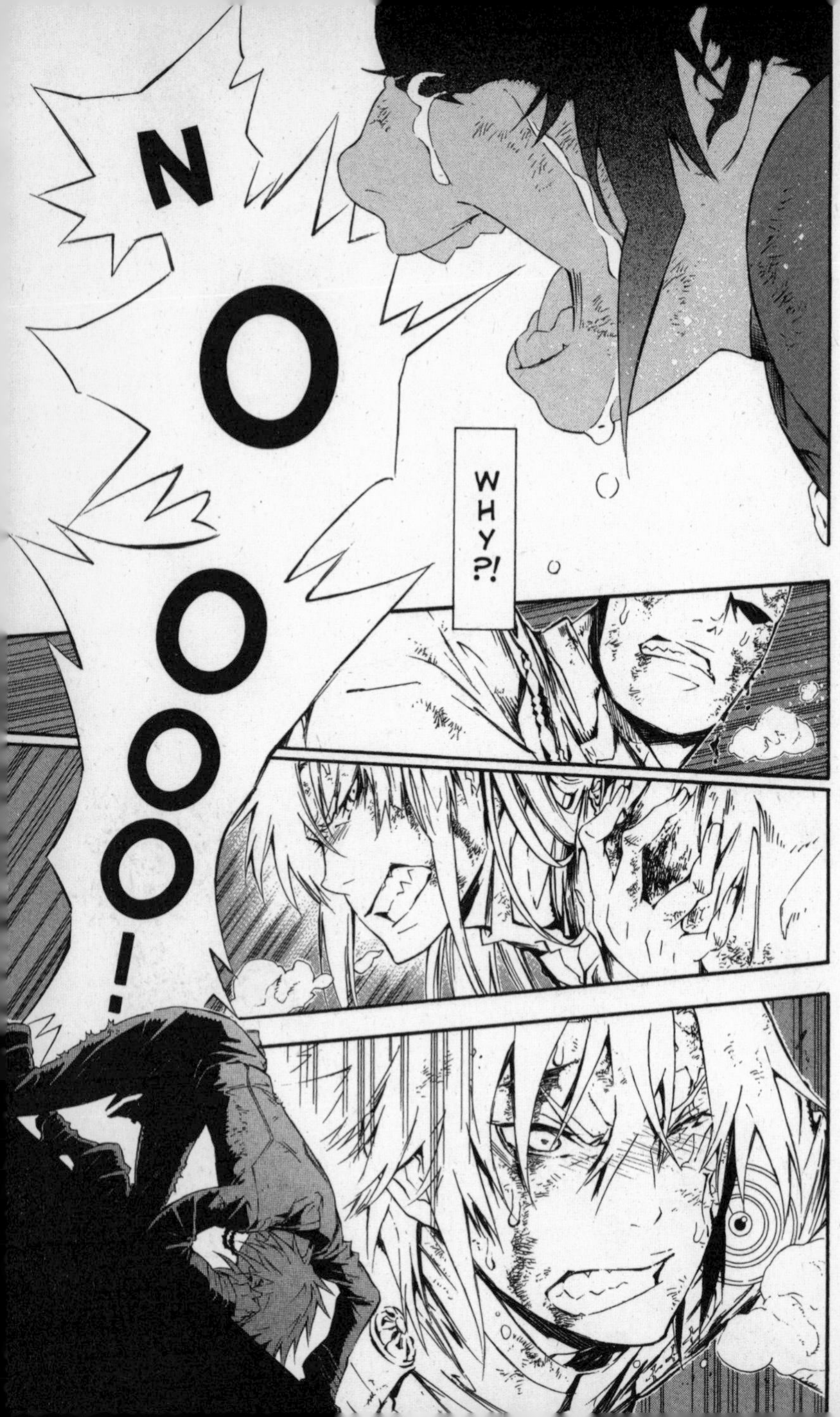
NOOOOO!
WHY?!

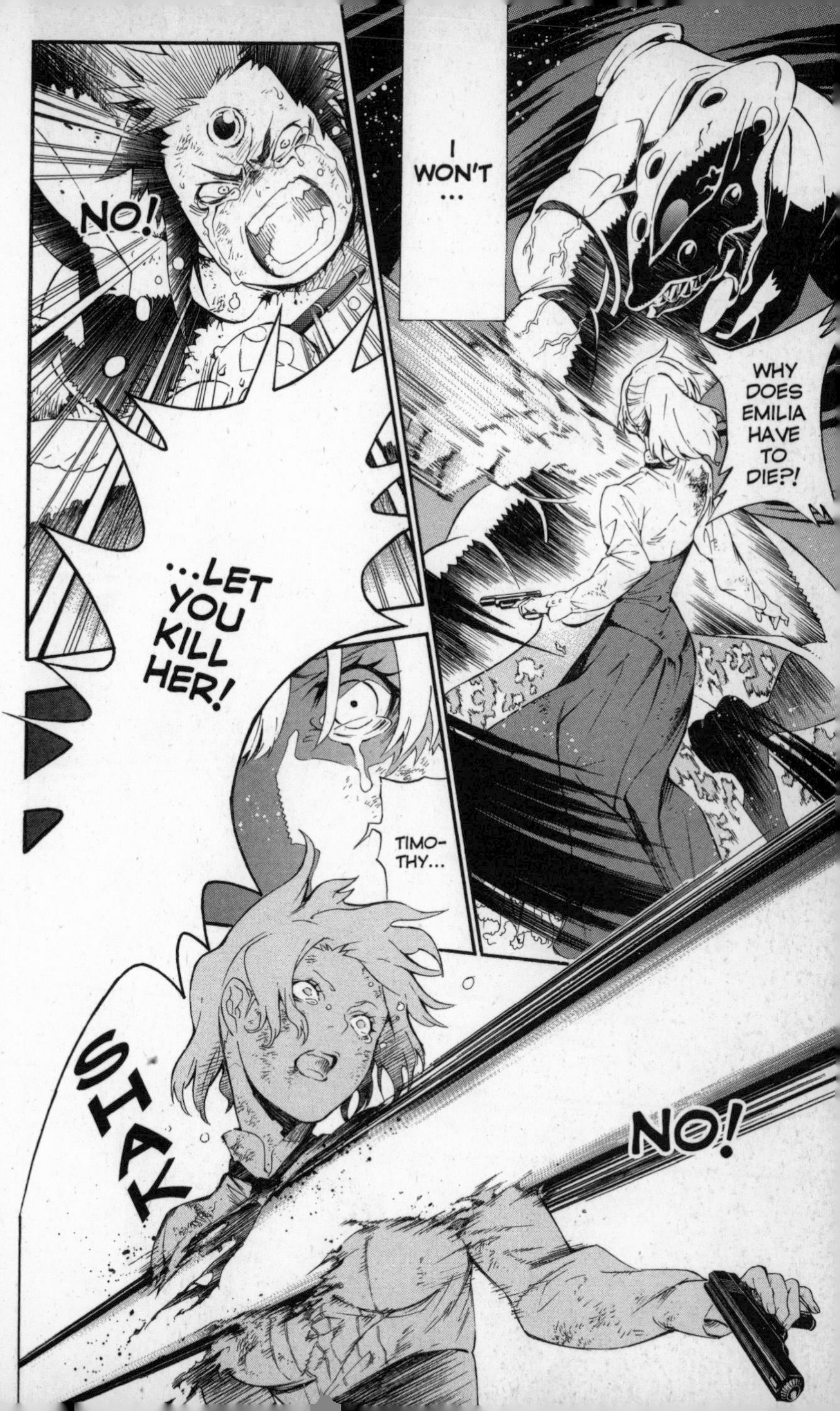
WHY DOES EMILIA HAVE TO DIE?!
I WON'T ...
NO!
...LET YOU KILL HER!
TIMOTHY...
NO!
SHAK

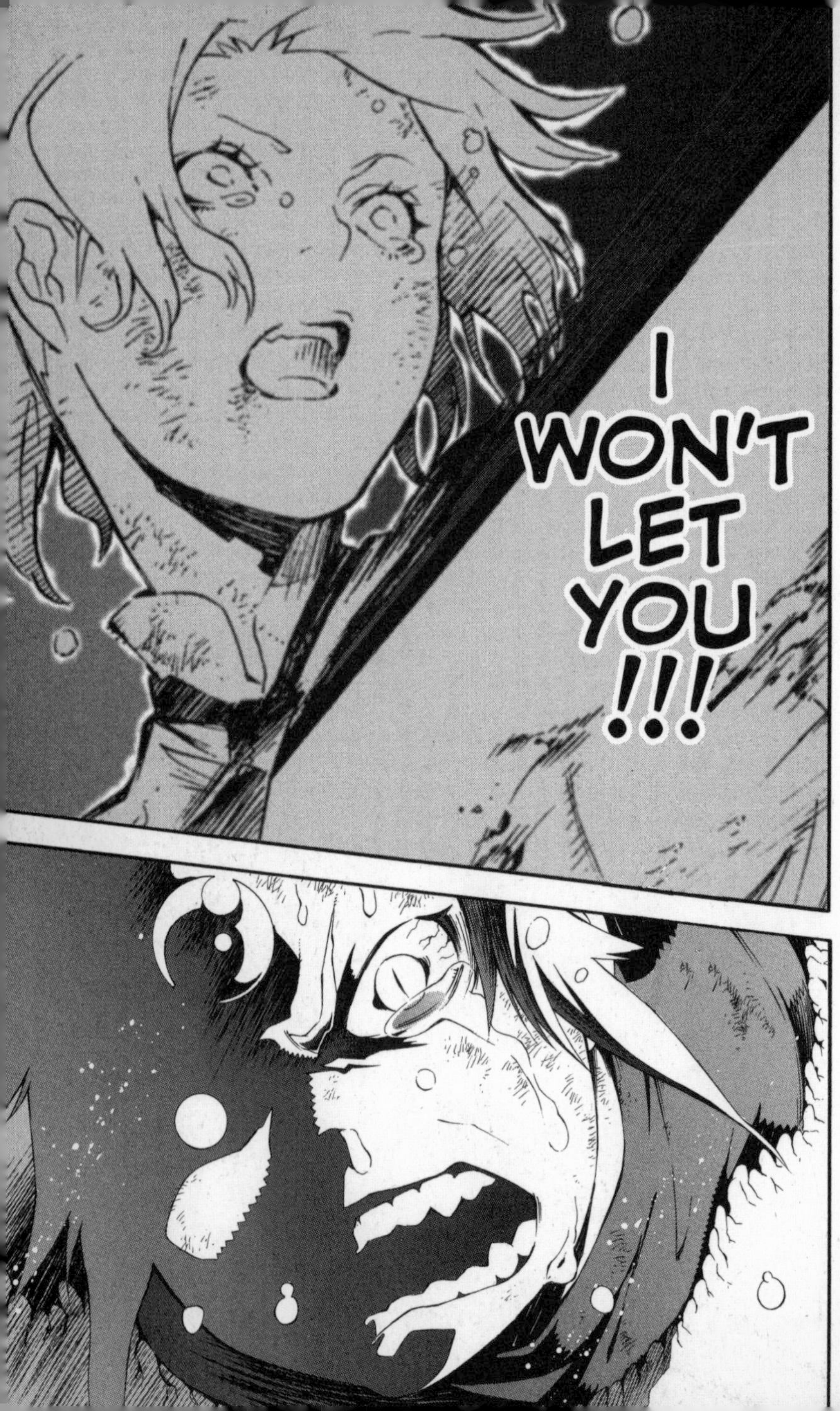
I WON'T LET YOU!!!

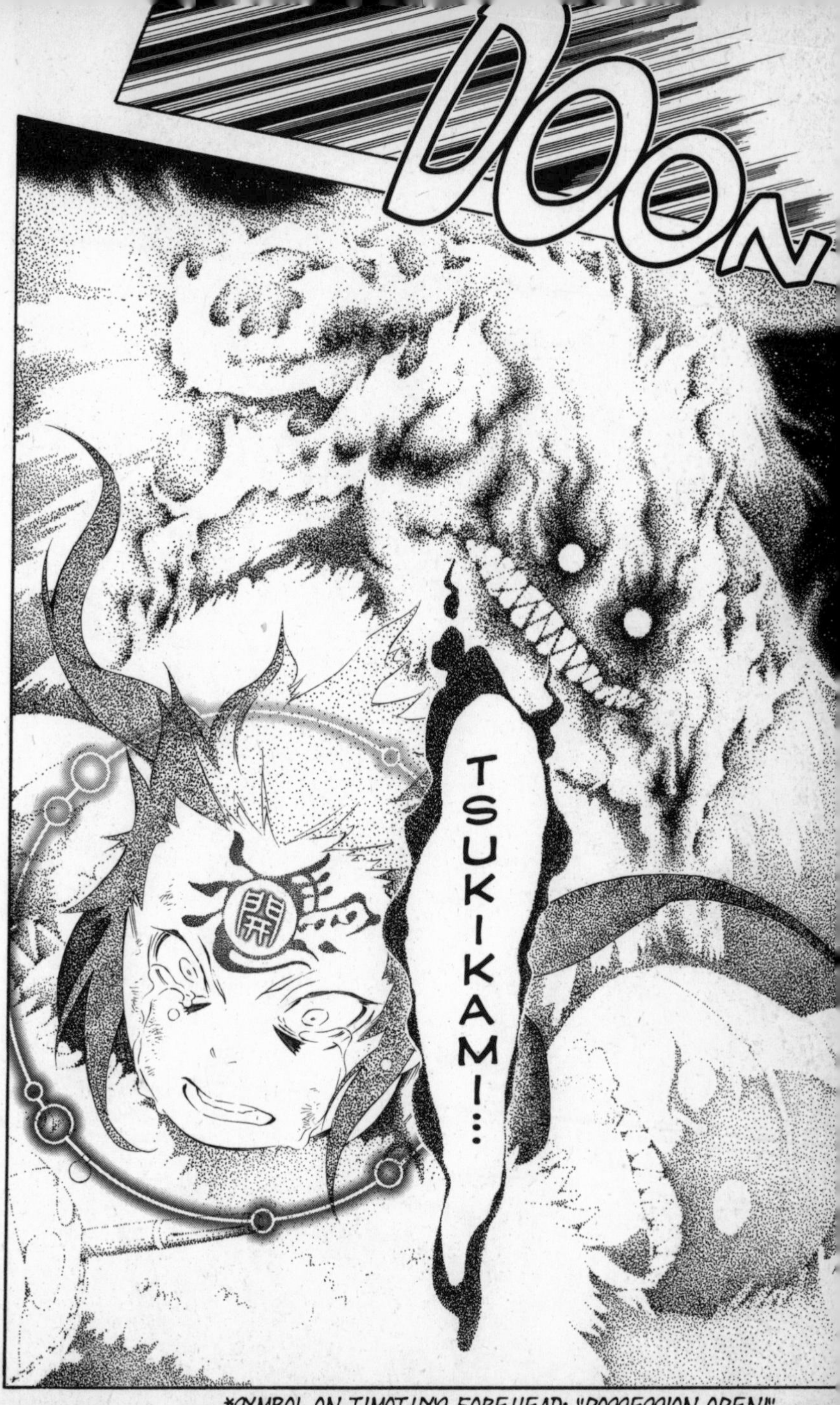
DOOON
TSUKIKAMI...

*SYMBOL ON TIMOTHY'S FOREHEAD: "POSSESSION OPEN!"

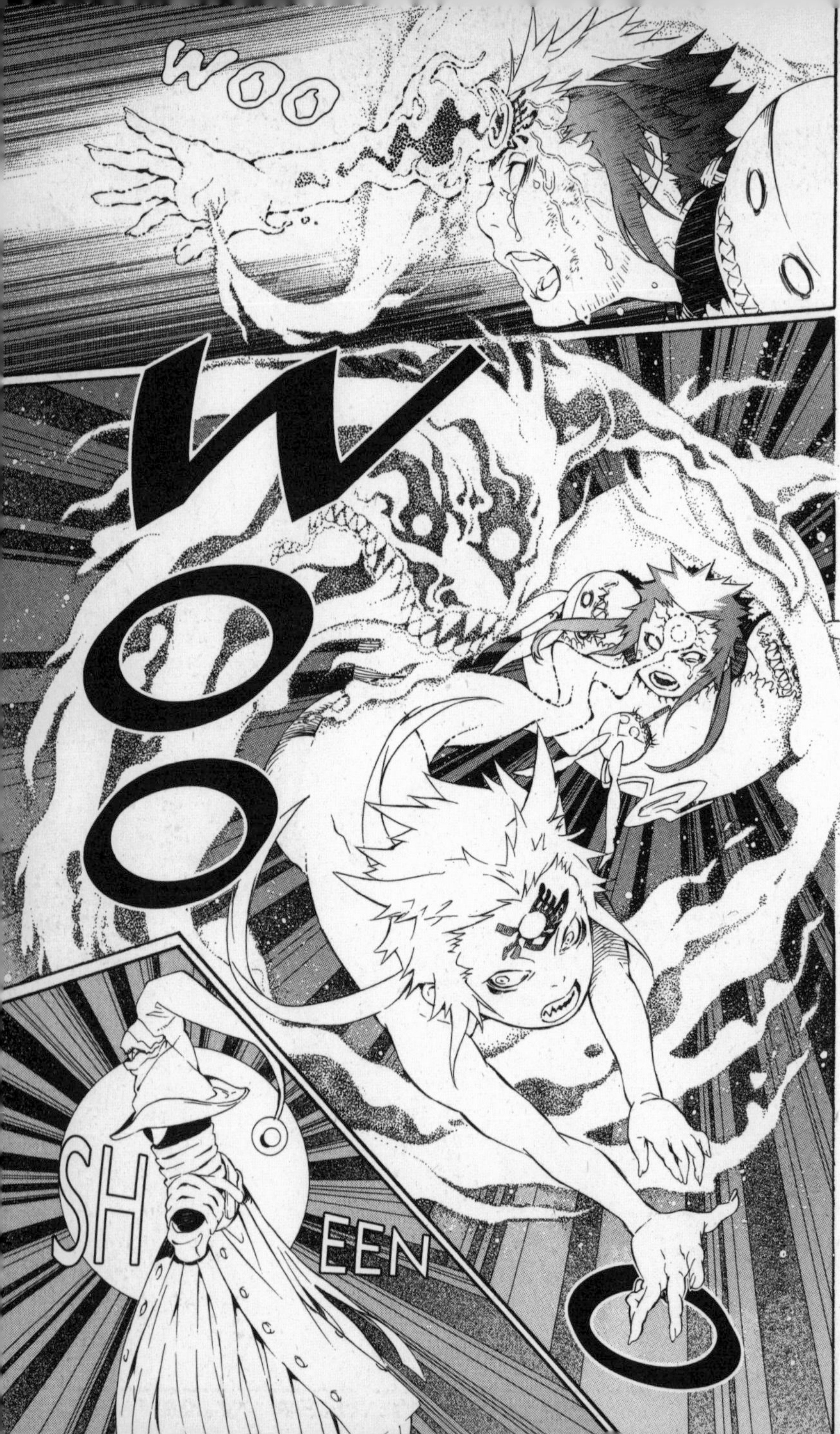
WOO
SH
EEN

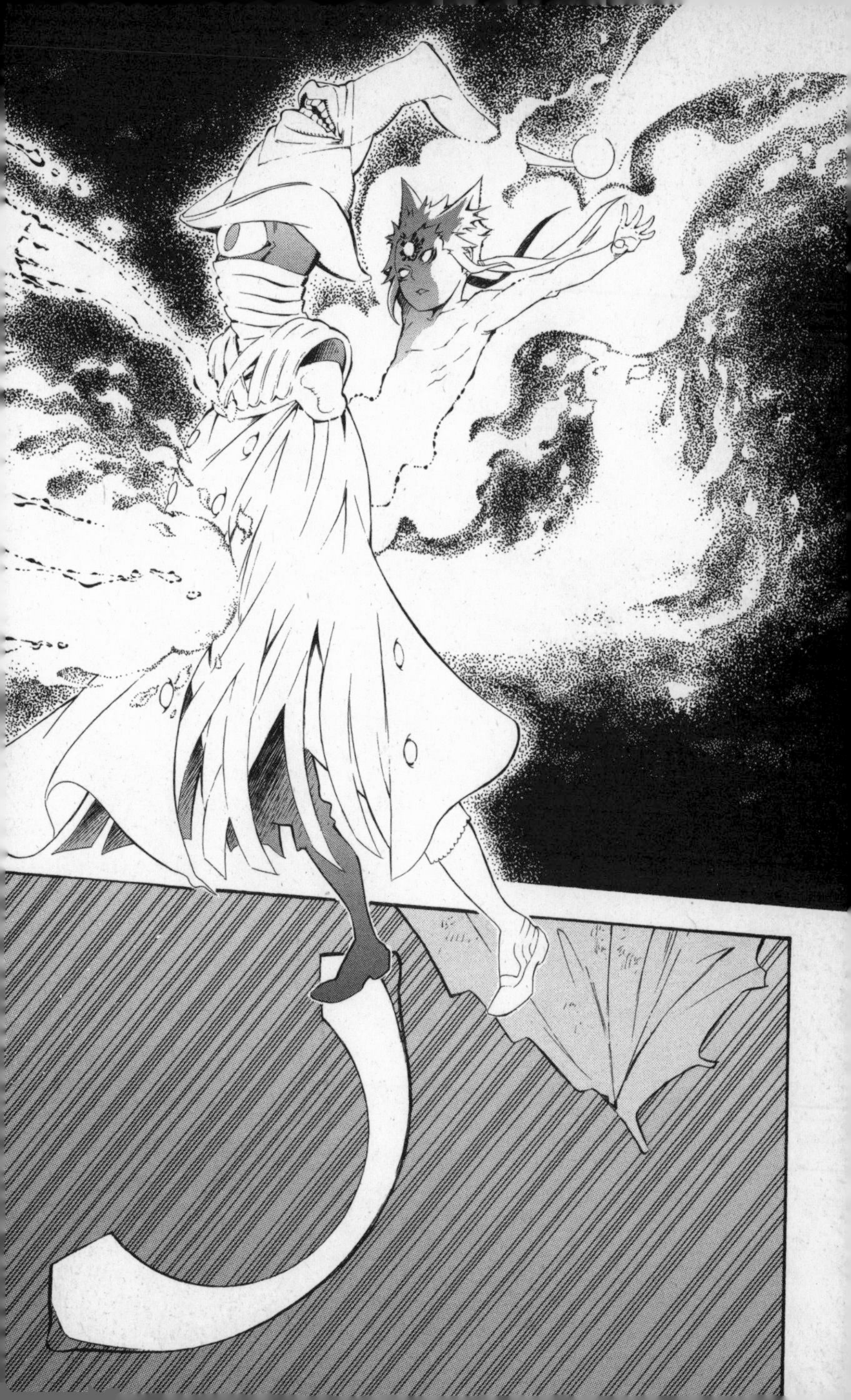

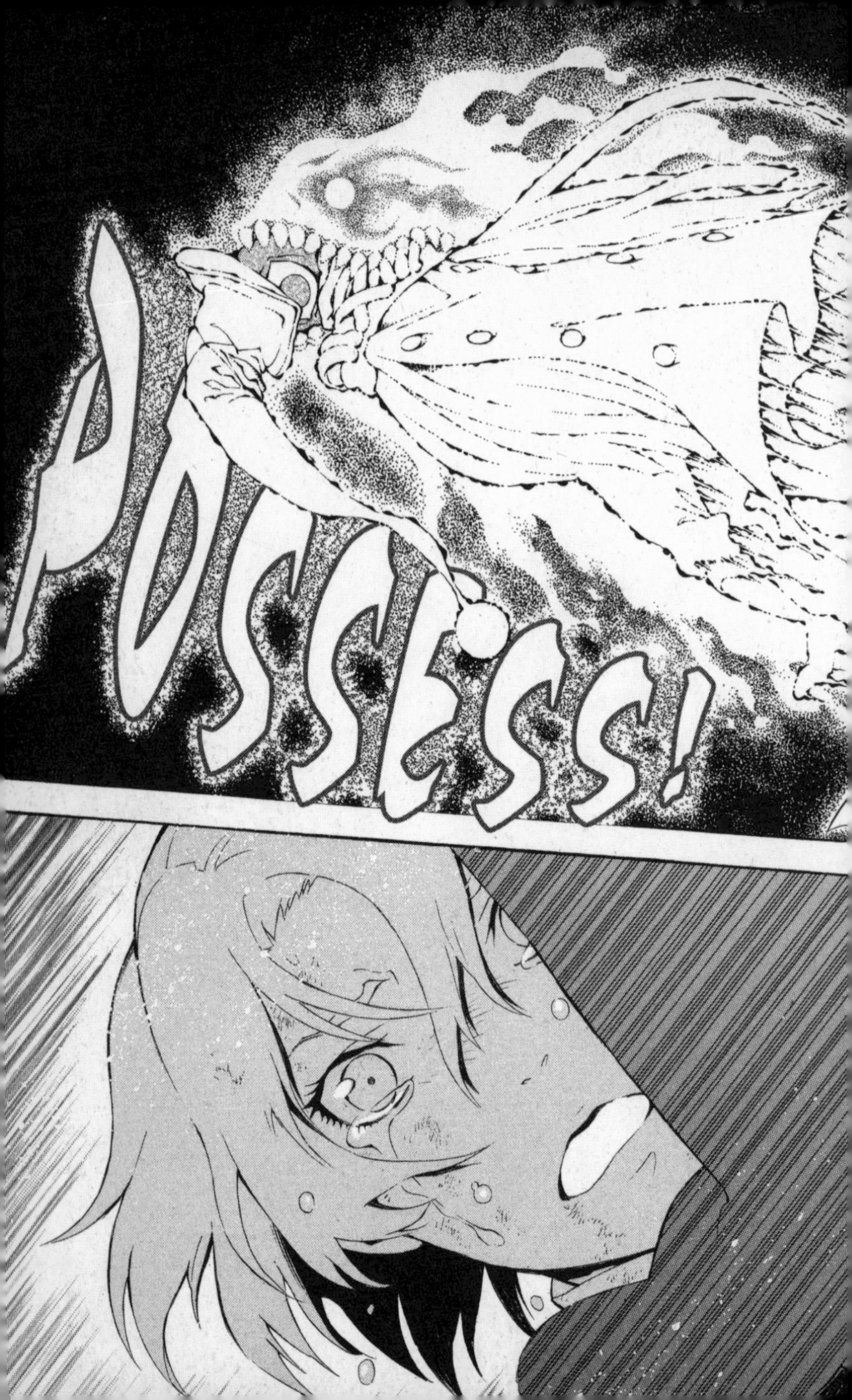
POSSESS!

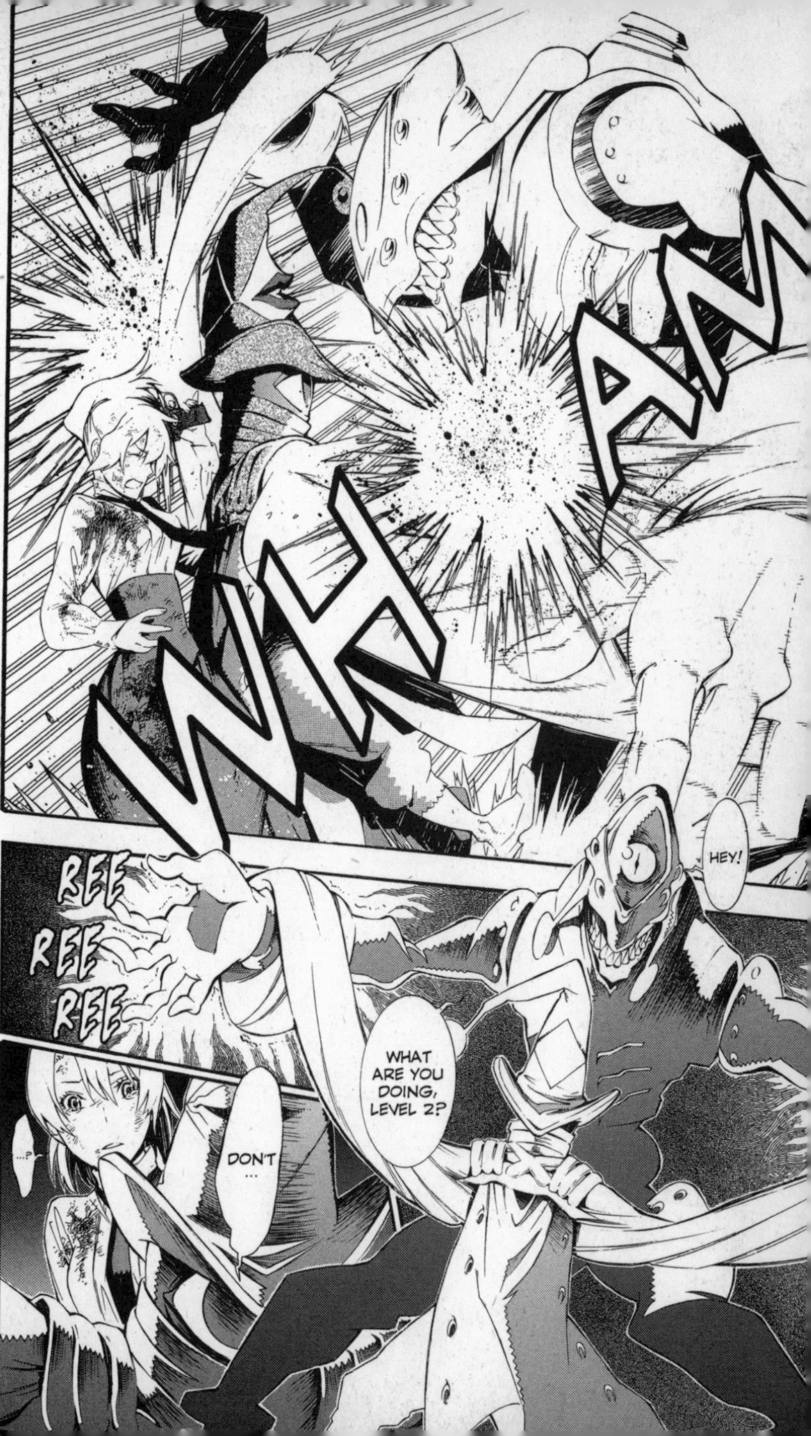
WHAM
HEY!
REE REE REE
WHAT ARE YOU DOING, LEVEL 2?
DON'T ...
...?

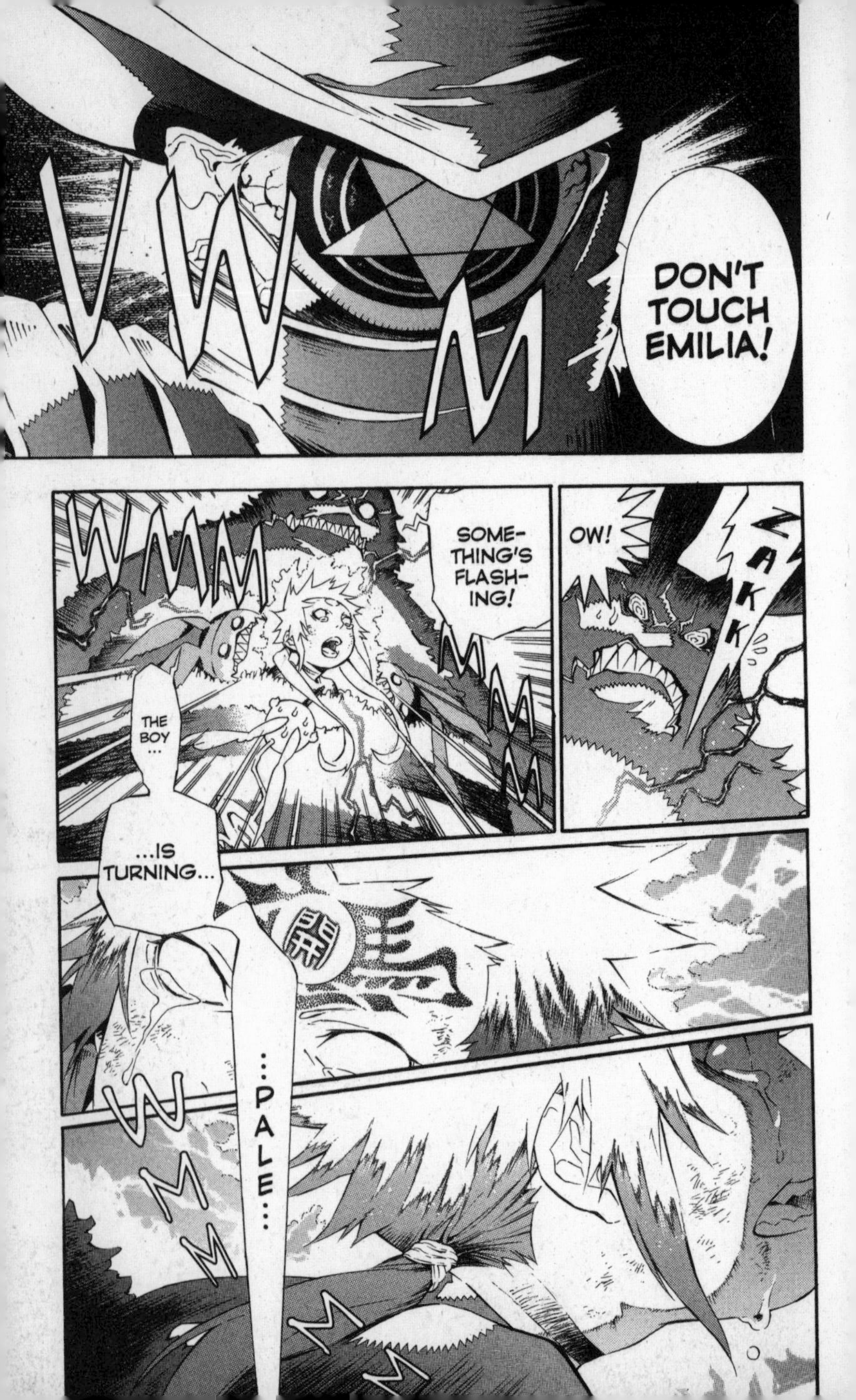
VWWM
DON'T TOUCH EMILIA!
OW!
ZAKK
SOME-THING'S FLASH-ING!
WMMM
MMMM
THE BOY...
...IS TURNING...
...PALE...
WWMMMM

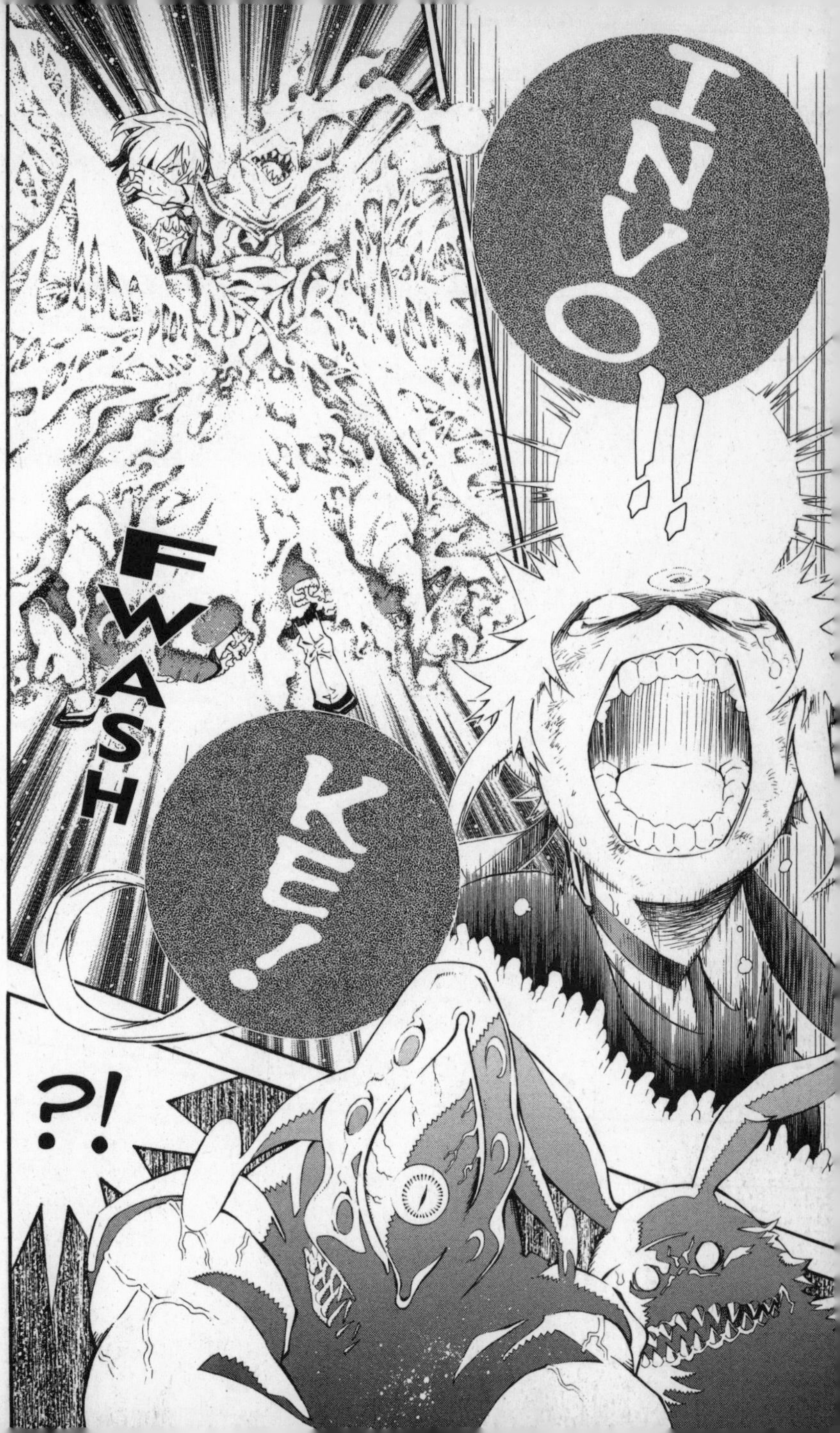
INUO!!
KE!
FWASH
?!

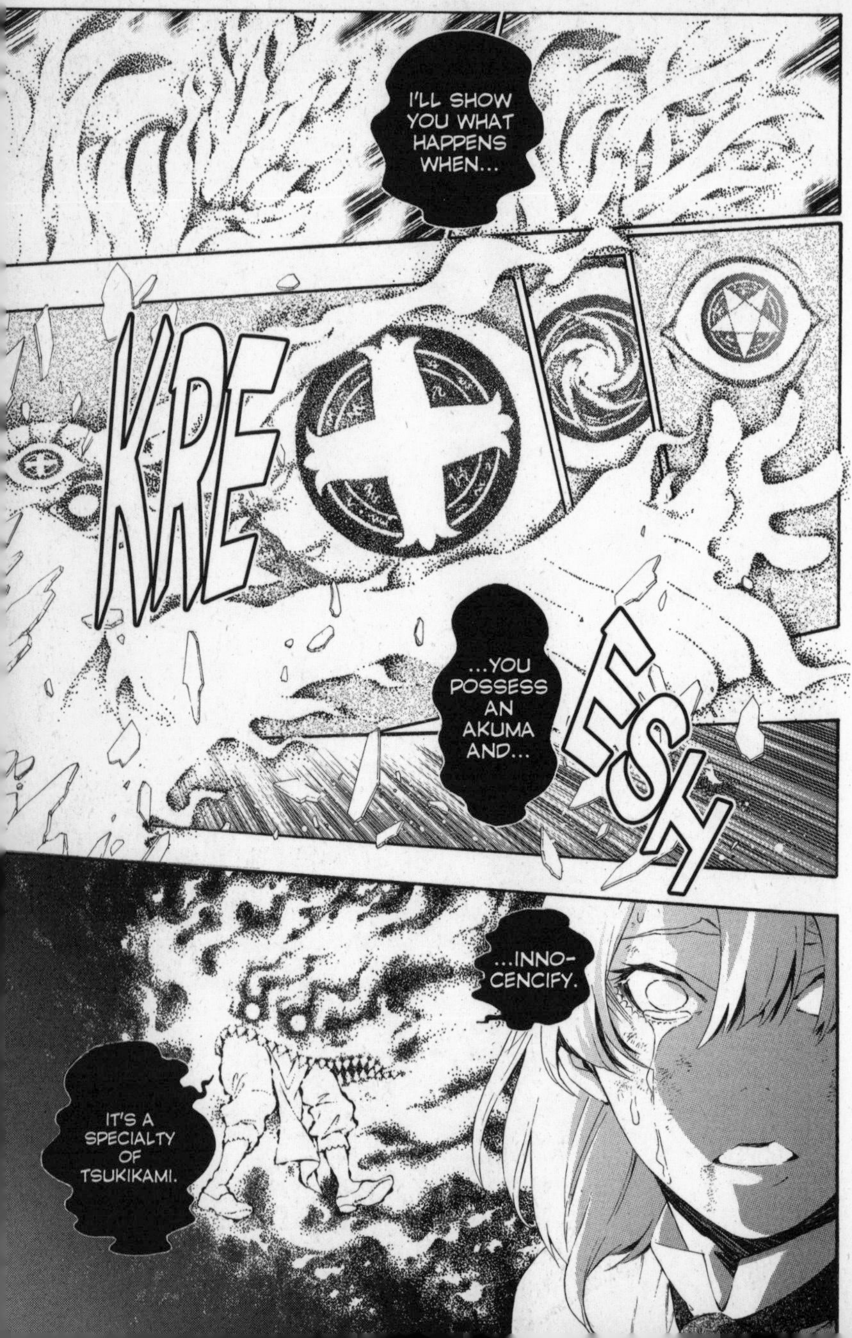
I'LL SHOW YOU WHAT HAPPENS WHEN...
KREESH
...YOU POSSESS AN AKUMA AND...
...INNO-CENCIFY.
IT'S A SPECIALTY OF TSUKIKAMI.

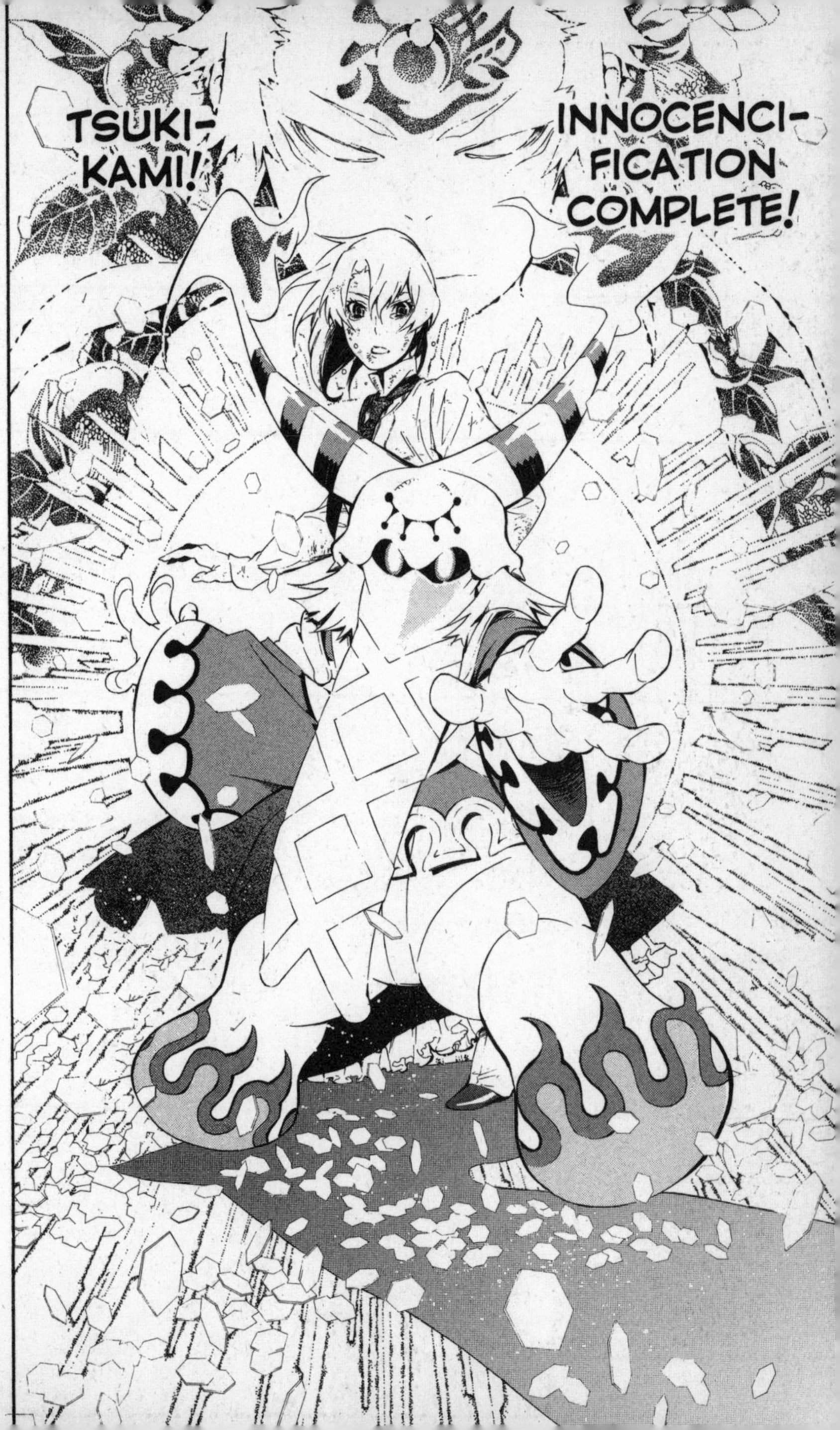
INNOCENCI-FICATION COMPLETE!
TSUKI-KAMI!

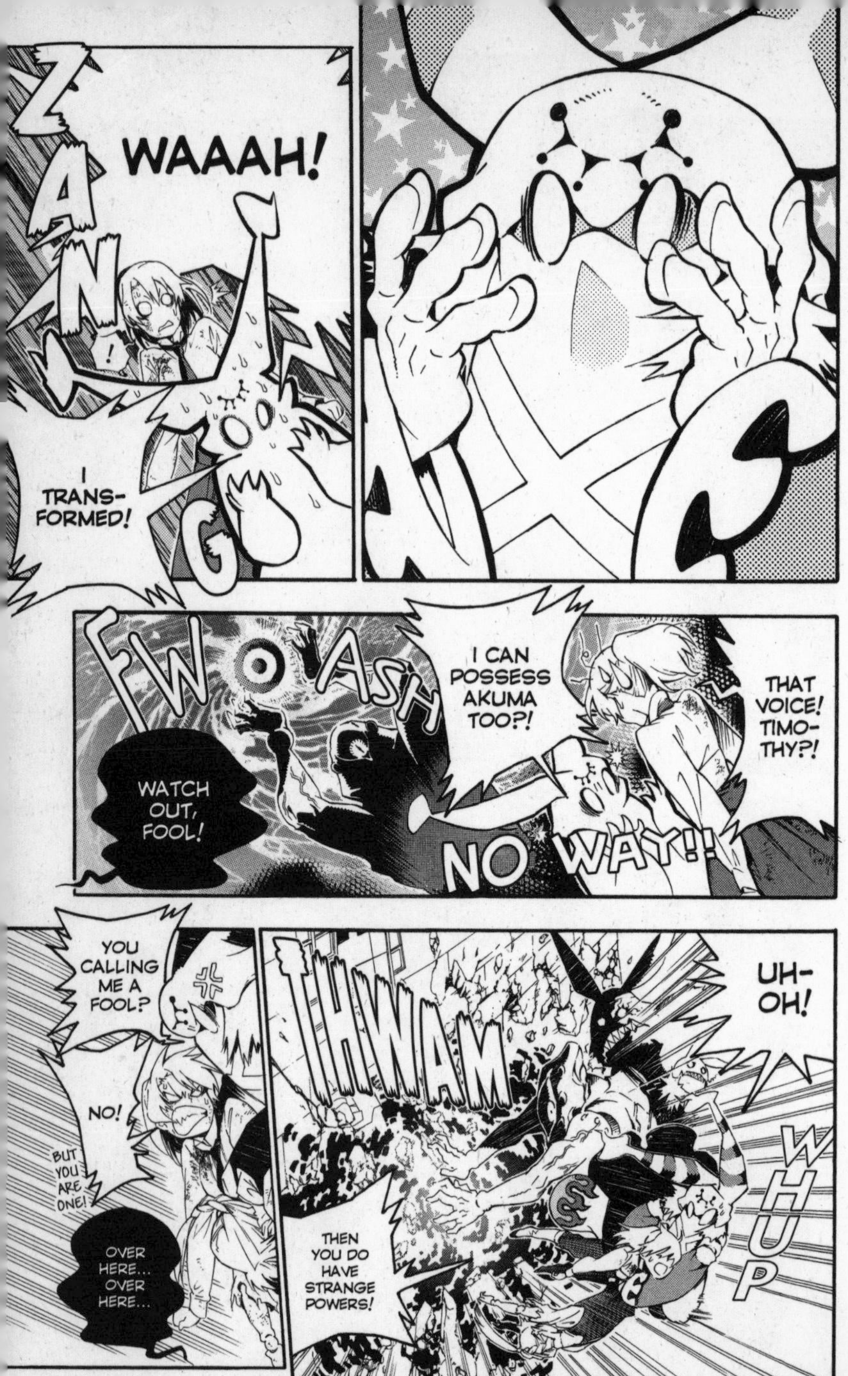
ZANG
WAAAH!
I TRANSFORMED!
THAT VOICE! TIMOTHY?!
I CAN POSSESS AKUMA TOO?!
NO WAY!!
FWOASH
WATCH OUT, FOOL!
UH-OH!
WHUP
THWAM
THEN YOU DO HAVE STRANGE POWERS!
YOU CALLING ME A FOOL?
NO!
BUT YOU ARE ONE!
OVER HERE... OVER HERE...

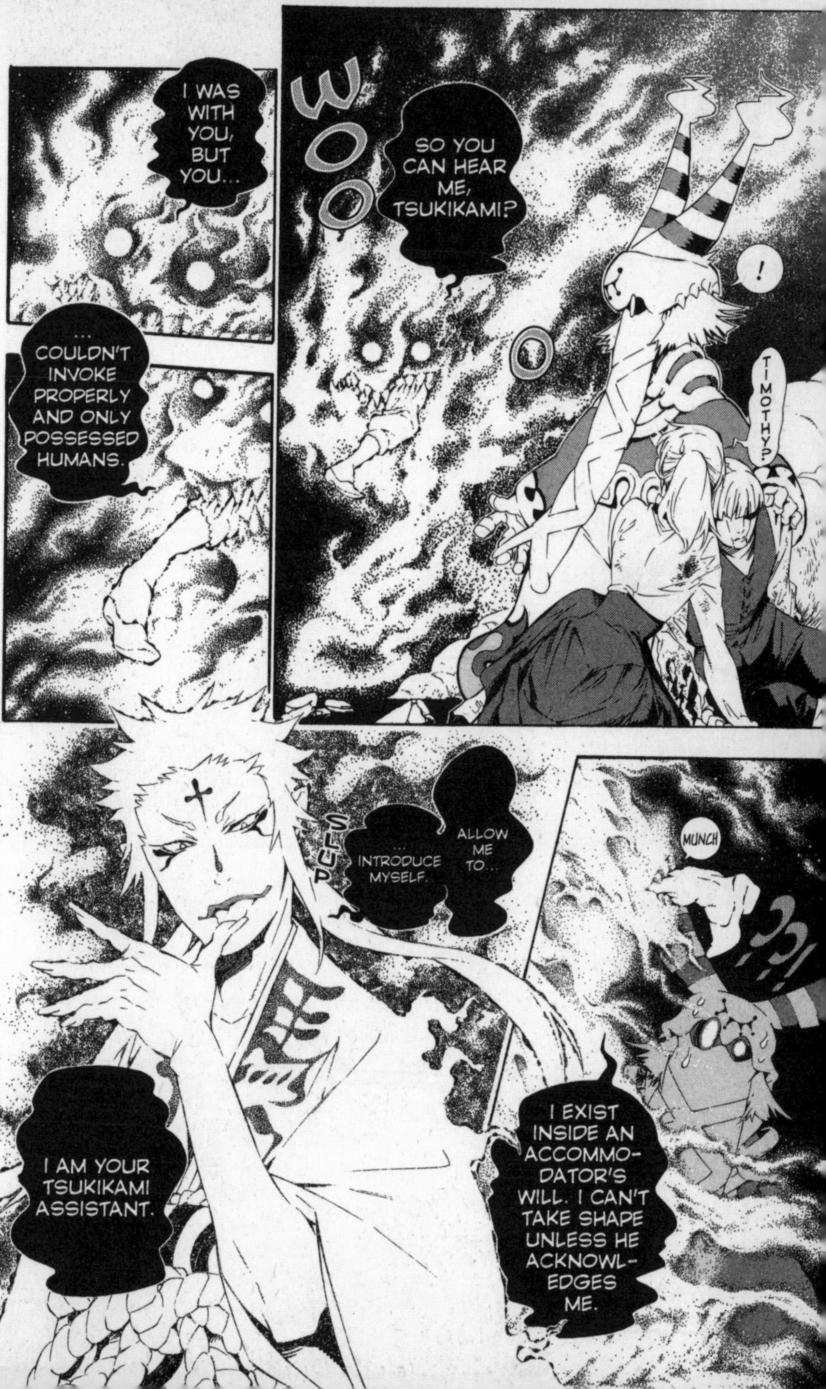
WOO
SO YOU CAN HEAR ME, TSUKIKAMI?
O
!
TIMOTHY?
I WAS WITH YOU, BUT YOU...
... COULDN'T INVOKE PROPERLY AND ONLY POSSESSED HUMANS.
MUNCH
SLUP
ALLOW ME TO...
... INTRODUCE MYSELF.
I AM YOUR TSUKIKAMI ASSISTANT.
I EXIST INSIDE AN ACCOMMO-DATOR'S WILL. I CAN'T TAKE SHAPE UNLESS HE ACKNOWL-EDGES ME.

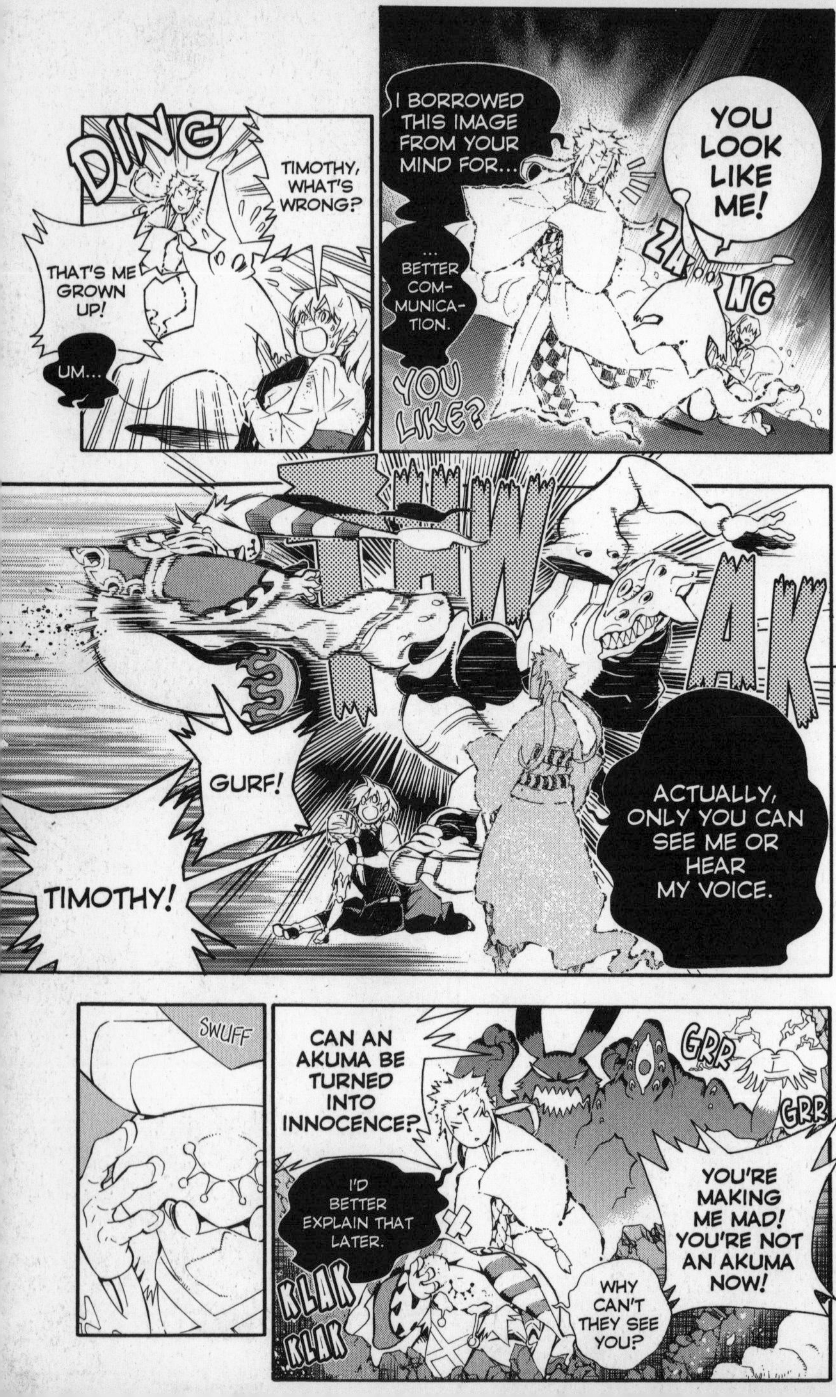
YOU LOOK LIKE ME!
I BORROWED THIS IMAGE FROM YOUR MIND FOR...
... BETTER COM-MUNICA-TION.
ZA...NG
YOU LIKE?
DING
TIMOTHY, WHAT'S WRONG?
THAT'S ME GROWN UP!
UM...
THWAK
ACTUALLY, ONLY YOU CAN SEE ME OR HEAR MY VOICE.
GURF!
TIMOTHY!
GRR
GRR
CAN AN AKUMA BE TURNED INTO INNOCENCE?
YOU'RE MAKING ME MAD! YOU'RE NOT AN AKUMA NOW!
I'D BETTER EXPLAIN THAT LATER.
WHY CAN'T THEY SEE YOU?
KLAK KLAK
SWUFF

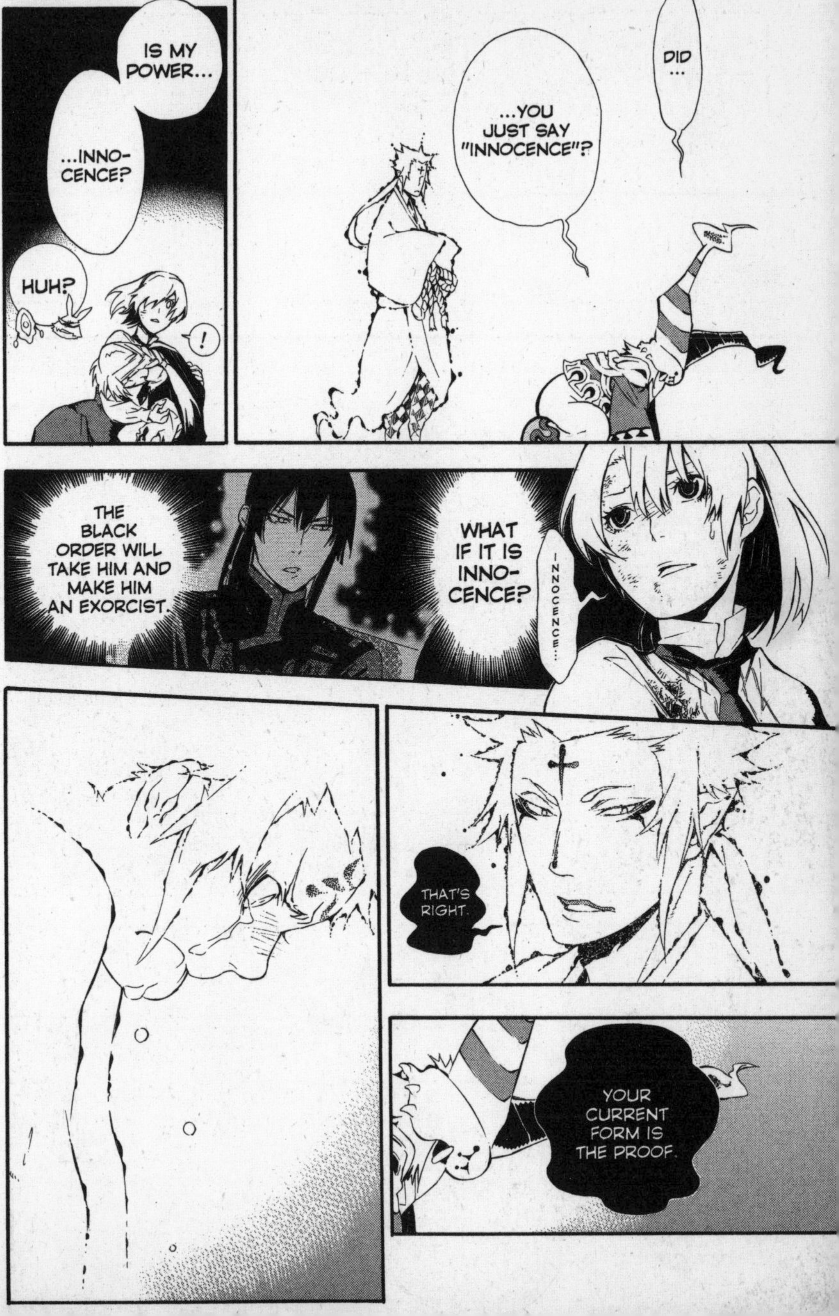
DID...
...YOU JUST SAY "INNOCENCE"?
IS MY POWER...
...INNO-CENCE?
HUH?
!
INNOCENCE...
WHAT IF IT IS INNO-CENCE?
THE BLACK ORDER WILL TAKE HIM AND MAKE HIM AN EXORCIST.
THAT'S RIGHT.
YOUR CURRENT FORM IS THE PROOF.

READ THIS WAY

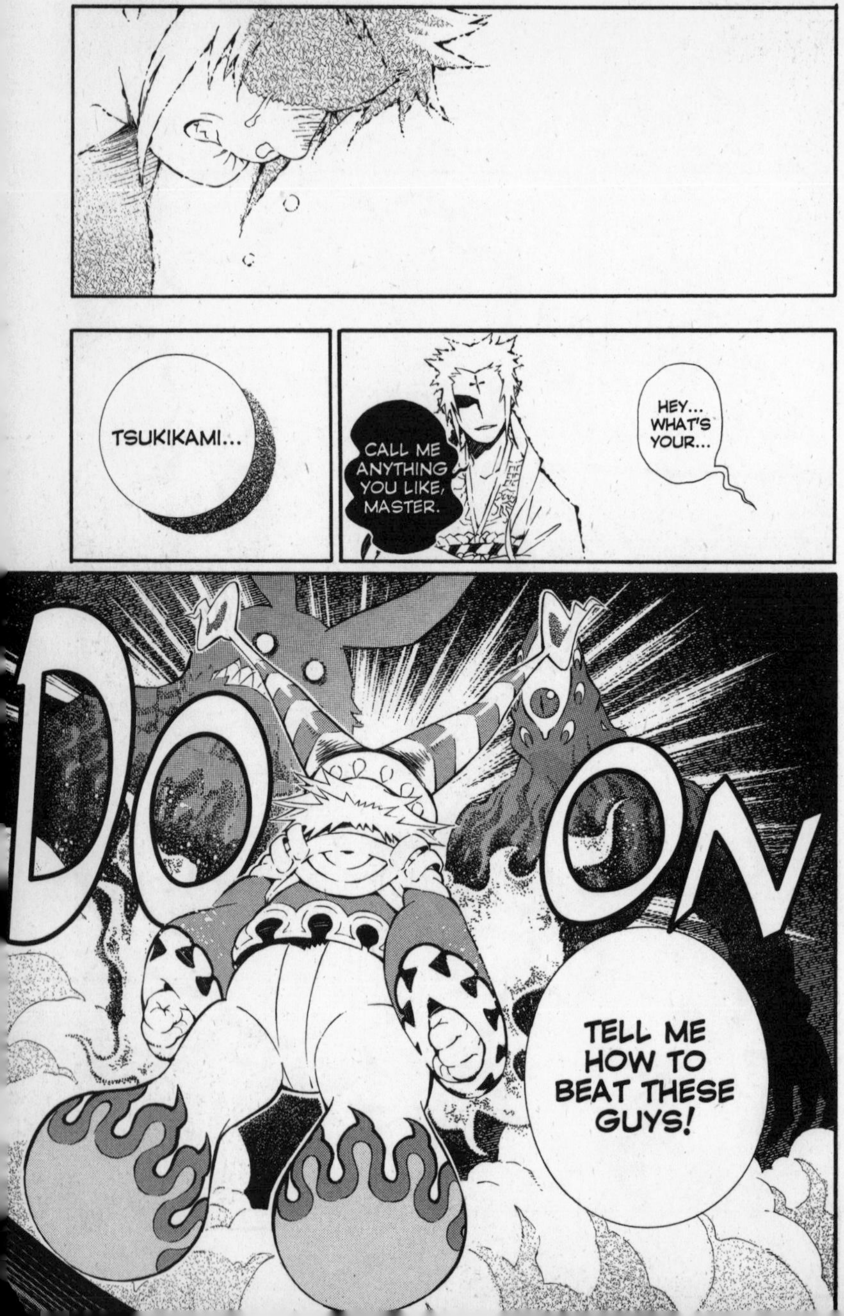
HEY... WHAT'S YOUR...
CALL ME ANYTHING YOU LIKE, MASTER.
TSUKIKAMI...
DOON
TELL ME HOW TO BEAT THESE GUYS!

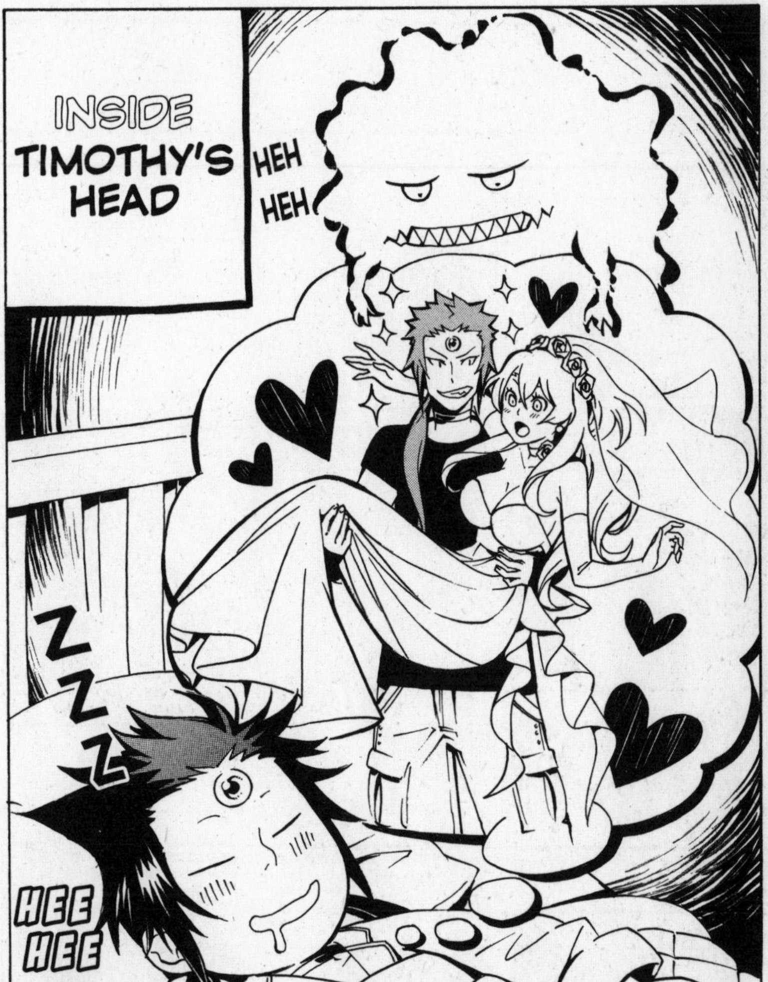
INSIDE TIMOTHY'S HEAD
HEH HEH
Z Z Z
HEE HEE

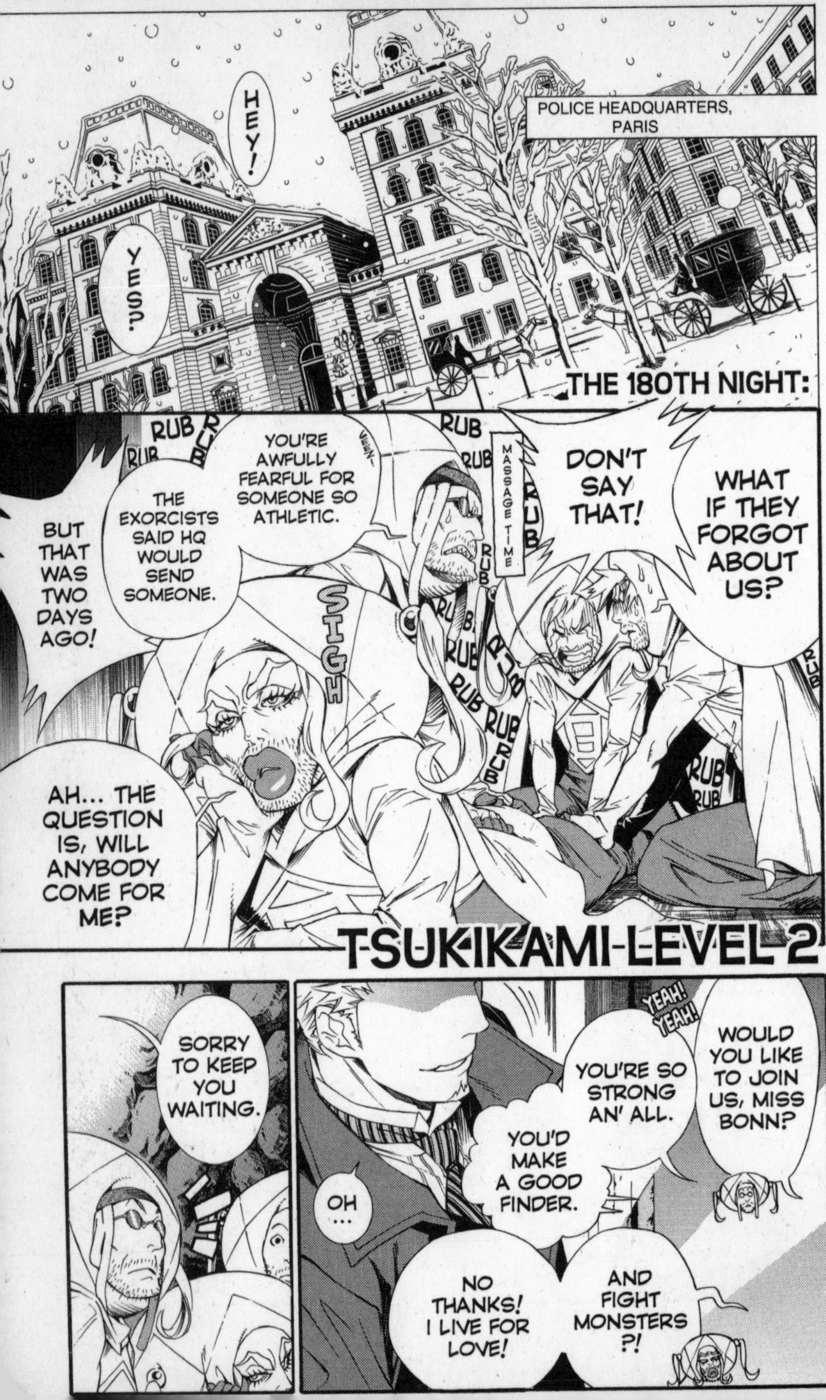
POLICE HEADQUARTERS, PARIS
HEY!
YES?
THE 180TH NIGHT:
TSUKIKAMI-LEVEL 2
WHAT IF THEY FORGOT ABOUT US?
DON'T SAY THAT!
MASSAGE TIME
RUB RUB
YOU'RE AWFULLY FEARFUL FOR SOMEONE SO ATHLETIC.
THE EXORCISTS SAID HQ WOULD SEND SOMEONE.
BUT THAT WAS TWO DAYS AGO!
SIGH
AH... THE QUESTION IS, WILL ANYBODY COME FOR ME?
YEAH! YEAH!
WOULD YOU LIKE TO JOIN US, MISS BONN?
YOU'RE SO STRONG AN' ALL.
YOU'D MAKE A GOOD FINDER.
OH ...
AND FIGHT MONSTERS?!
NO THANKS! I LIVE FOR LOVE!
SORRY TO KEEP YOU WAITING.

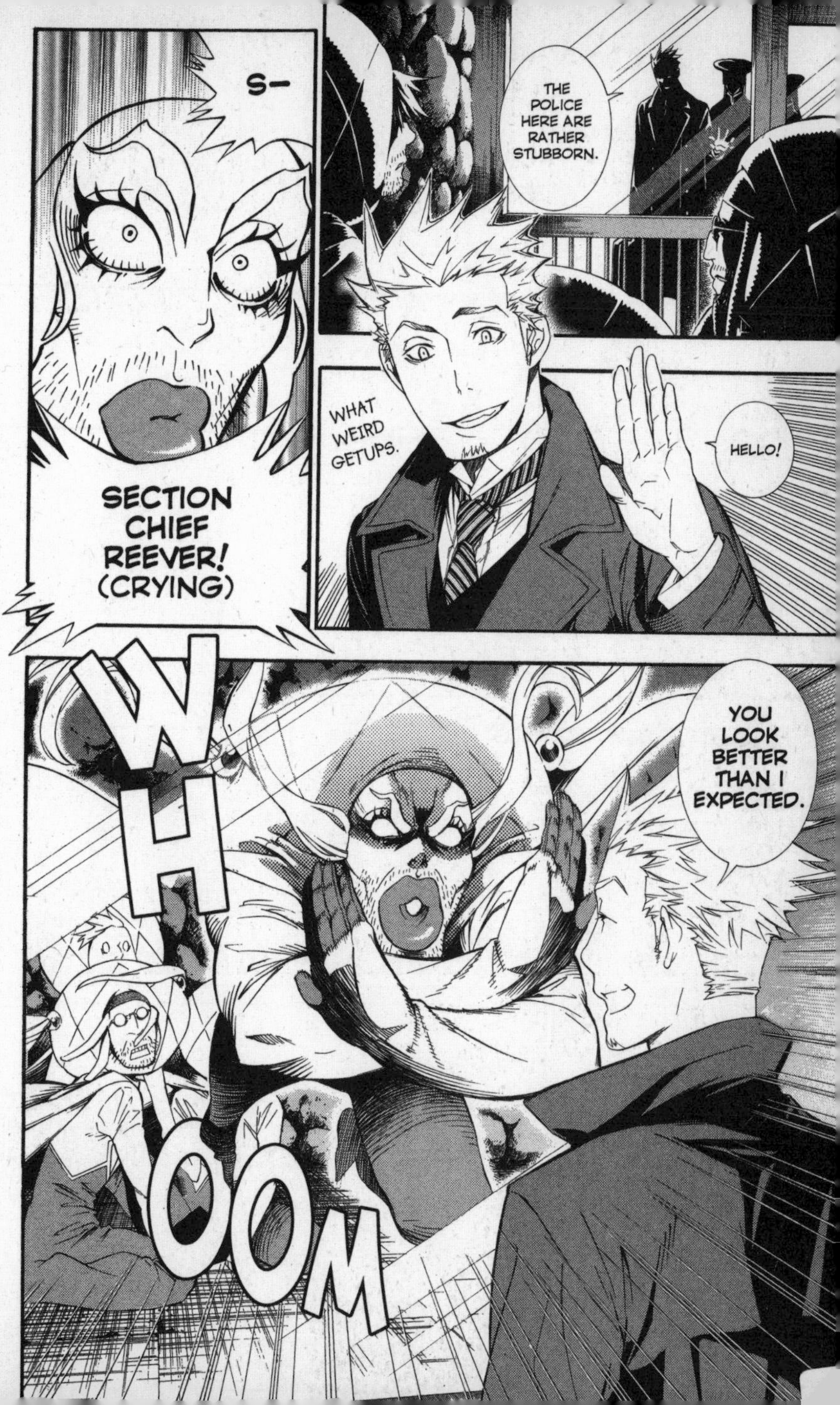
THE POLICE HERE ARE RATHER STUBBORN.
HELLO!
WHAT WEIRD GETUPS.
S–
SECTION CHIEF REEVER! (CRYING)
YOU LOOK BETTER THAN I EXPECTED.
WHOOM

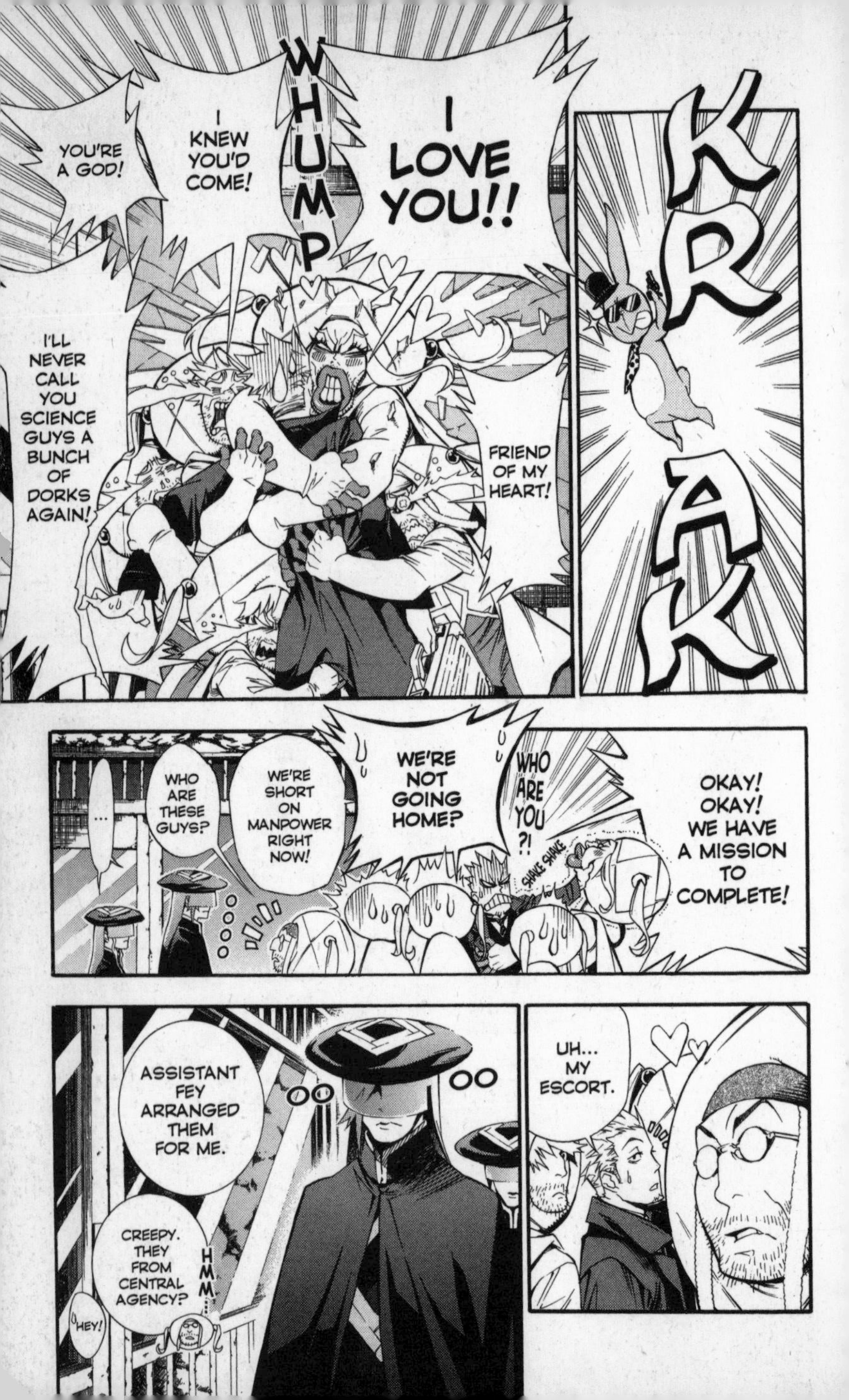
KRAK
I LOVE YOU!!
WHUMP
I KNEW YOU'D COME!
YOU'RE A GOD!
FRIEND OF MY HEART!
I'LL NEVER CALL YOU SCIENCE GUYS A BUNCH OF DORKS AGAIN!
OKAY! OKAY! WE HAVE A MISSION TO COMPLETE!
WHO ARE YOU?!
SHAKE SHAKE
WE'RE NOT GOING HOME?
WE'RE SHORT ON MANPOWER RIGHT NOW!
WHO ARE THESE GUYS?
...
UH... MY ESCORT.
ASSISTANT FEY ARRANGED THEM FOR ME.
HMM...
CREEPY. THEY FROM CENTRAL AGENCY?
HEY!

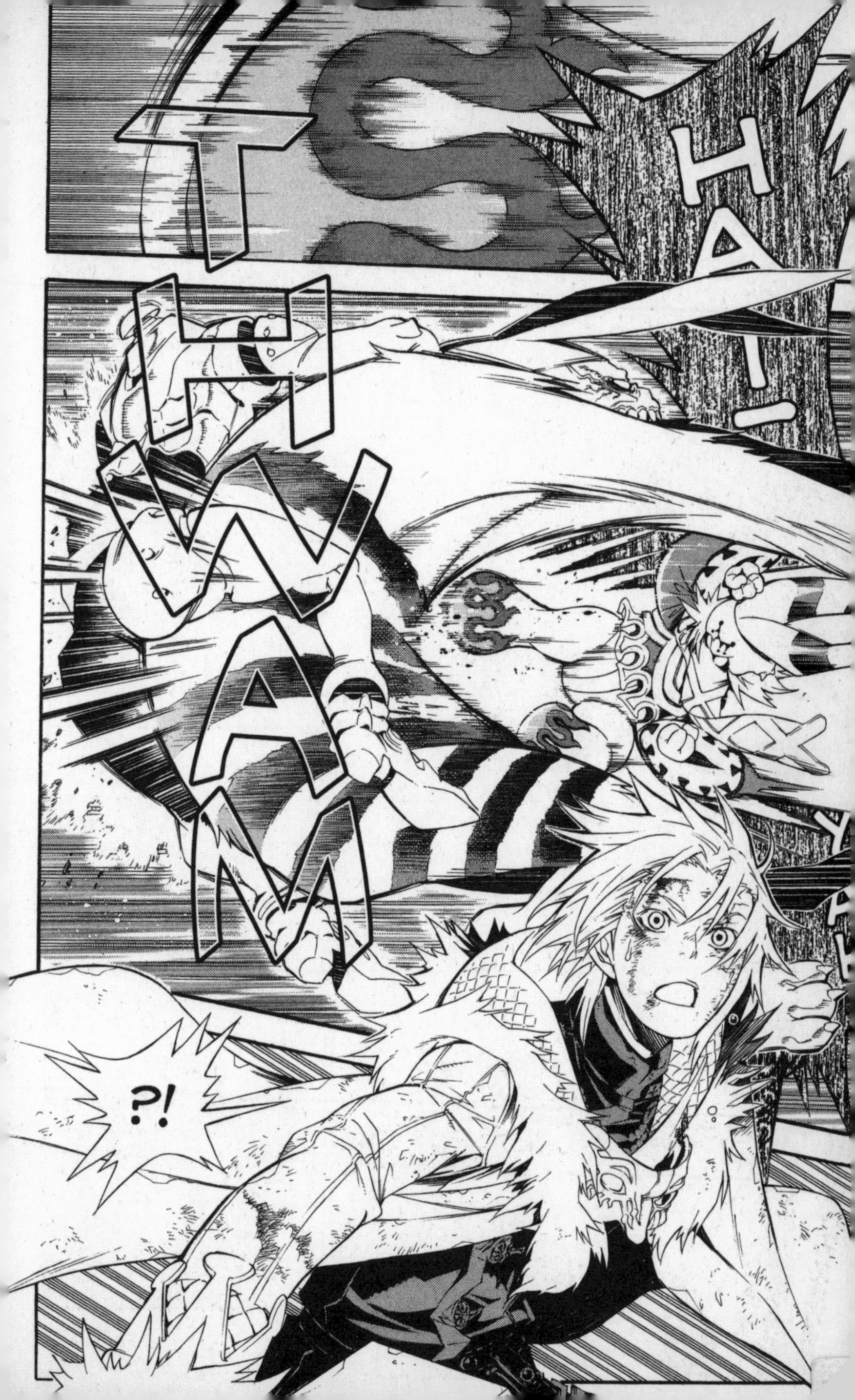
HAI-
THWAM
?!

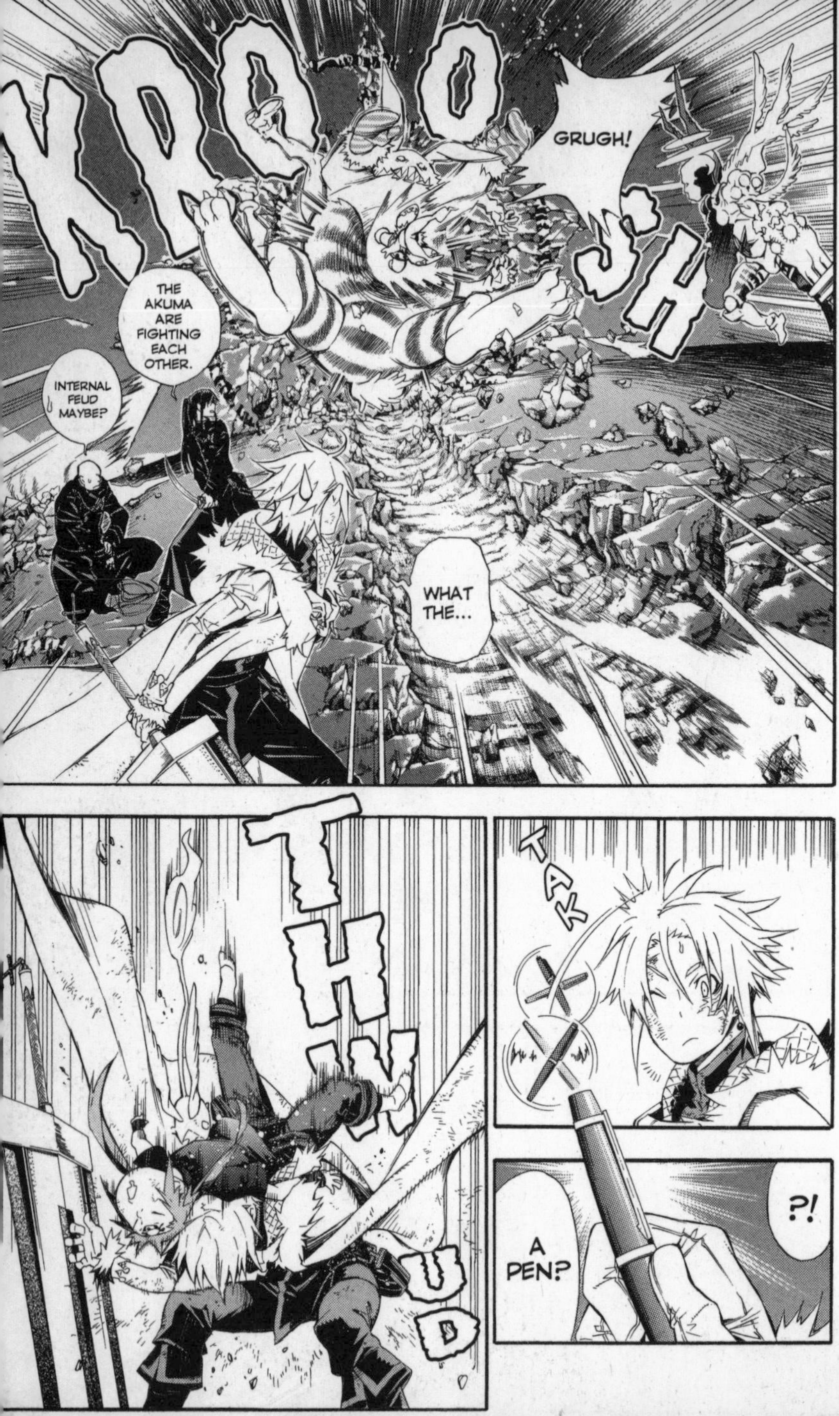
GRUGH!
KROOOSH
THE AKUMA ARE FIGHTING EACH OTHER.
INTERNAL FEUD MAYBE?
WHAT THE...
TAK
?!
A PEN?
THWUD

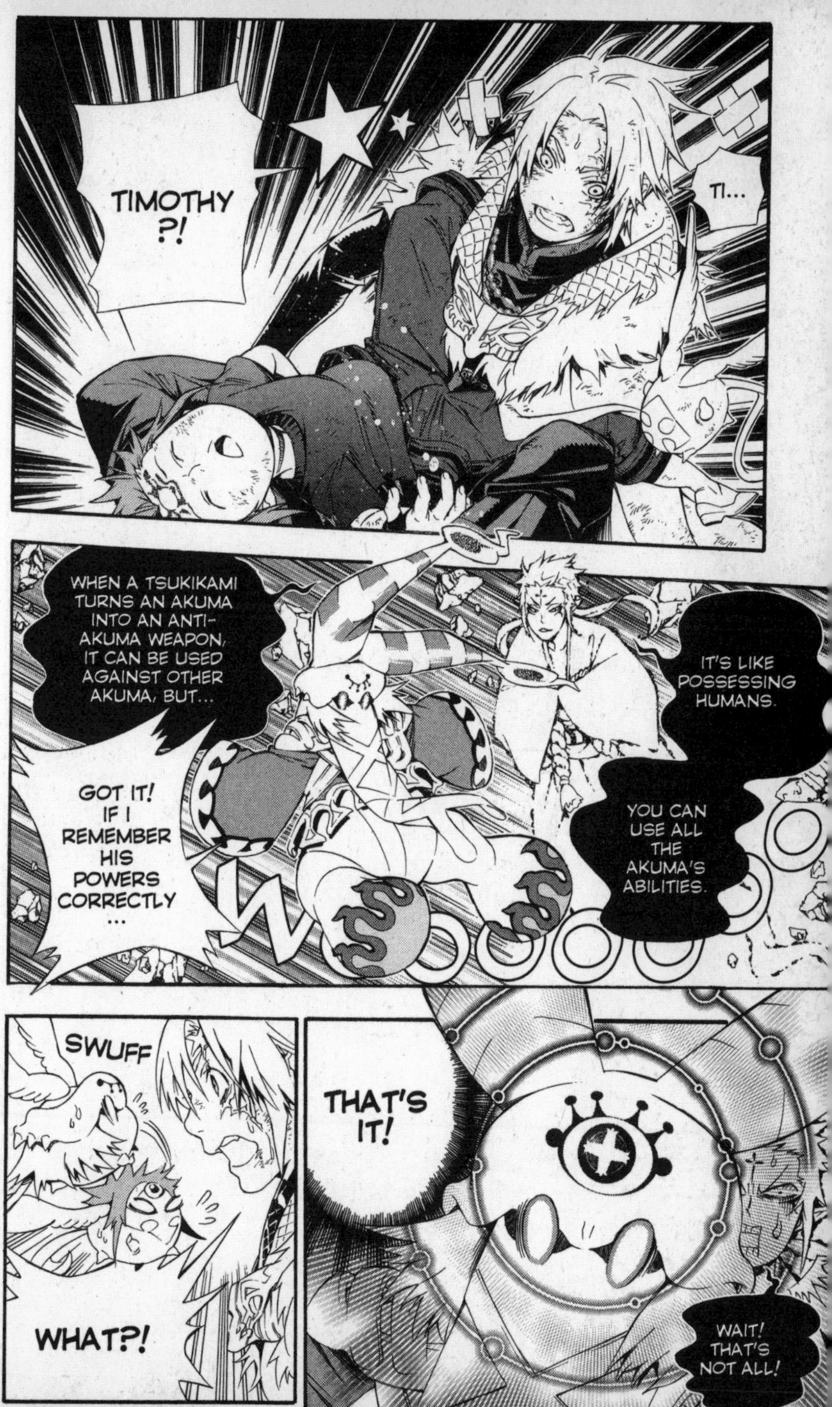
TI...
TIMOTHY ?!
WHEN A TSUKIKAMI TURNS AN AKUMA INTO AN ANTI-AKUMA WEAPON, IT CAN BE USED AGAINST OTHER AKUMA, BUT...
IT'S LIKE POSSESSING HUMANS.
YOU CAN USE ALL THE AKUMA'S ABILITIES.
GOT IT! IF I REMEMBER HIS POWERS CORRECTLY...
THAT'S IT!
WAIT! THAT'S NOT ALL!
SWUFF
WHAT?!

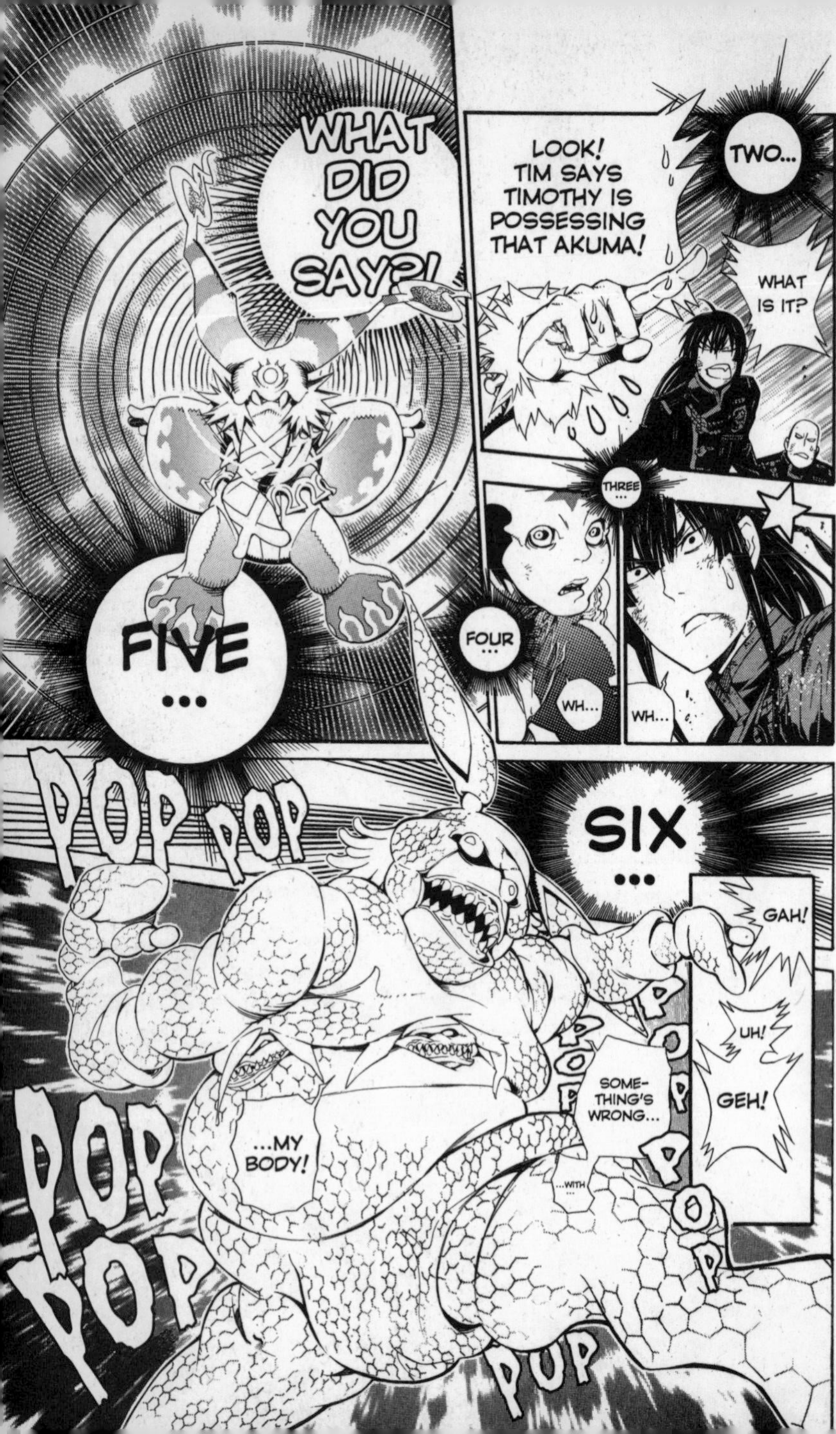
TWO...
LOOK! TIM SAYS TIMOTHY IS POSSESSING THAT AKUMA!
WHAT IS IT?
THREE...
WH...
FOUR...
WH...
WHAT DID YOU SAY?!
FIVE...
SIX...
GAH!
UH!
GEH!
POP POP POP POP
SOME-THING'S WRONG...
...WITH...
...MY BODY!
POP POP
POP POP
PUP

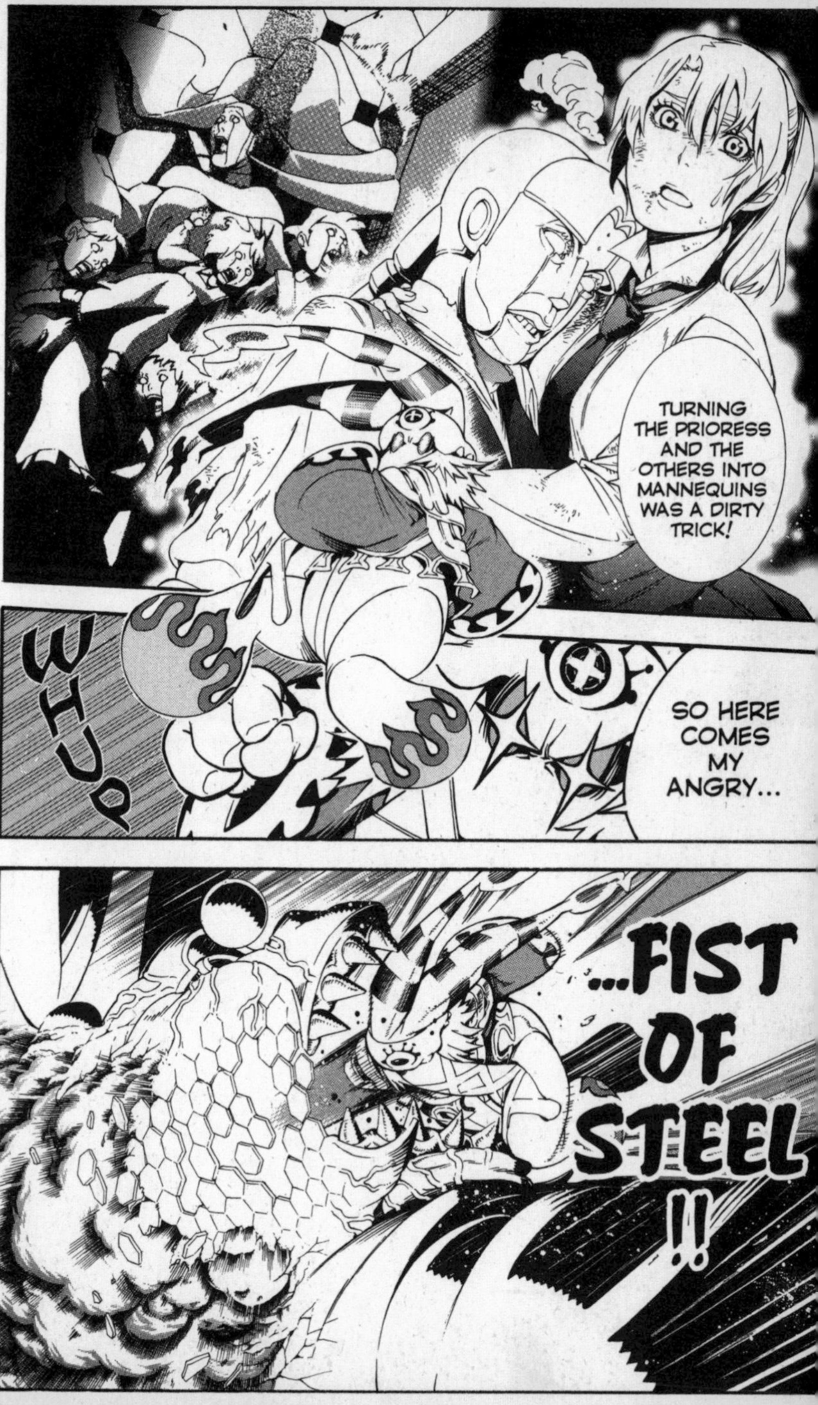
TURNING THE PRIORESS AND THE OTHERS INTO MANNEQUINS WAS A DIRTY TRICK!
SO HERE COMES MY ANGRY...
WHUP
...FIST OF STEEL!!

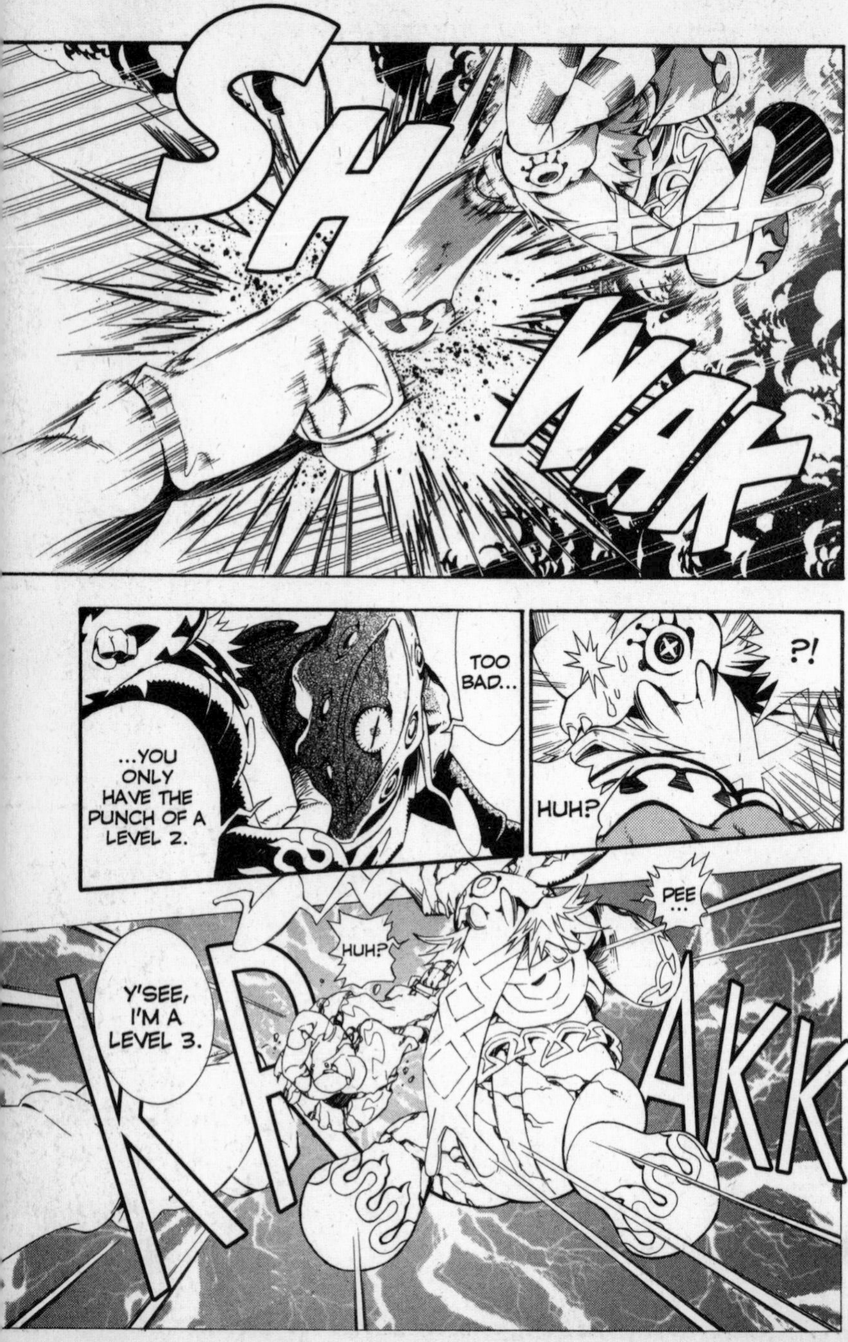
SHWAK
?!
HUH?
TOO BAD...
...YOU ONLY HAVE THE PUNCH OF A LEVEL 2.
PEE ...
HUH?
Y'SEE, I'M A LEVEL 3.
KRAKK

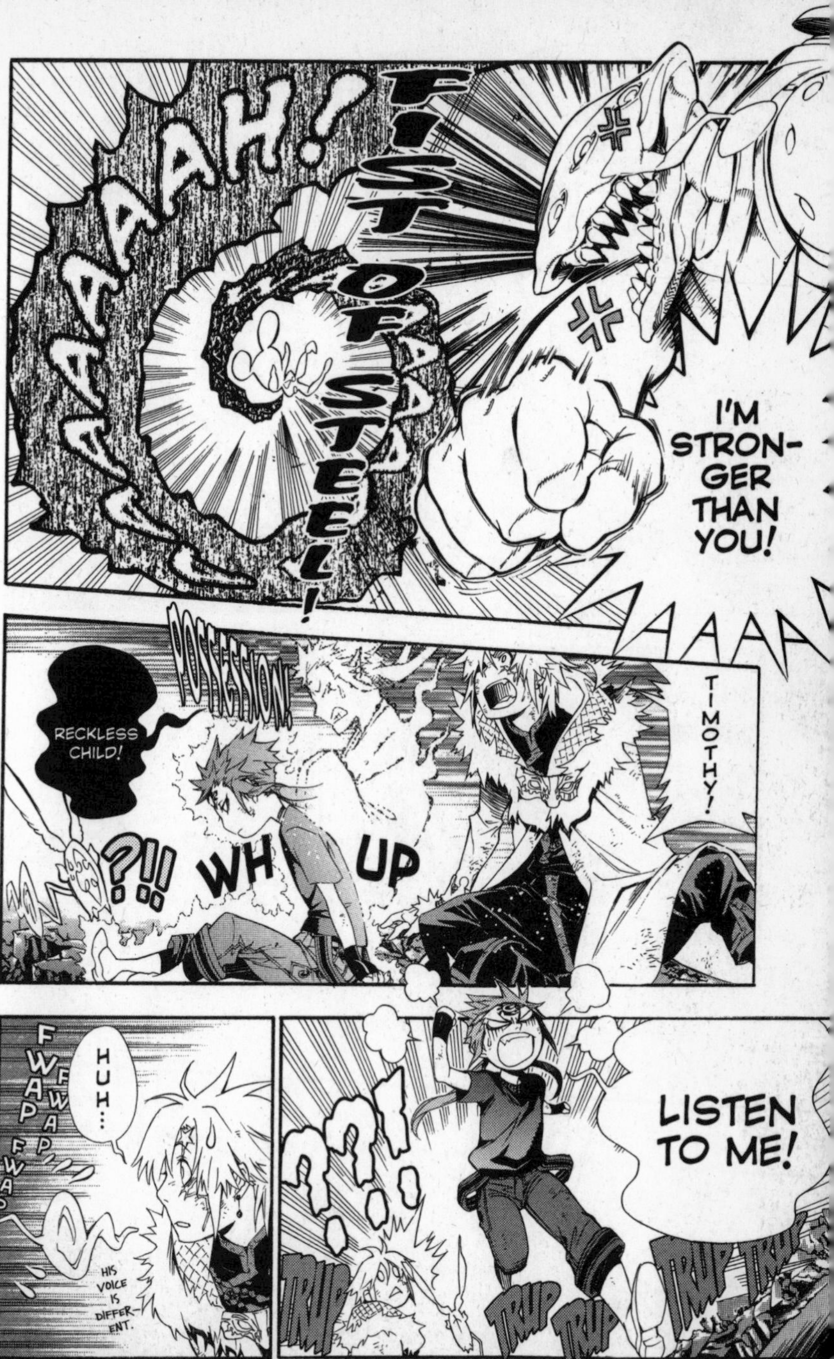
I'M STRONGER THAN YOU!
FIST OF STEEL!
AAAAH!
AAAA
TIMOTHY!
POSSESSION!!
RECKLESS CHILD!
WHUP
?!!
LISTEN TO ME!
?!
TRUP TRUP TRUP TRUP TRUP
HUH...
HIS VOICE IS DIFFERENT.
FWAP FWAP FWAP FWAP

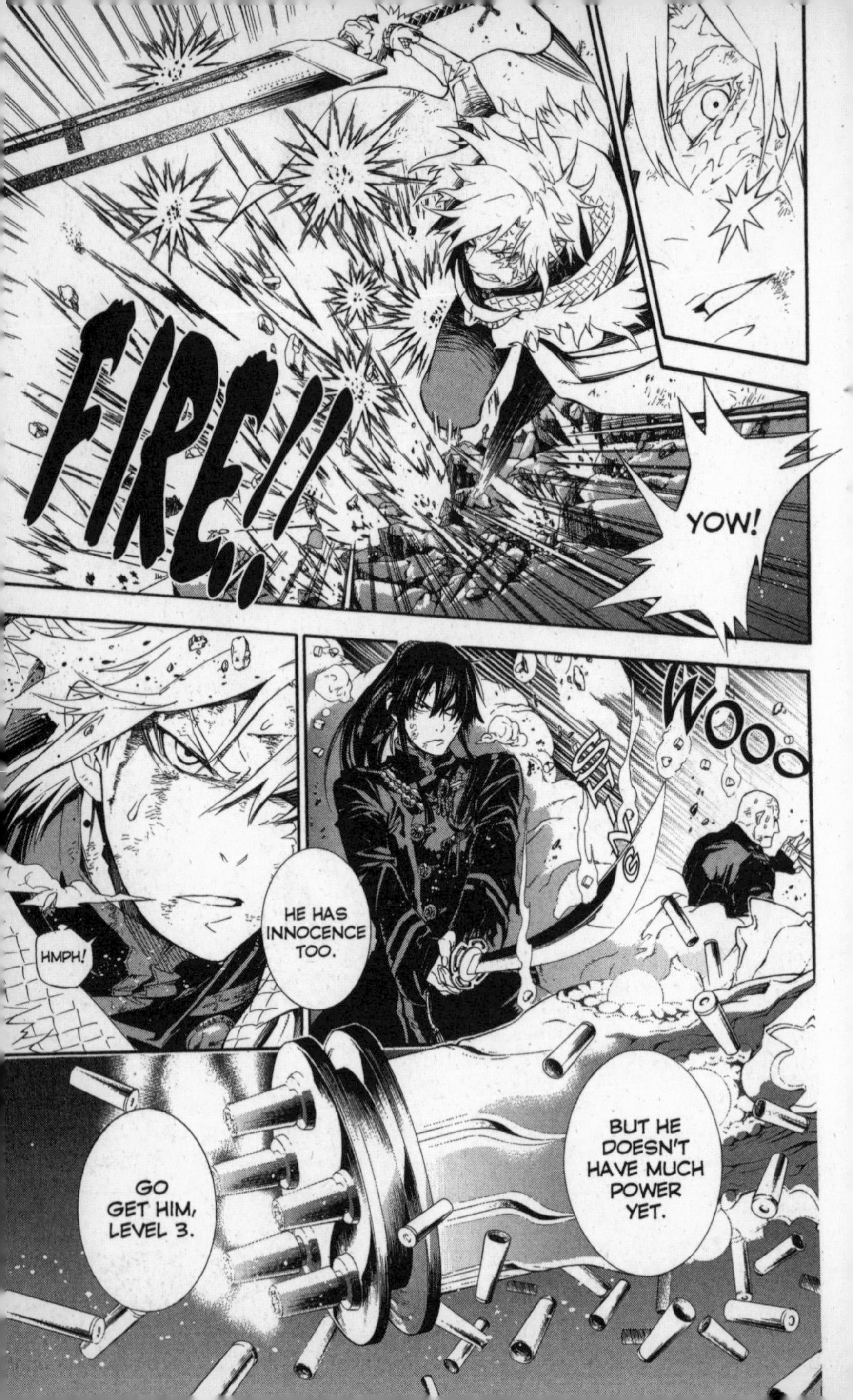
FIRE!!
YOW!
WOOO
HE HAS INNOCENCE TOO.
HMPH!
BUT HE DOESN'T HAVE MUCH POWER YET.
GO GET HIM, LEVEL 3.

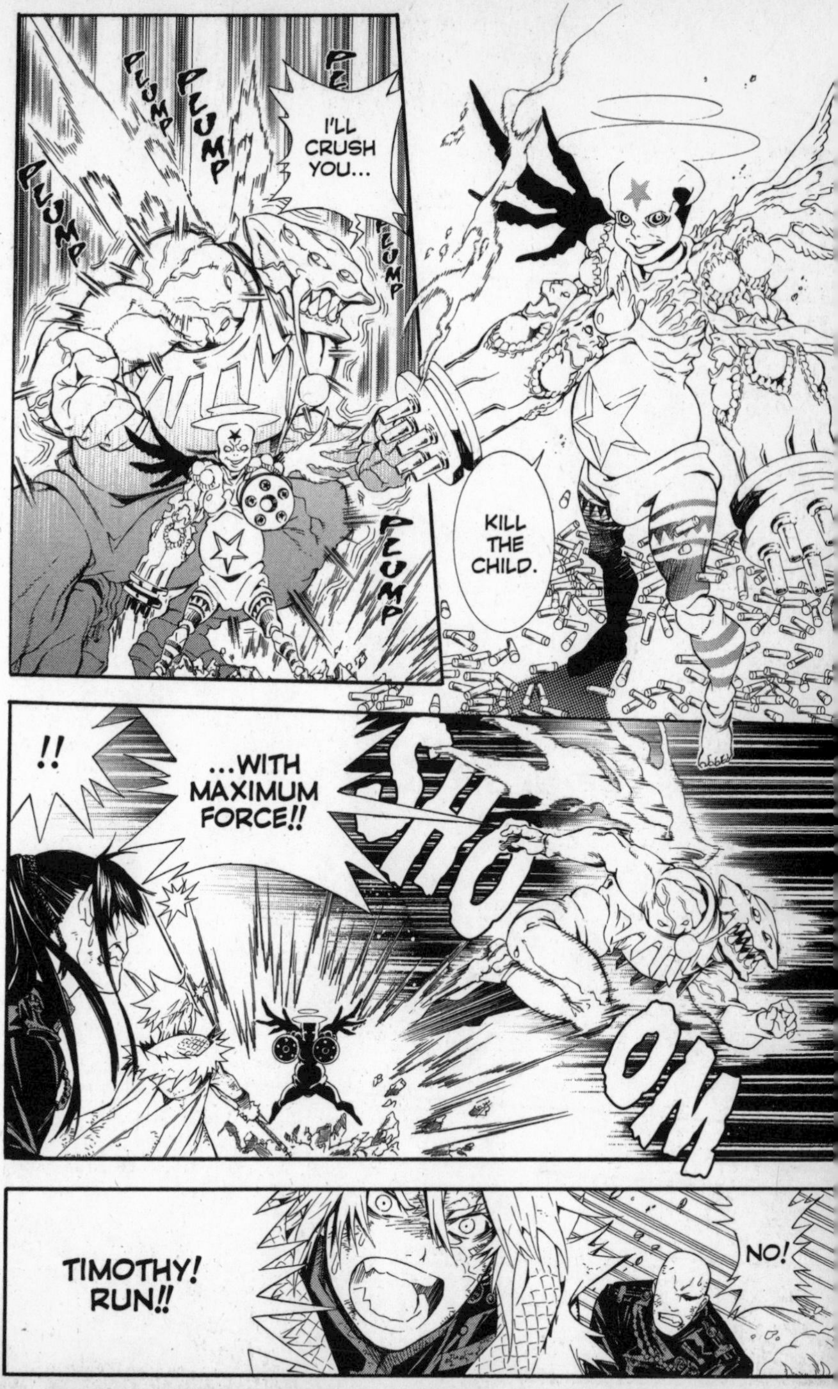
KILL THE CHILD.
PLUMP
PLUMP
I'LL CRUSH YOU...
PLUMP
PLUMP
PLUMP
PLUMP
...WITH MAXIMUM FORCE!!
SHOOOM
!!
NO!
TIMOTHY! RUN!!

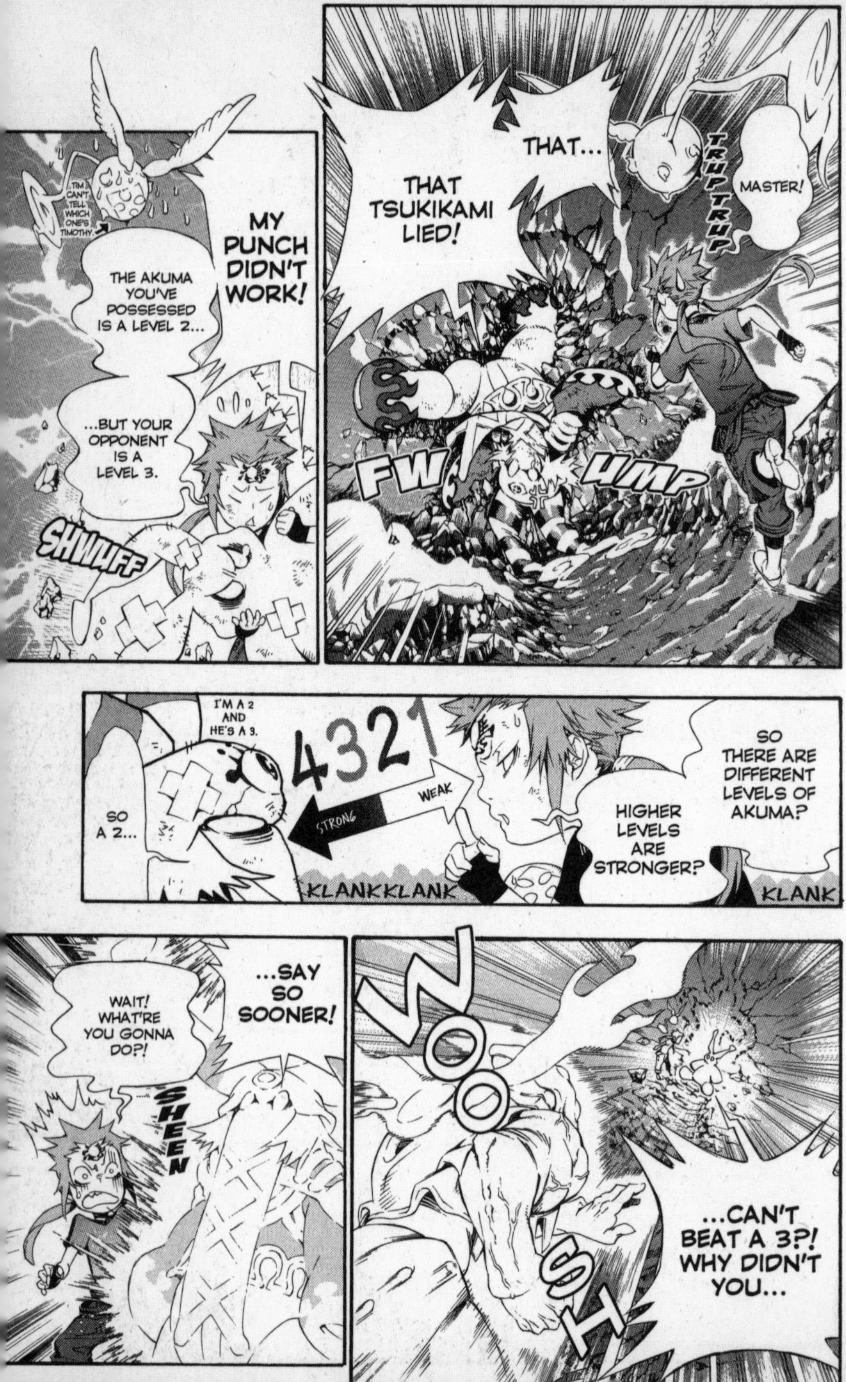
MASTER!
TRUP TRUP
THAT...
THAT TSUKIKAMI LIED!
FW UMP
MY PUNCH DIDN'T WORK!
THE AKUMA YOU'VE POSSESSED IS A LEVEL 2...
...BUT YOUR OPPONENT IS A LEVEL 3.
TIM CAN'T TELL WHICH ONE'S TIMOTHY.
SHWUFF
SO THERE ARE DIFFERENT LEVELS OF AKUMA?
KLANK
HIGHER LEVELS ARE STRONGER?
4321
WEAK
STRONG
I'M A 2 AND HE'S A 3.
SO A 2...
KLANKKLANK
WOOOSH
...CAN'T BEAT A 3?! WHY DIDN'T YOU...
...SAY SO SOONER!
WAIT! WHAT'RE YOU GONNA DO?!
SHEEN

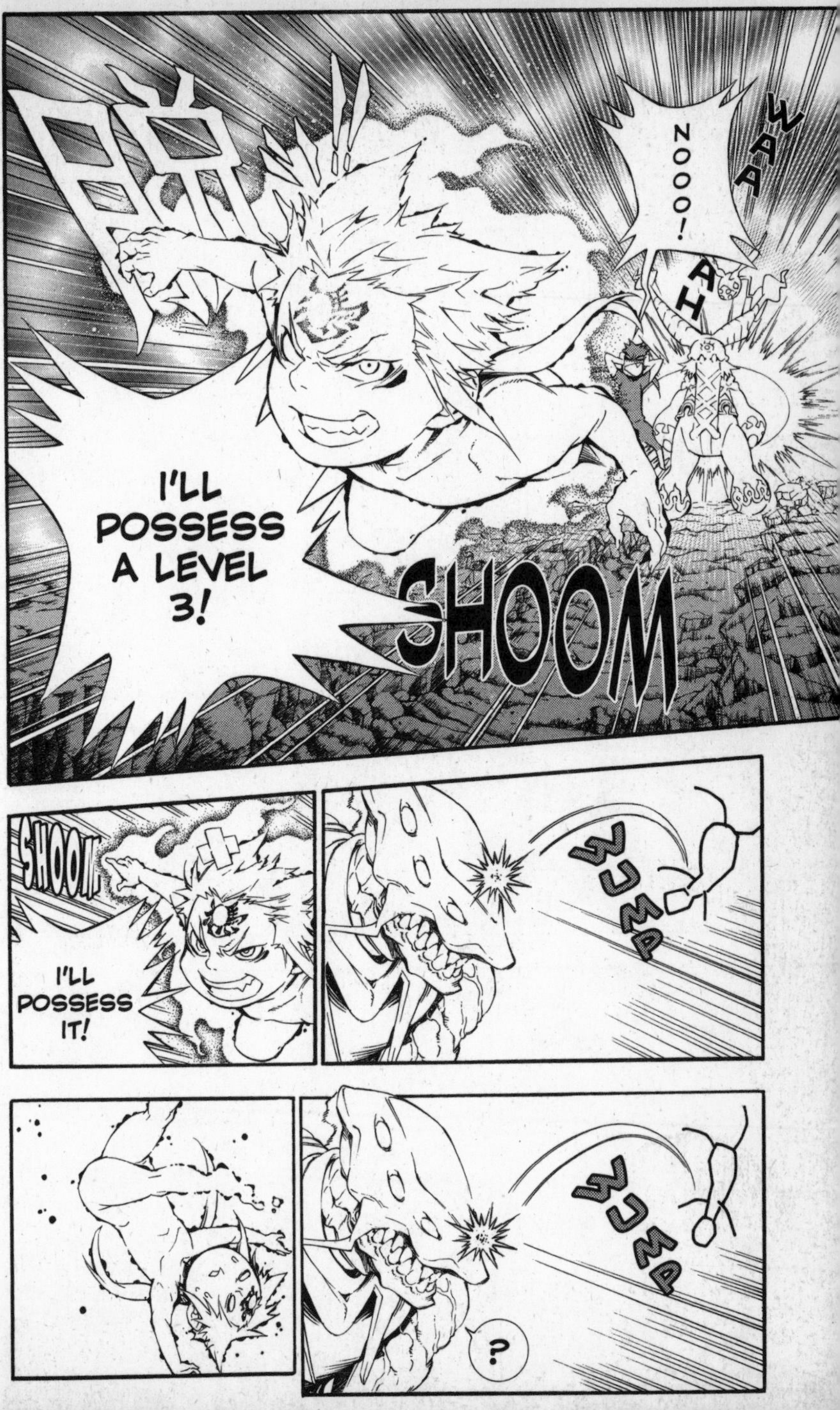
WAAA
NOOO!
AH
I'LL POSSESS A LEVEL 3!
SHOOM
WUMP
SHOOM
I'LL POSSESS IT!
WUMP
?

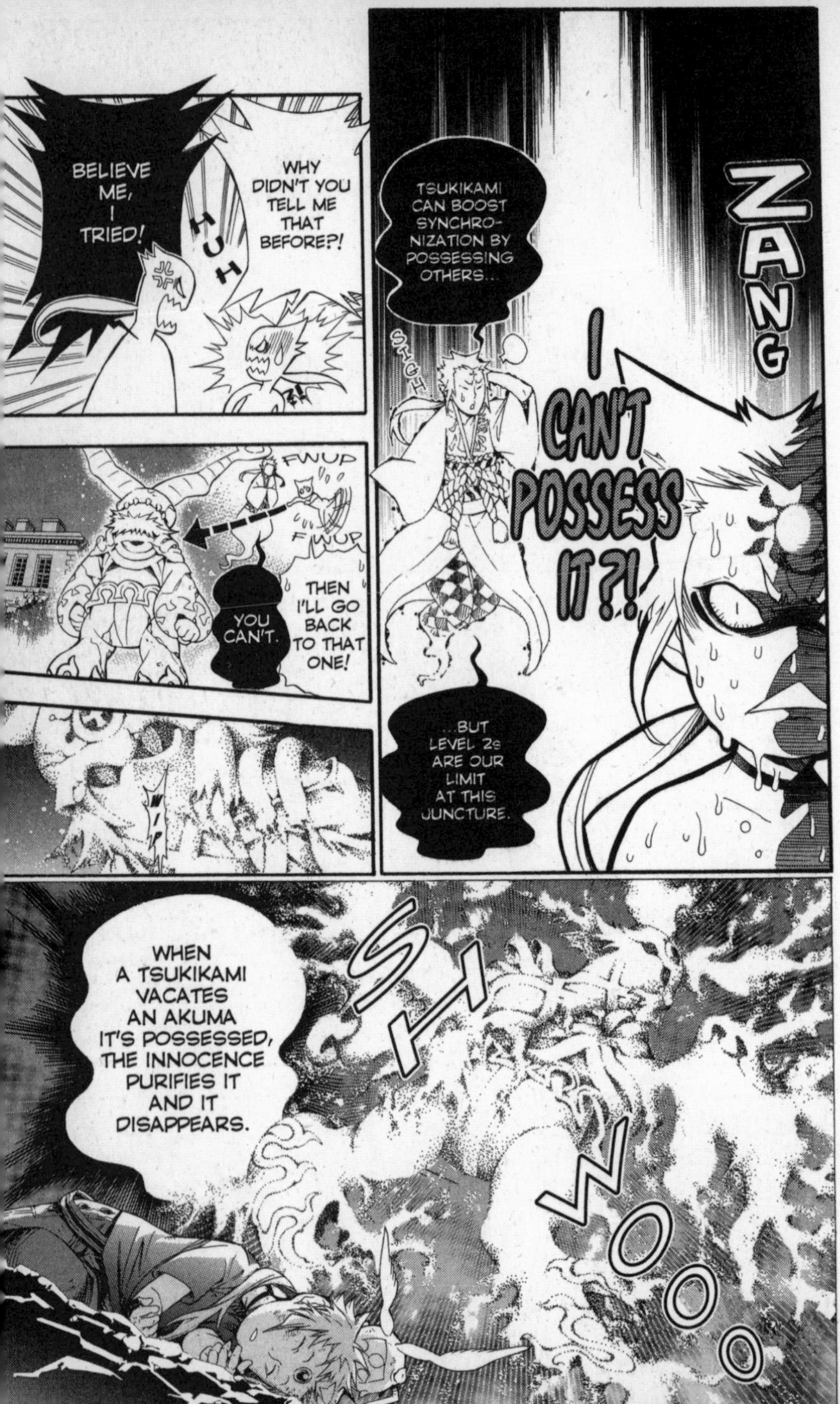
ZANG
I CAN'T POSSESS IT?!
TSUKIKAMI CAN BOOST SYNCHRO-NIZATION BY POSSESSING OTHERS...
SIGH
...BUT LEVEL 2s ARE OUR LIMIT AT THIS JUNCTURE.
WHY DIDN'T YOU TELL ME THAT BEFORE?!
HUH
BELIEVE ME, I TRIED!
?!
FWUP
FWUP
THEN I'LL GO BACK TO THAT ONE!
YOU CAN'T.
WIP
SHH
WOOOO
WHEN A TSUKIKAMI VACATES AN AKUMA IT'S POSSESSED, THE INNOCENCE PURIFIES IT AND IT DISAPPEARS.

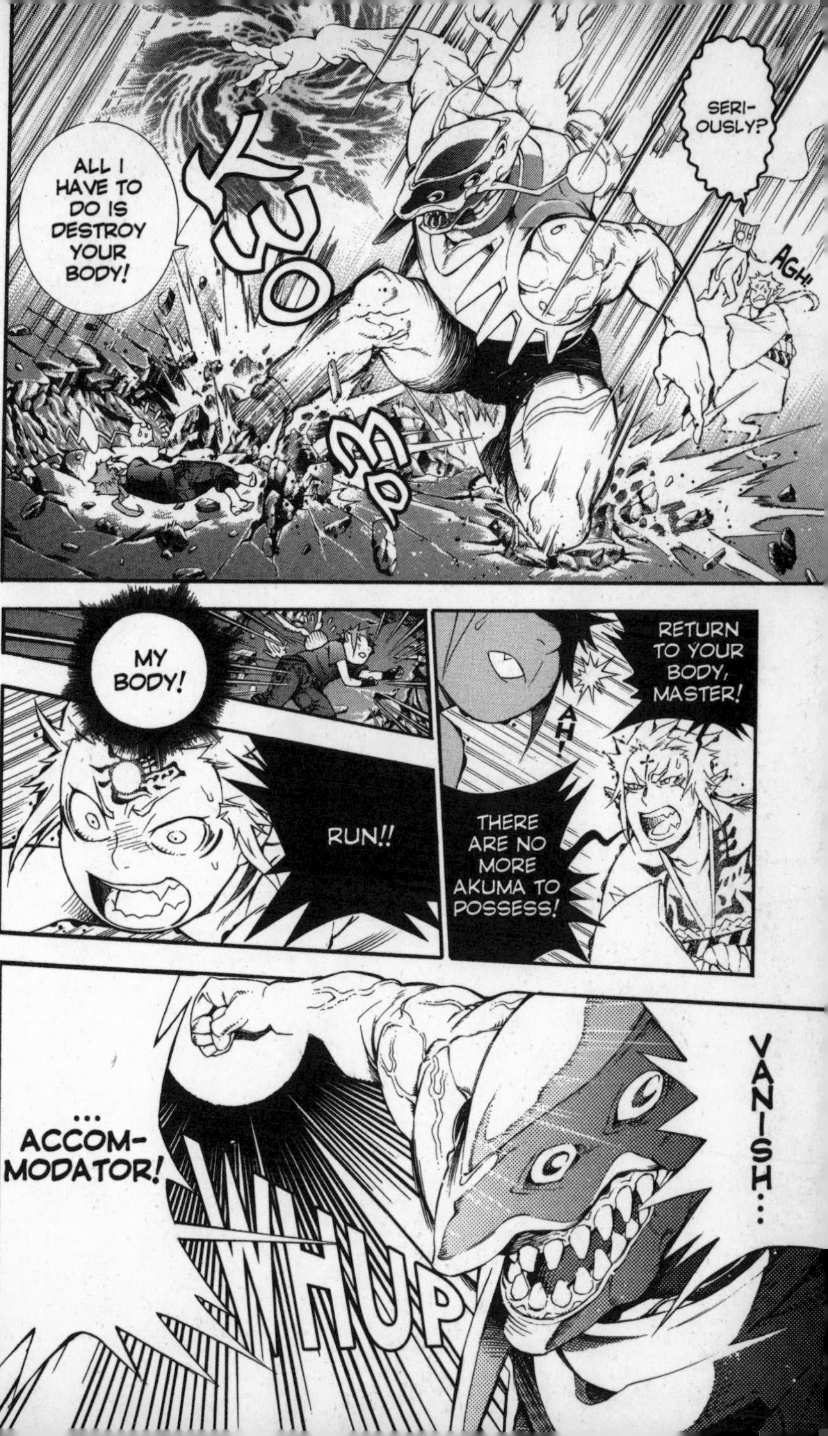
SERI-OUSLY?
AGH!
ALL I HAVE TO DO IS DESTROY YOUR BODY!
RETURN TO YOUR BODY, MASTER!
AH!
THERE ARE NO MORE AKUMA TO POSSESS!
MY BODY!
RUN!!
VANISH...
WHUP
... ACCOM-MODATOR!

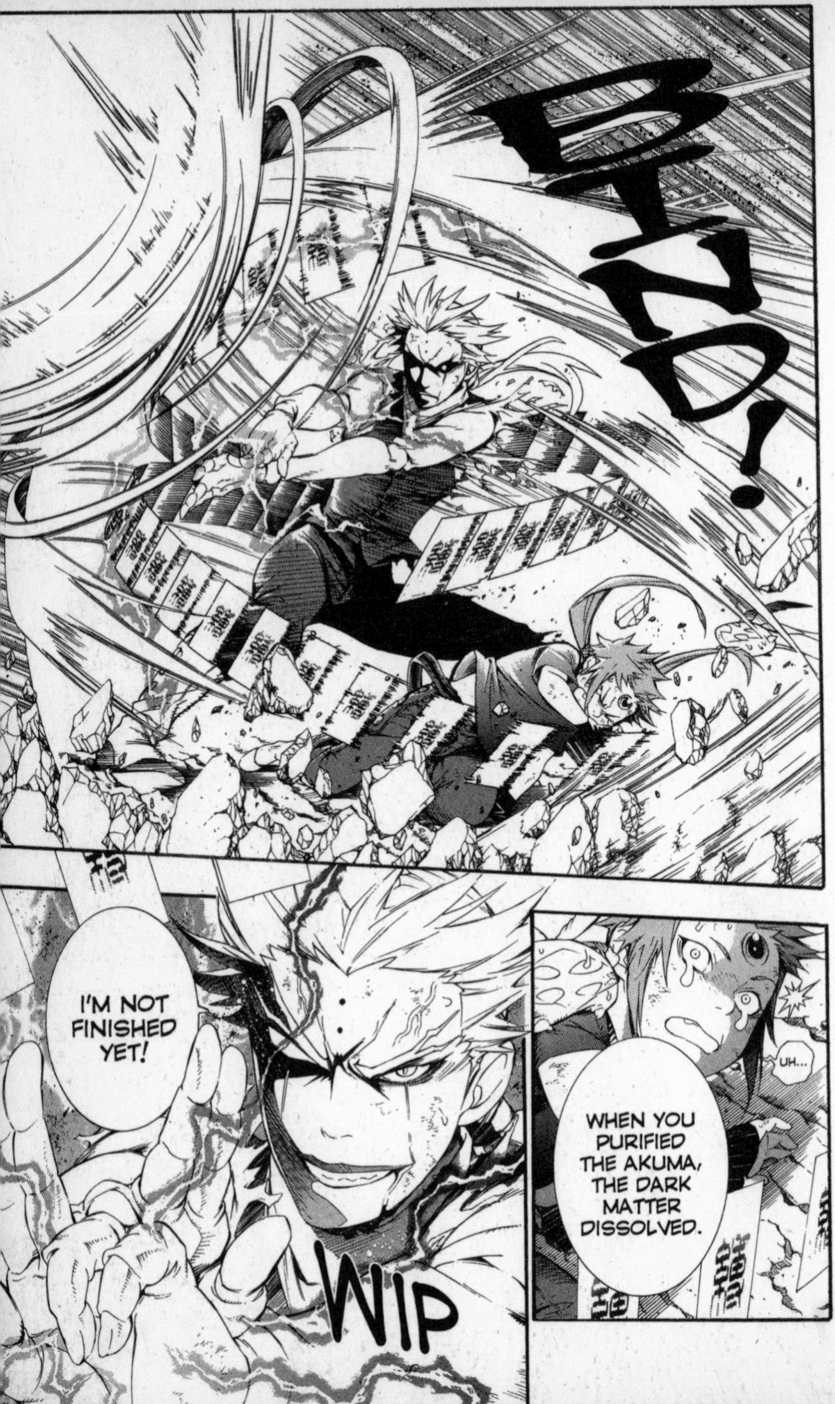
BANG!
UH...
WHEN YOU PURIFIED THE AKUMA, THE DARK MATTER DISSOLVED.
I'M NOT FINISHED YET!
WIP

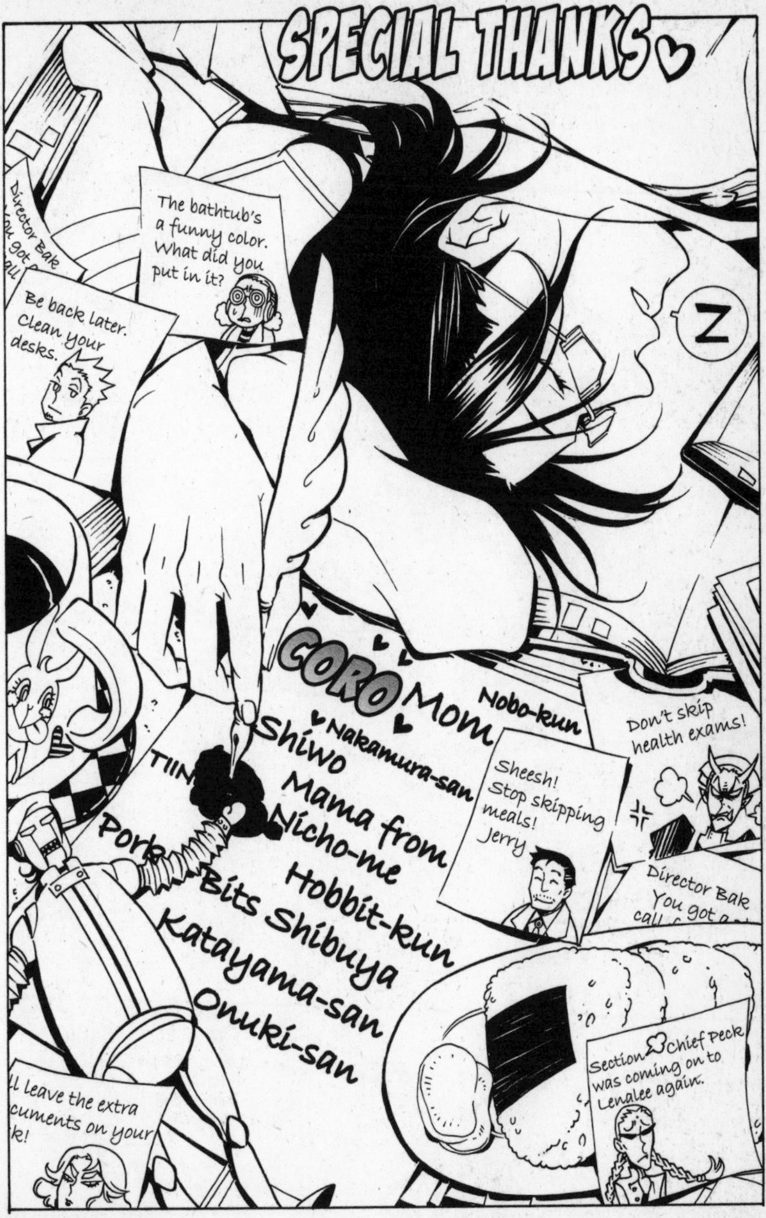

SPECIAL THANKS
The bathtub's a funny color. What did you put in it?
Director Bak
Be back later. Clean your desks.
Z
CORO
Mom
Nobo-kun
Nakamura-san
Shiwo
TIIN
Mama from Nicho-me
Pork
Hobbit-kun
Bits Shibuya
Katayama-san
Onuki-san
Don't skip health exams!
Sheesh! Stop skipping meals! Jerry
Director Bak You got a
Section Chief Peck was coming on to Lenalee again.
ll leave the extra cuments on your k!

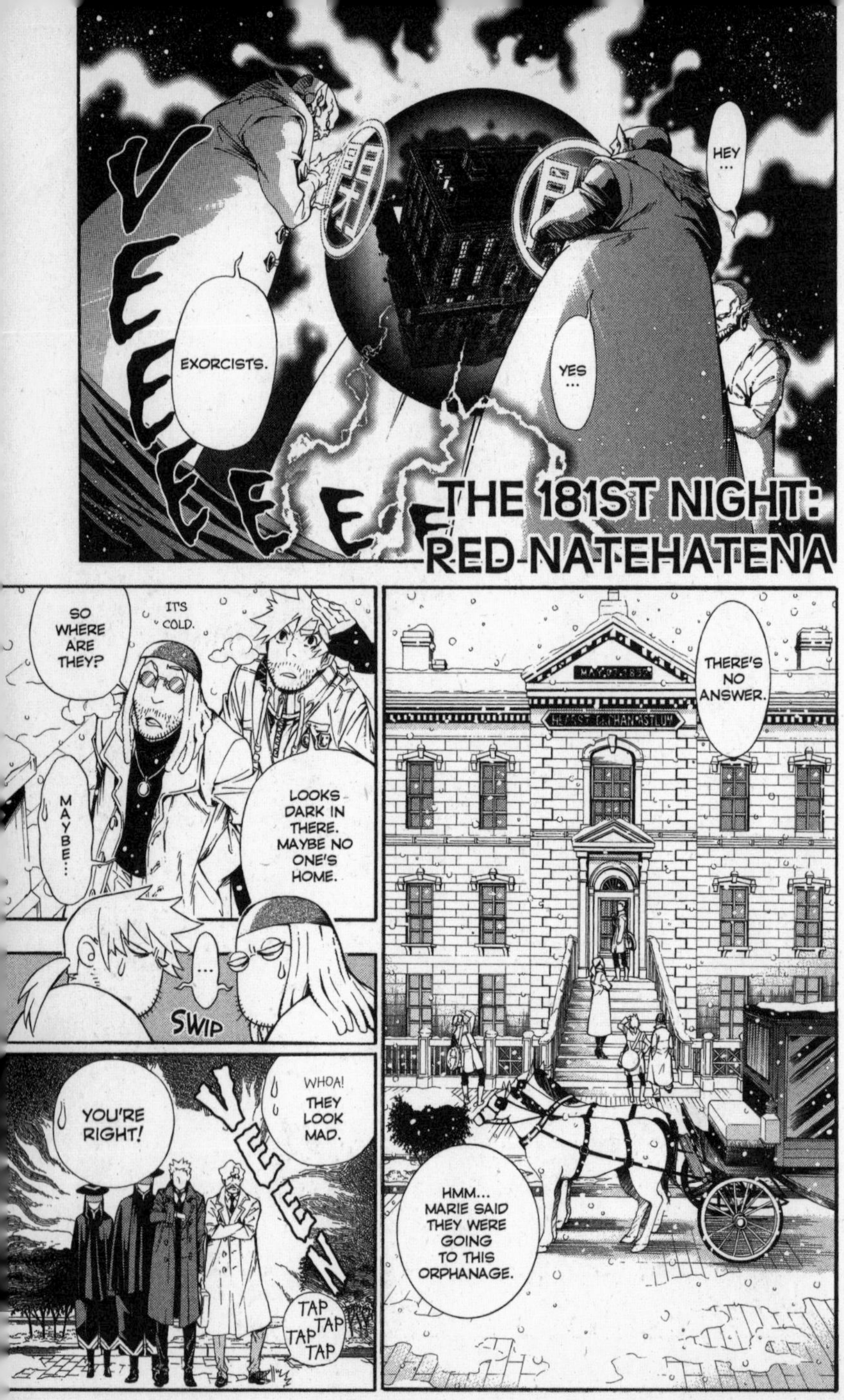
HEY...
YES...
EXORCISTS.
VEEEEEE
THE 181ST NIGHT: RED NATEHATENA
THERE'S NO ANSWER.
HMM... MARIE SAID THEY WERE GOING TO THIS ORPHANAGE.
IT'S COLD.
SO WHERE ARE THEY?
LOOKS DARK IN THERE. MAYBE NO ONE'S HOME.
MAYBE...
...
SWIP
WHOA! THEY LOOK MAD.
YOU'RE RIGHT!
VEEEN
TAP TAP TAP TAP

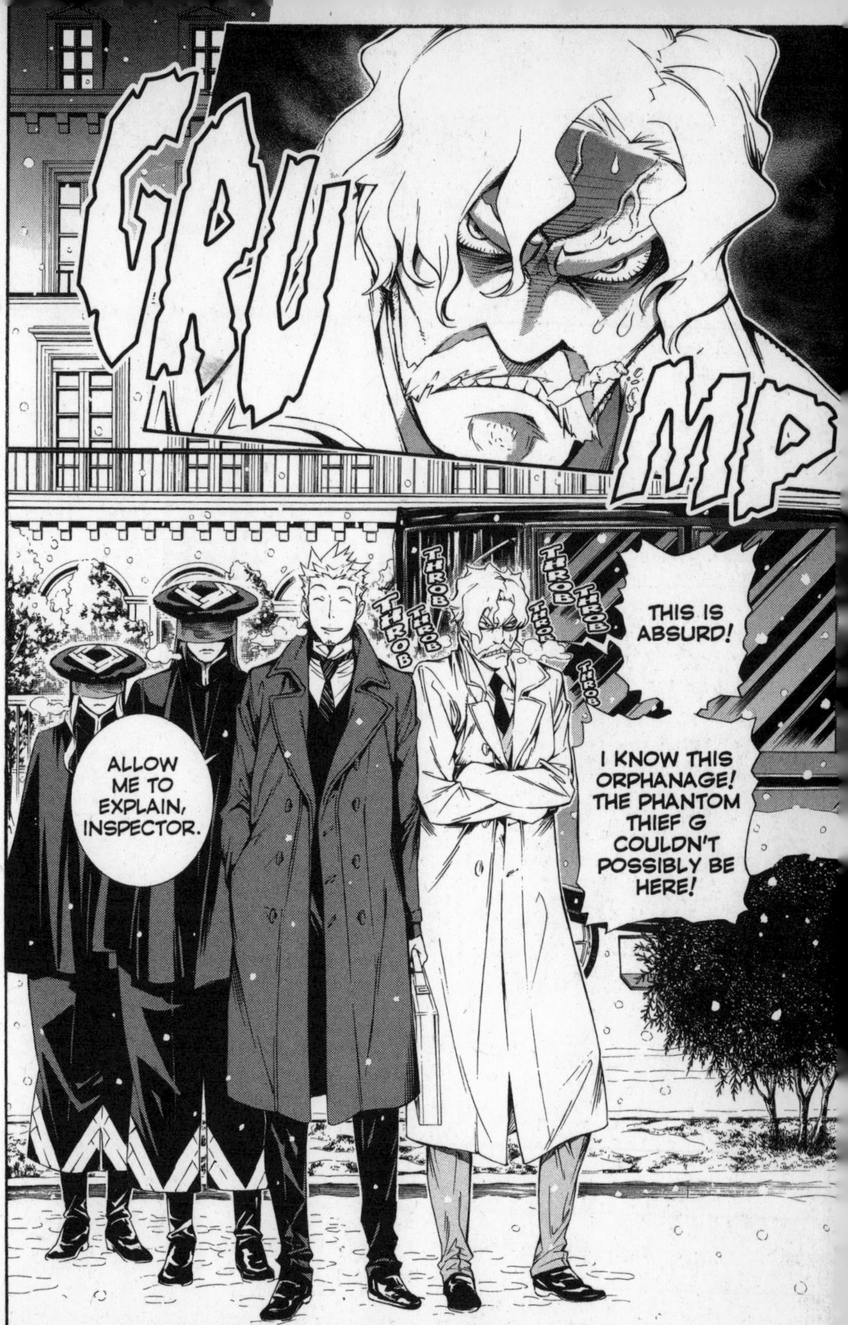
GRUMP
THIS IS ABSURD!
THROB THROB THROB THROB
THROB THROB THROB
I KNOW THIS ORPHANAGE! THE PHANTOM THIEF G COULDN'T POSSIBLY BE HERE!
ALLOW ME TO EXPLAIN, INSPECTOR.

THE 181ST NIGHT: RED NATEHATENA

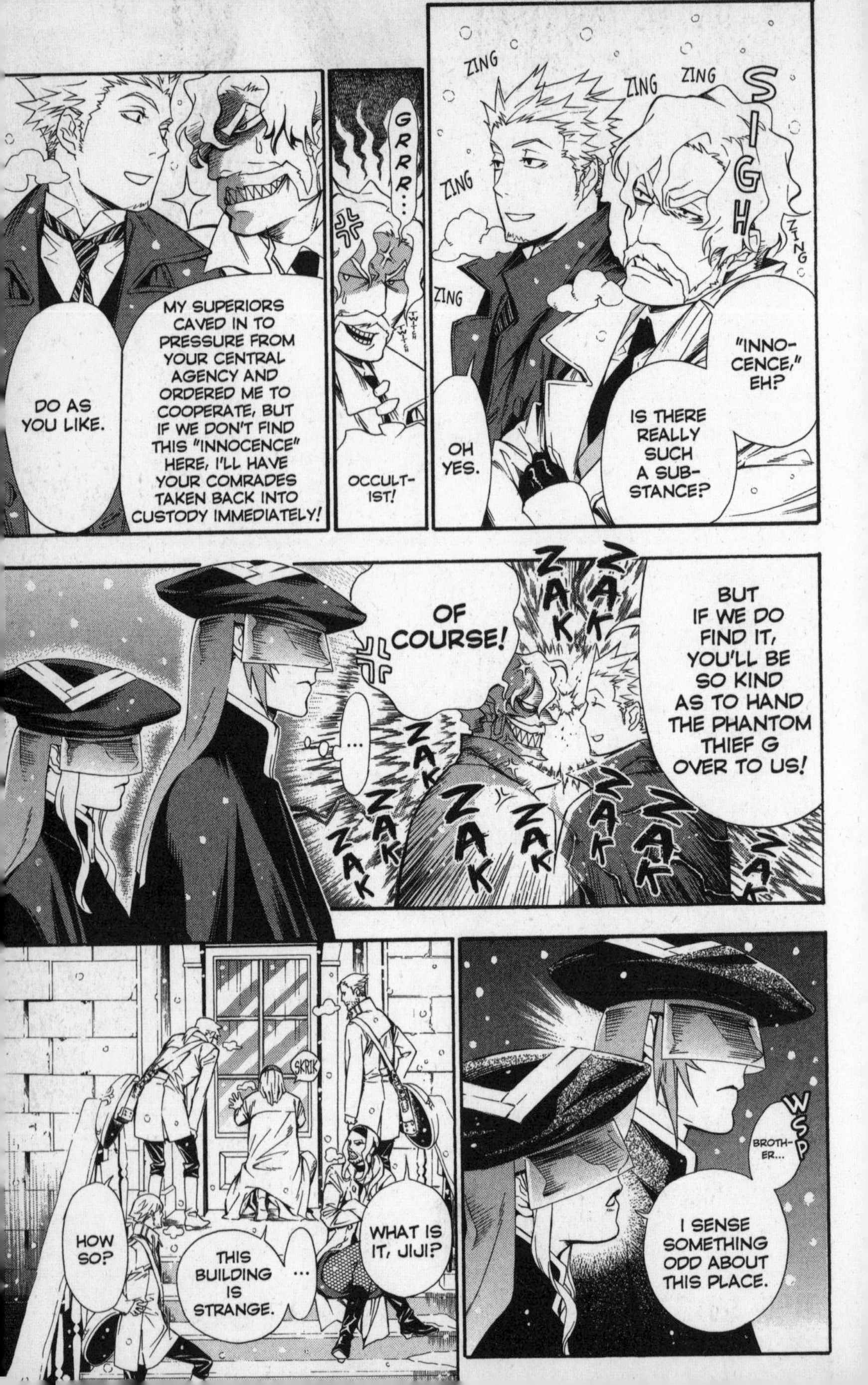
ZING
ZING ZING
SIGH
ZING
"INNO-CENCE," EH?
IS THERE REALLY SUCH A SUB-STANCE?
ZING
ZING
OH YES.
GRRR...
TWITCH TWITCH
OCCULT-IST!
MY SUPERIORS CAVED IN TO PRESSURE FROM YOUR CENTRAL AGENCY AND ORDERED ME TO COOPERATE, BUT IF WE DON'T FIND THIS "INNOCENCE" HERE, I'LL HAVE YOUR COMRADES TAKEN BACK INTO CUSTODY IMMEDIATELY!
DO AS YOU LIKE.
BUT IF WE DO FIND IT, YOU'LL BE SO KIND AS TO HAND THE PHANTOM THIEF G OVER TO US!
ZAK ZAK
OF COURSE!
ZAK ZAK ZAK ZAK ZAK ZAK ZAK ZAK ZAK ZAK
...
WSP
BROTH-ER...
I SENSE SOMETHING ODD ABOUT THIS PLACE.
SKRIK
WHAT IS IT, JIJI?
...
THIS BUILDING IS STRANGE.
HOW SO?

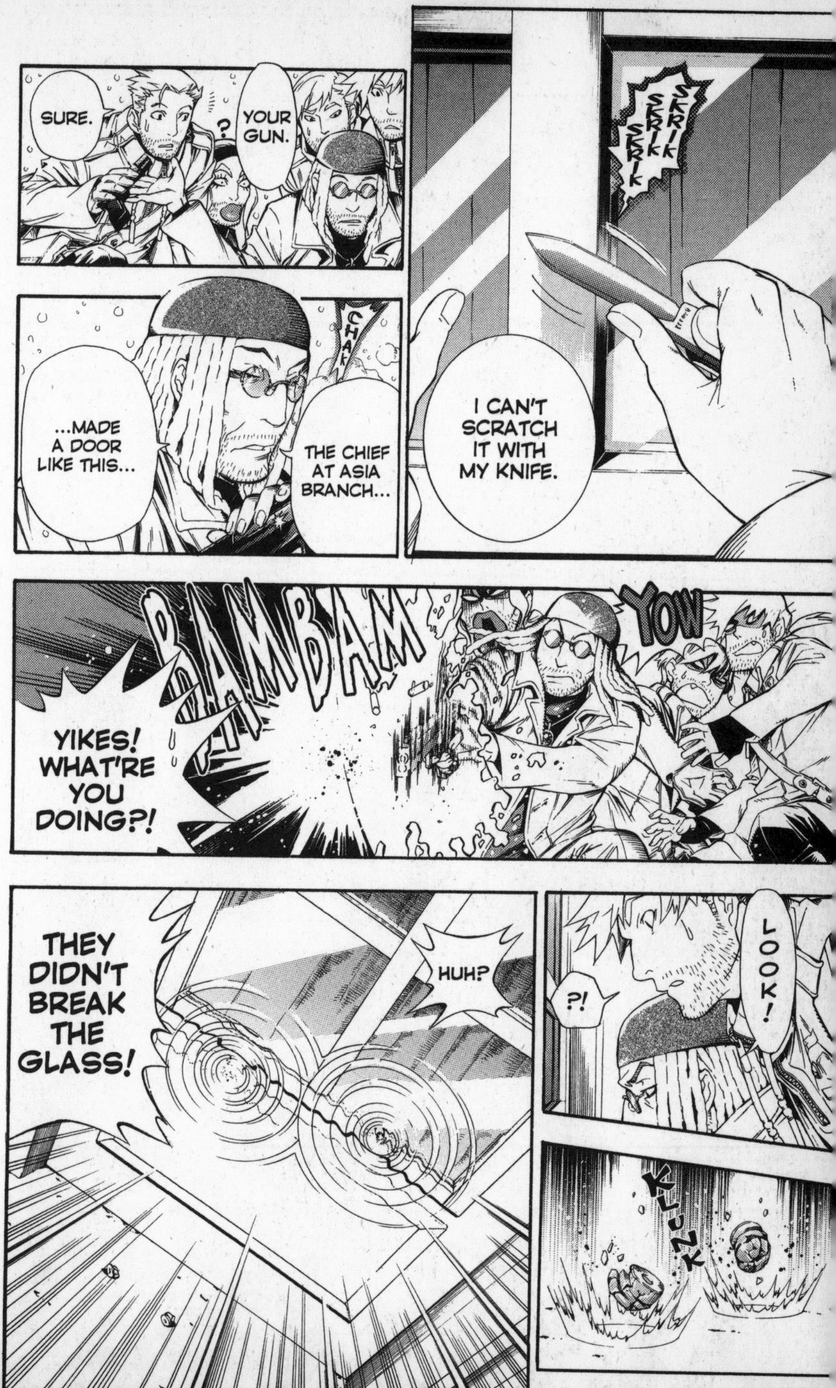
SKRIK SKRIK SKRIK
I CAN'T SCRATCH IT WITH MY KNIFE.
YOUR GUN.
?
SURE.
CHAK
THE CHIEF AT ASIA BRANCH...
...MADE A DOOR LIKE THIS...
YOW
BAMBAM
YIKES! WHAT'RE YOU DOING?!
LOOK!
?!
KLUNK
HUH?
THEY DIDN'T BREAK THE GLASS!

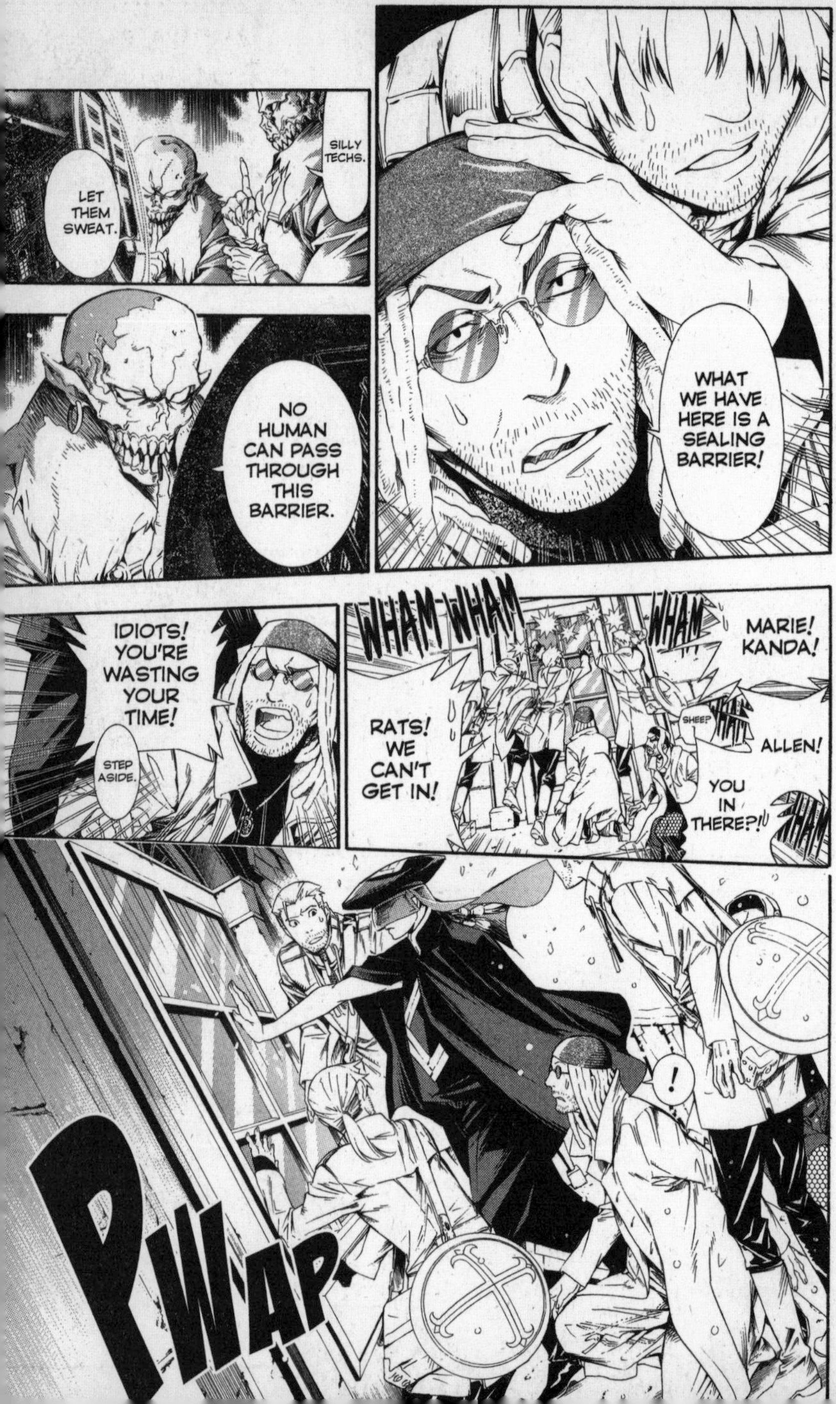
WHAT WE HAVE HERE IS A SEALING BARRIER!
SILLY TECHS.
LET THEM SWEAT.
NO HUMAN CAN PASS THROUGH THIS BARRIER.
WHAM
MARIE! KANDA!
WHAM WHAM
SHEP?
WHAM
ALLEN!
YOU IN THERE?!
WHAM
RATS! WE CAN'T GET IN!
IDIOTS! YOU'RE WASTING YOUR TIME!
STEP ASIDE.
!
PWAP

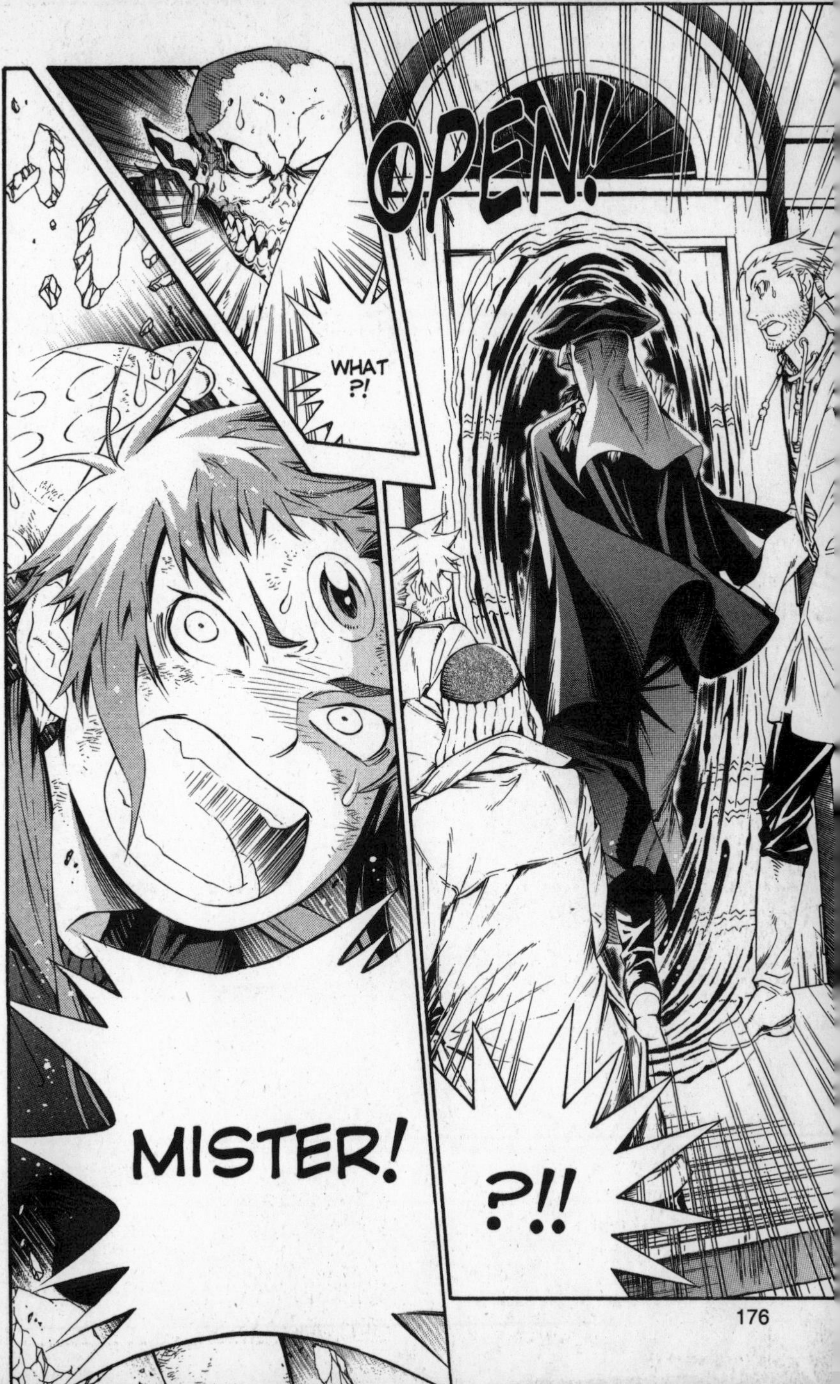
OPEN!
?!!
WHAT ?!
MISTER!

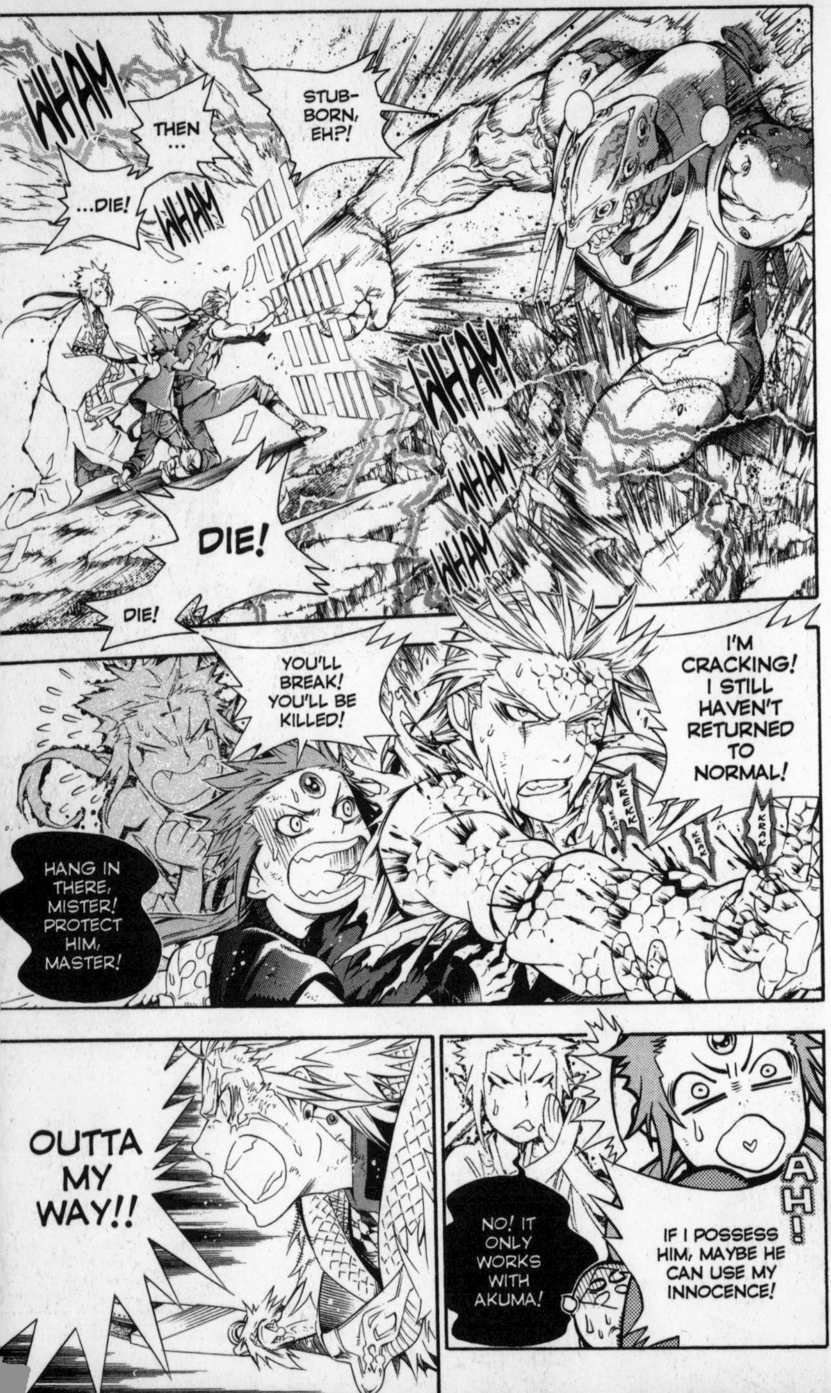
STUB-BORN, EH?!
THEN ...
WHAM
...DIE!
WHAM
WHAM
WHAM
WHAM
DIE!
DIE!
I'M CRACKING! I STILL HAVEN'T RETURNED TO NORMAL!
KRAK
KRAK
KREKK
KRAK
YOU'LL BREAK! YOU'LL BE KILLED!
HANG IN THERE, MISTER! PROTECT HIM, MASTER!
AH!
IF I POSSESS HIM, MAYBE HE CAN USE MY INNOCENCE!
NO! IT ONLY WORKS WITH AKUMA!
OUTTA MY WAY!!

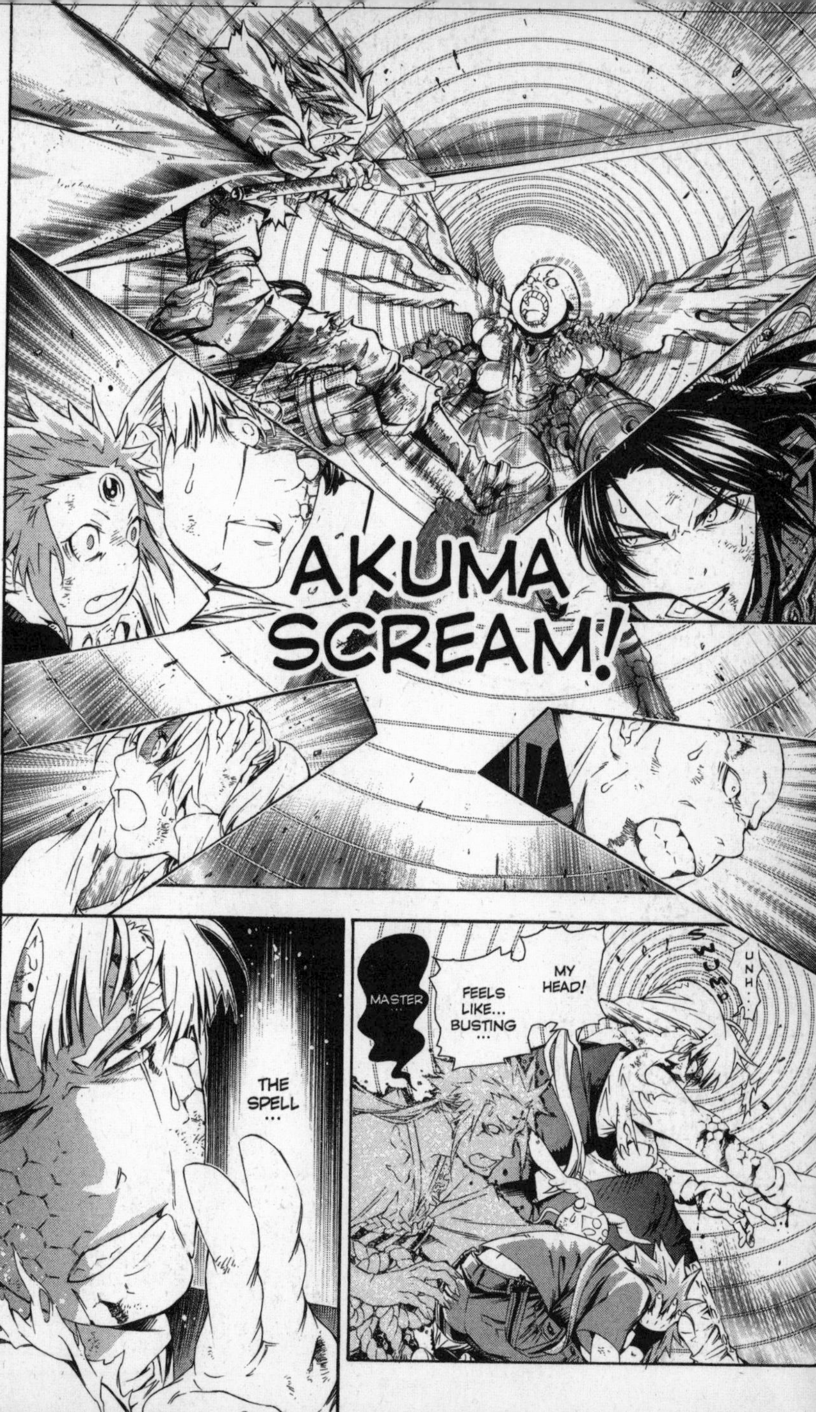
AKUMA SCREAM!
UNH...
SWUMP
MY HEAD!
FEELS LIKE... BUSTING...
MASTER...
THE SPELL...

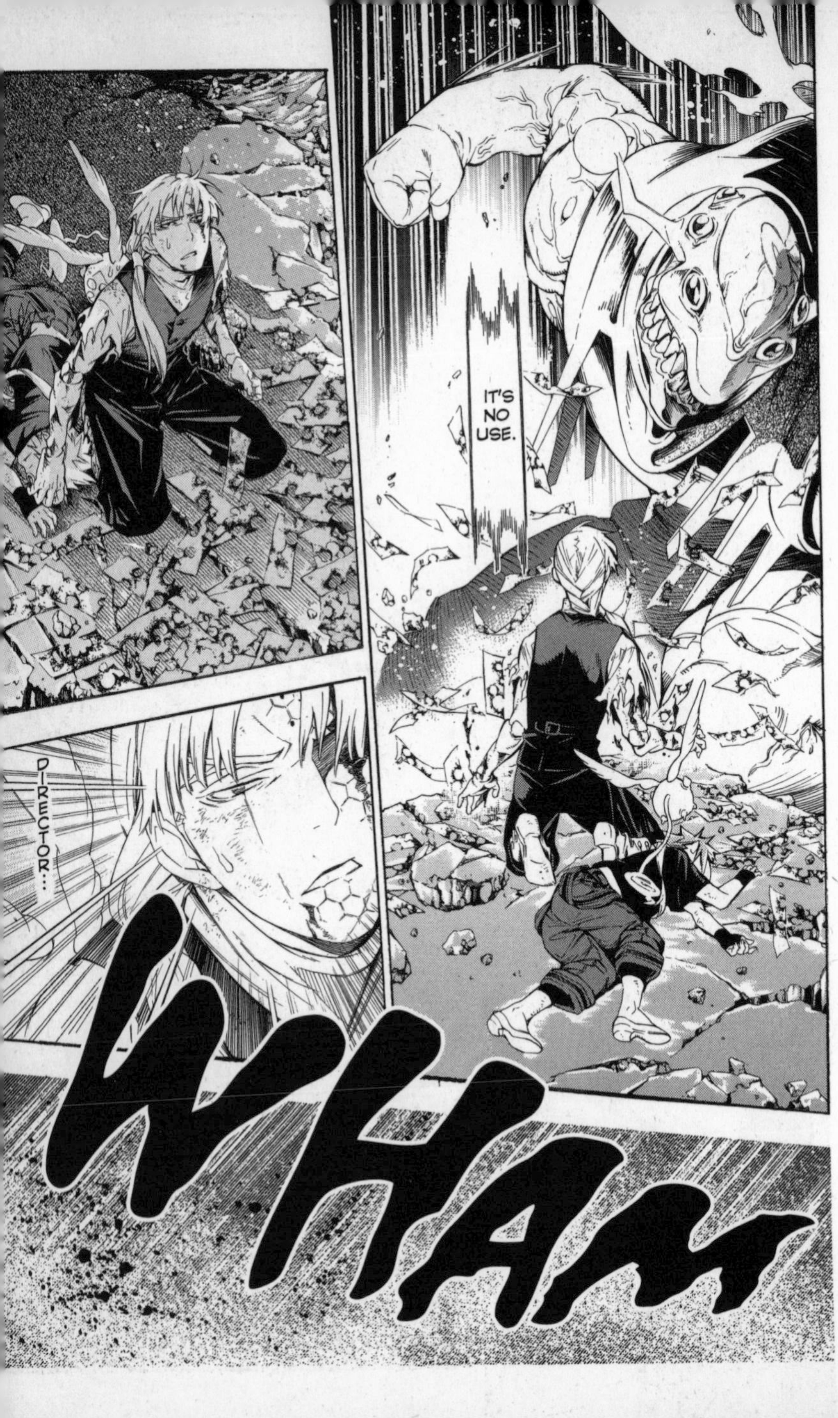

IT'S NO USE.
DIRECTOR...
WHAM

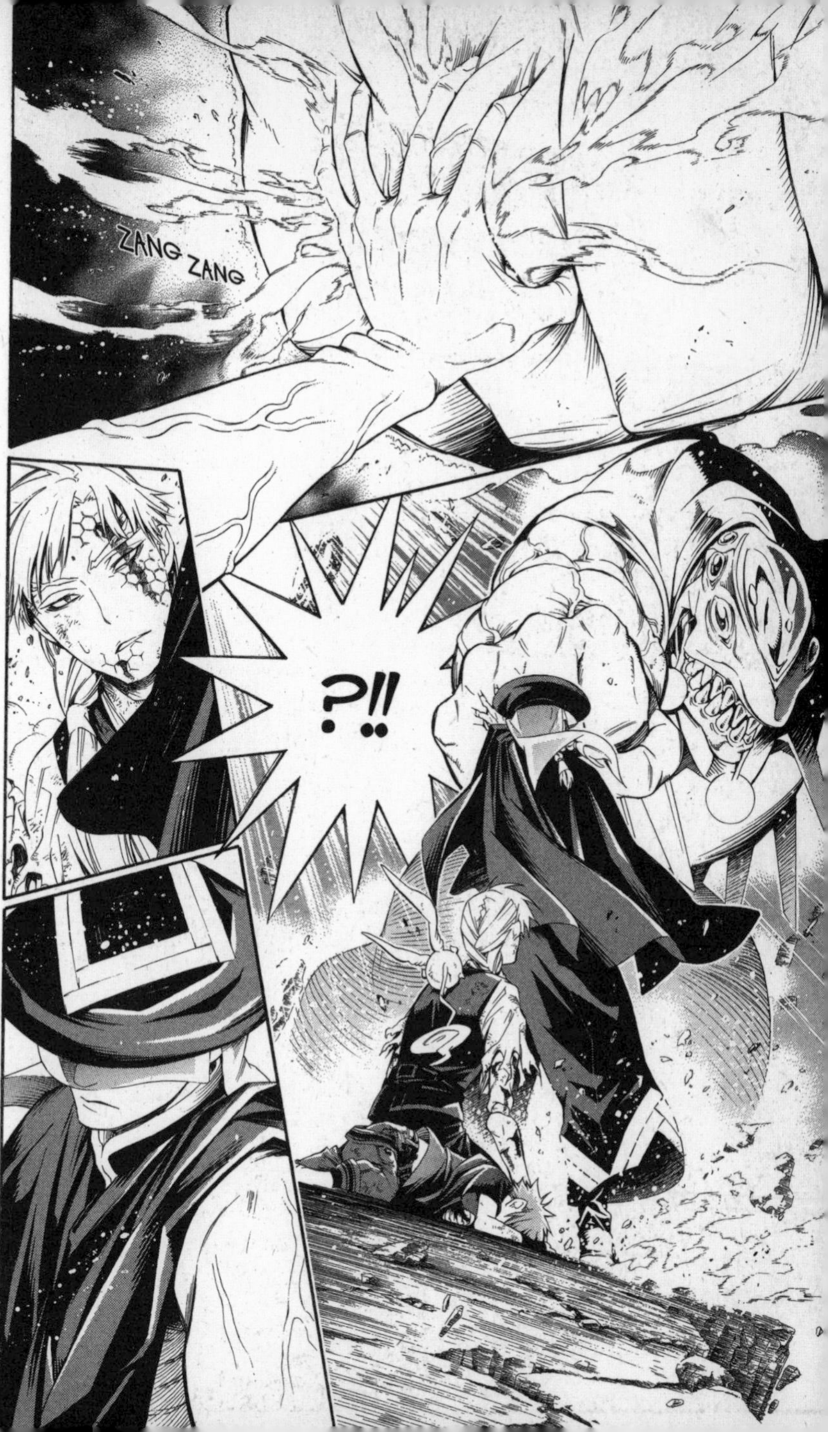
ZANG ZANG
?!!

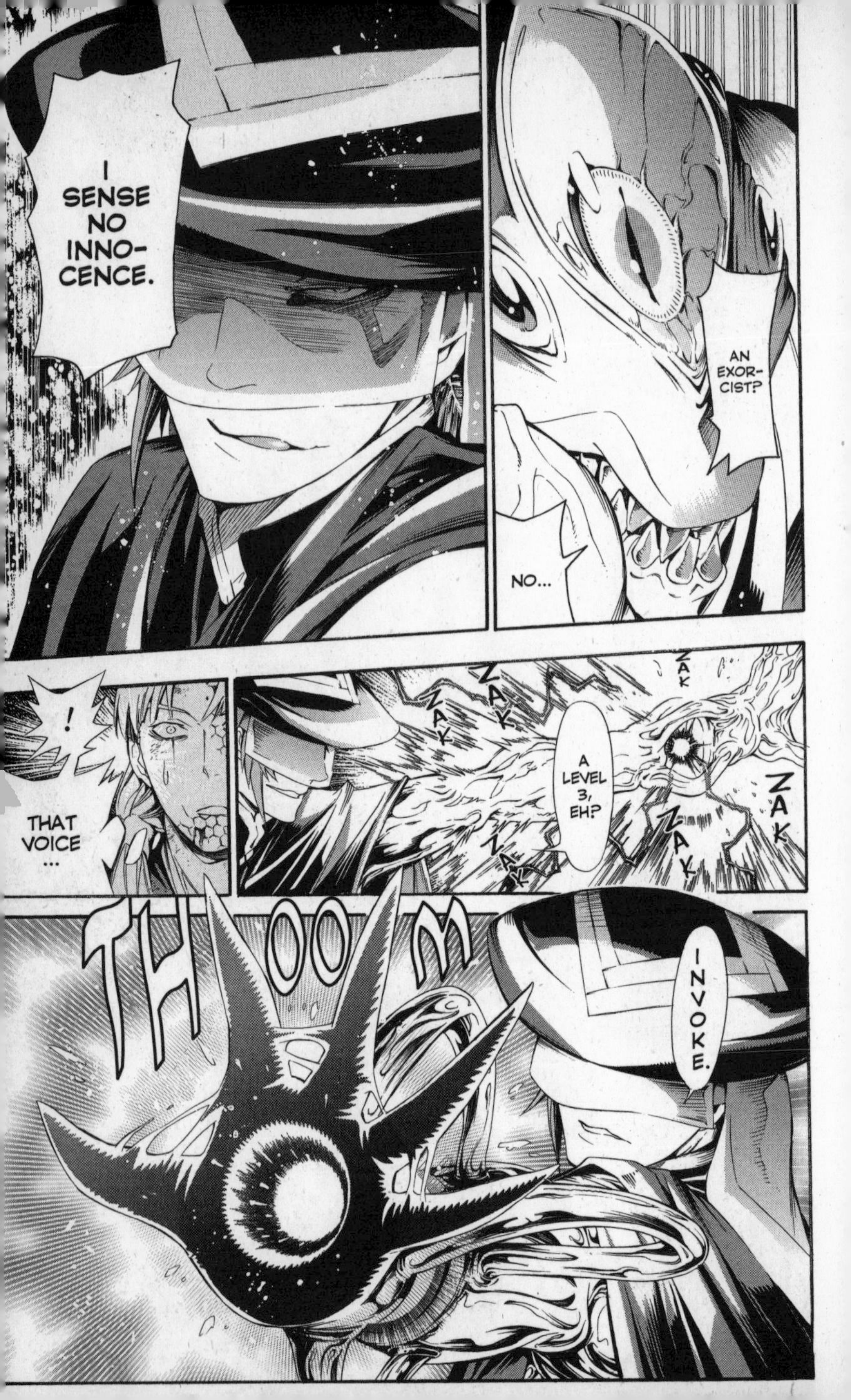
AN EXORCIST?
NO...
I SENSE NO INNOCENCE.
ZAK
ZAK
ZAK
A LEVEL 3, EH?
ZAK
ZAK
ZAK
!
THAT VOICE...
INVOKE.
THOOM

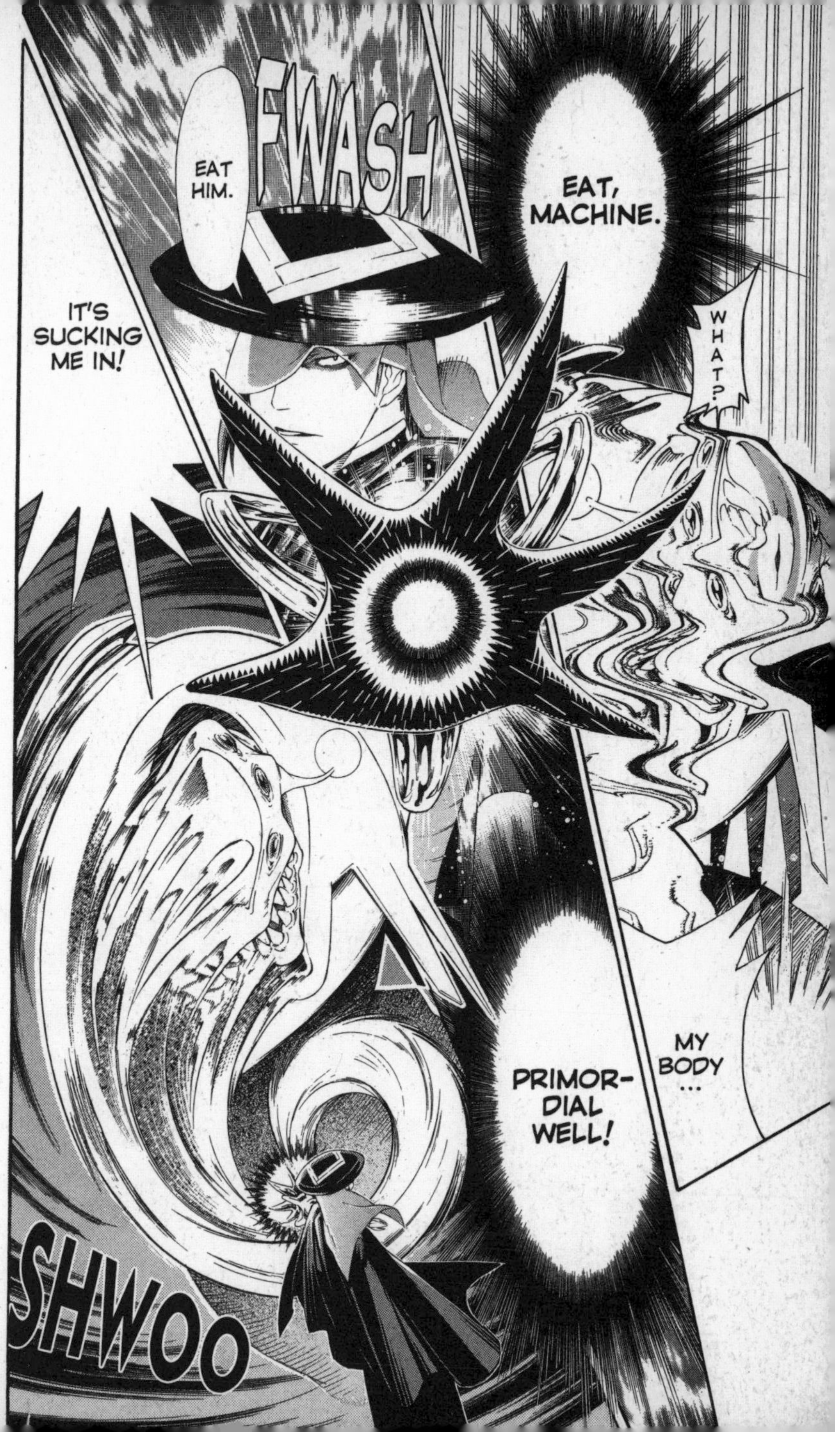
EAT, MACHINE.
WHAT?!
EAT HIM.
FWASH
IT'S SUCKING ME IN!
MY BODY...
PRIMOR-DIAL WELL!
SHWOO

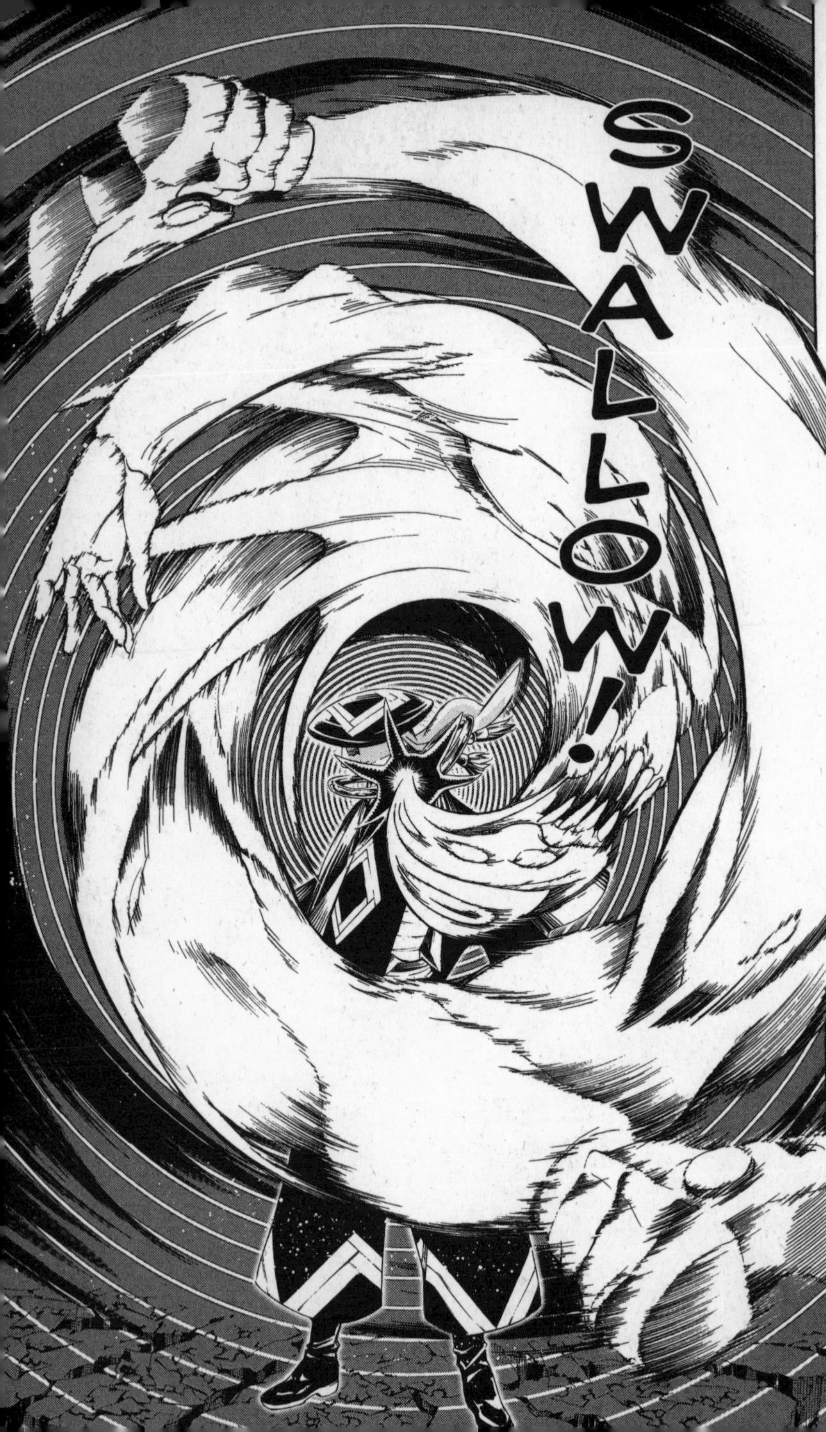
SWALLOW!

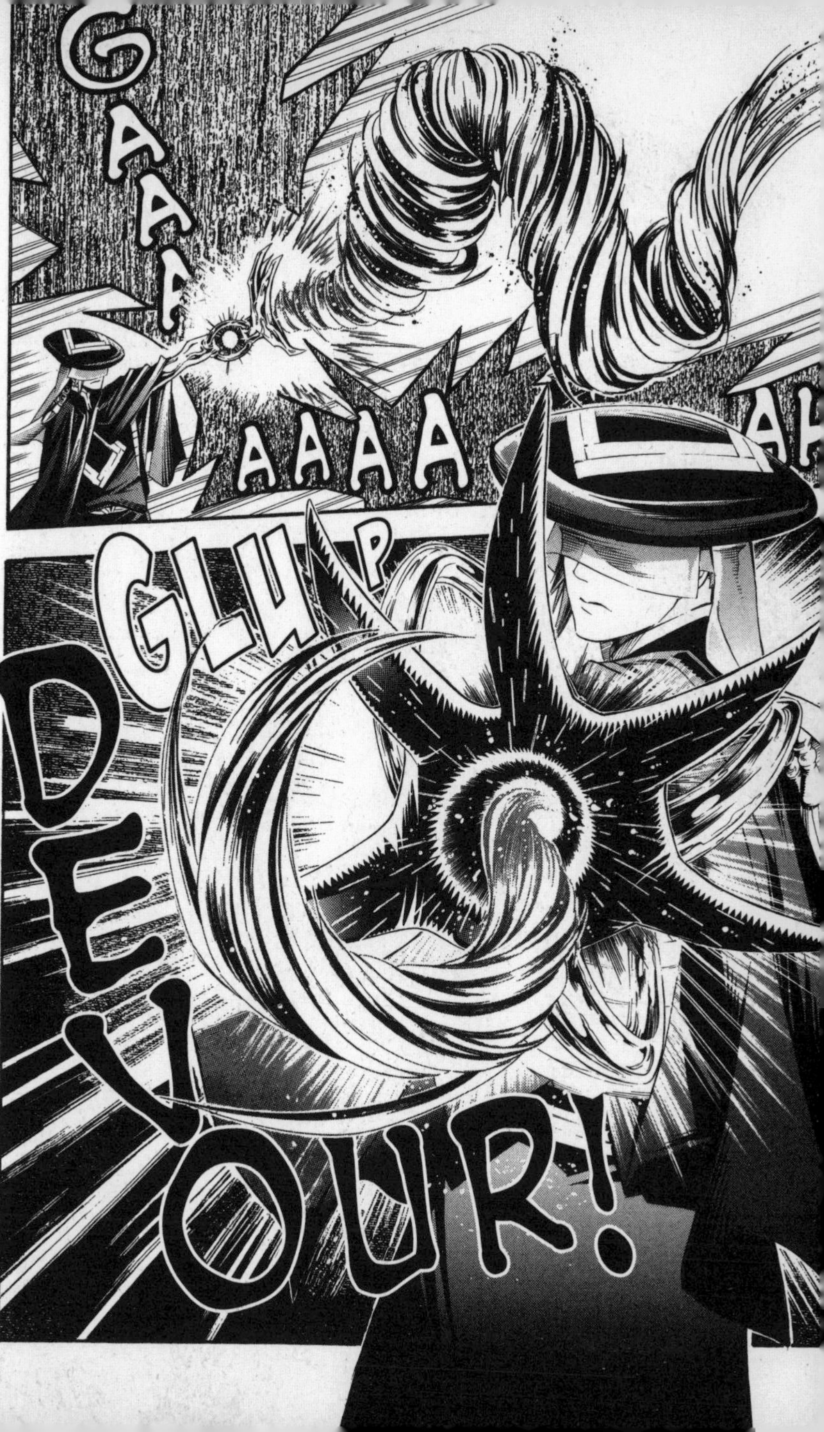
GAAAAAAAAH
GLUP
DEVOUR!

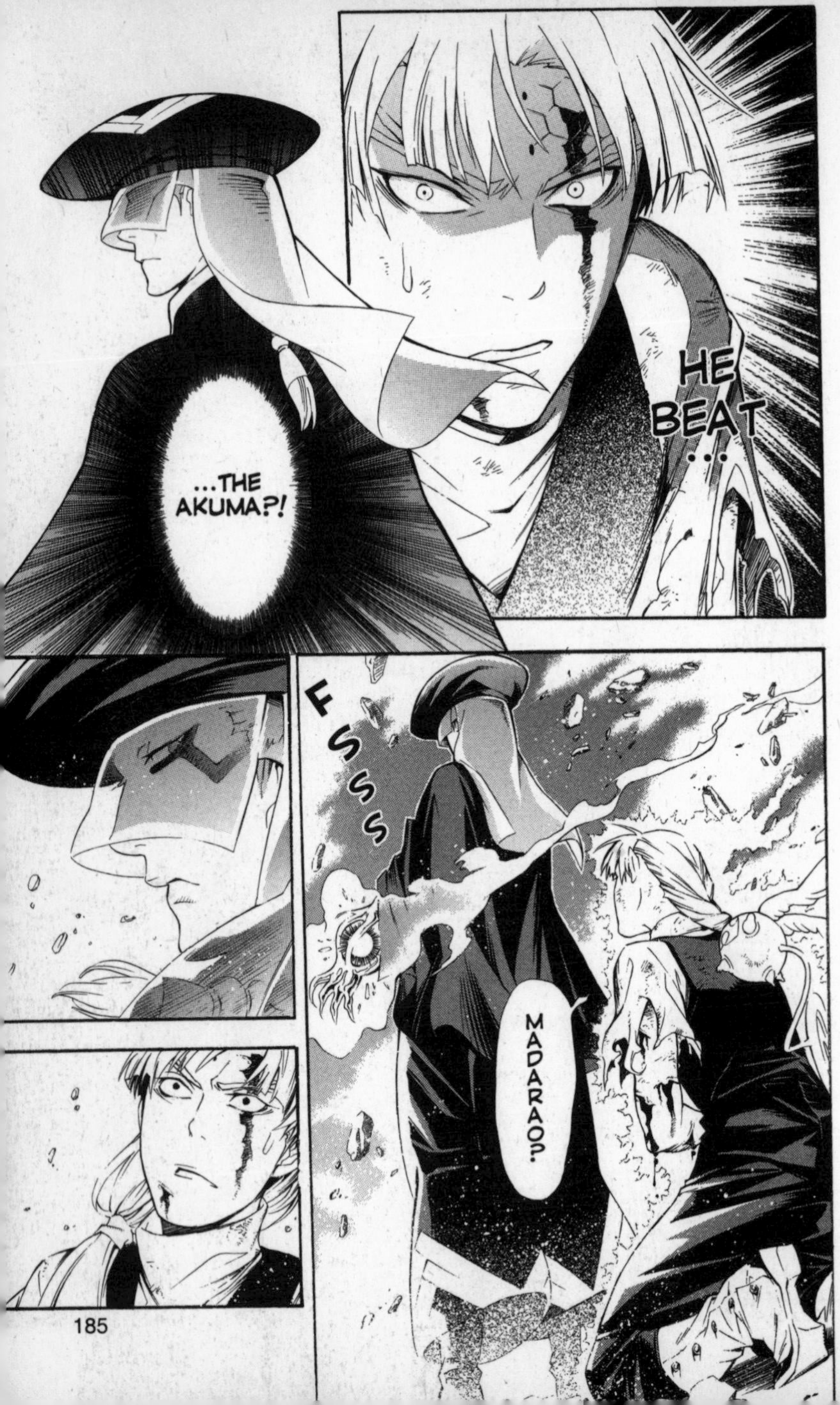
HE BEAT...
...THE AKUMA?!
FSSS
MADARAO?

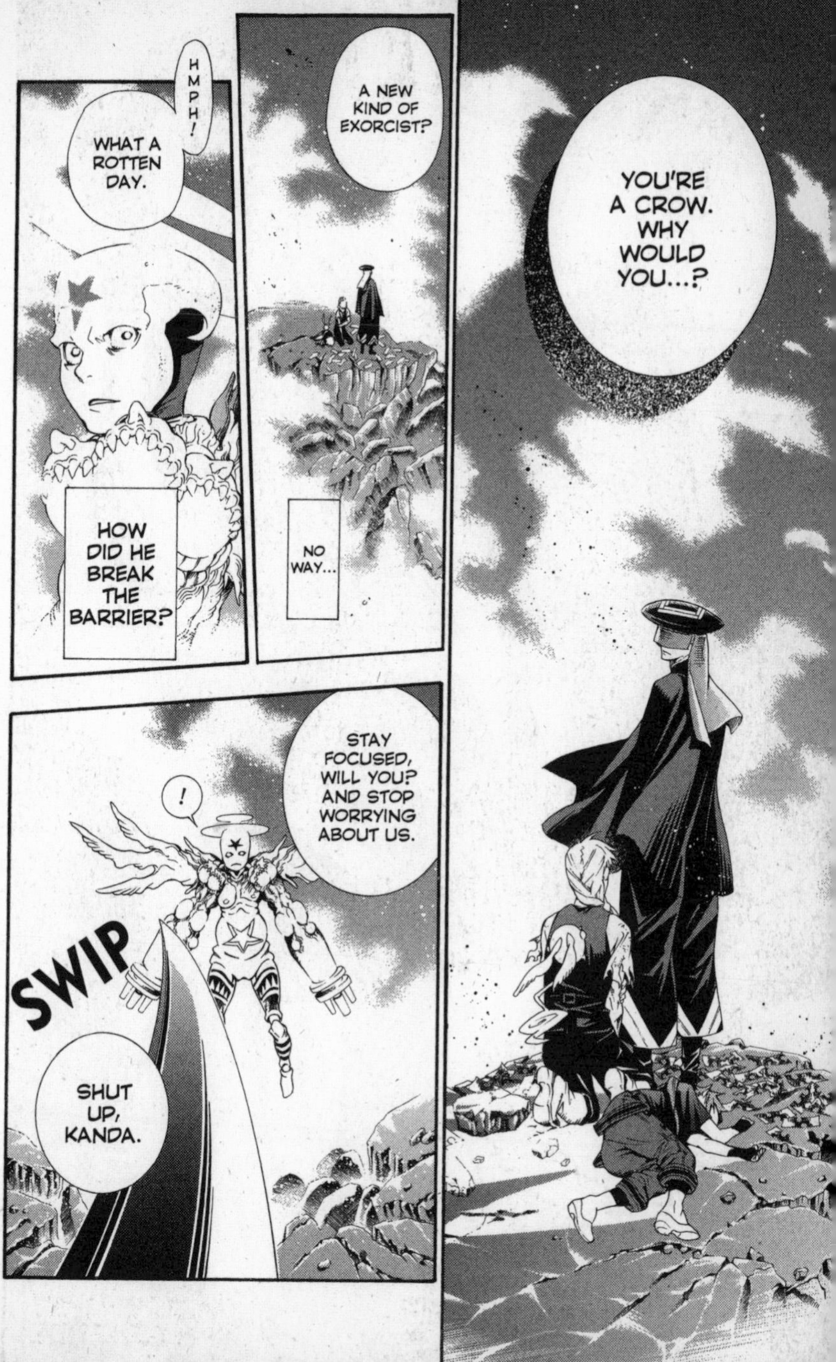
YOU'RE A CROW. WHY WOULD YOU...?
A NEW KIND OF EXORCIST?
NO WAY...
HMPH!
WHAT A ROTTEN DAY.
HOW DID HE BREAK THE BARRIER?
STAY FOCUSED, WILL YOU? AND STOP WORRYING ABOUT US.
!
SWIP
SHUT UP, KANDA.

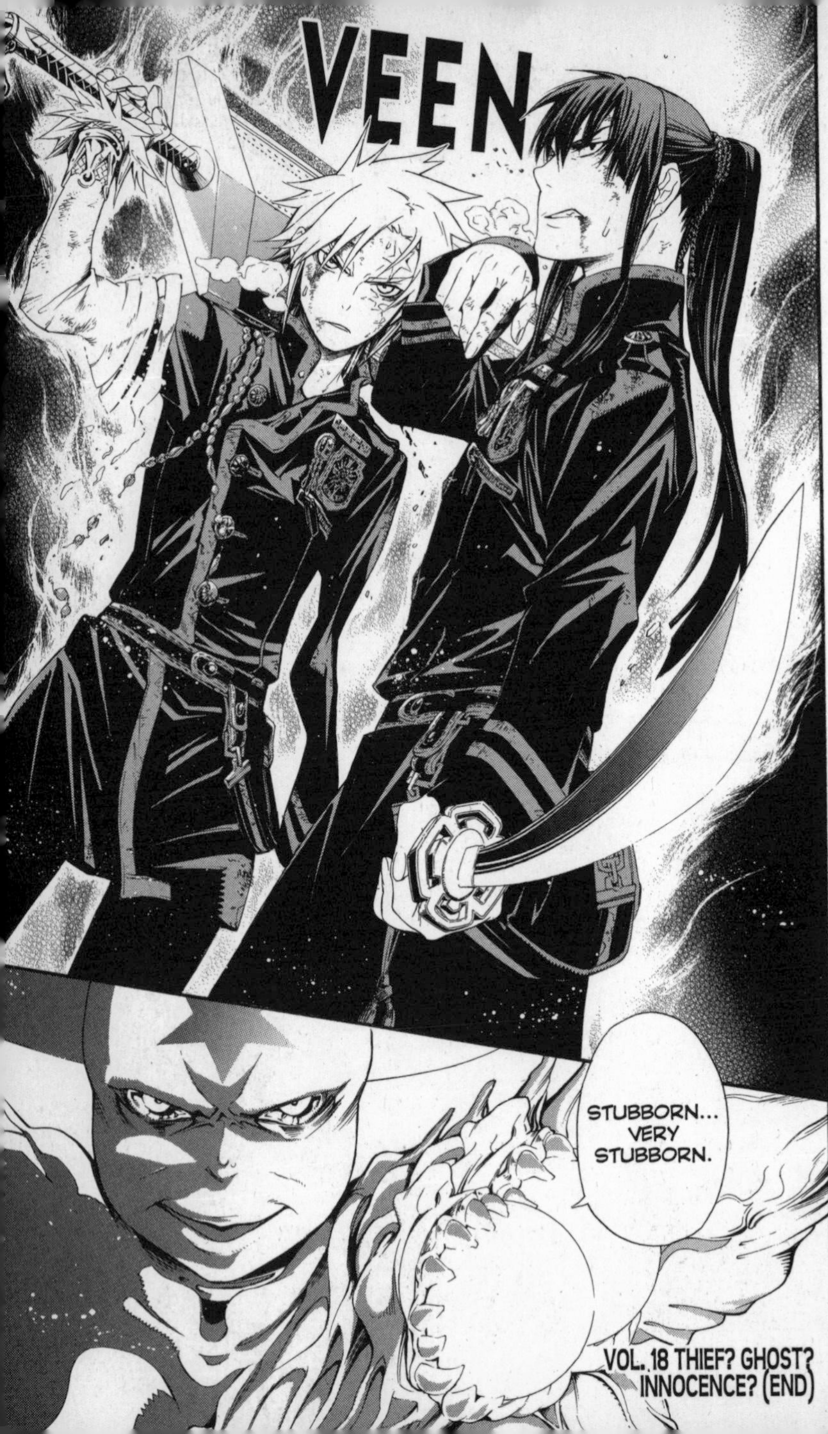
VEEN
STUBBORN... VERY STUBBORN.
VOL. 18 THIEF? GHOST? INNOCENCE? (END)

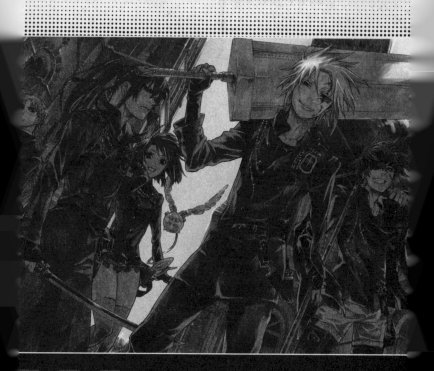

N THE NEXT VOLUME...

After battling a Level 4 akuma, Allen begins to exhibit signs of a change that may be affecting his very nature. Attention at Black Order headquarters, however, is focused on the introduction of a radical new breed of Exorcist. Meanwhile, at Asia Branch, Kanda learns something significant about his background. What a time for the servants of the Millennium Earl to start popping up all over the world!

Available November 2010!

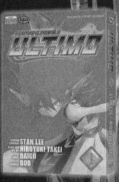

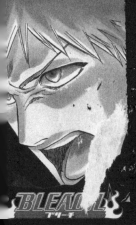

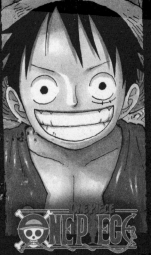

BLEACH

ONE PIECE

Tegami Bachi

STORY AND ART BY
TITE KUBO

STORY AND ART BY
EIICHIRO ODA

STORY AND ART BY
HIROYUKI ASADA

JUMP INTO THE ACTION BY TELLING US WHAT YOU LOVE (AND WHAT YOU DON'T)

LET YOUR VOICE BE HEARD!

SHONENJUMP.VIZ.COM/MANGASURVEY

HELP US MAKE MORE OF THE WORLD'S MOST POPULAR MANGA!

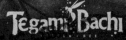

RATED
TEEN

VIZ
media

www.viz.com